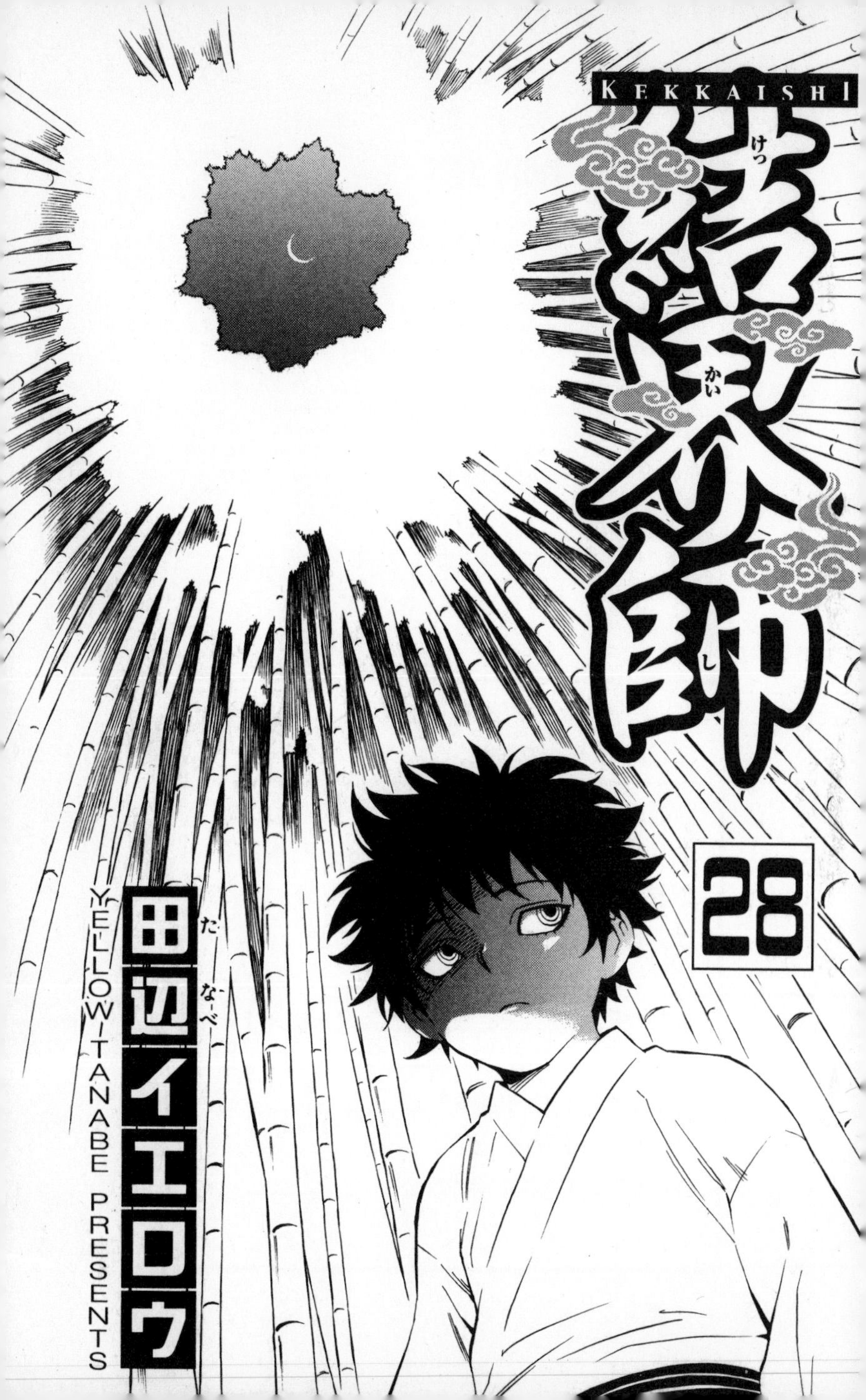
KEKKAISHI
結界師
けっかいし
28
田辺イエロウ
たなべ
YELLOW TANABE PRESENTS

The Story Thus Far

Two witches, Michiru and Kakeru, use their powerful magic to viciously attack the Karasumori Site while holding the entire nearby town hostage!

Yoshimori and his Night Troops attempt to repel the attack, but their chances seem even more remote when the witches' partners, warriors No. 1 and No. 2, arrive.

Meanwhile, Masamori pays a visit to Hisaomi Yumeji, a key member of the Council of Twelve, at his residence. There, Masamori learns of a longstanding feud between Yumeji and his elder brother, Nichinaga Omi, the Shadow Organization's supreme leader. Masamori's meeting with Yumeji ends abruptly when Zero, a hit man sent by Nichinaga, raids Yumeji's home.

Back at Karasumori, the battling kekkaishi and their allies are overwhelmed. Will Yoshimori's power be enough to repel them?

KEKKAISHI VOL. 28
TABLE OF CONTENTS

CHAPTER 266: Ultimate Mind Emptying............ 5

CHAPTER 267: Magic Spell Neutralization...... 25

CHAPTER 268: Magic Spell Neutralized............ 43

CHAPTER 269: Face-to-Face........................ 61

CHAPTER 270: Let's Make a Deal 79

CHAPTER 271: Denial.............................. 97

CHAPTER 272: Prepared To Be Equal............. 115

CHAPTER 273: Karasumori 133

CHAPTER 274: True End.......................... 151

CHAPTER 275: Grim Reaper 169

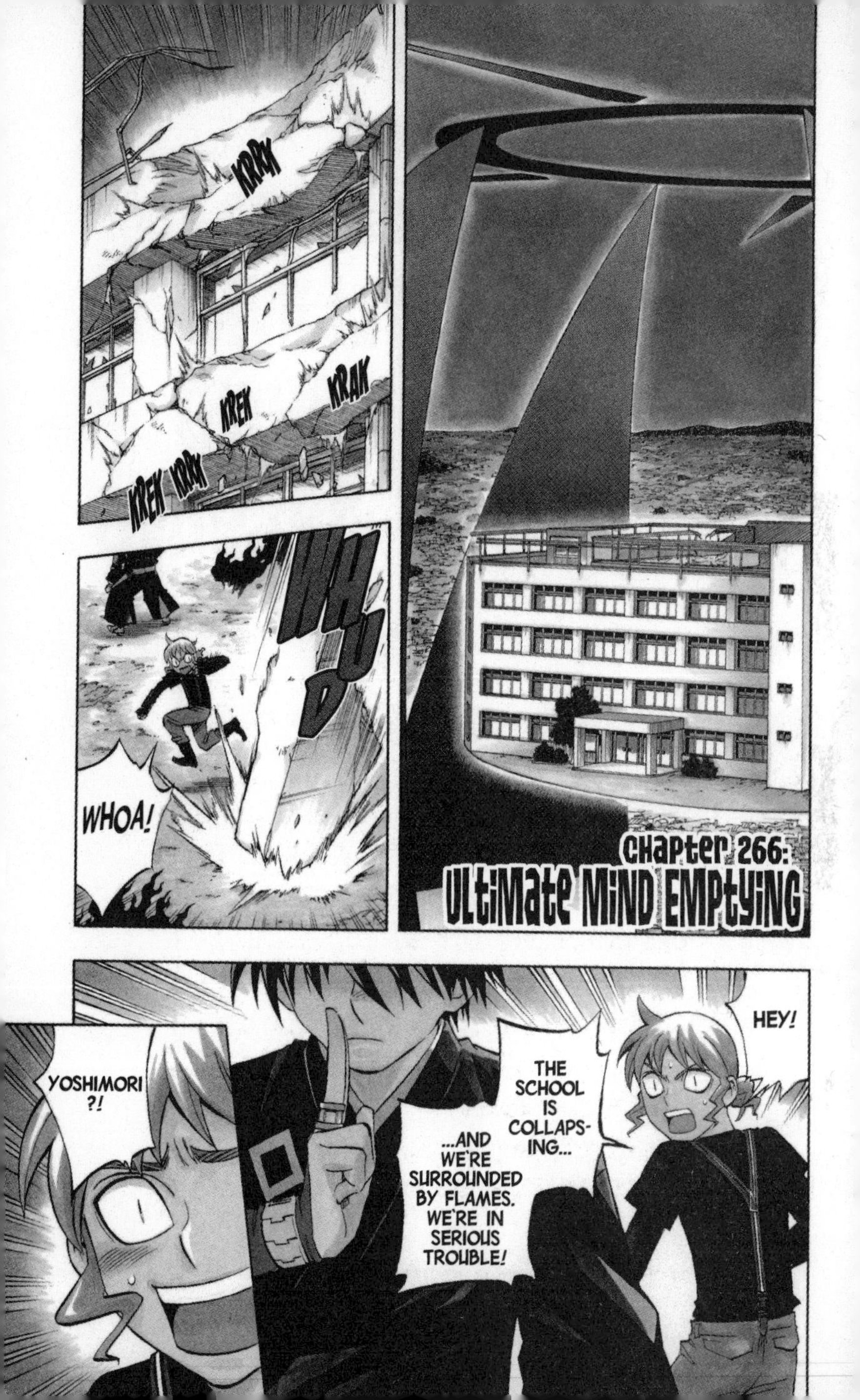
Chapter 266:
Ultimate Mind Emptying
KRRK
KRAK
KREK
KRRK
KREK
WHUD
WHOA!
HEY!
THE SCHOOL IS COLLAPSING...
...AND WE'RE SURROUNDED BY FLAMES. WE'RE IN SERIOUS TROUBLE!
YOSHIMORI ?!

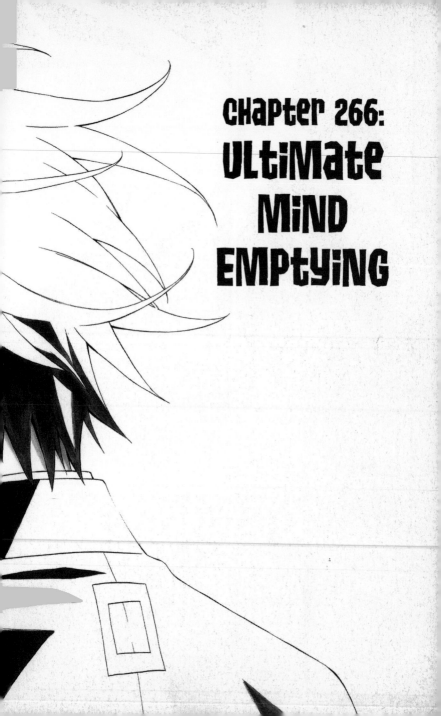

Chapter 266: Ultimate Mind Emptying

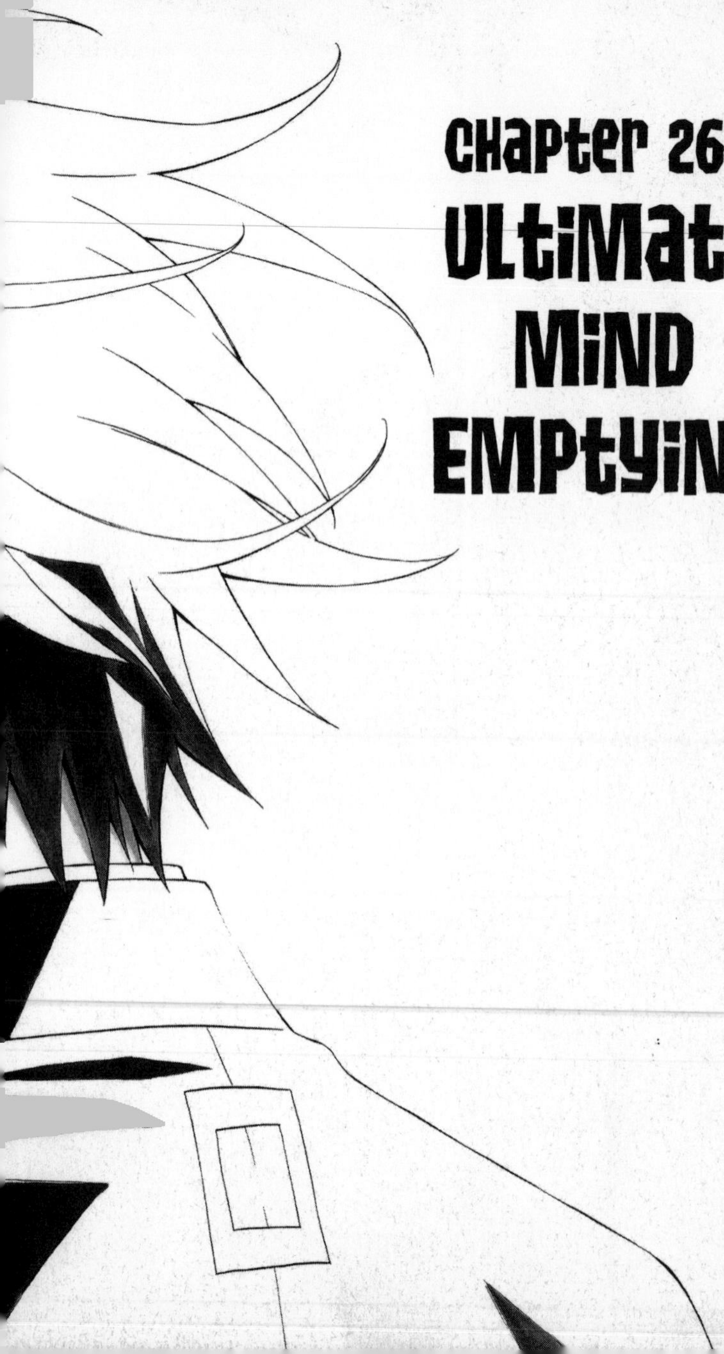

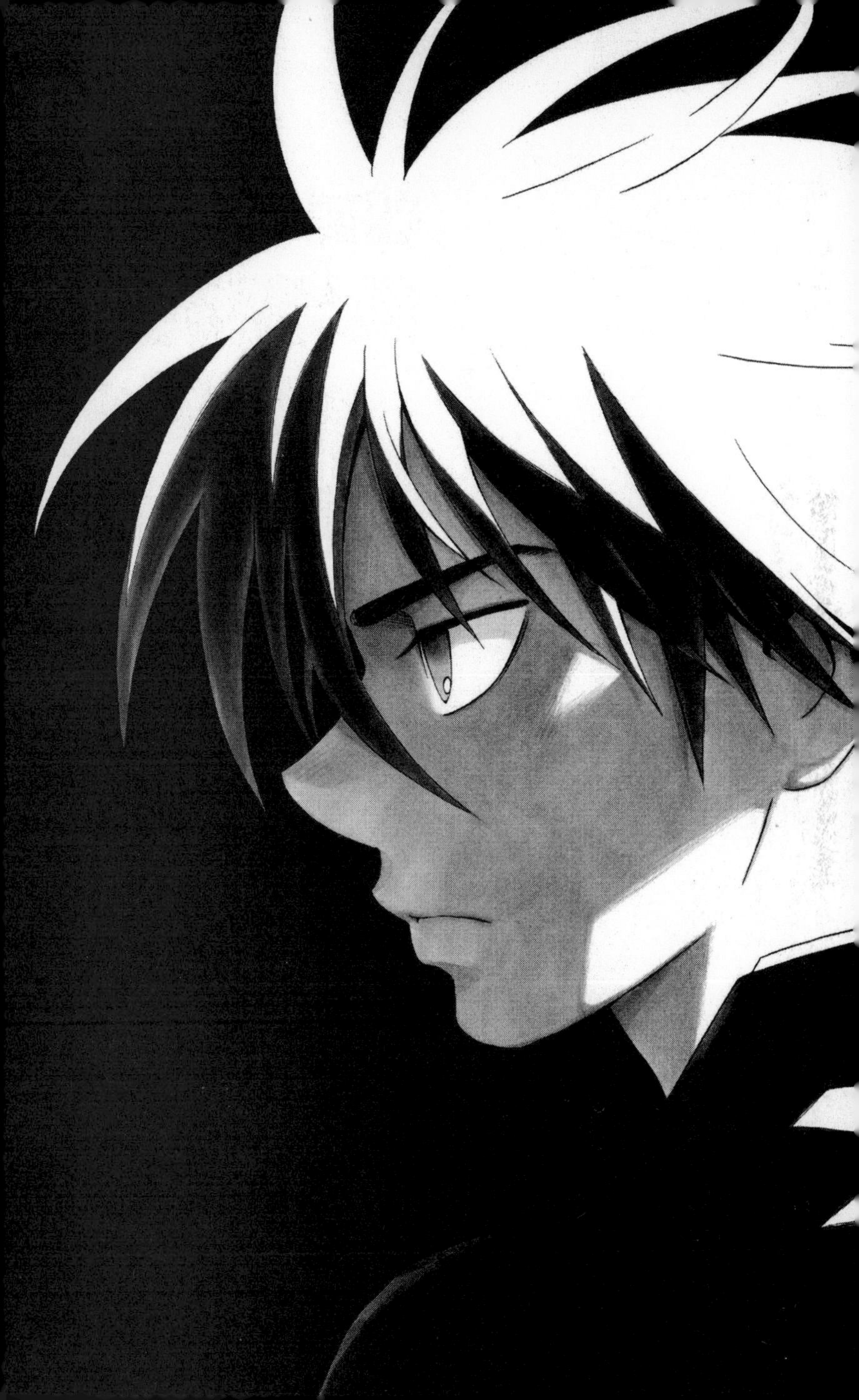

結界師

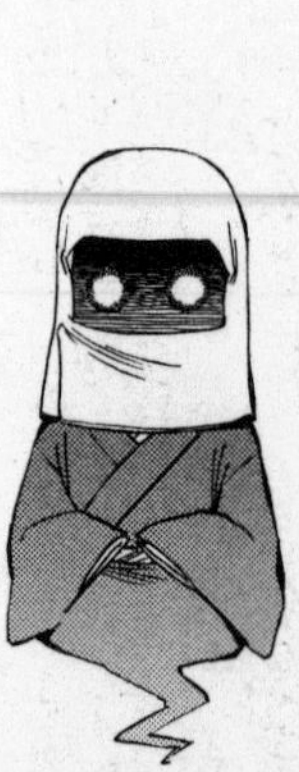

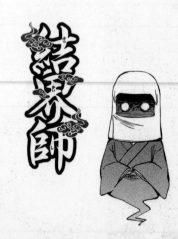

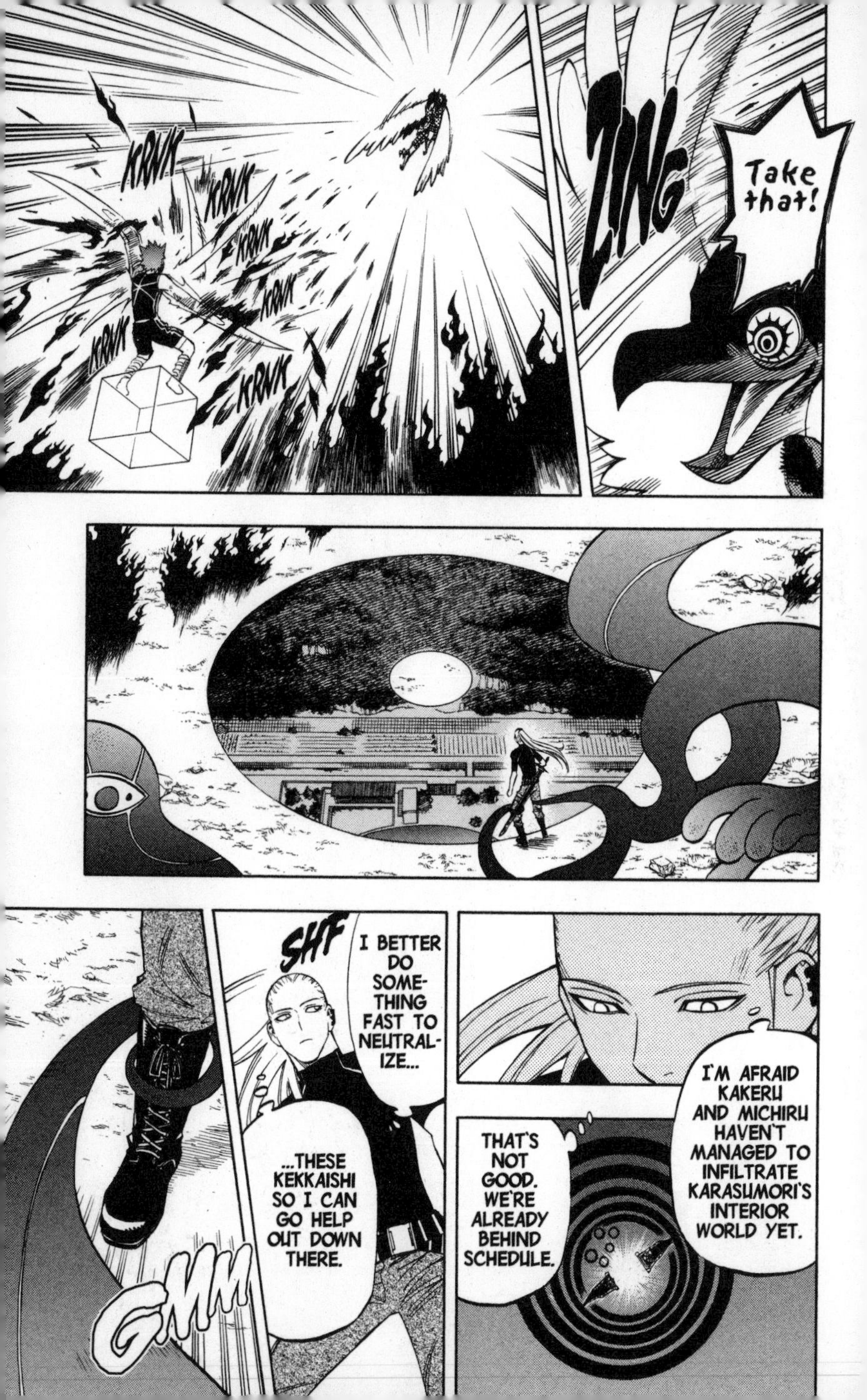
ZING
Take that!
KRNK
KRNK
KRNK
KRNK
KRNK
KRNK
I'M AFRAID KAKERU AND MICHIRU HAVEN'T MANAGED TO INFILTRATE KARASUMORI'S INTERIOR WORLD YET.
THAT'S NOT GOOD. WE'RE ALREADY BEHIND SCHEDULE.
SHF
I BETTER DO SOME-THING FAST TO NEUTRAL-IZE...
...THESE KEKKAISHI SO I CAN GO HELP OUT DOWN THERE.
GMM

SH DD R

ACK...

SEE ...?

THIS IS WHY I TOLD YOU TO HURRY UP...!

FORGIVE ME, ITO.

I HATE TO ASK YOU TO PUT YOURSELF IN THE PATH OF DANGER, BUT...

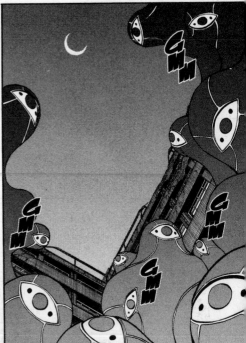

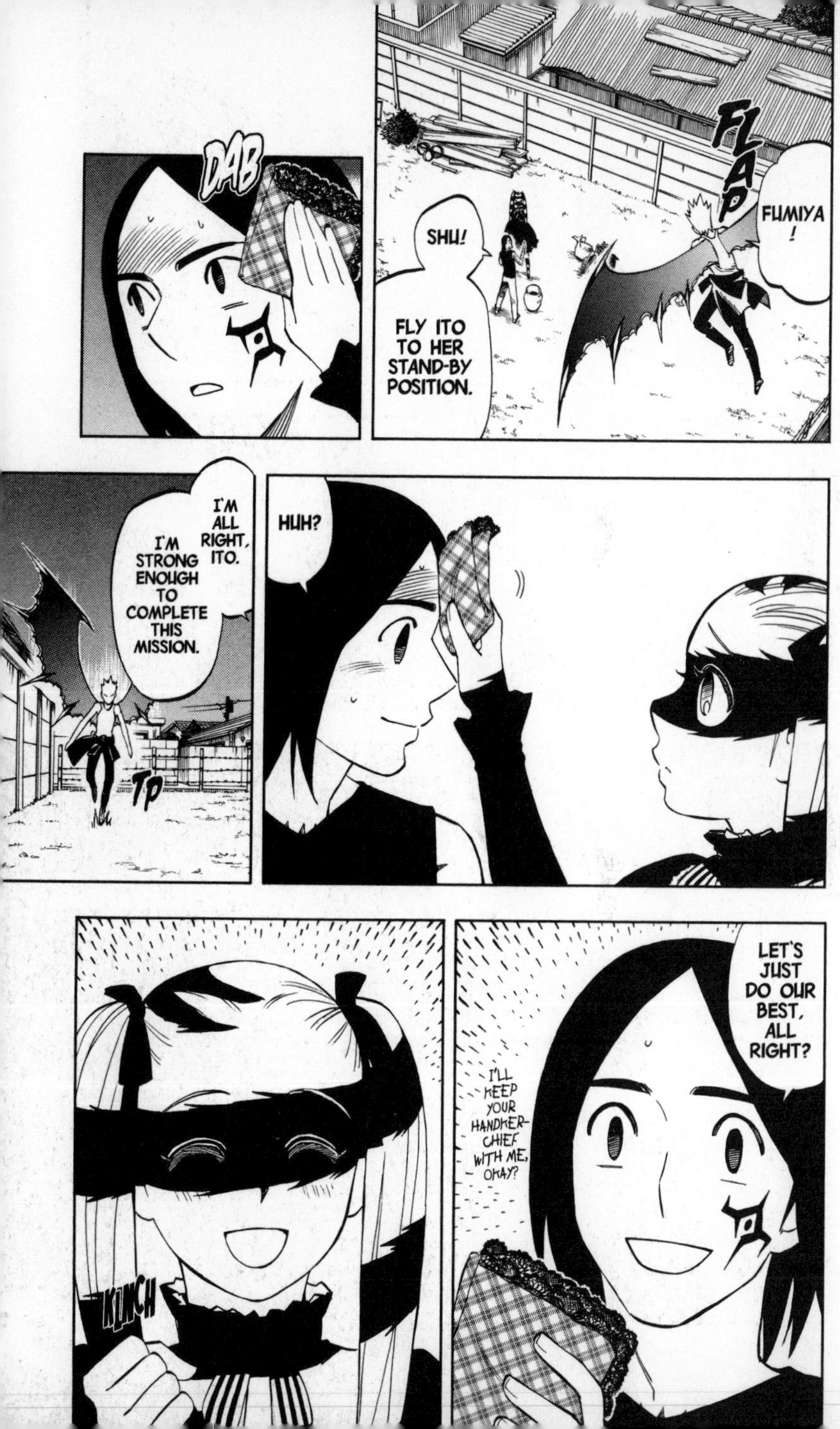
FLAP
FUMIYA!
SHU!
FLY ITO TO HER STAND-BY POSITION.
DAB
HUH?
I'M ALL RIGHT, ITO.
I'M STRONG ENOUGH TO COMPLETE THIS MISSION.
TP
LET'S JUST DO OUR BEST, ALL RIGHT?
I'LL KEEP YOUR HANDKER-CHIEF WITH ME, OKAY?
KLINCH

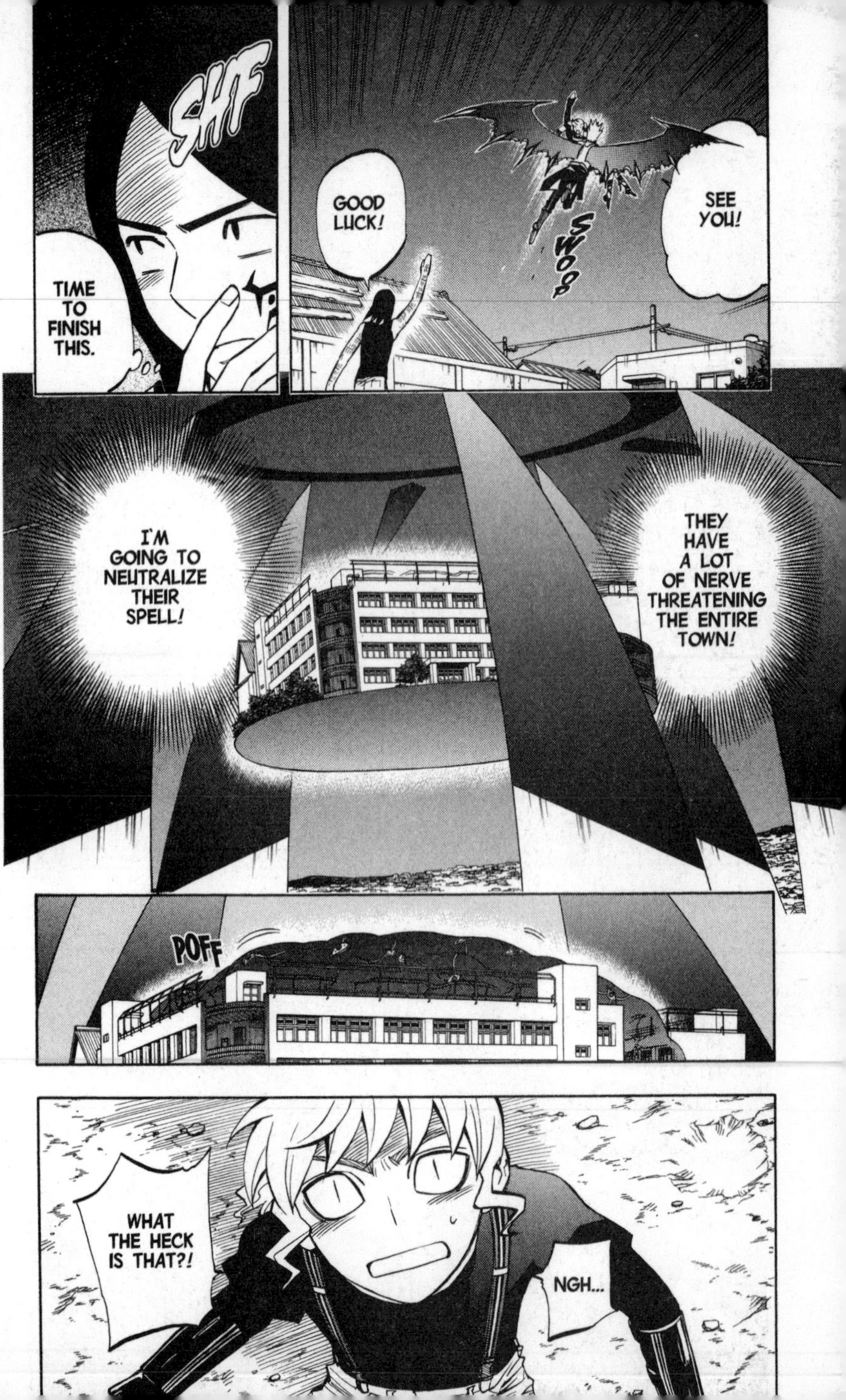
SEE YOU!
SWOOP
GOOD LUCK!
SHF
TIME TO FINISH THIS.
THEY HAVE A LOT OF NERVE THREATENING THE ENTIRE TOWN!
I'M GOING TO NEUTRALIZE THEIR SPELL!
POFF
NGH...
WHAT THE HECK IS THAT?!

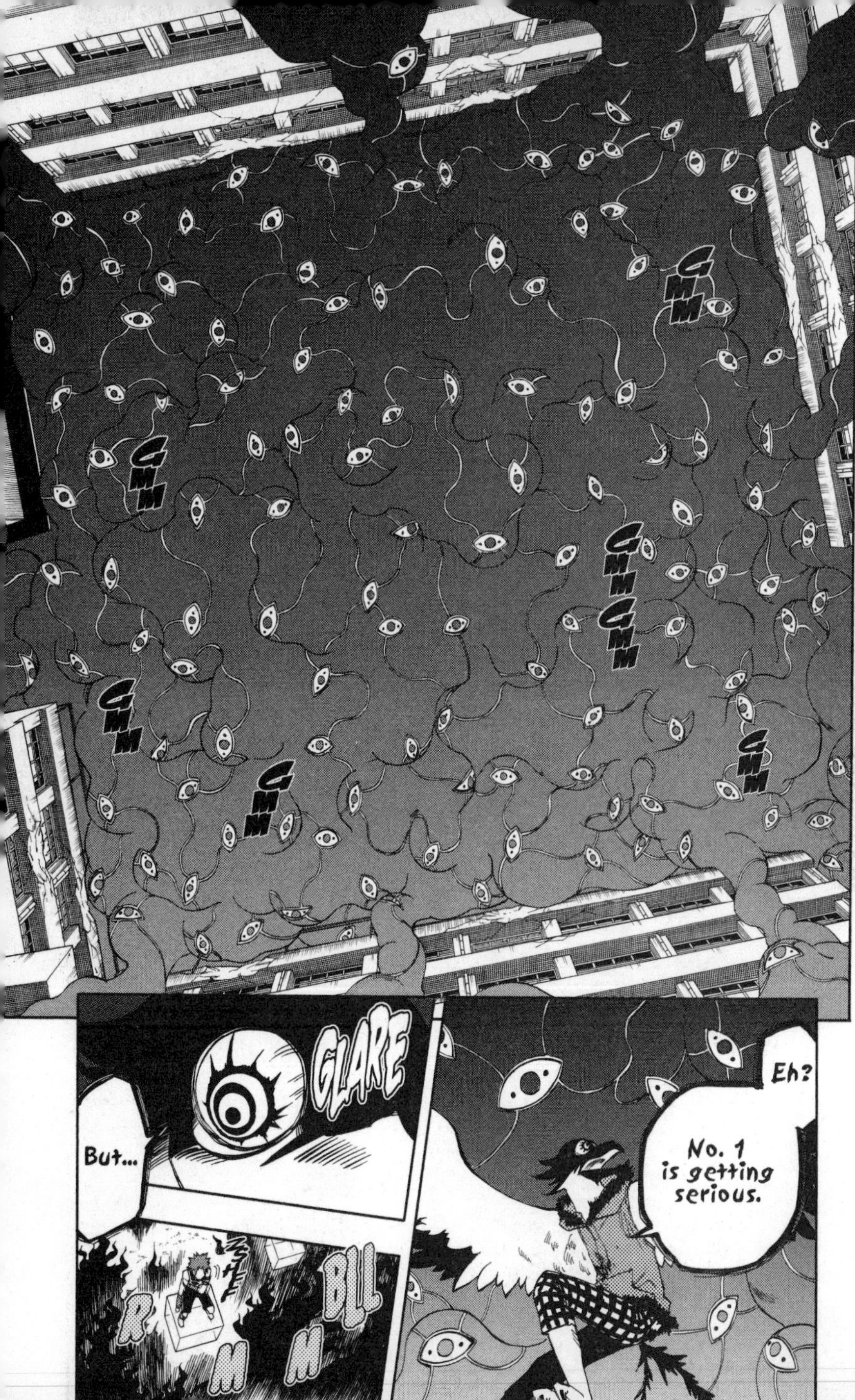
GMM
GMMGMM
GMM
GMM
GMM
GMM
Eh?
No. 1 is getting serious.
GLARE
But...

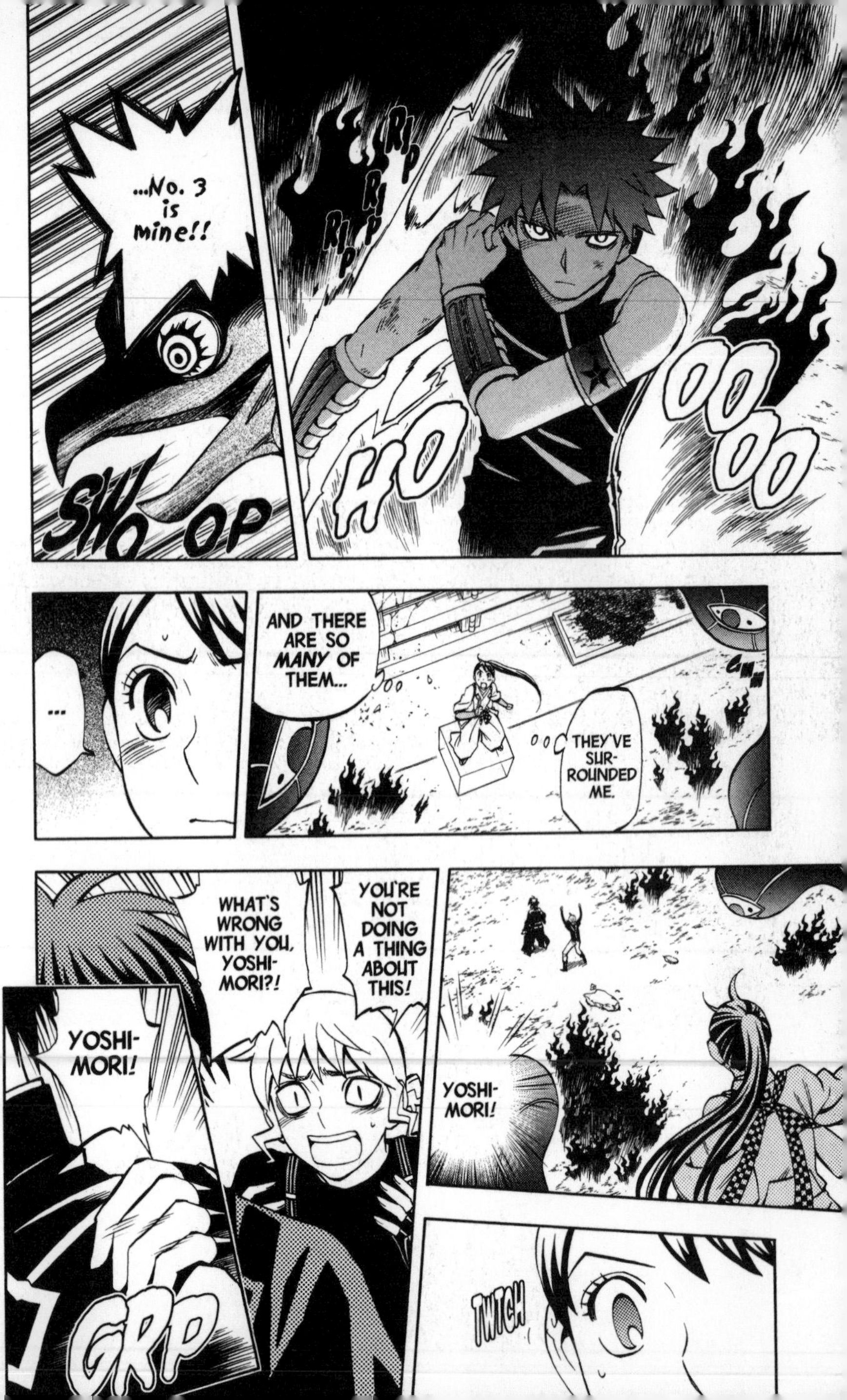

RIP
RIP
RIP
HOOOOOOO
...No. 3 is mine!!
SWOOP
AND THERE ARE SO MANY OF THEM...
THEY'VE SURROUNDED ME.
...
YOSHIMORI!
TWTCH
YOU'RE NOT DOING A THING ABOUT THIS!
WHAT'S WRONG WITH YOU, YOSHIMORI?!
YOSHIMORI!
GRP

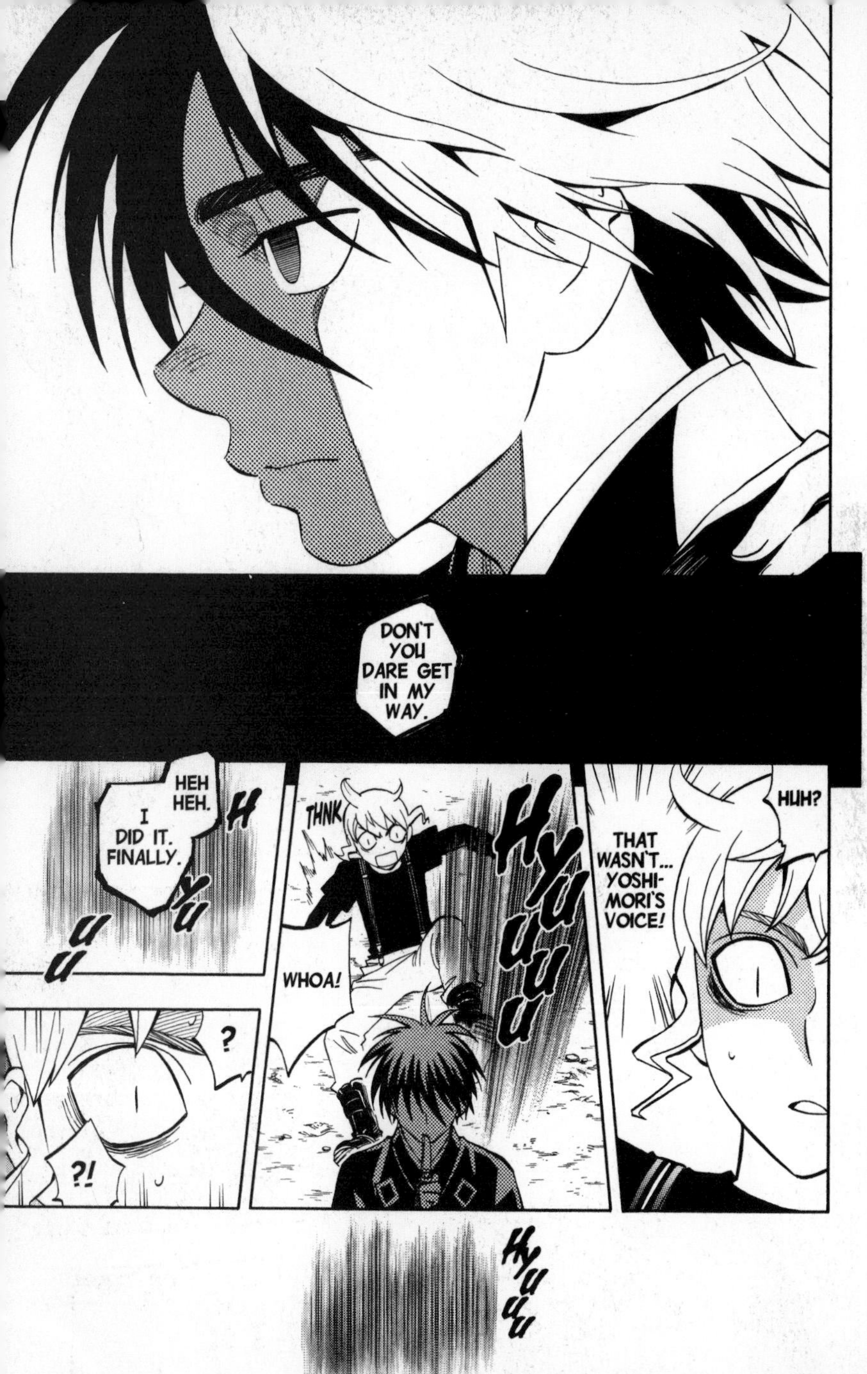
DON'T YOU DARE GET IN MY WAY.
HUH?
THAT WASN'T... YOSHIMORI'S VOICE!
THNK
HYUUUUU
WHOA!
HEH HEH.
I DID IT. FINALLY.
HYUUU
?
?!
HYUUUU

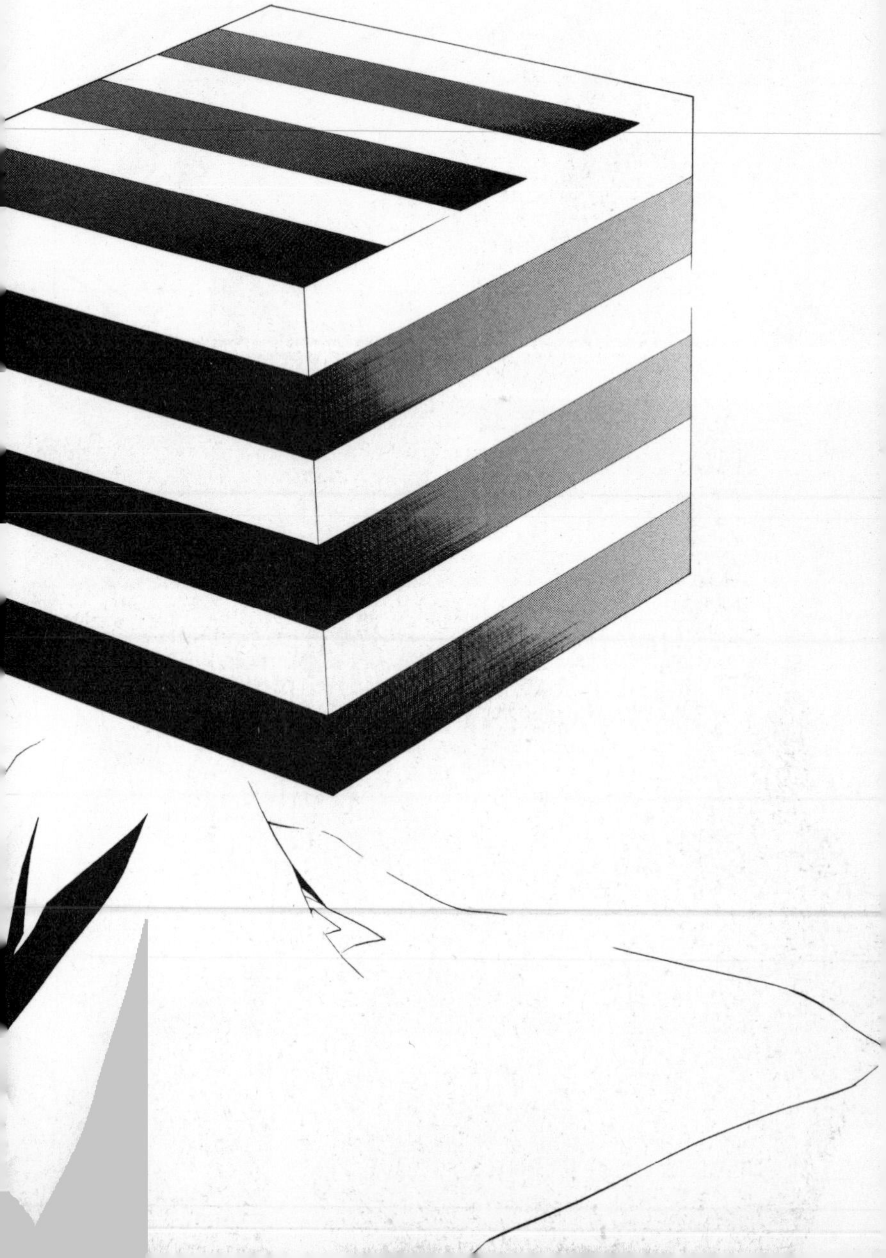

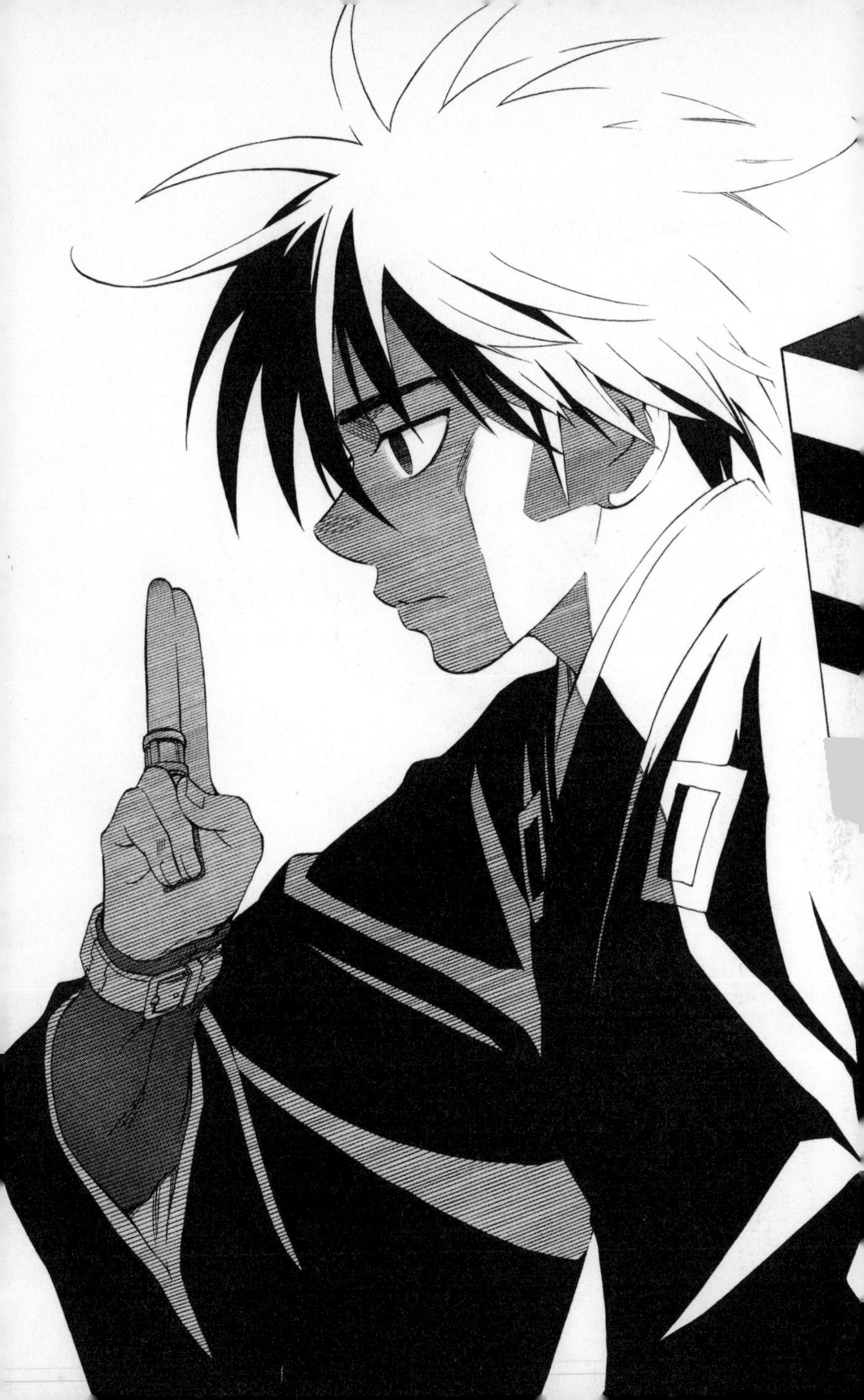

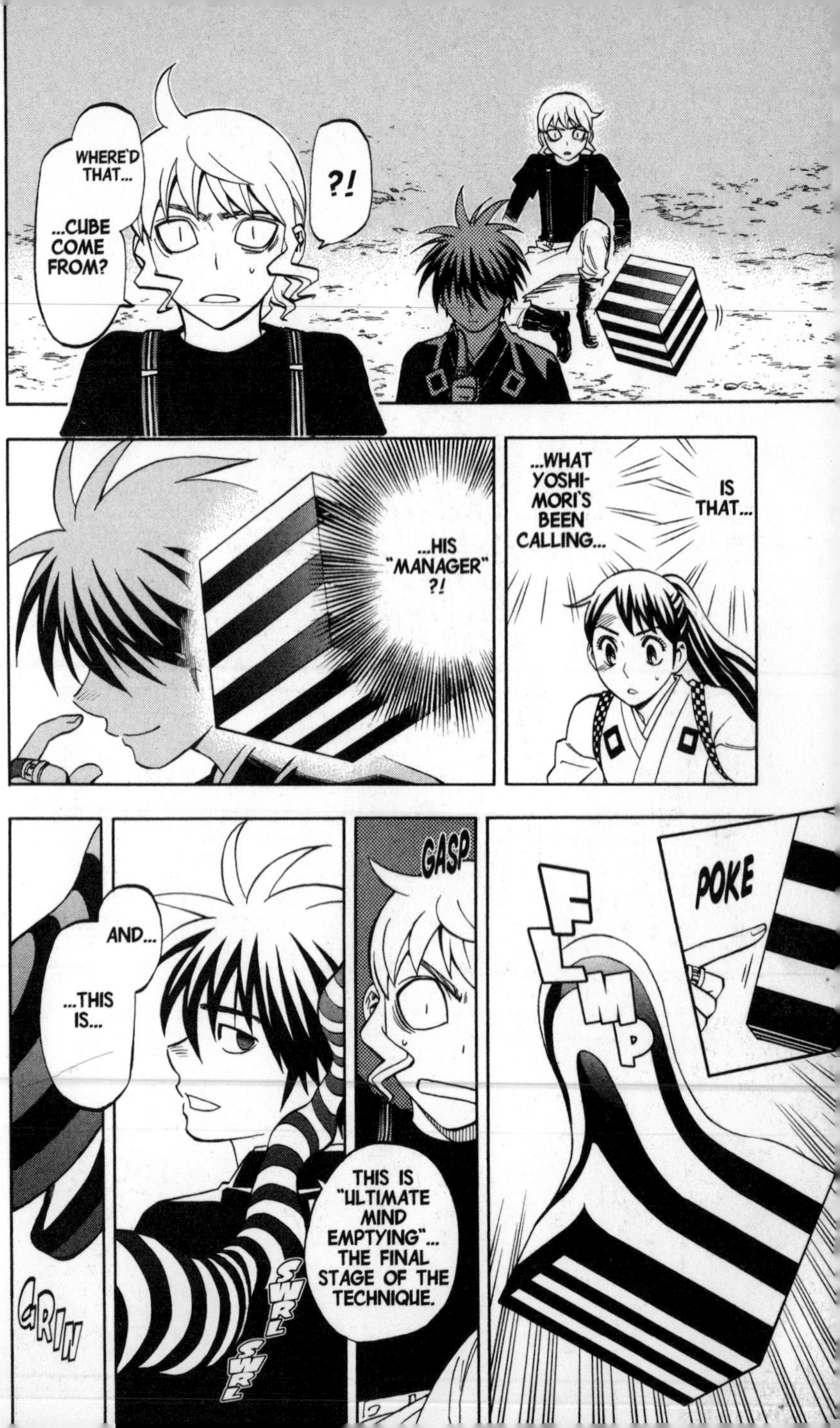
?!
WHERE'D THAT...
...CUBE COME FROM?
IS THAT...
...WHAT YOSHI-MORI'S BEEN CALLING...
...HIS "MANAGER" ?!
POKE
FLMP
GASP
AND...
...THIS IS...
THIS IS "ULTIMATE MIND EMPTYING"... THE FINAL STAGE OF THE TECHNIQUE.
SWRL SWRL
GRIN

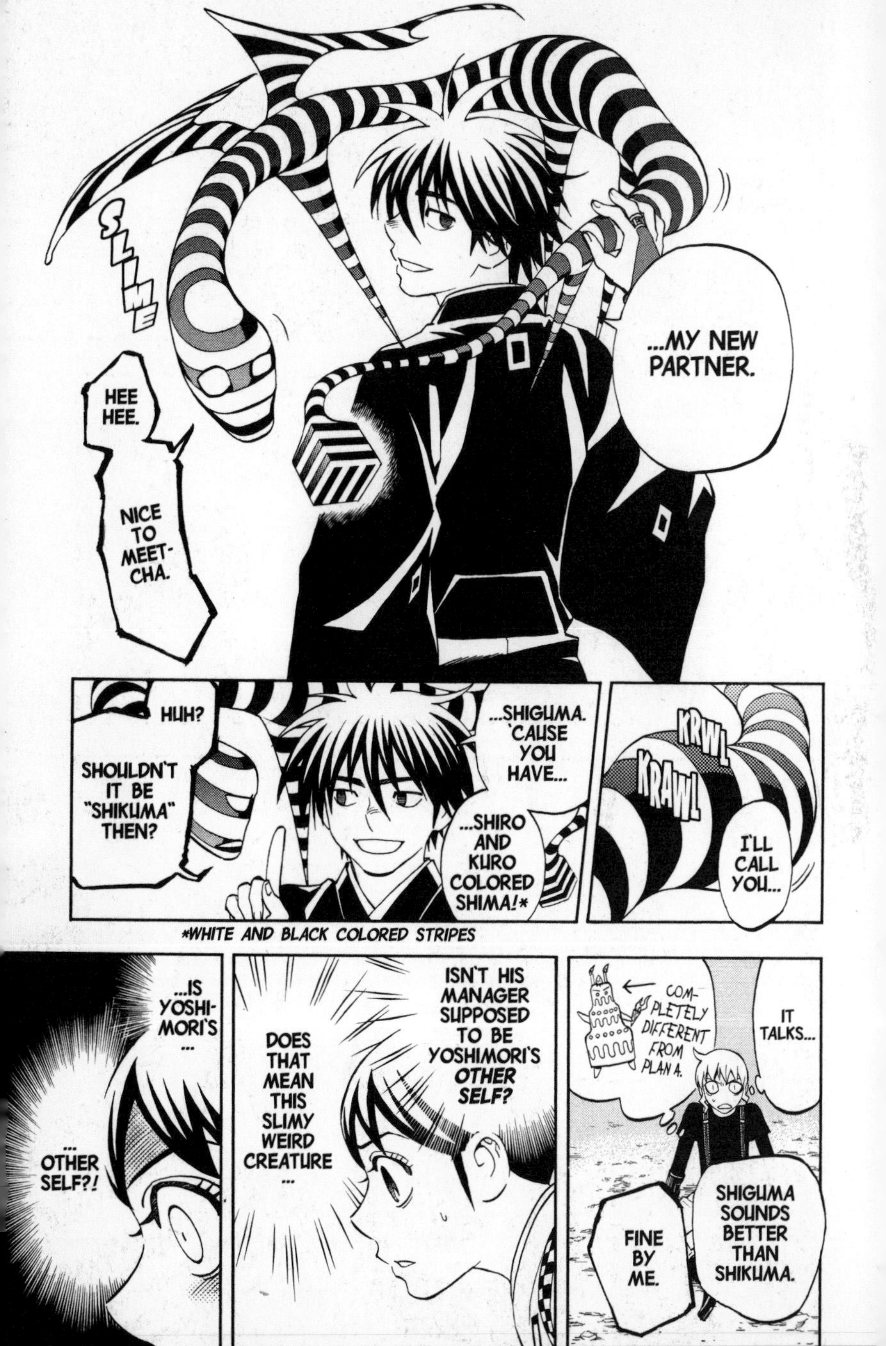
...MY NEW PARTNER.
SLIME
HEE HEE.
NICE TO MEET-CHA.
KRWL
KRAWL
I'LL CALL YOU...
...SHIGUMA. 'CAUSE YOU HAVE...
...SHIRO AND KURO COLORED SHIMA!*
HUH?
SHOULDN'T IT BE "SHIKUMA" THEN?
*WHITE AND BLACK COLORED STRIPES
IT TALKS...
COMPLETELY DIFFERENT FROM PLAN A.
SHIGUMA SOUNDS BETTER THAN SHIKUMA.
FINE BY ME.
ISN'T HIS MANAGER SUPPOSED TO BE YOSHIMORI'S OTHER SELF?
DOES THAT MEAN THIS SLIMY WEIRD CREATURE...
...IS YOSHIMORI'S...
...OTHER SELF?!

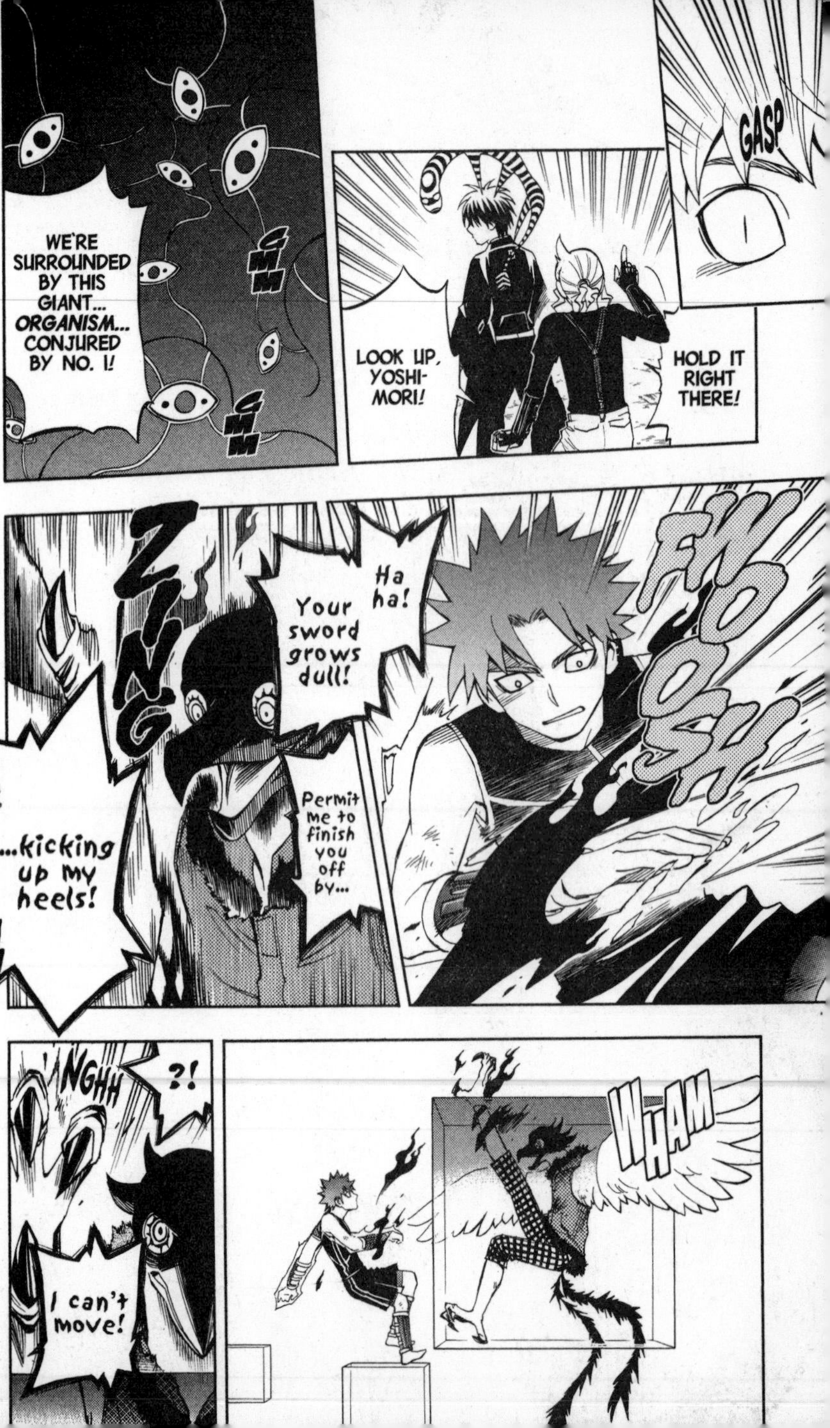
GASP
HOLD IT RIGHT THERE!
LOOK UP, YOSHIMORI!
WE'RE SURROUNDED BY THIS GIANT... ORGANISM... CONJURED BY NO. 1!
GMM
GMM
FWOOSH
Ha ha! Your sword grows dull!
ZING
Permit me to finish you off by...
...kicking up my heels!
WHAM
?!
NGHH
I can't move!

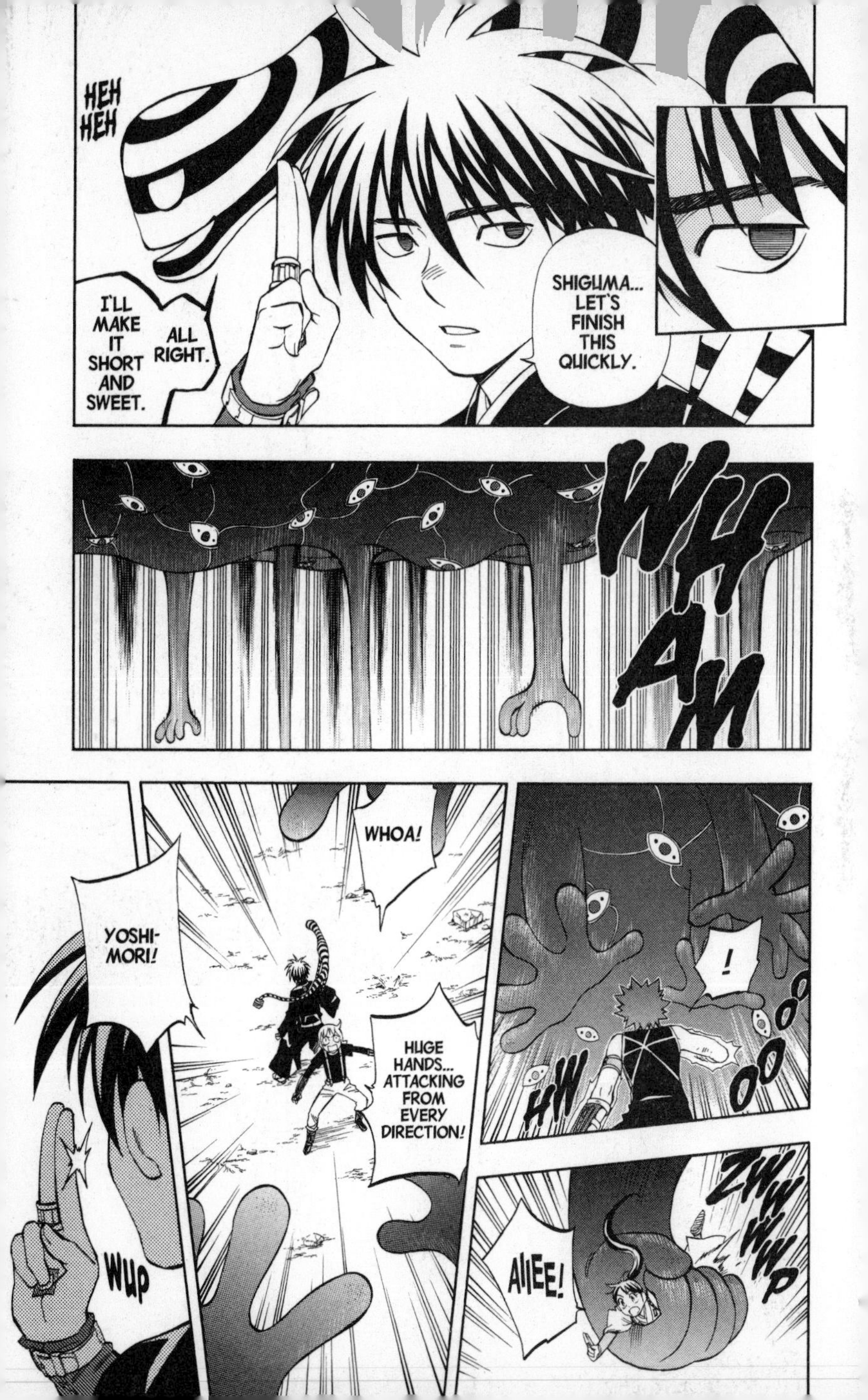
SHIGUMA... LET'S FINISH THIS QUICKLY.
ALL RIGHT.
I'LL MAKE IT SHORT AND SWEET.
HEH HEH
WHAM
!
WHOOOO
ZWWWWP
AIIEE!
WHOA!
HUGE HANDS... ATTACKING FROM EVERY DIRECTION!
YOSHIMORI!
WUP

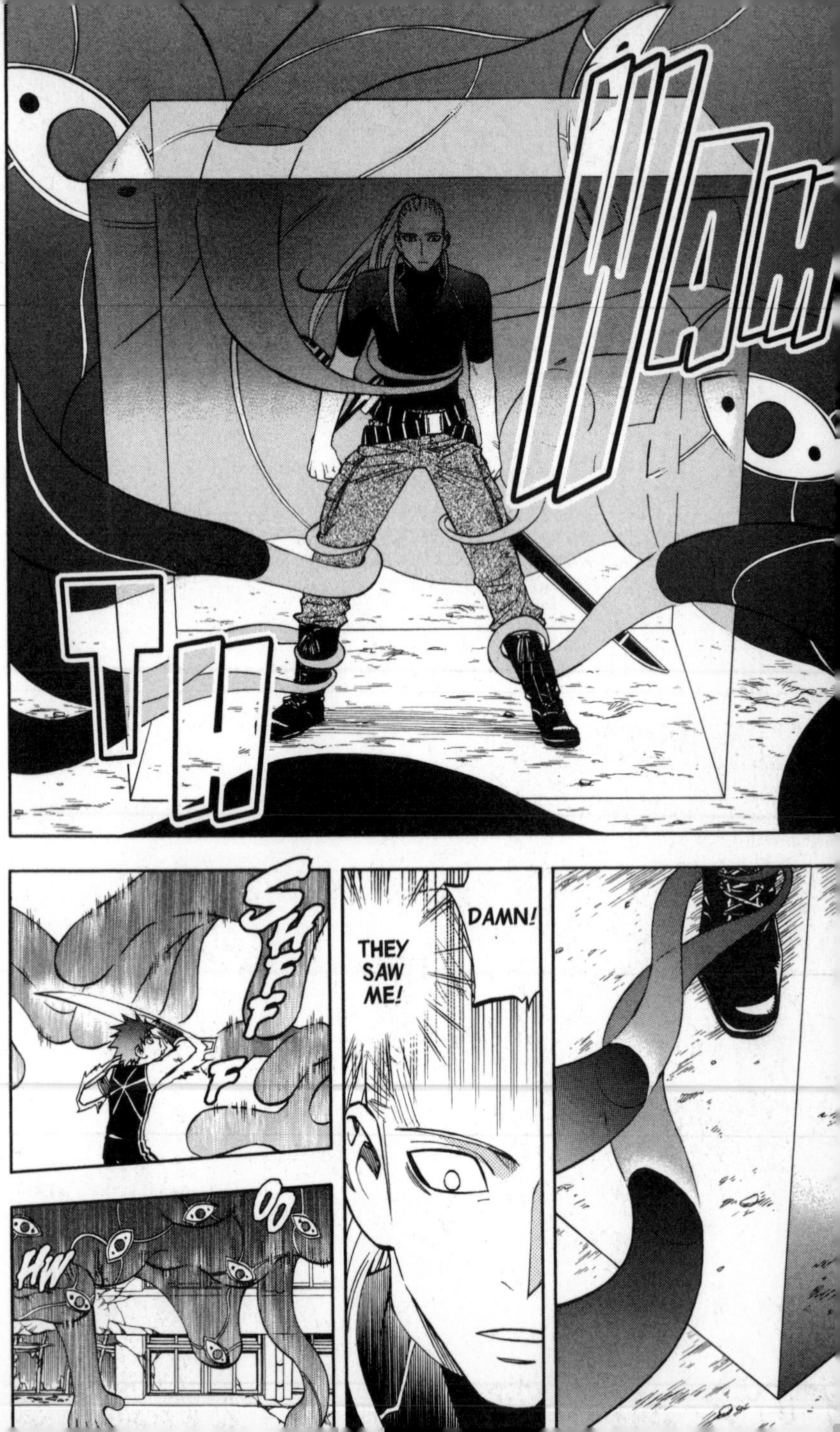
WHAM
TH
DAMN!
THEY SAW ME!
SHFF
F
OO
HW

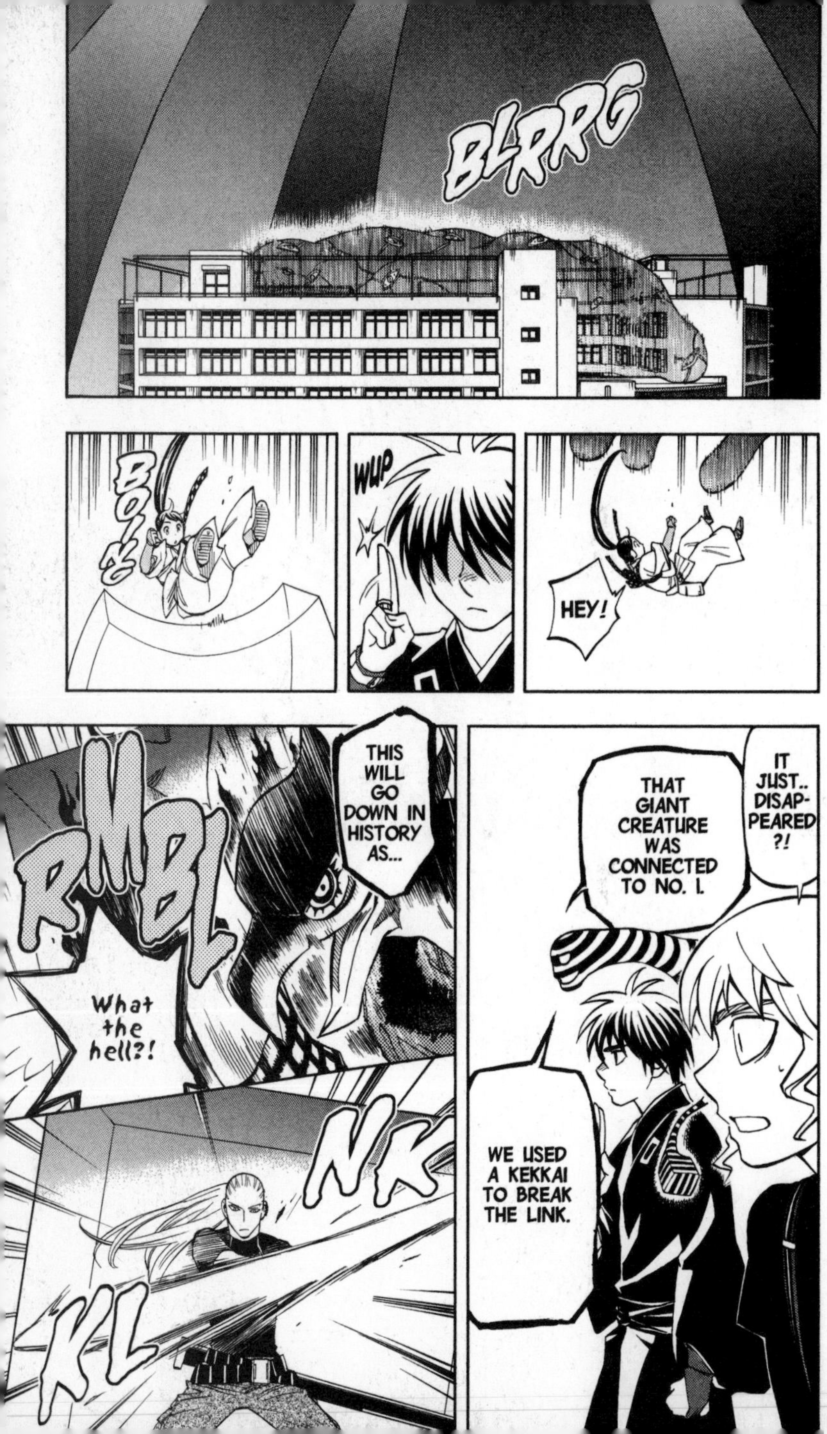
BLRRG
HEY!
WUP
BOING
IT JUST.. DISAPPEARED?!
THAT GIANT CREATURE WAS CONNECTED TO NO. 1.
WE USED A KEKKAI TO BREAK THE LINK.
RMBL
THIS WILL GO DOWN IN HISTORY AS...
What the hell?!
NK
KL

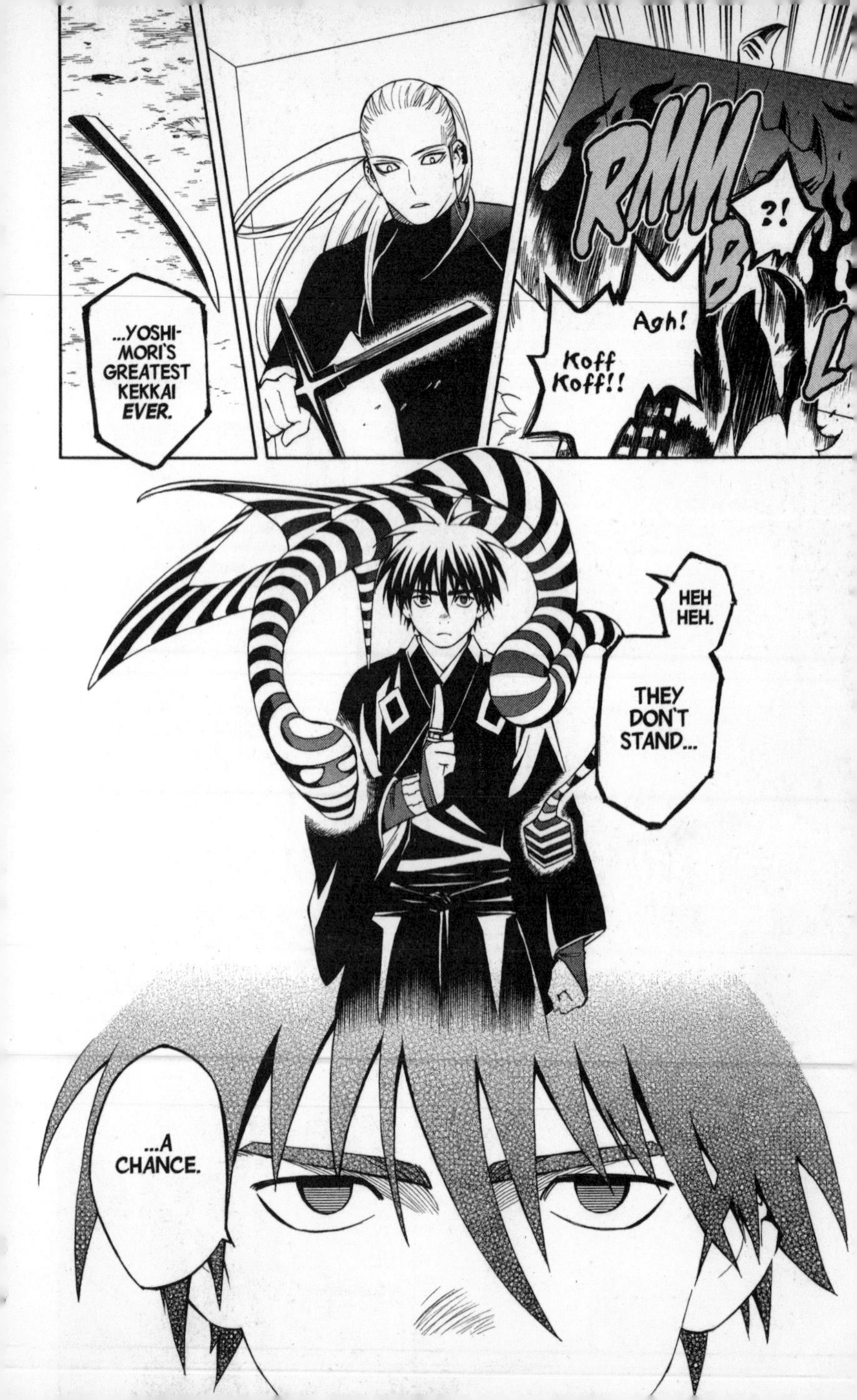
RMMBL
?!
Agh!
Koff Koff!!
...YOSHIMORI'S GREATEST KEKKAI *EVER.*
HEH HEH.
THEY DON'T STAND...
...A CHANCE.

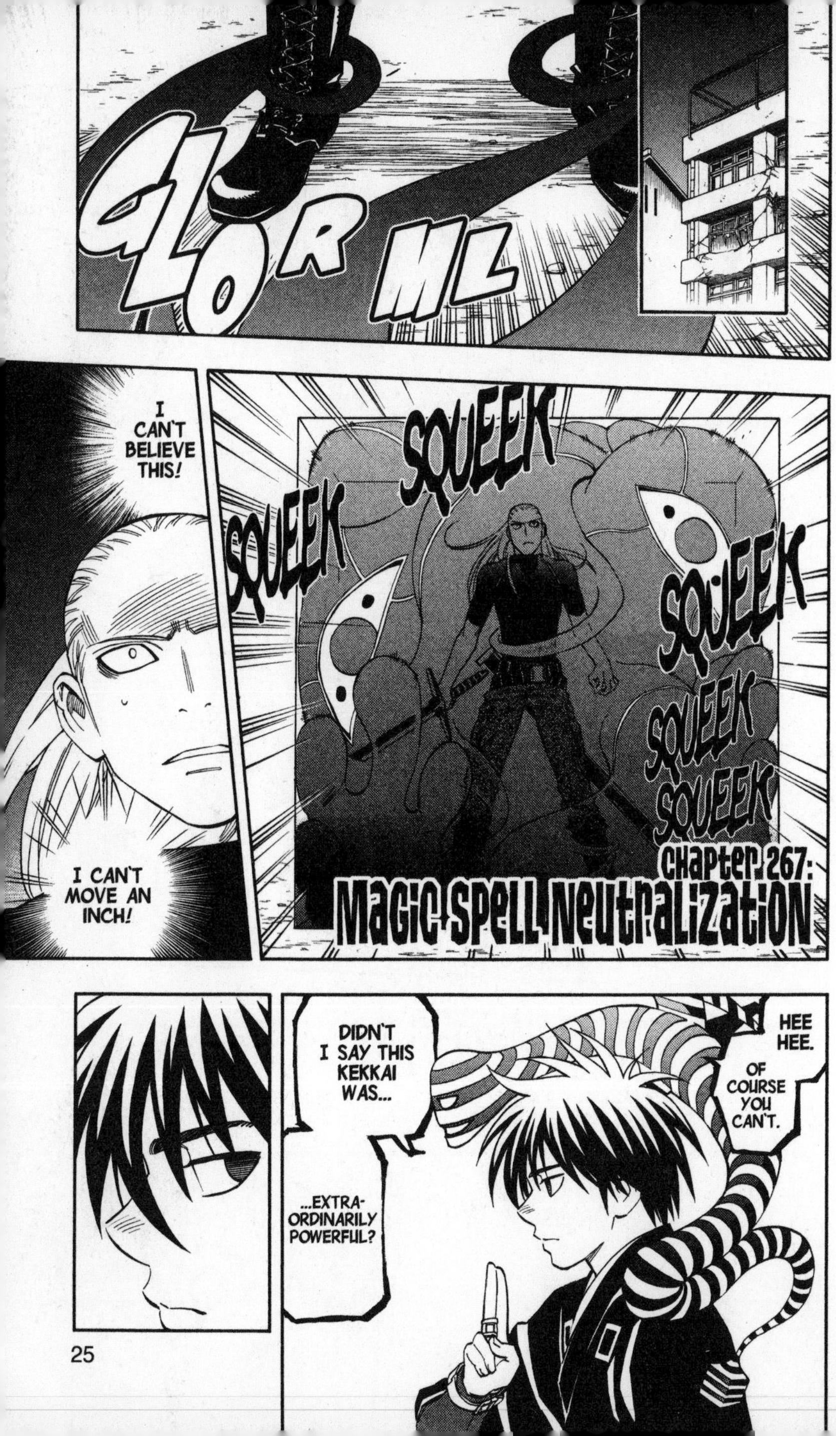
GLORML
SQUEEK
SQUEEK
SQUEEK
SQUEEK
SQUEEK
Chapter 267:
Magic Spell Neutralization
I CAN'T BELIEVE THIS!
I CAN'T MOVE AN INCH!
HEE HEE.
OF COURSE YOU CAN'T.
DIDN'T I SAY THIS KEKKAI WAS...
...EXTRA-ORDINARILY POWERFUL?

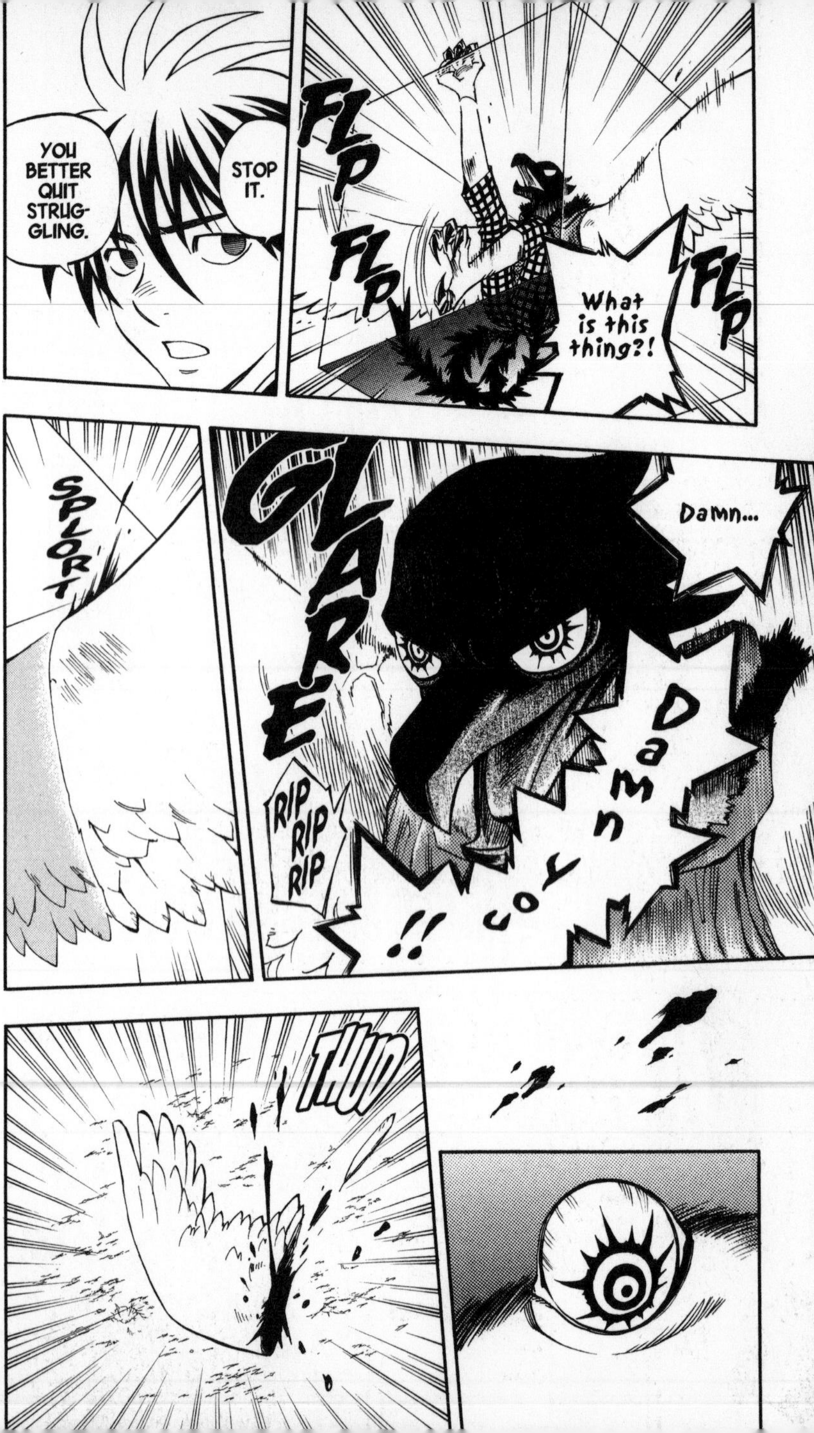
FLP
FLP
What is this thing?!
FLP
STOP IT.
YOU BETTER QUIT STRUG-GLING.
GLARE
Damn...
Damn you!!
RIP RIP RIP
SPLORT
THUD

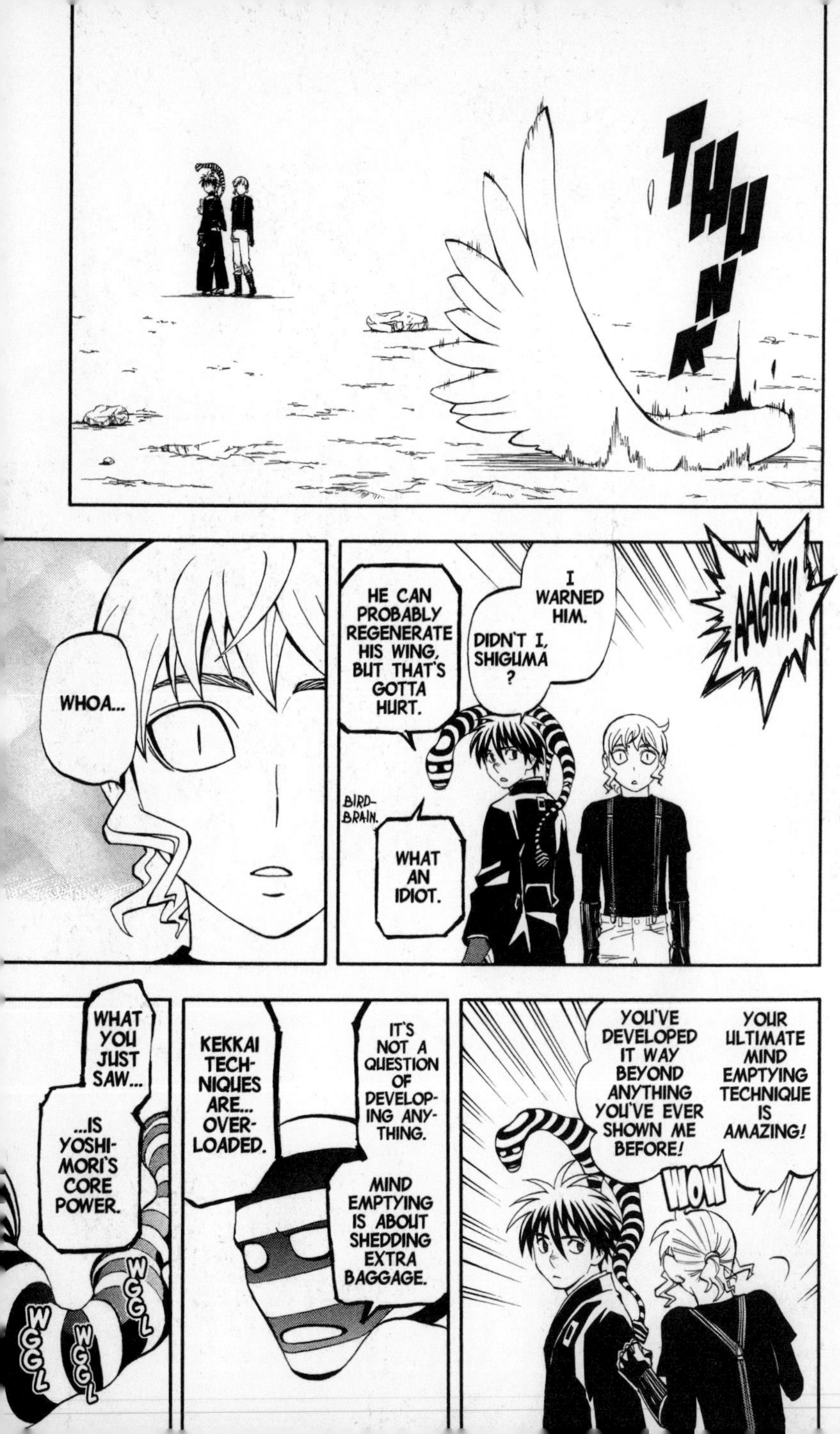
THUNK
AAGHH!
I WARNED HIM.
DIDN'T I, SHIGUMA?
HE CAN PROBABLY REGENERATE HIS WING, BUT THAT'S GOTTA HURT.
BIRD-BRAIN.
WHAT AN IDIOT.
WHOA...
YOUR ULTIMATE MIND EMPTYING TECHNIQUE IS AMAZING!
YOU'VE DEVELOPED IT WAY BEYOND ANYTHING YOU'VE EVER SHOWN ME BEFORE!
WOW
IT'S NOT A QUESTION OF DEVELOPING ANYTHING.
KEKKAI TECHNIQUES ARE... OVERLOADED.
MIND EMPTYING IS ABOUT SHEDDING EXTRA BAGGAGE.
WHAT YOU JUST SAW...
...IS YOSHIMORI'S CORE POWER.
WGGL
WGGL
WGGL

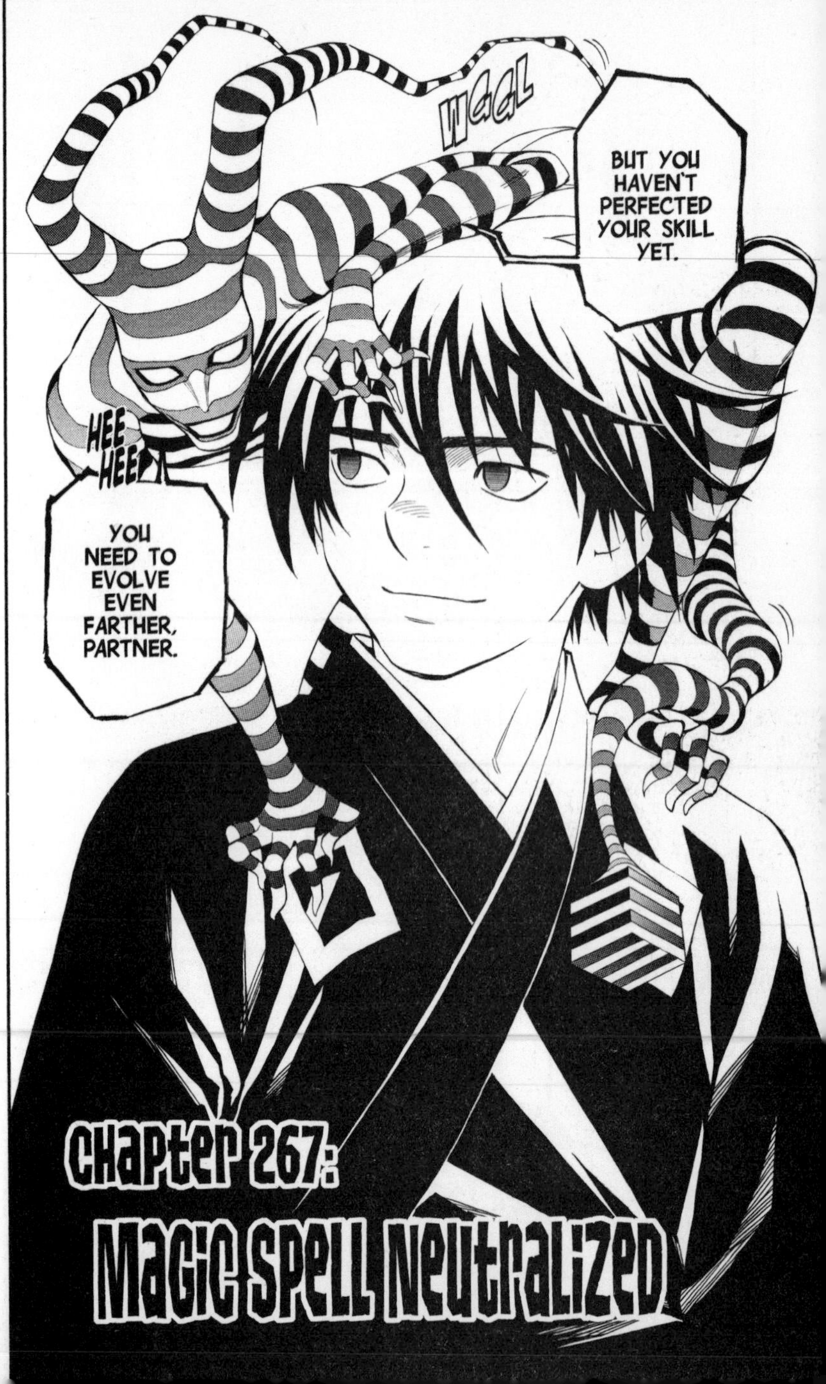
WGGL
BUT YOU HAVEN'T PERFECTED YOUR SKILL YET.
HEE HEE
YOU NEED TO EVOLVE EVEN FARTHER, PARTNER.
CHAPTER 267:
MAGIC SPELL NEUTRALIZED

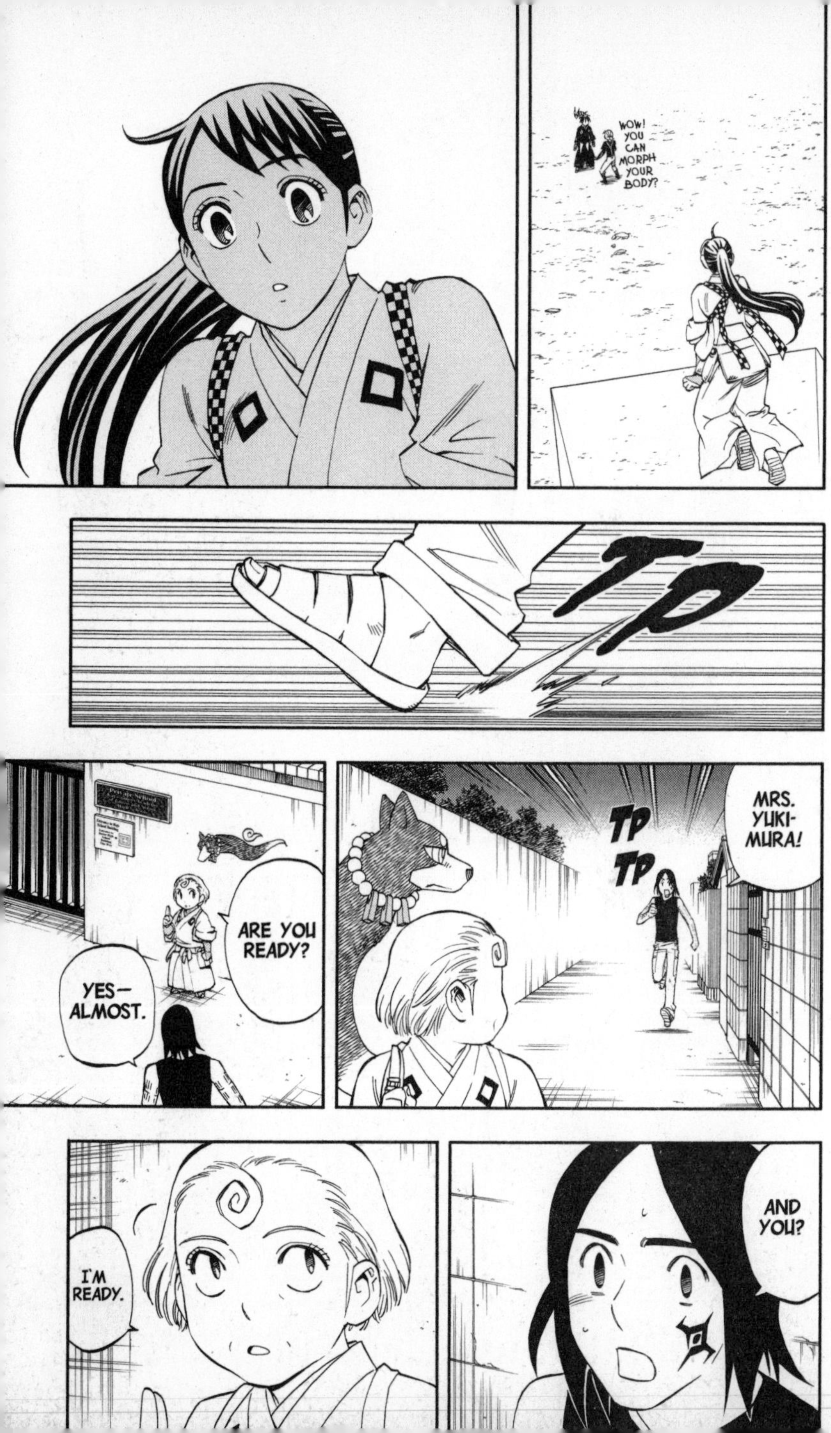
WOW! YOU CAN MORPH YOUR BODY?
TP
MRS. YUKI-MURA!
TP TP
ARE YOU READY?
YES— ALMOST.
AND YOU?
I'M READY.

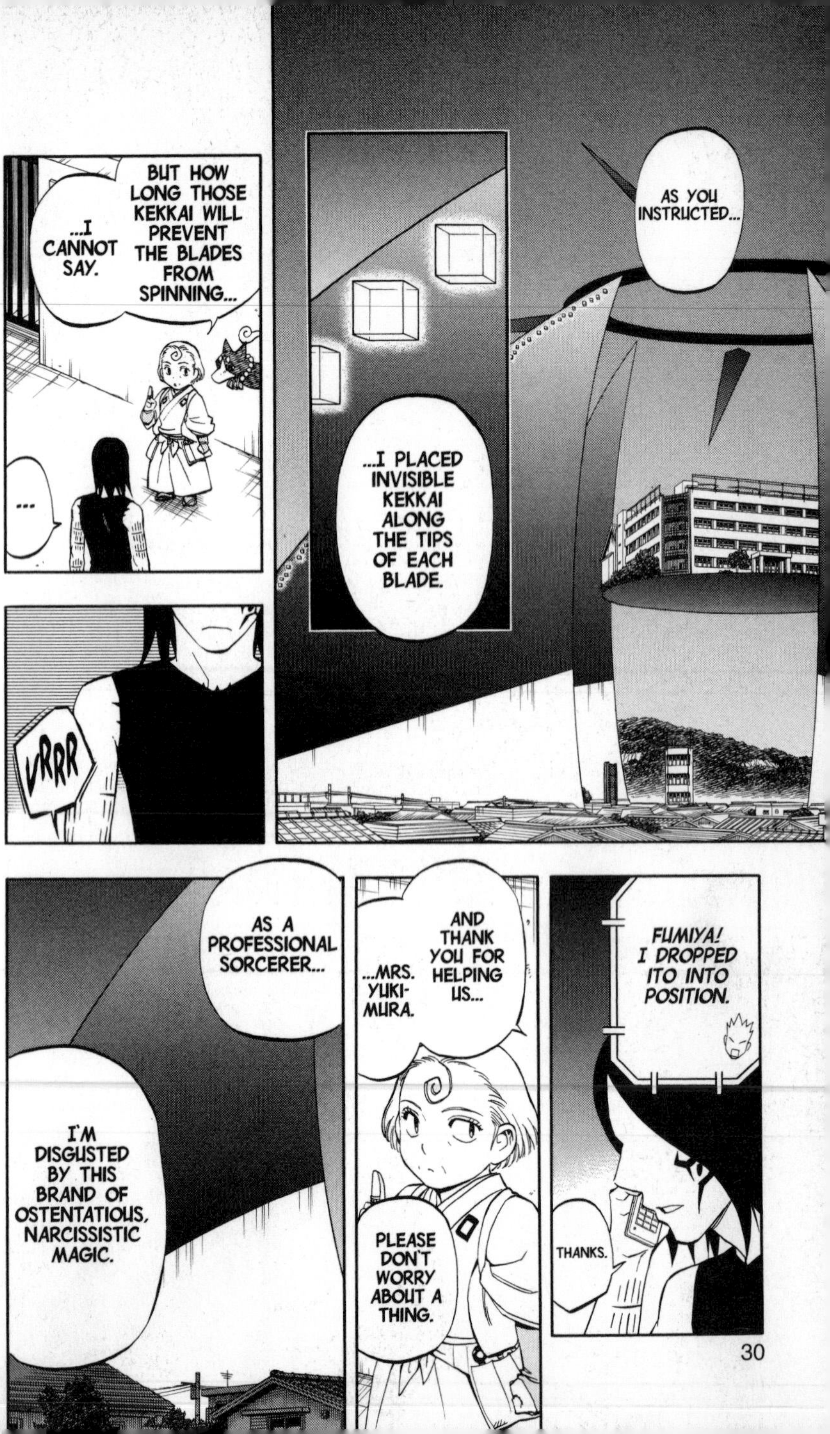
AS YOU INSTRUCTED...
...I PLACED INVISIBLE KEKKAI ALONG THE TIPS OF EACH BLADE.
BUT HOW LONG THOSE KEKKAI WILL PREVENT THE BLADES FROM SPINNING...
...I CANNOT SAY.
...
VRRR
FUMIYA! I DROPPED ITO INTO POSITION.
THANKS.
AND THANK YOU FOR HELPING US...
...MRS. YUKIMURA.
PLEASE DON'T WORRY ABOUT A THING.
AS A PROFESSIONAL SORCERER...
I'M DISGUSTED BY THIS BRAND OF OSTENTATIOUS, NARCISSISTIC MAGIC.

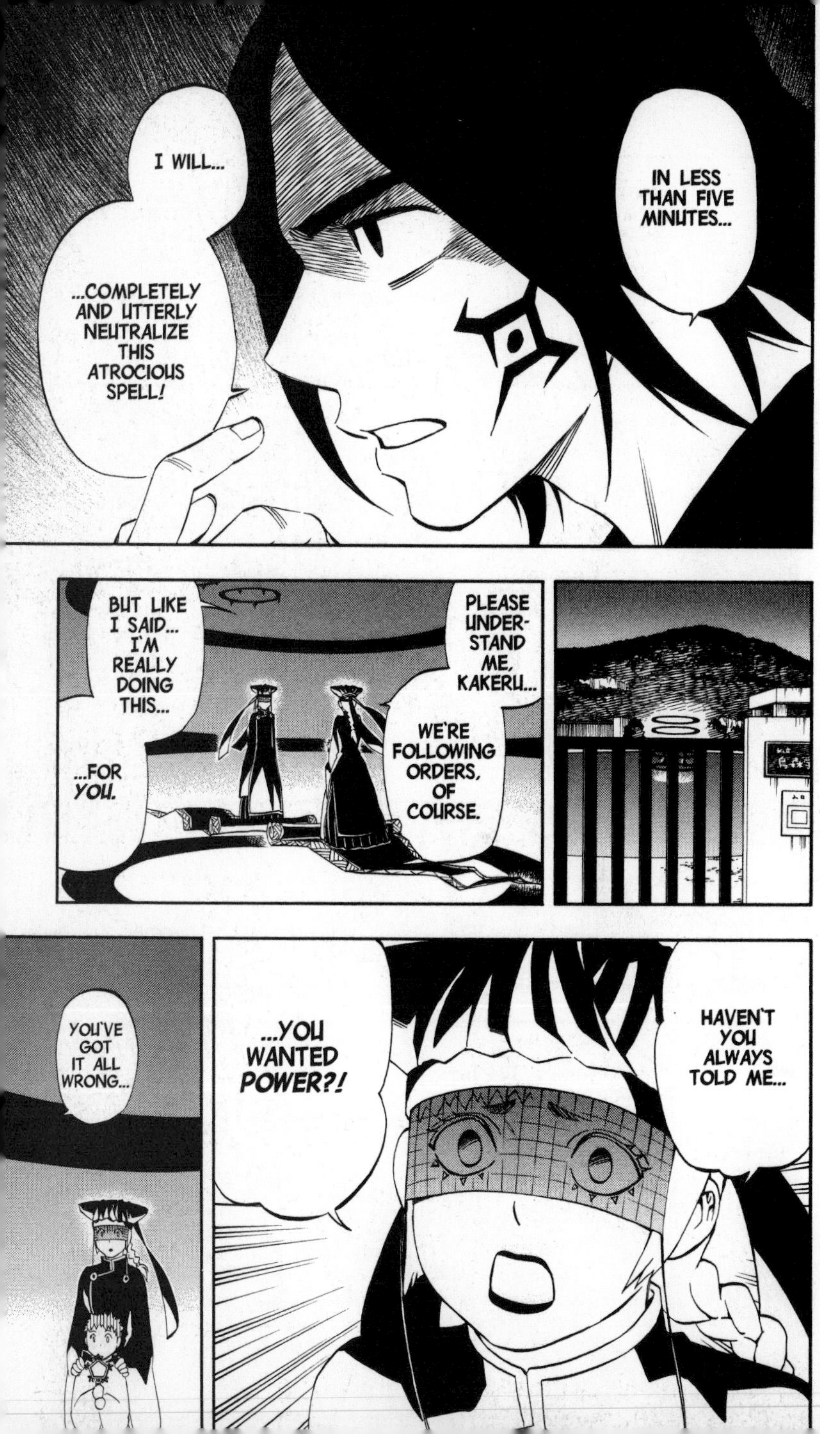
IN LESS THAN FIVE MINUTES...
I WILL...
...COMPLETELY AND UTTERLY NEUTRALIZE THIS ATROCIOUS SPELL!
PLEASE UNDERSTAND ME, KAKERU...
WE'RE FOLLOWING ORDERS, OF COURSE.
BUT LIKE I SAID... I'M REALLY DOING THIS...
...FOR *YOU*.
HAVEN'T YOU ALWAYS TOLD ME...
...YOU WANTED *POWER*?!
YOU'VE GOT IT ALL WRONG...

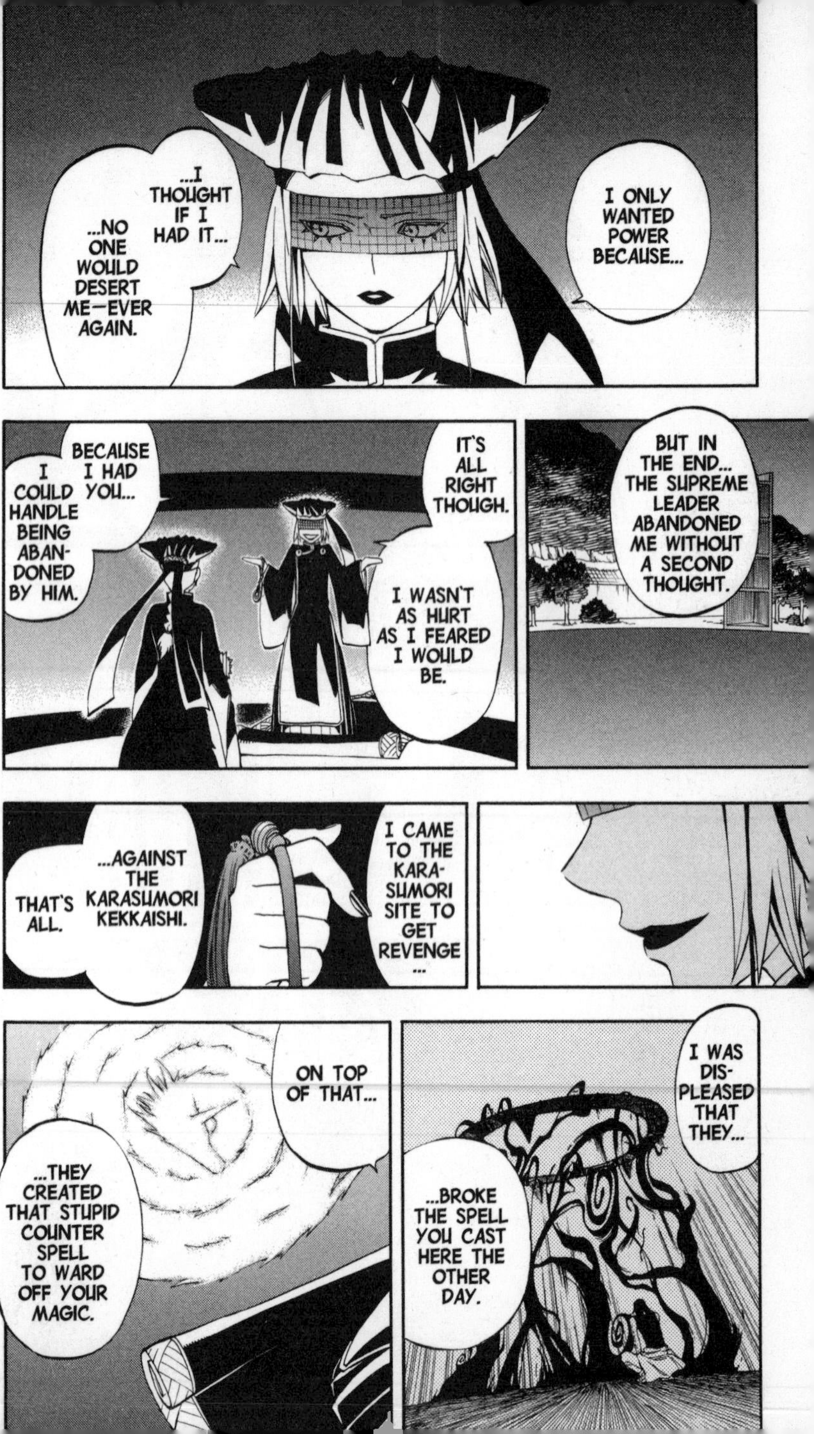
I ONLY WANTED POWER BECAUSE...
...I THOUGHT IF I HAD IT...
...NO ONE WOULD DESERT ME—EVER AGAIN.
BUT IN THE END... THE SUPREME LEADER ABANDONED ME WITHOUT A SECOND THOUGHT.
IT'S ALL RIGHT THOUGH.
I WASN'T AS HURT AS I FEARED I WOULD BE.
BECAUSE I HAD YOU...
I COULD HANDLE BEING ABAN-DONED BY HIM.
I CAME TO THE KARA-SUMORI SITE TO GET REVENGE...
...AGAINST THE KARASUMORI KEKKAISHI.
THAT'S ALL.
I WAS DIS-PLEASED THAT THEY...
...BROKE THE SPELL YOU CAST HERE THE OTHER DAY.
ON TOP OF THAT...
...THEY CREATED THAT STUPID COUNTER SPELL TO WARD OFF YOUR MAGIC.

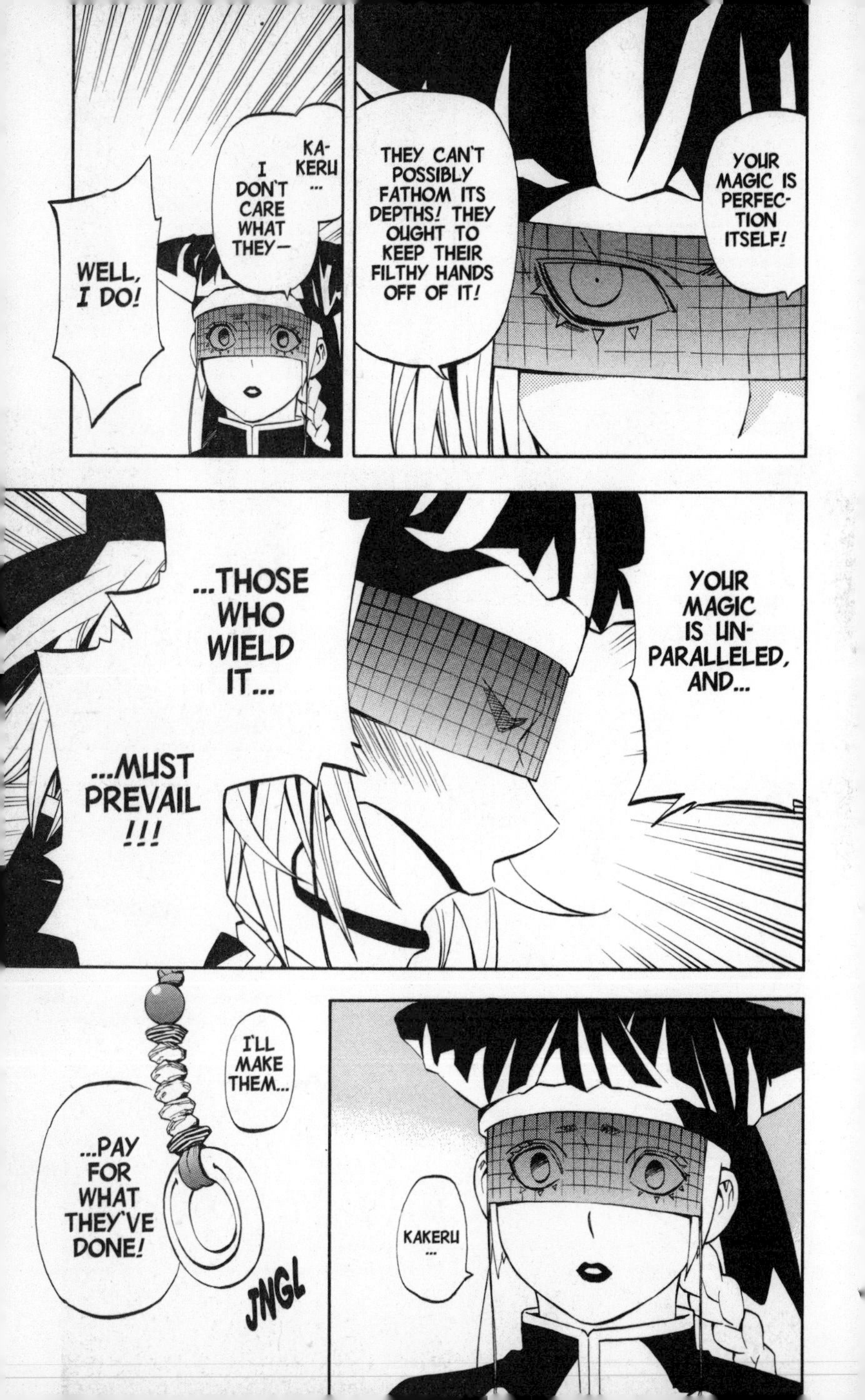
YOUR MAGIC IS PERFECTION ITSELF!
THEY CAN'T POSSIBLY FATHOM ITS DEPTHS! THEY OUGHT TO KEEP THEIR FILTHY HANDS OFF OF IT!
KAKERU...
I DON'T CARE WHAT THEY—
WELL, I DO!
YOUR MAGIC IS UNPARALLELED, AND...
...THOSE WHO WIELD IT...
...MUST PREVAIL!!!
KAKERU...
I'LL MAKE THEM...
...PAY FOR WHAT THEY'VE DONE!
JNGL

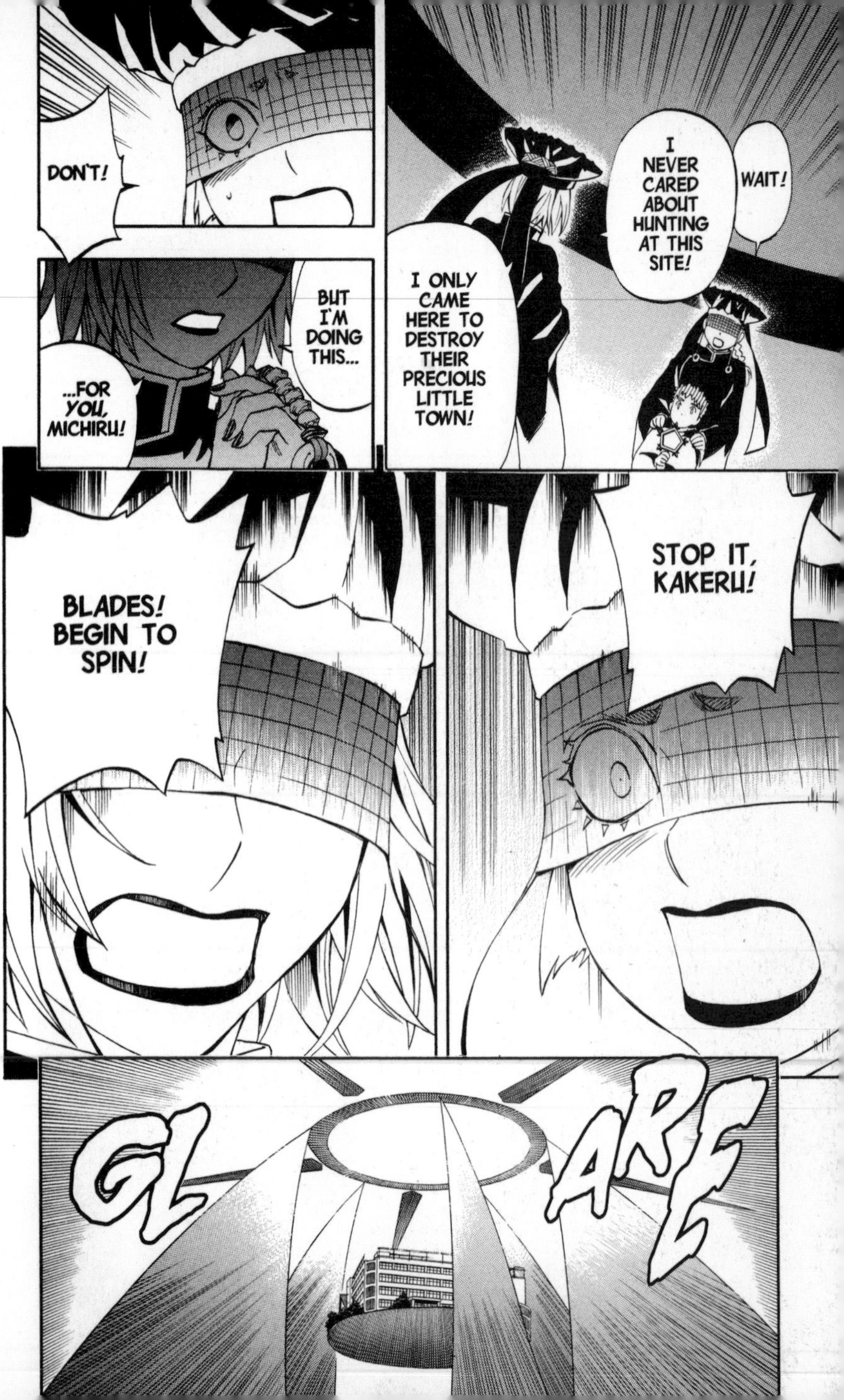
WAIT!
I NEVER CARED ABOUT HUNTING AT THIS SITE!
I ONLY CAME HERE TO DESTROY THEIR PRECIOUS LITTLE TOWN!
DON'T!
BUT I'M DOING THIS...
...FOR YOU, MICHIRU!
STOP IT, KAKERU!
BLADES! BEGIN TO SPIN!
GLARE

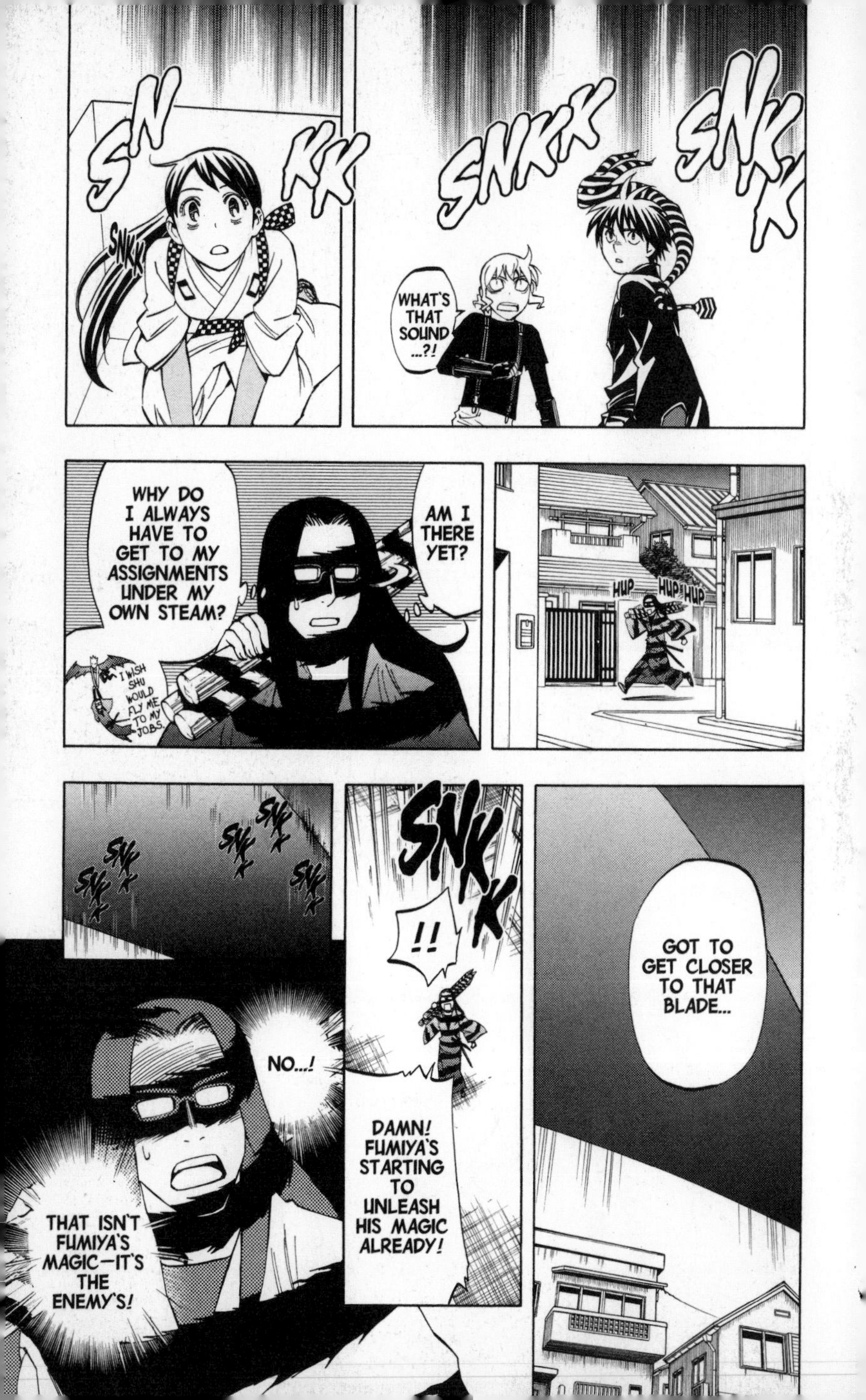
SNKK
SNKK
WHAT'S THAT SOUND ...?!
SNKK
SNKK
HUP HUP HUP
AM I THERE YET?
WHY DO I ALWAYS HAVE TO GET TO MY ASSIGNMENTS UNDER MY OWN STEAM?
I WISH SHU WOULD FLY ME TO MY JOBS.
GOT TO GET CLOSER TO THAT BLADE...
SNKK
!!
DAMN! FUMIYA'S STARTING TO UNLEASH HIS MAGIC ALREADY!
SNKK
SNKK
SNKK
SNKK
NO...!
THAT ISN'T FUMIYA'S MAGIC—IT'S THE ENEMY'S!

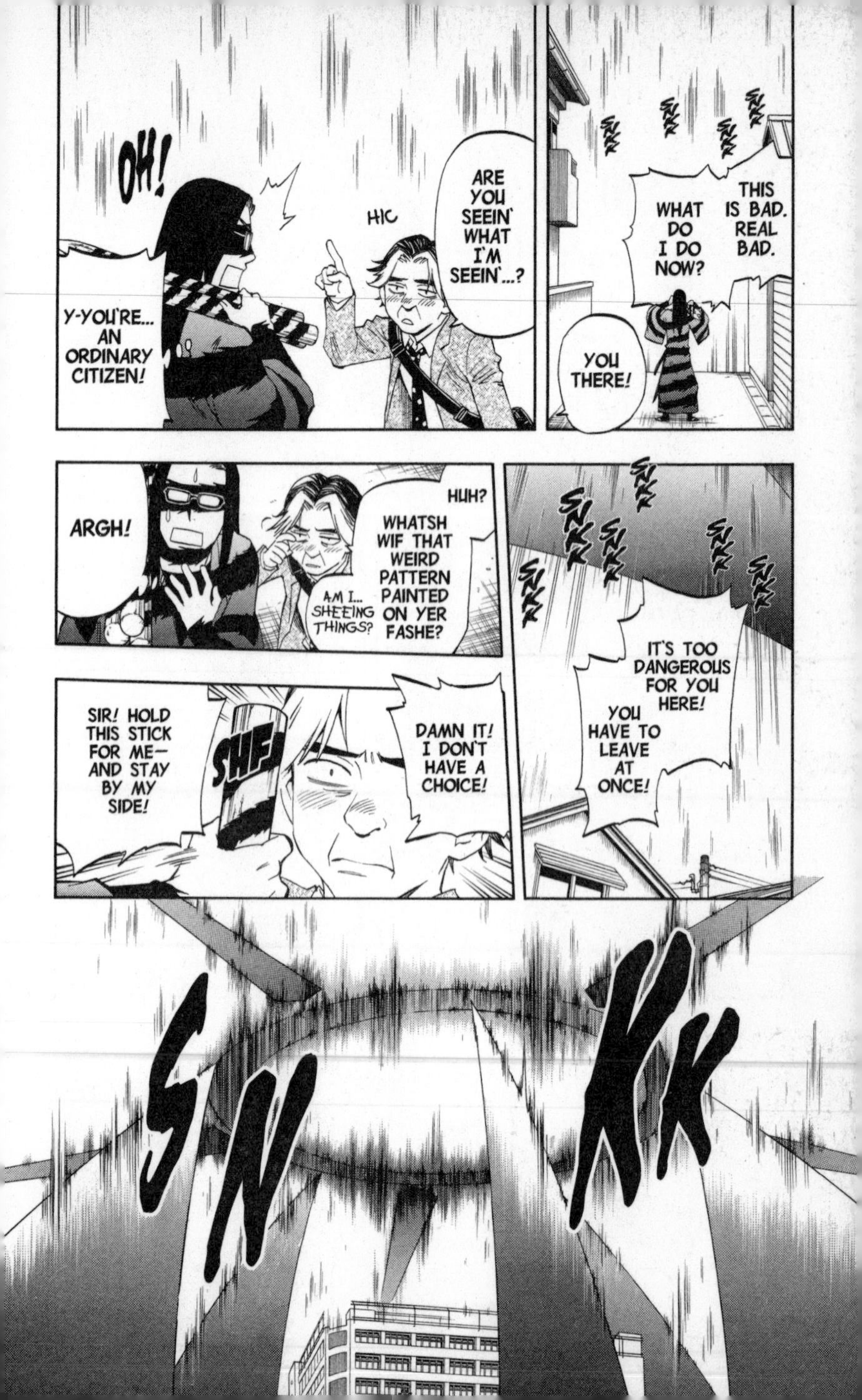
SNKK SNKK SNKK SNKK
THIS IS BAD. REAL BAD.
WHAT DO I DO NOW?
YOU THERE!
ARE YOU SEEIN' WHAT I'M SEEIN'...?
HIC
OH!
Y-YOU'RE... AN ORDINARY CITIZEN!
SNKK SNKK SNKK SNKK SNKK SNKK
IT'S TOO DANGEROUS FOR YOU HERE!
YOU HAVE TO LEAVE AT ONCE!
HUH?
WHATSH WIF THAT WEIRD PATTERN PAINTED ON YER FASHE?
AM I... SHEEING THINGS?
ARGH!
DAMN IT! I DON'T HAVE A CHOICE!
SHF
SIR! HOLD THIS STICK FOR ME—AND STAY BY MY SIDE!
SNKK

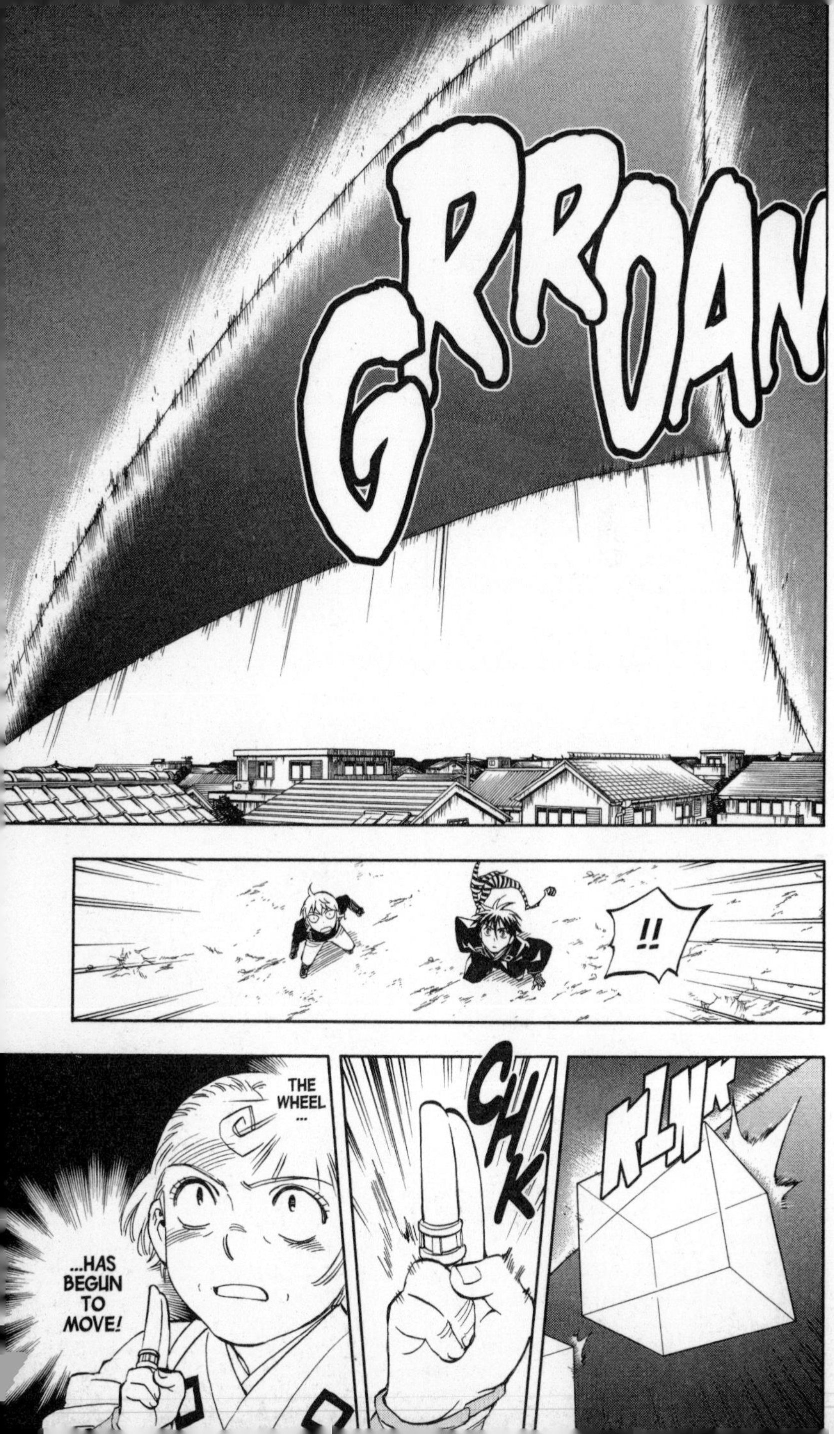
GRROAN
!!
KLINK
CHK
THE WHEEL ...
...HAS BEGUN TO MOVE!

RMBL

KRESH

RMBL

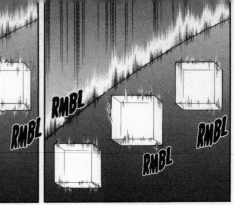
RMBL

RMBL

RMBL

!!

WHAT TREMENDOUS POWER!

NGH

MY KEKKAI MIGHT NOT BE ABLE TO WITHSTAND SUCH FORCE!

...IT SURVIVES LONG ENOUGH FOR FUMIYA'S MAGIC TO TAKE EFFECT!

I ONLY HOPE...

KWICH

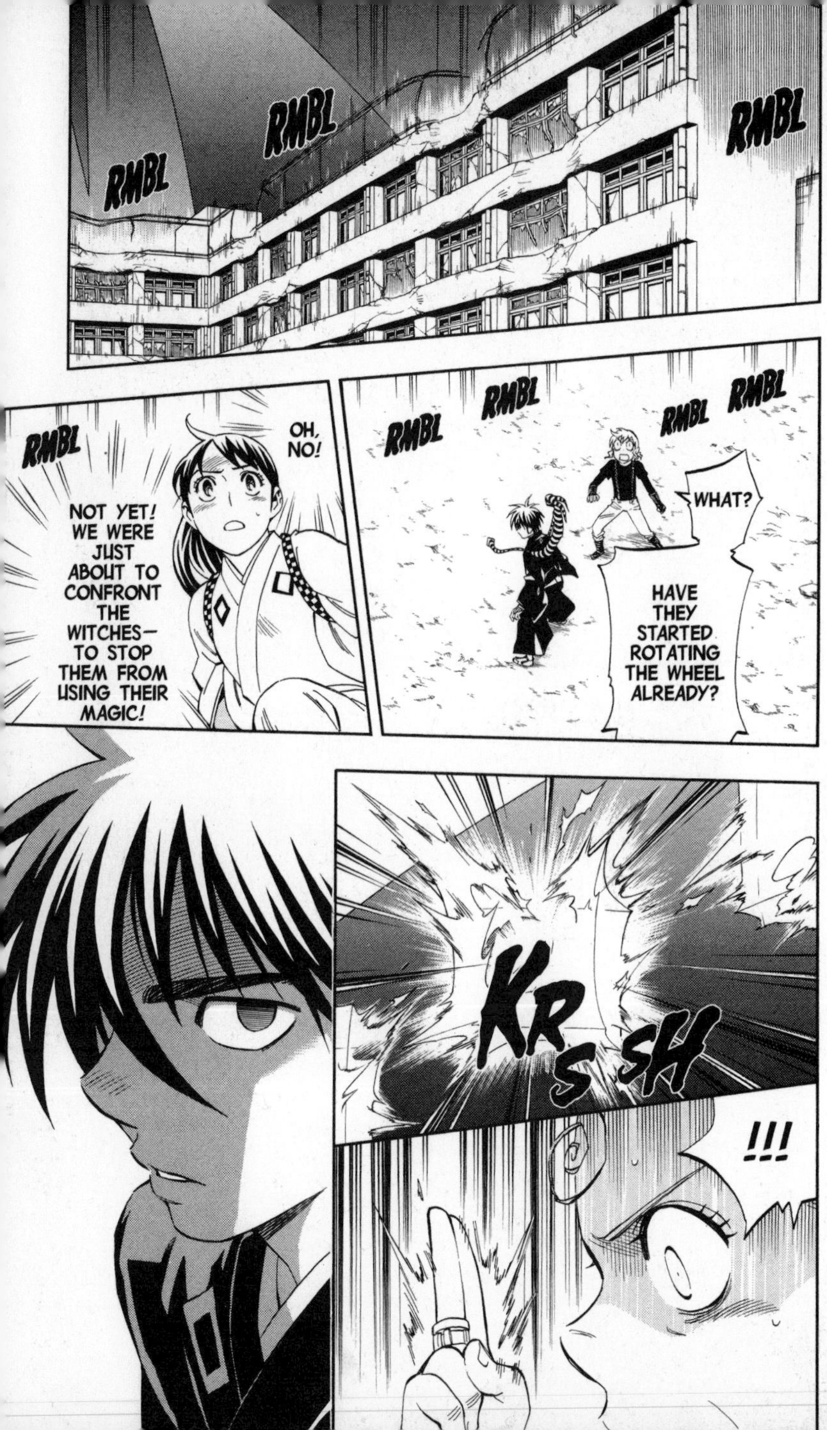
RMBL
RMBL
RMBL
RMBL
RMBL
RMBL
RMBL
WHAT?
HAVE THEY STARTED ROTATING THE WHEEL ALREADY?
OH, NO!
NOT YET! WE WERE JUST ABOUT TO CONFRONT THE WITCHES—TO STOP THEM FROM USING THEIR MAGIC!
RMBL
KRSSH
!!!

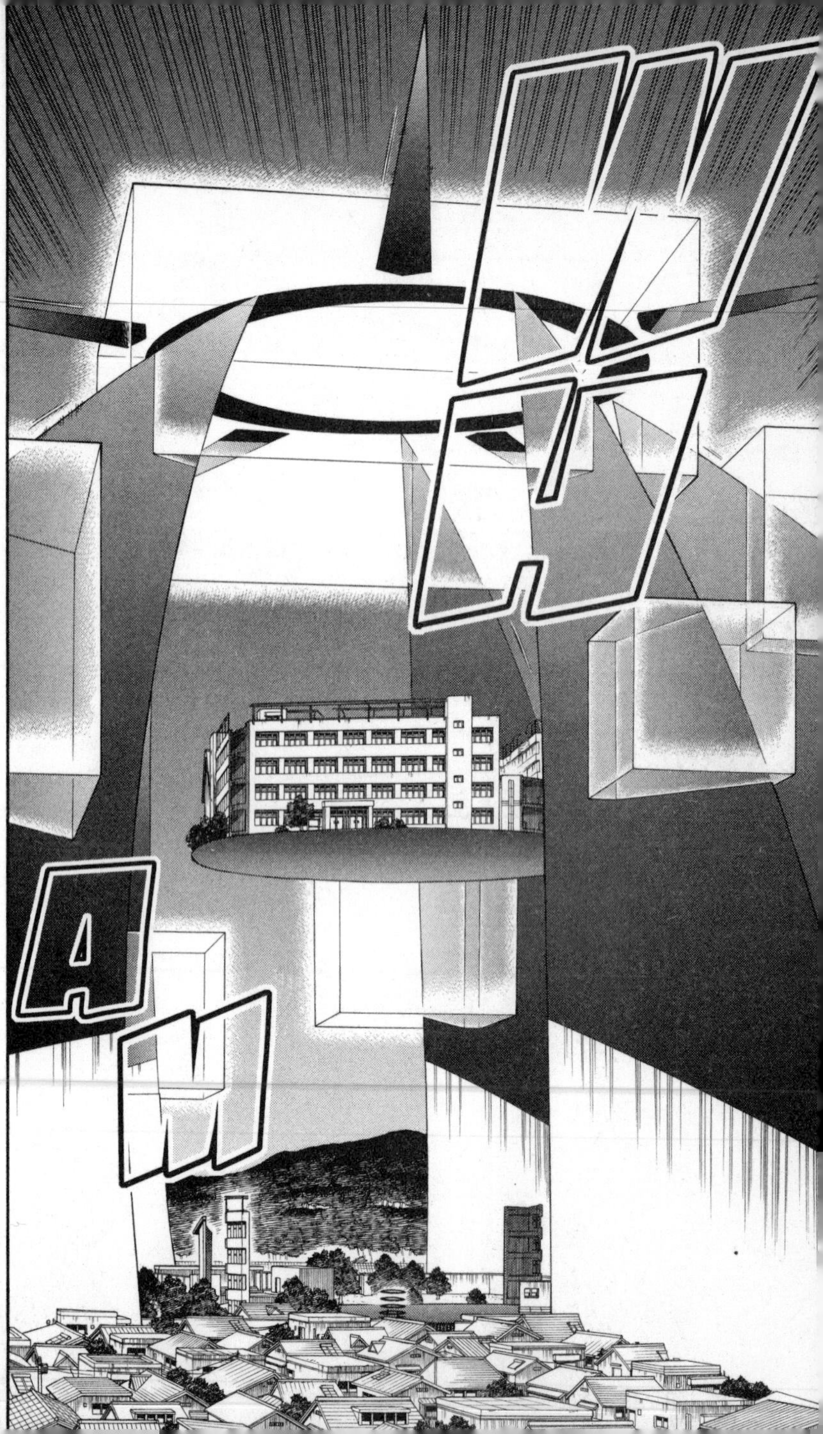
WHAM

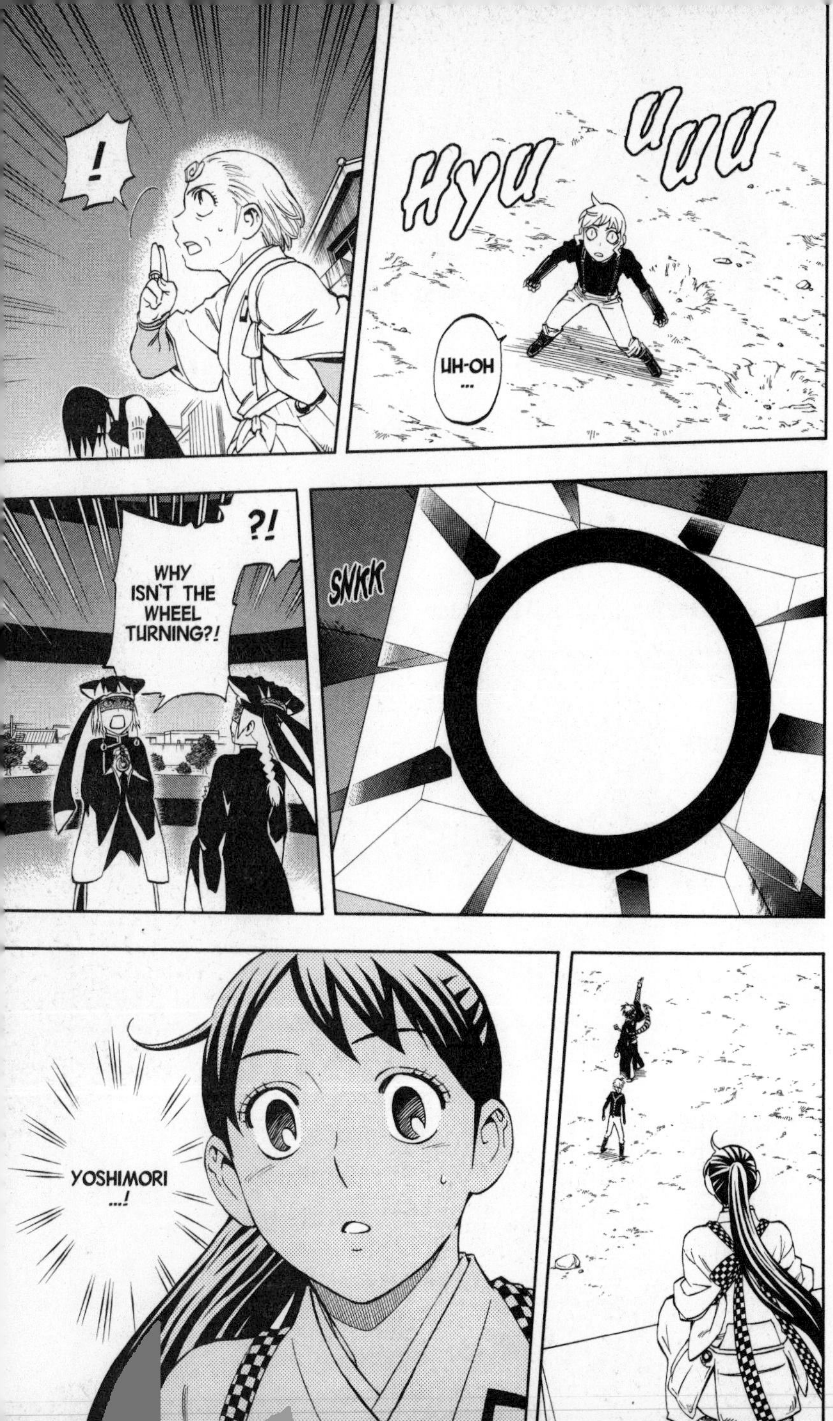
HYU UUU
UH-OH ...
!
SNKK
?!
WHY ISN'T THE WHEEL TURNING?!
YOSHIMORI ...!

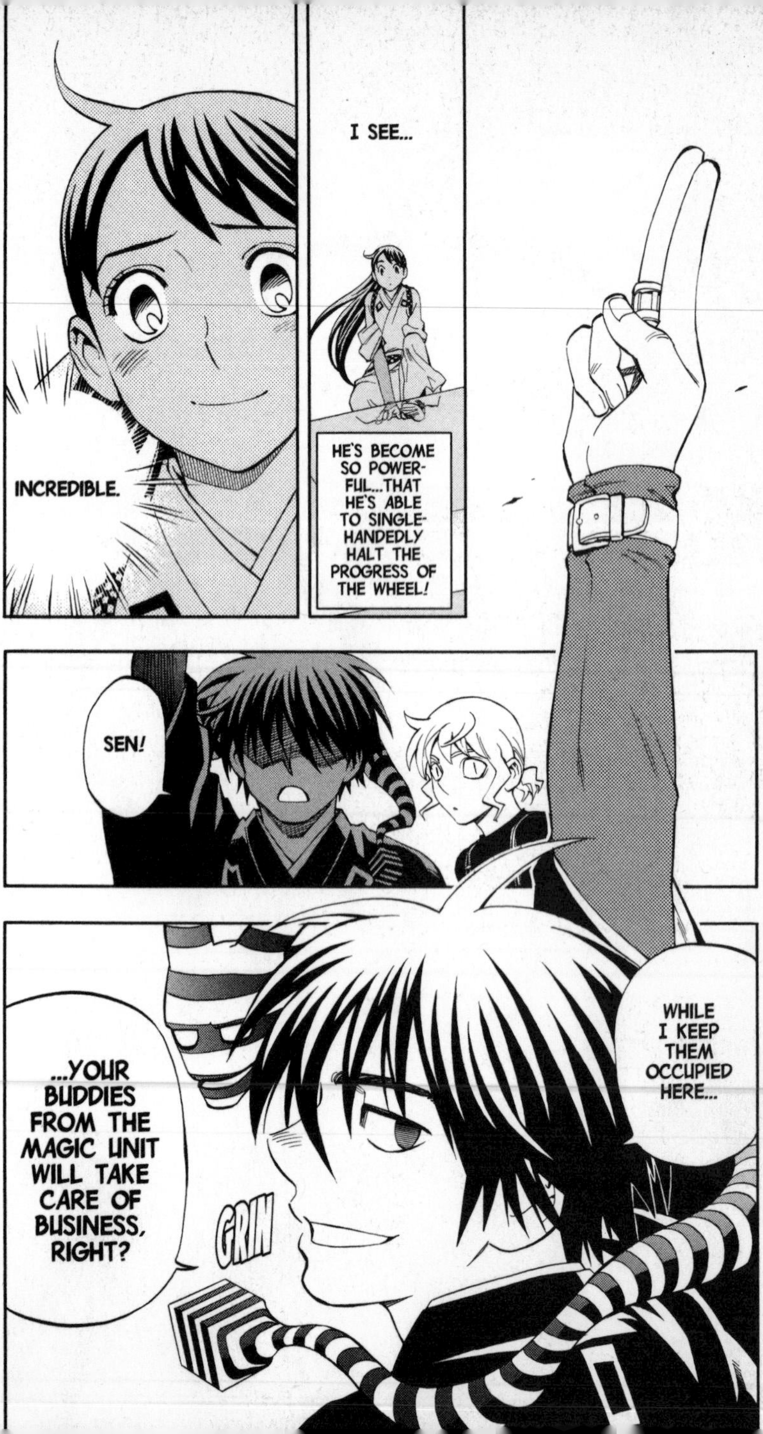
I SEE...
HE'S BECOME SO POWER-FUL...THAT HE'S ABLE TO SINGLE-HANDEDLY HALT THE PROGRESS OF THE WHEEL!
INCREDIBLE.
SEN!
WHILE I KEEP THEM OCCUPIED HERE...
...YOUR BUDDIES FROM THE MAGIC UNIT WILL TAKE CARE OF BUSINESS, RIGHT?
GRIN

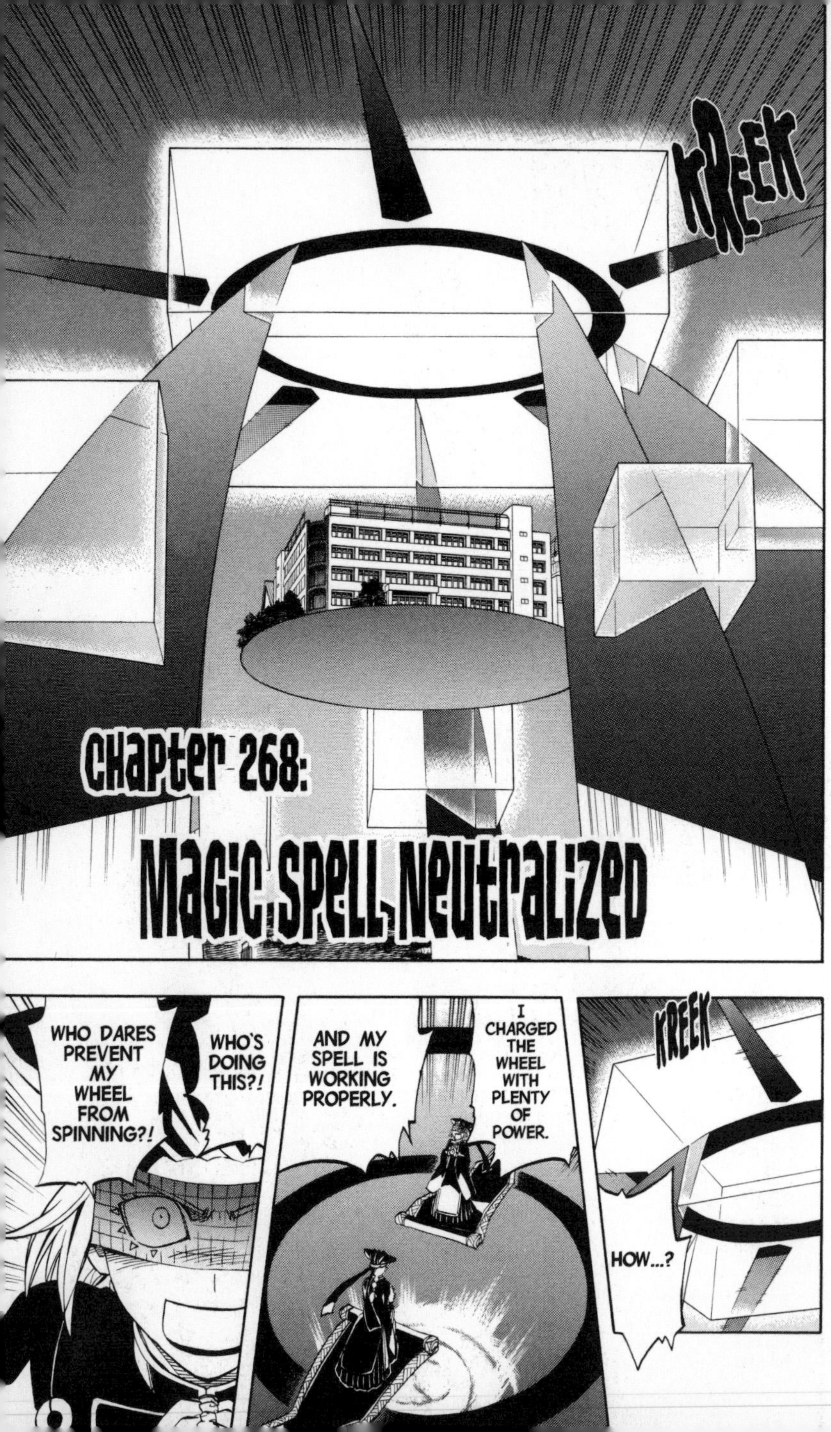
KREEK
Chapter 268:
Magic Spell Neutralized
KREEK
HOW...?
I CHARGED THE WHEEL WITH PLENTY OF POWER.
AND MY SPELL IS WORKING PROPERLY.
WHO'S DOING THIS?!
WHO DARES PREVENT MY WHEEL FROM SPINNING?!

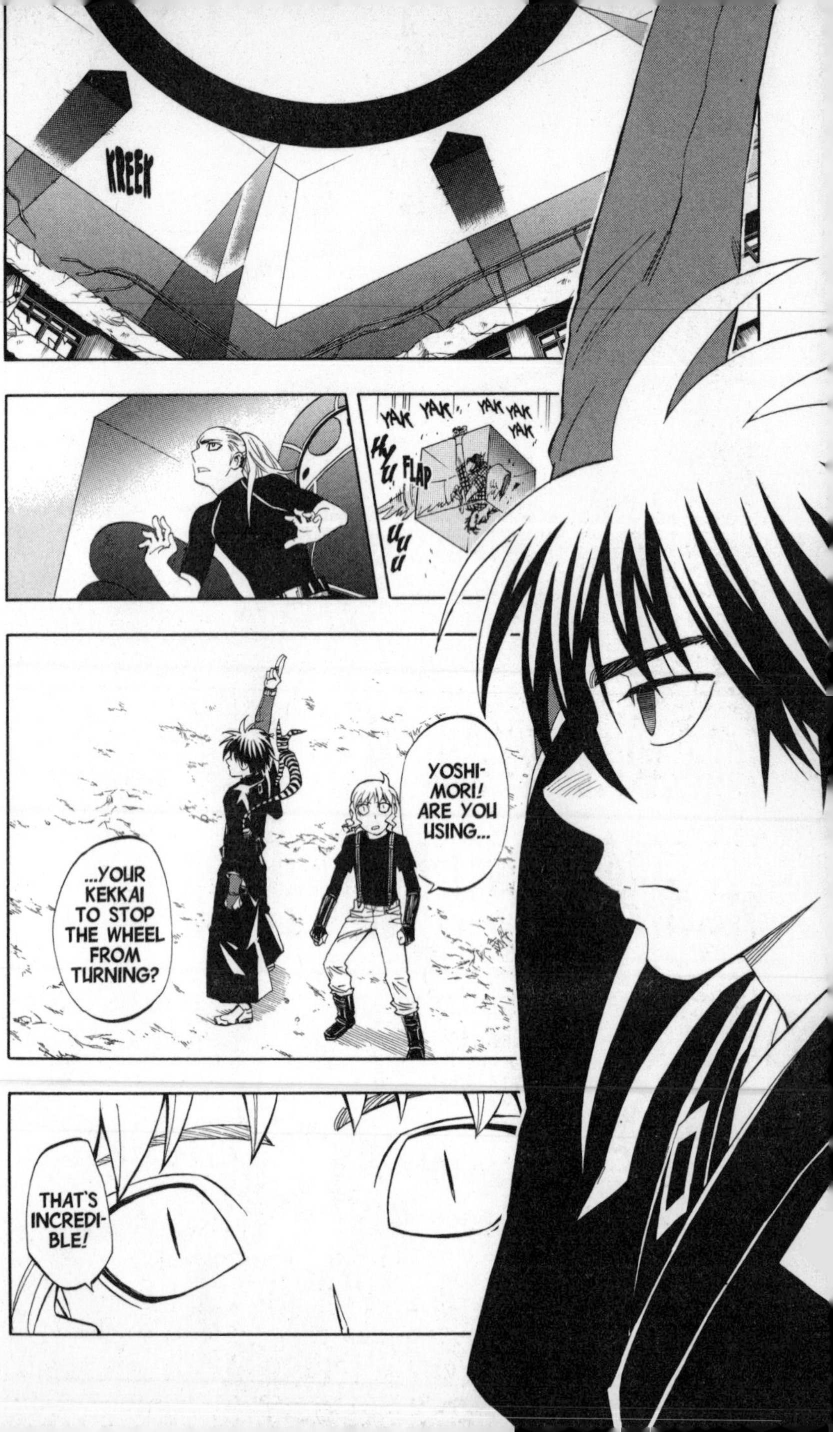
KREEK
YAK YAK YAK YAK YAK
FLAP
HYUUUU
YOSHI-MORI! ARE YOU USING...
...YOUR KEKKAI TO STOP THE WHEEL FROM TURNING?
THAT'S INCREDI-BLE!

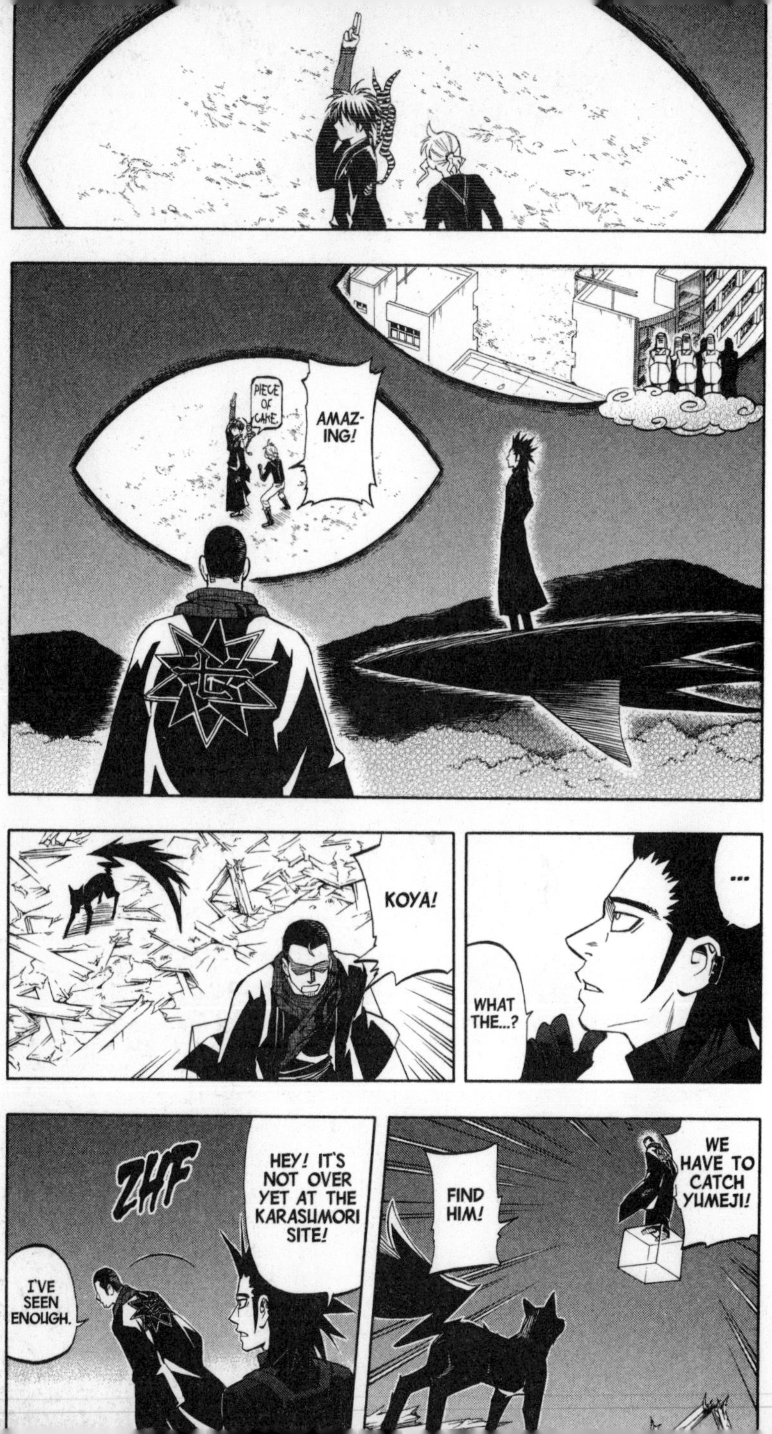
AMAZ-ING!
PIECE OF CAKE.
...
WHAT THE...?
KOYA!
WE HAVE TO CATCH YUMEJI!
FIND HIM!
HEY! IT'S NOT OVER YET AT THE KARASUMORI SITE!
ZHF
I'VE SEEN ENOUGH.

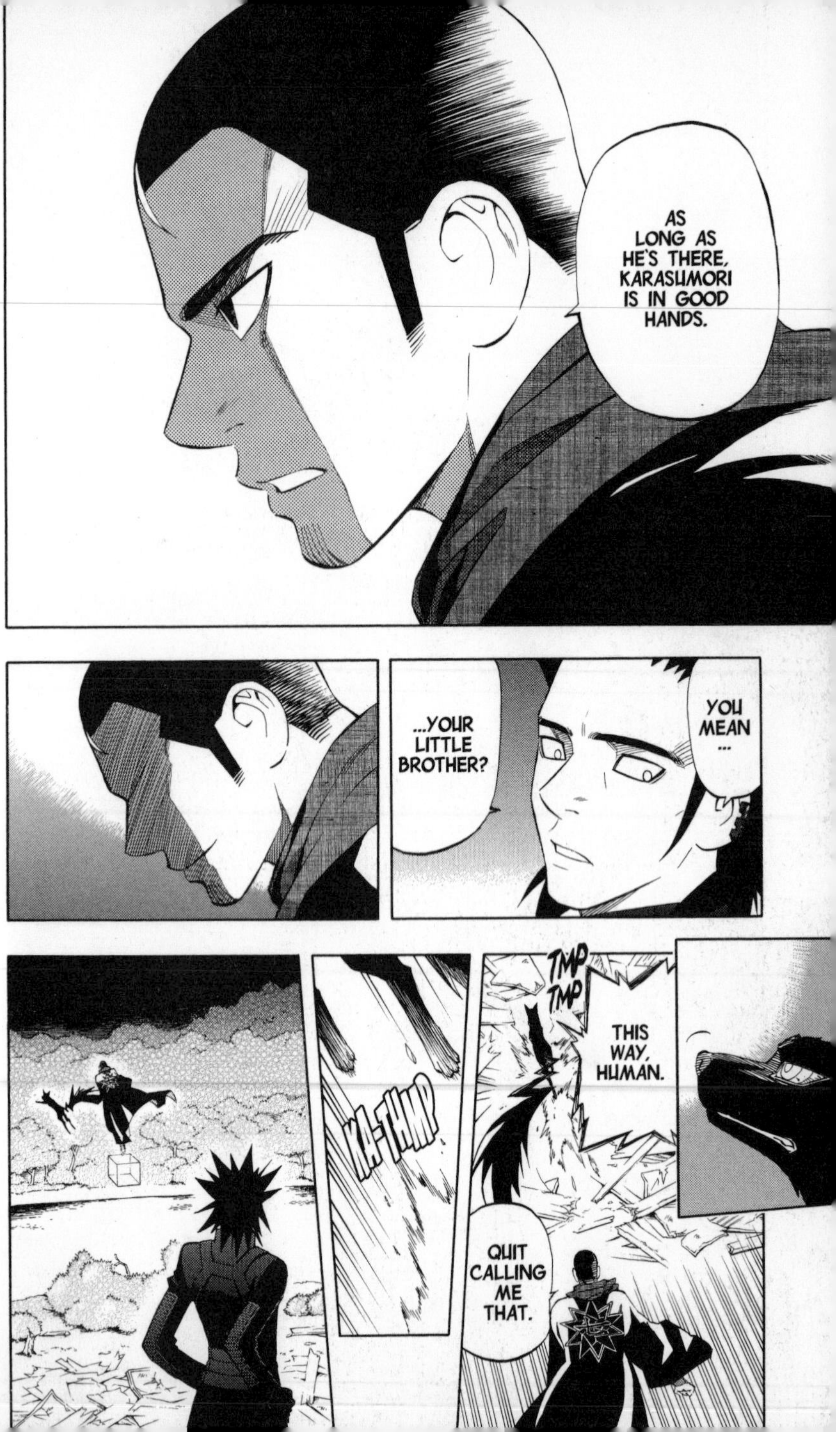

AS LONG AS HE'S THERE, KARASUMORI IS IN GOOD HANDS.
YOU MEAN ...
...YOUR LITTLE BROTHER?
TMP TMP
THIS WAY, HUMAN.
QUIT CALLING ME THAT.
KA-THMP

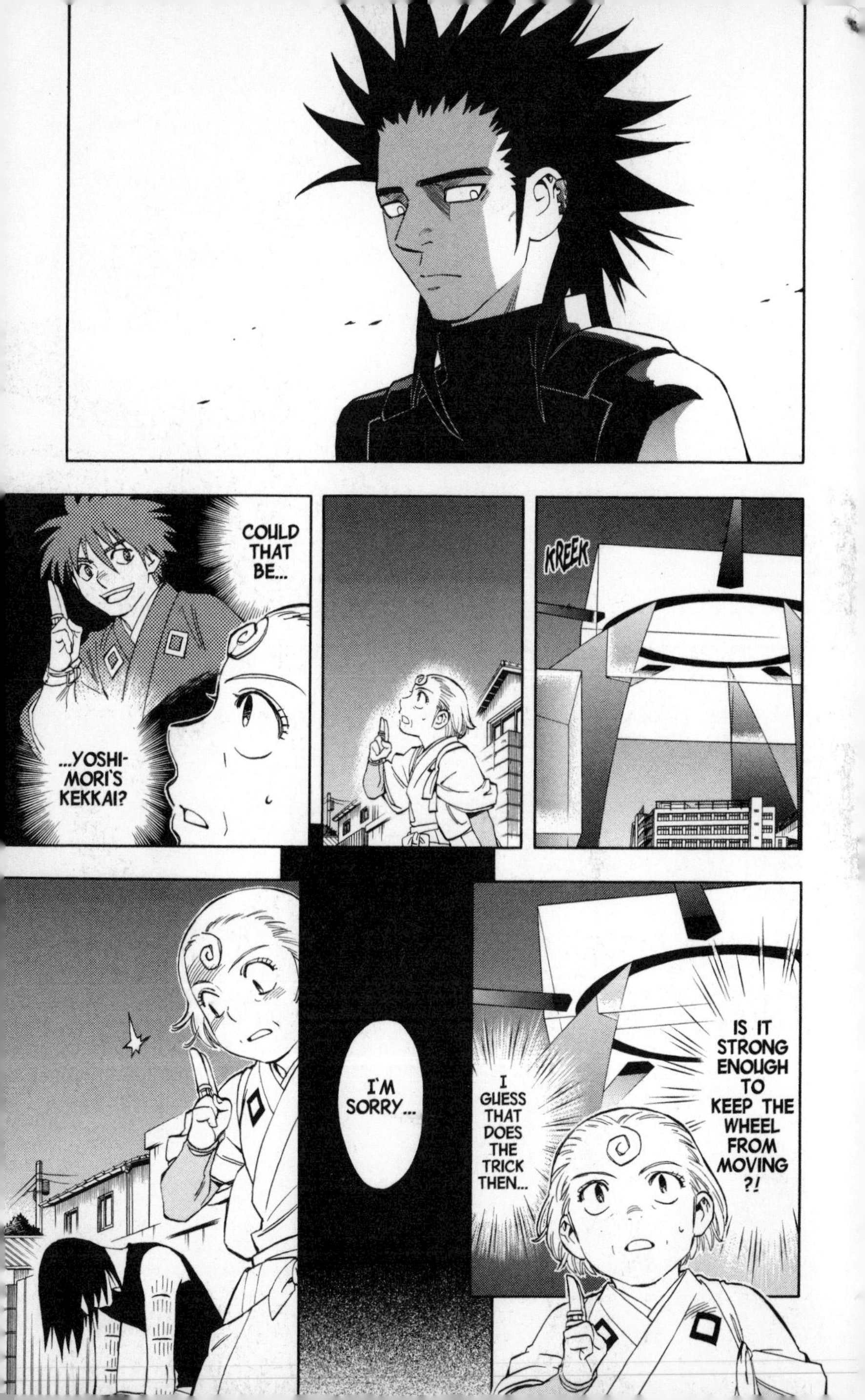
KREEK
COULD THAT BE...
...YOSHI-MORI'S KEKKAI?
IS IT STRONG ENOUGH TO KEEP THE WHEEL FROM MOVING ?!
I GUESS THAT DOES THE TRICK THEN...
I'M SORRY...

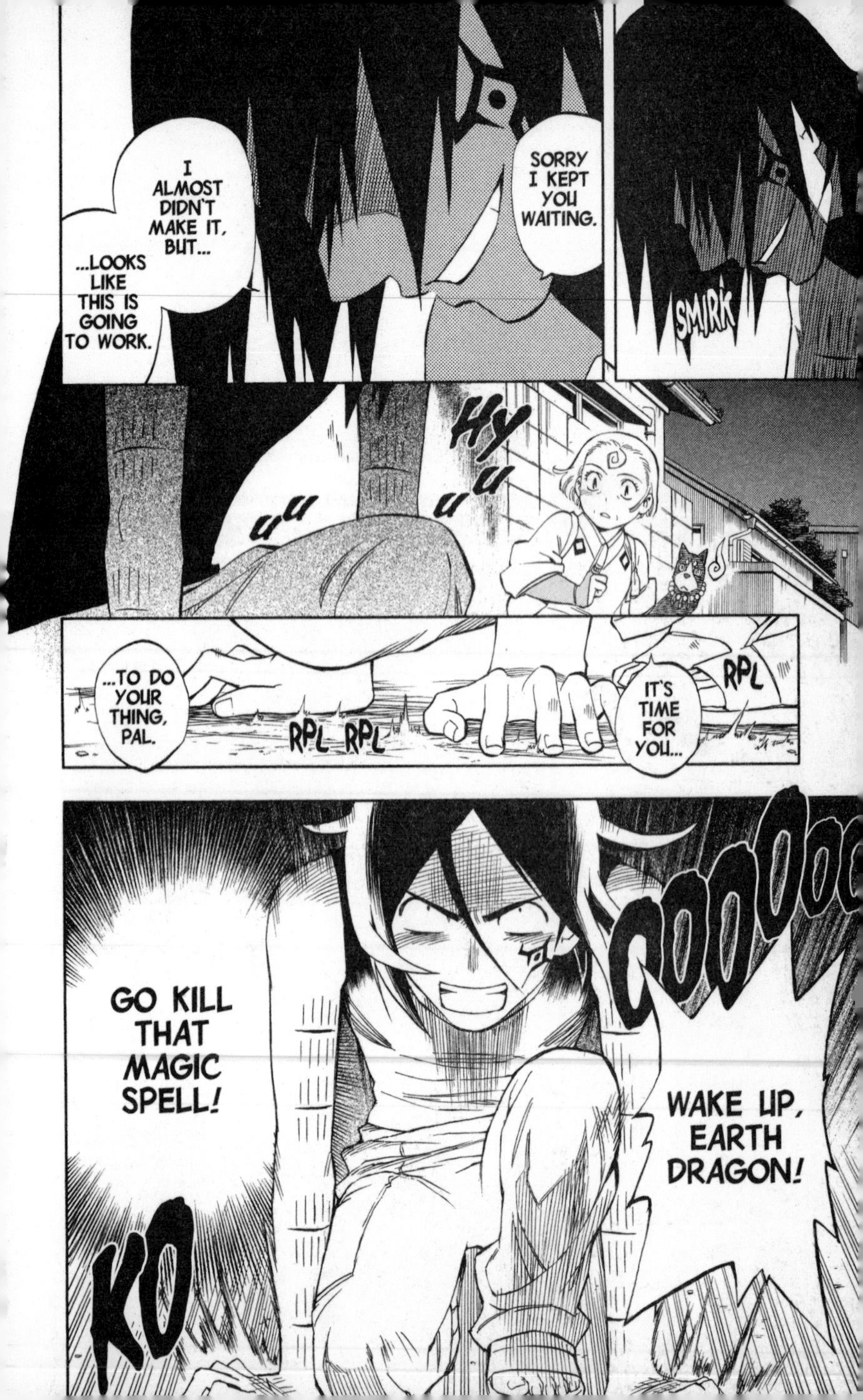
SMIRK
SORRY I KEPT YOU WAITING.
I ALMOST DIDN'T MAKE IT, BUT...
...LOOKS LIKE THIS IS GOING TO WORK.
HYUUU
UU
RPL
IT'S TIME FOR YOU...
RPL RPL
...TO DO YOUR THING, PAL.
OOOOOO
WAKE UP, EARTH DRAGON!
GO KILL THAT MAGIC SPELL!
KO

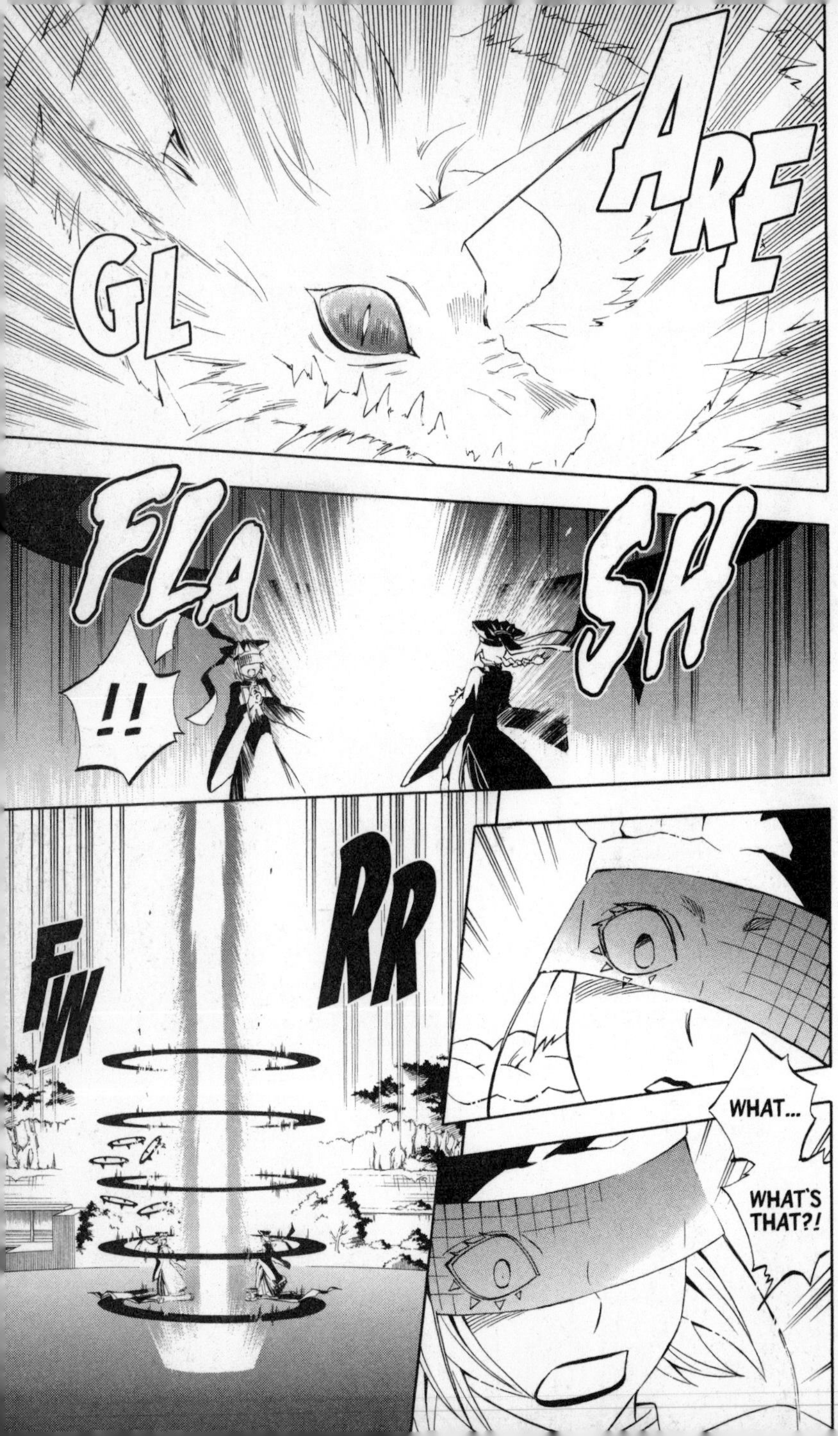
GLARE
FLASH
!!
WHAT...
WHAT'S THAT?!
FWRR

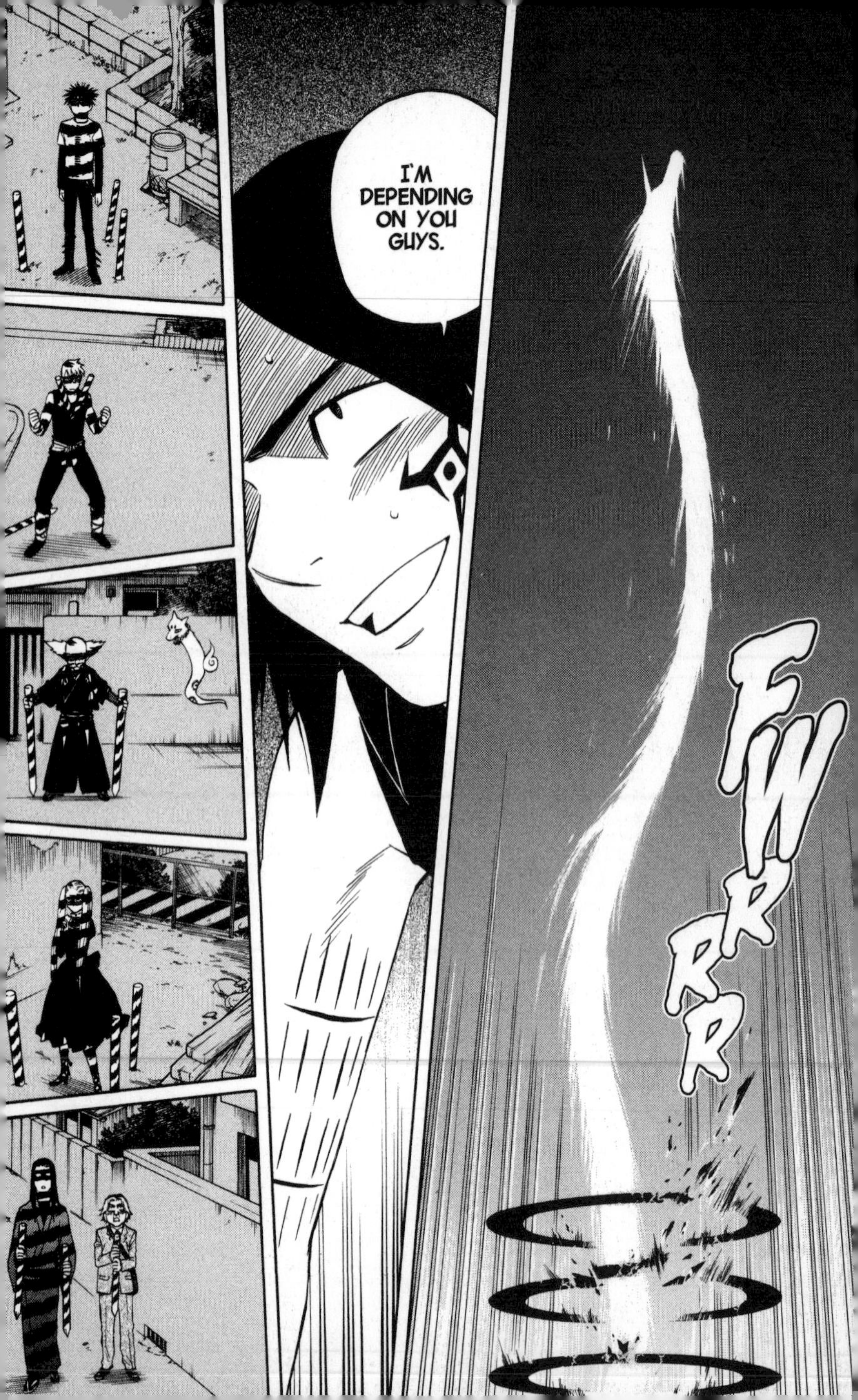
I'M DEPENDING ON YOU GUYS.
FWRRRR

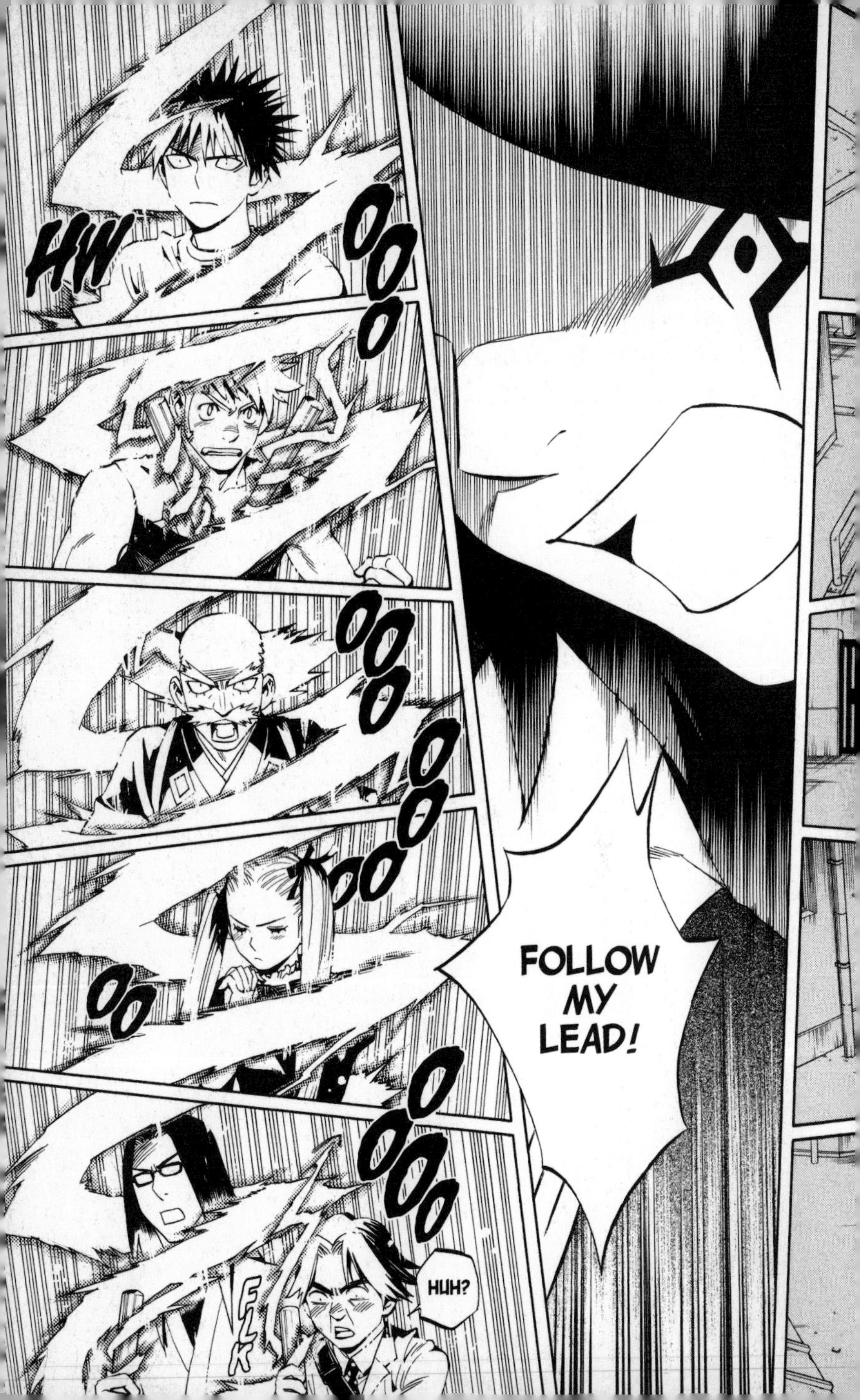
FOLLOW MY LEAD!
HW
OOOOO
OOOOOOO
OO
OOOOO
HUH?
FLK

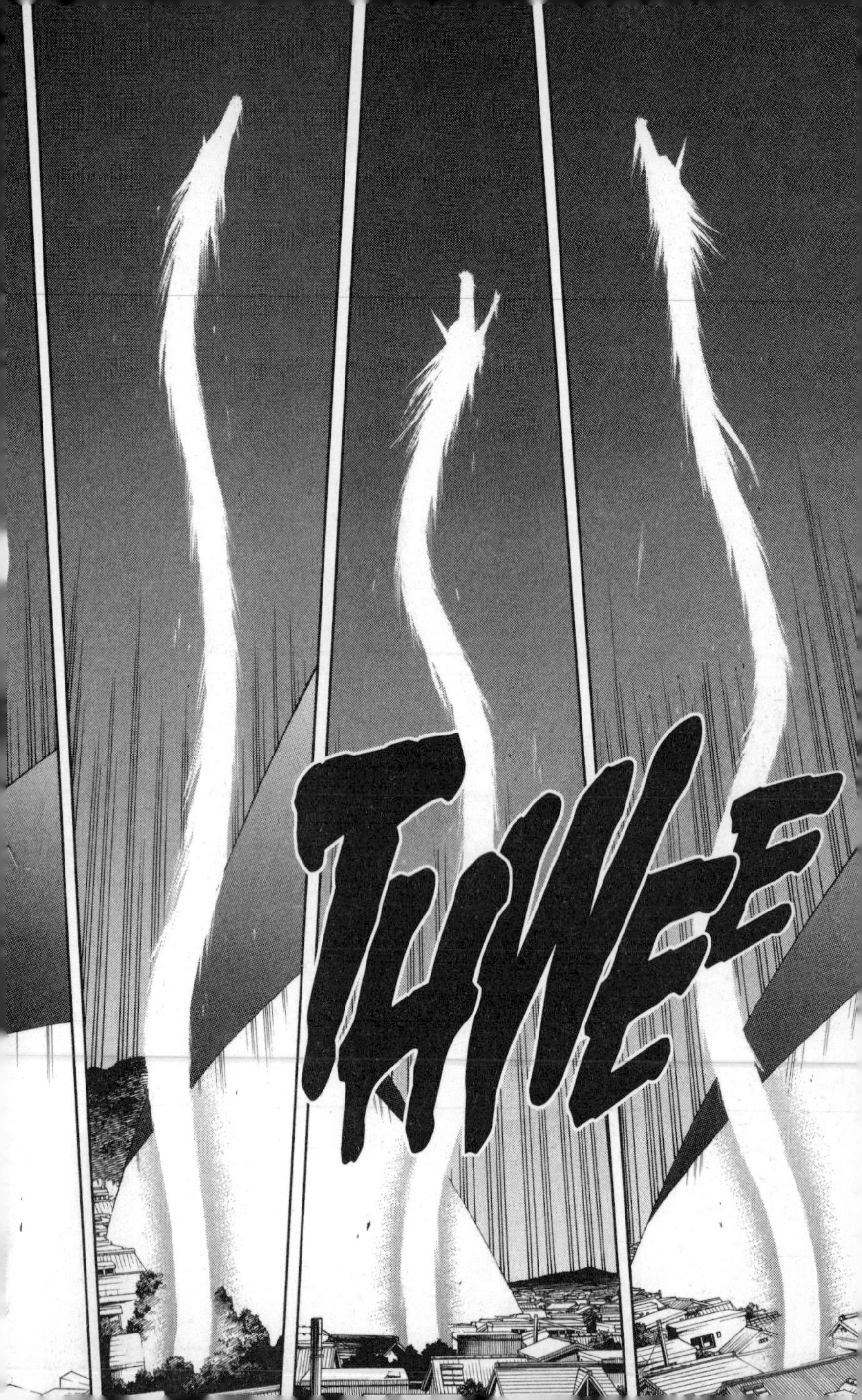
TWEE

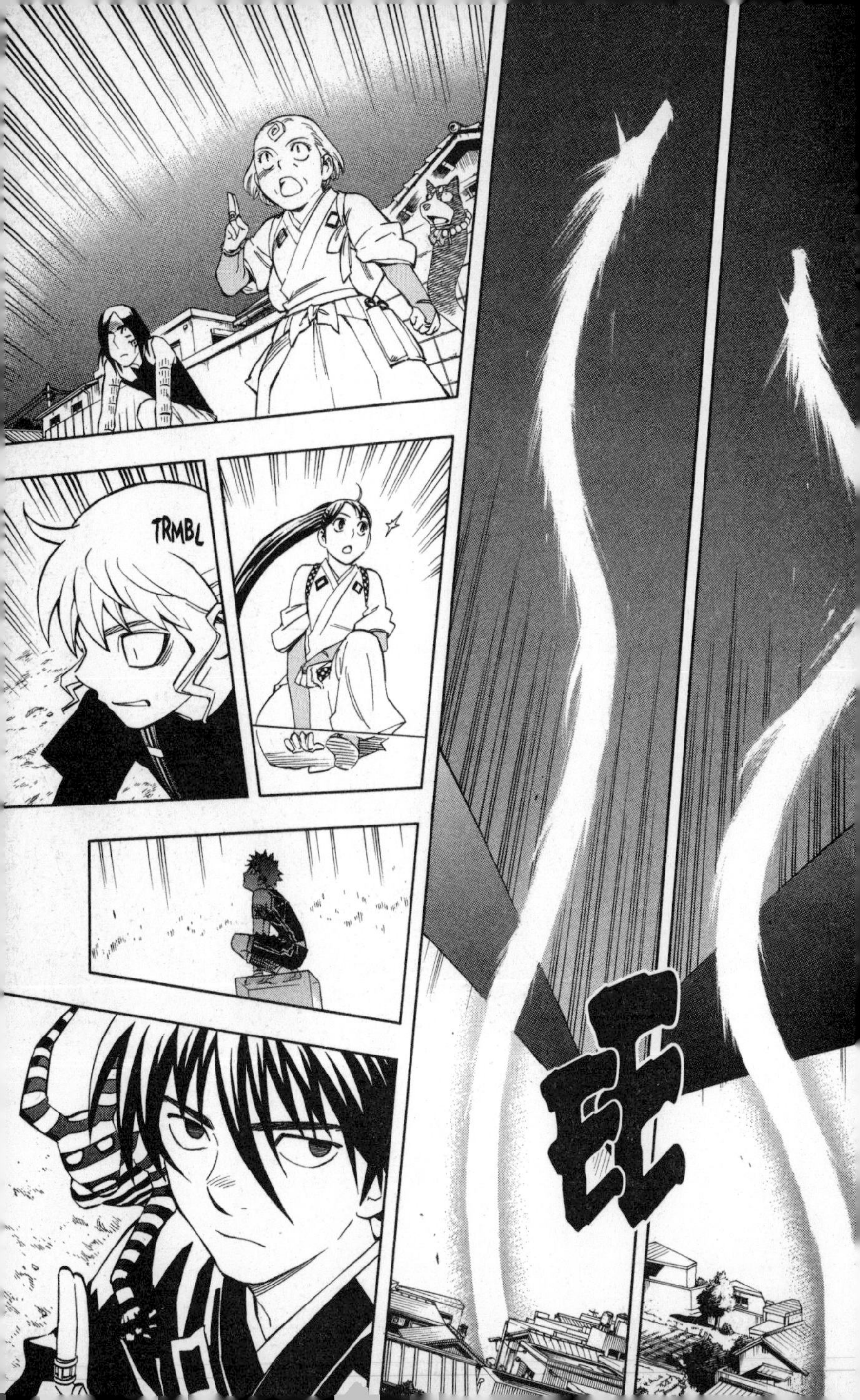
TRMBL

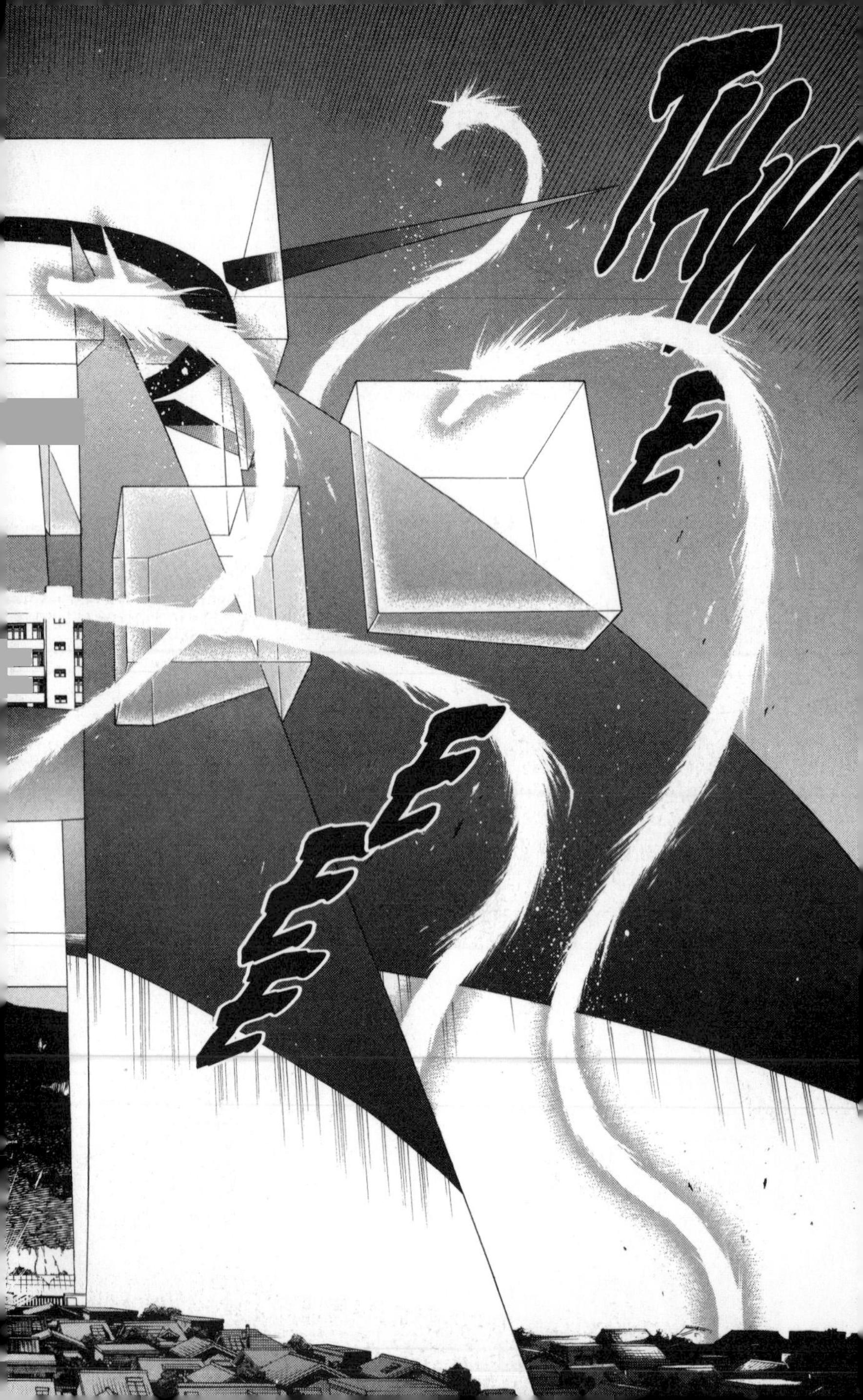
THWEEEEEE

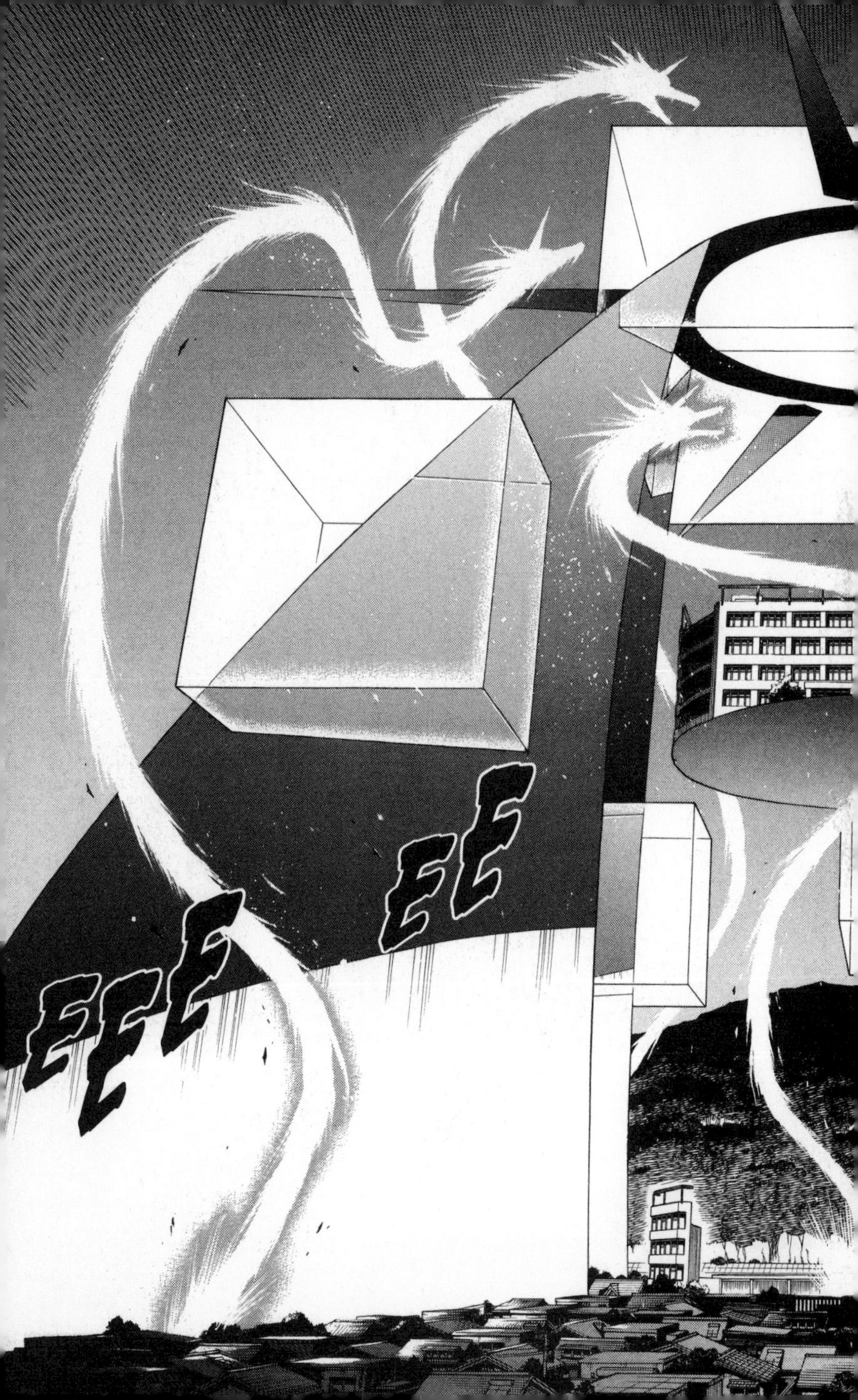
EEE
EEEE

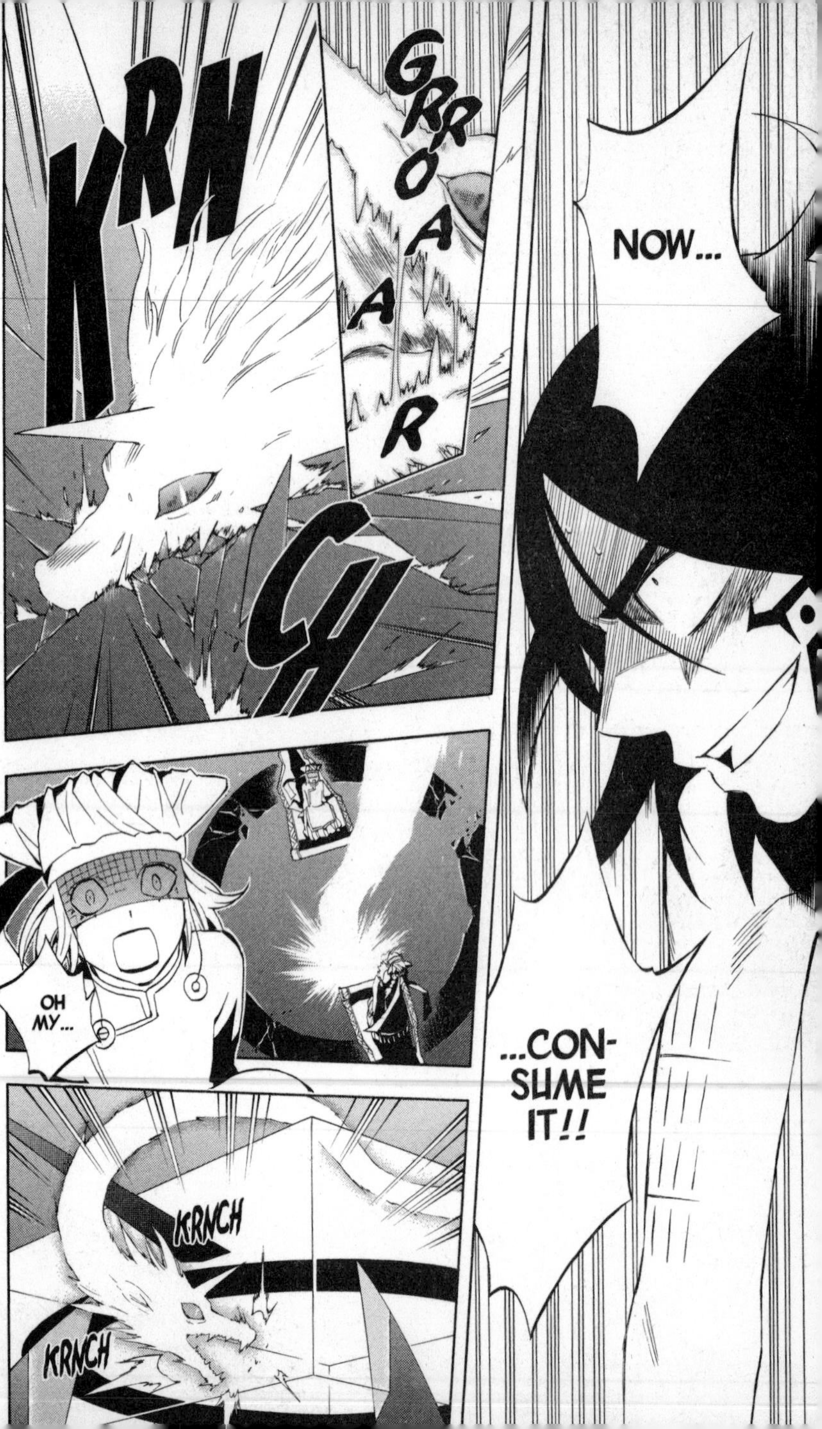
NOW...
...CON-
SUME
IT!!
GRROAAR
KRN
CH
OH
MY...
KRNCH
KRNCH

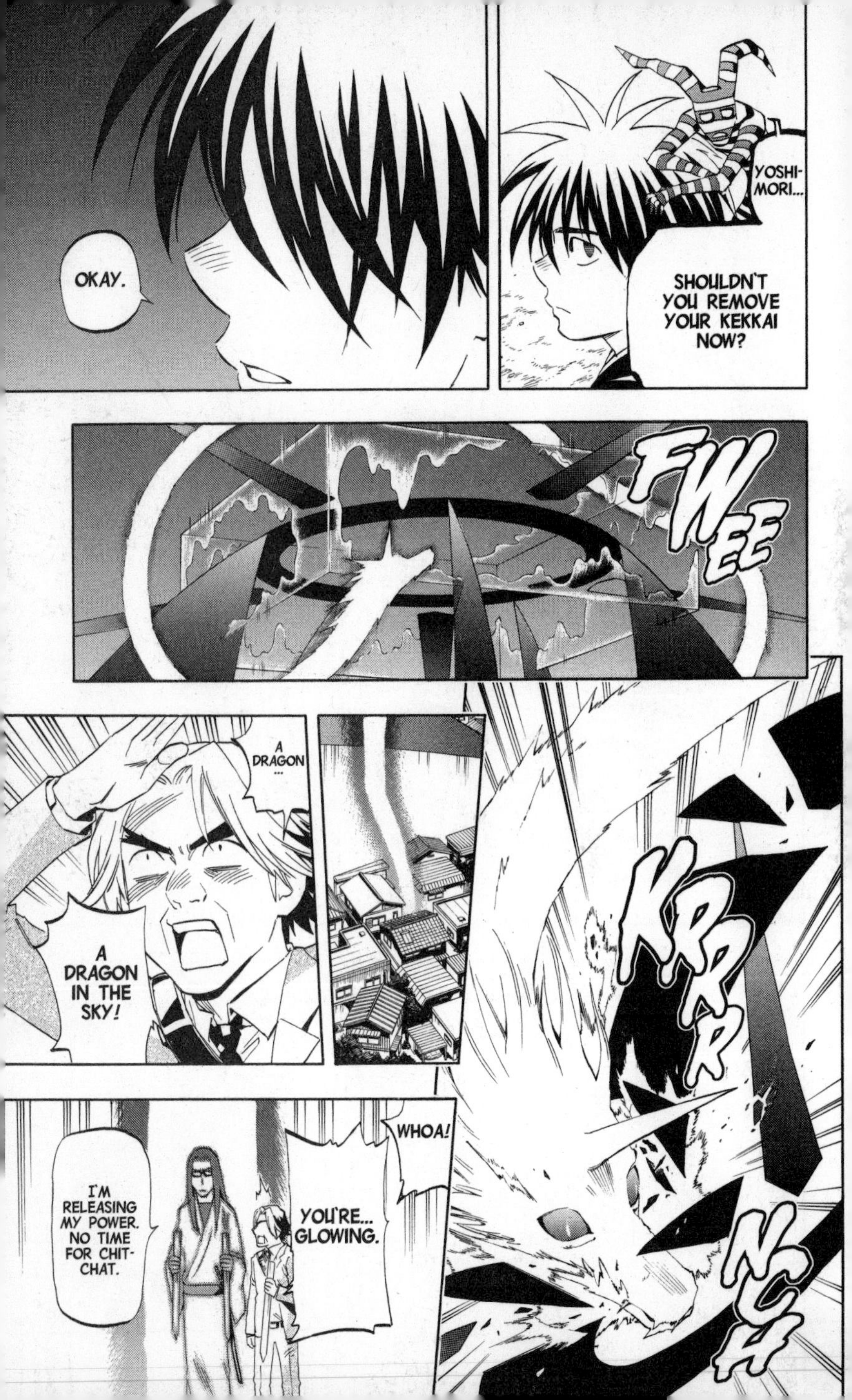
YOSHI-MORI...
SHOULDN'T YOU REMOVE YOUR KEKKAI NOW?
OKAY.
FWEE
KRRRNCH
A DRAGON...
A DRAGON IN THE SKY!
WHOA!
YOU'RE... GLOWING.
I'M RELEASING MY POWER. NO TIME FOR CHIT-CHAT.

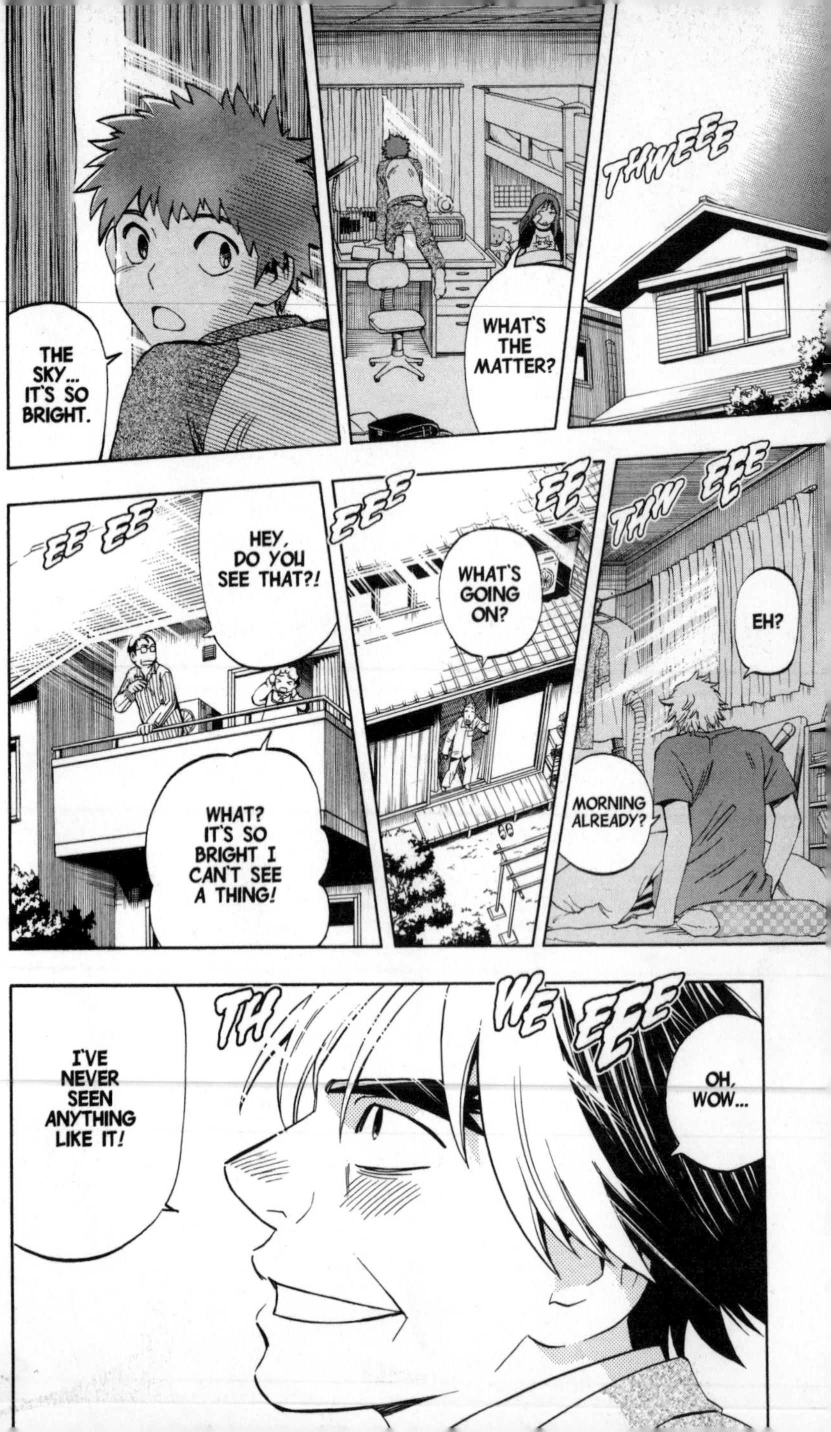
THWEEE
WHAT'S THE MATTER?
THE SKY... IT'S SO BRIGHT.
THW EEE
EH?
MORNING ALREADY?
EE
EEE
WHAT'S GOING ON?
EE EE
HEY, DO YOU SEE THAT?!
WHAT? IT'S SO BRIGHT I CAN'T SEE A THING!
TH WE EEE
OH, WOW...
I'VE NEVER SEEN ANYTHING LIKE IT!

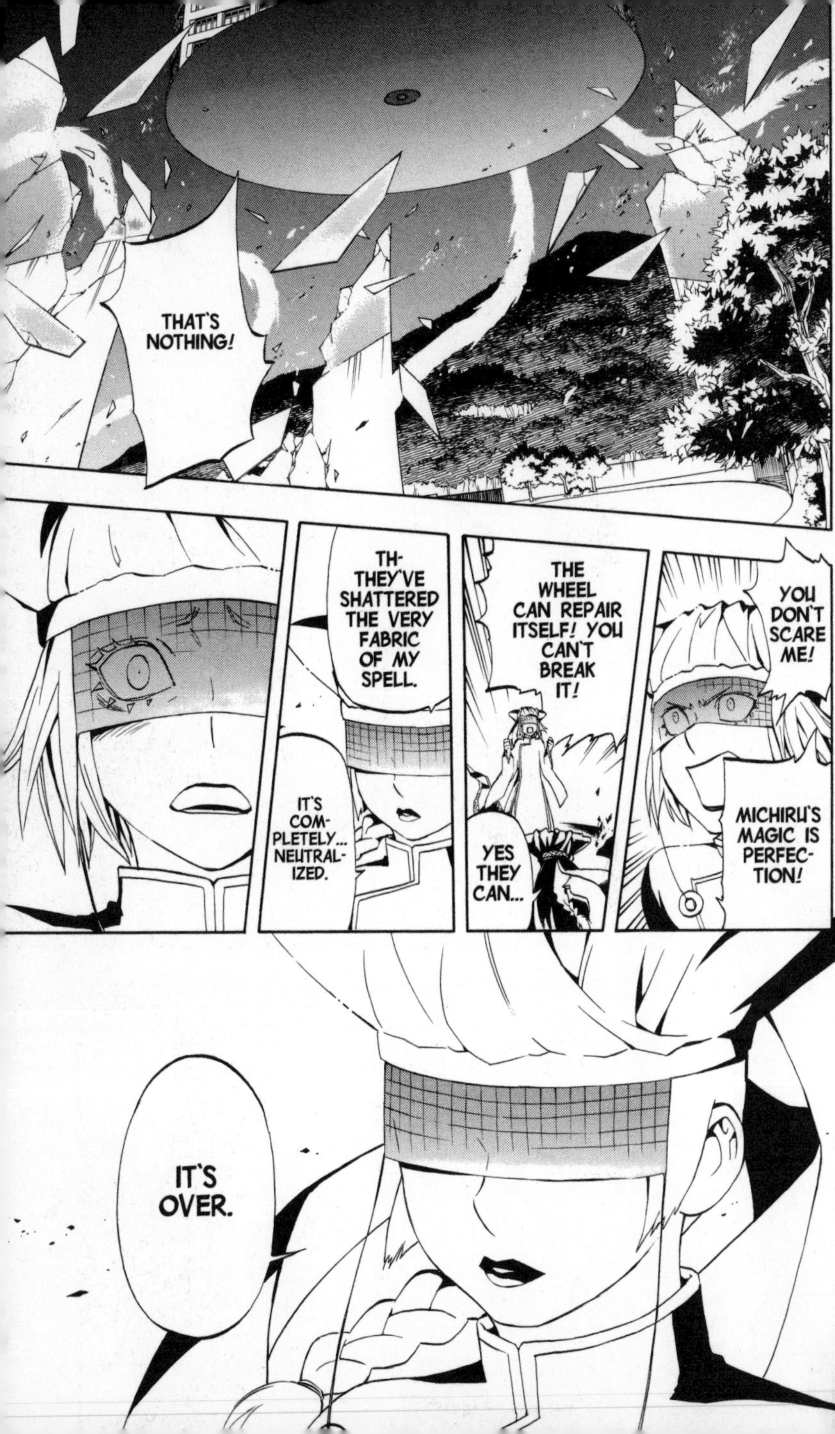
THAT'S NOTHING!
YOU DON'T SCARE ME!
MICHIRU'S MAGIC IS PERFECTION!
THE WHEEL CAN REPAIR ITSELF! YOU CAN'T BREAK IT!
YES THEY CAN...
TH-THEY'VE SHATTERED THE VERY FABRIC OF MY SPELL.
IT'S COMPLETELY... NEUTRALIZED.
IT'S OVER.

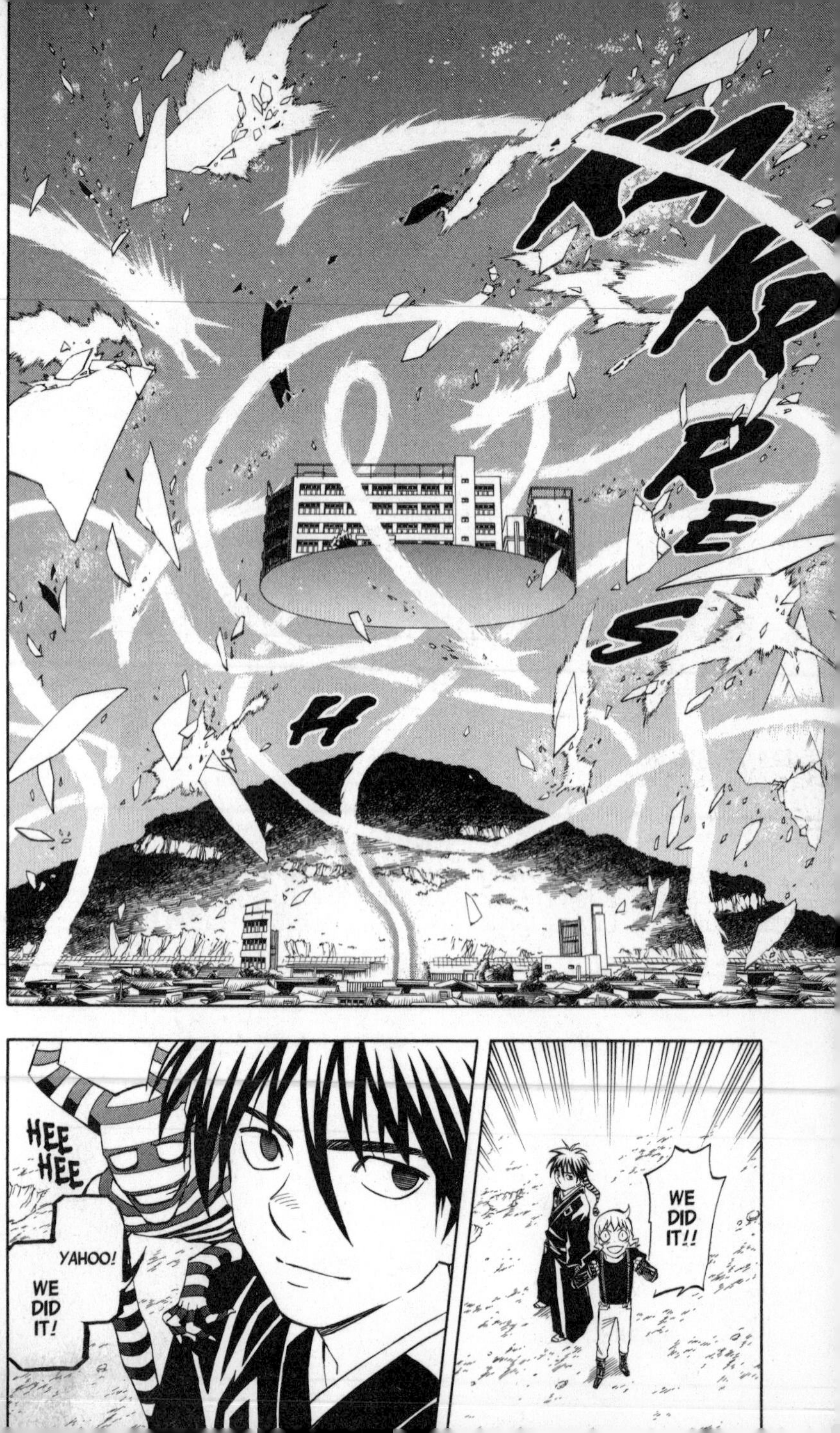
KRRESH
WE DID IT!!
HEE HEE
YAHOO!
WE DID IT!

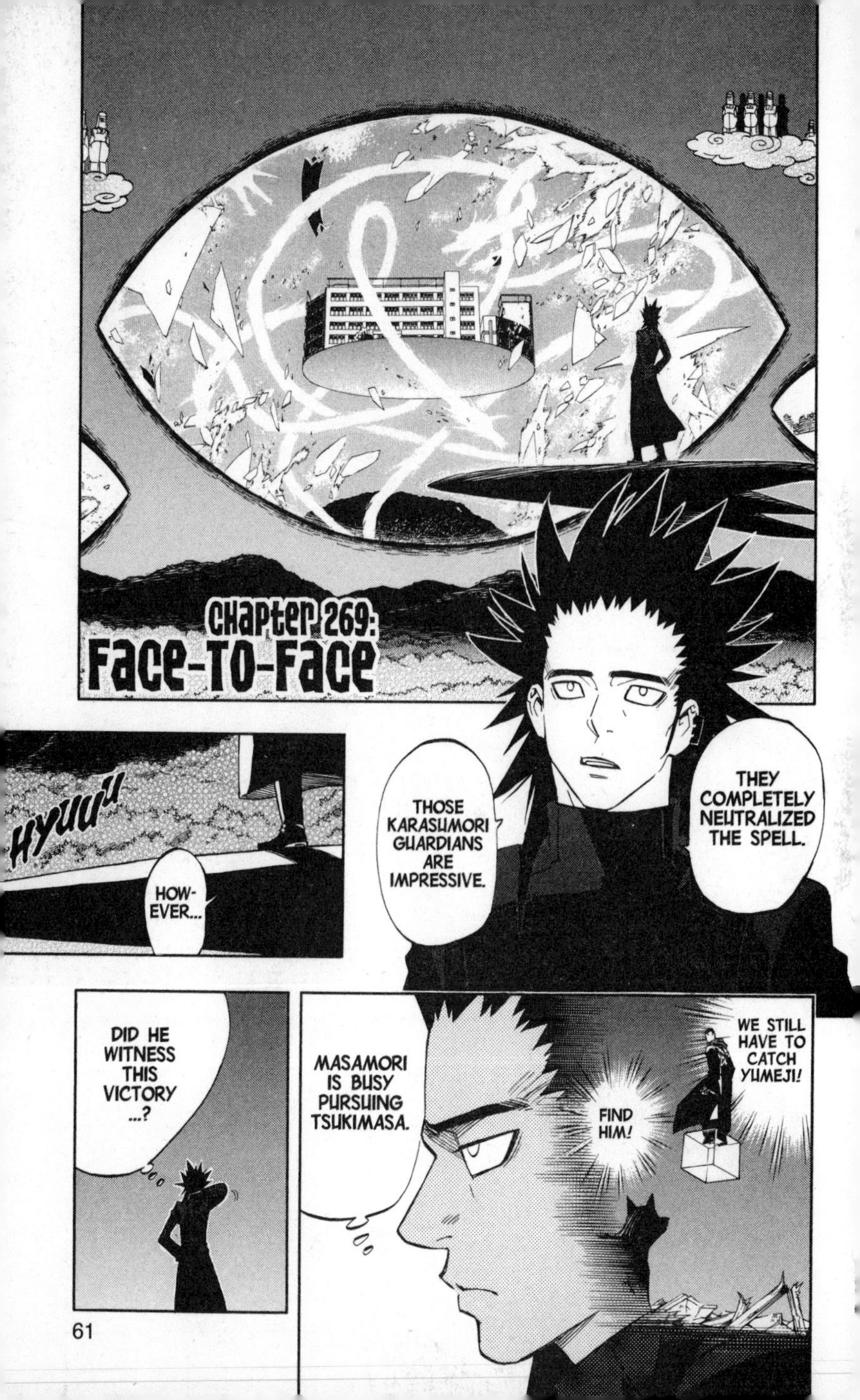
Chapter 269:
Face-to-Face
THEY COMPLETELY NEUTRALIZED THE SPELL.
THOSE KARASUMORI GUARDIANS ARE IMPRESSIVE.
HYUUU
HOW-EVER...
WE STILL HAVE TO CATCH YUMEJI!
FIND HIM!
MASAMORI IS BUSY PURSUING TSUKIMASA.
DID HE WITNESS THIS VICTORY ...?

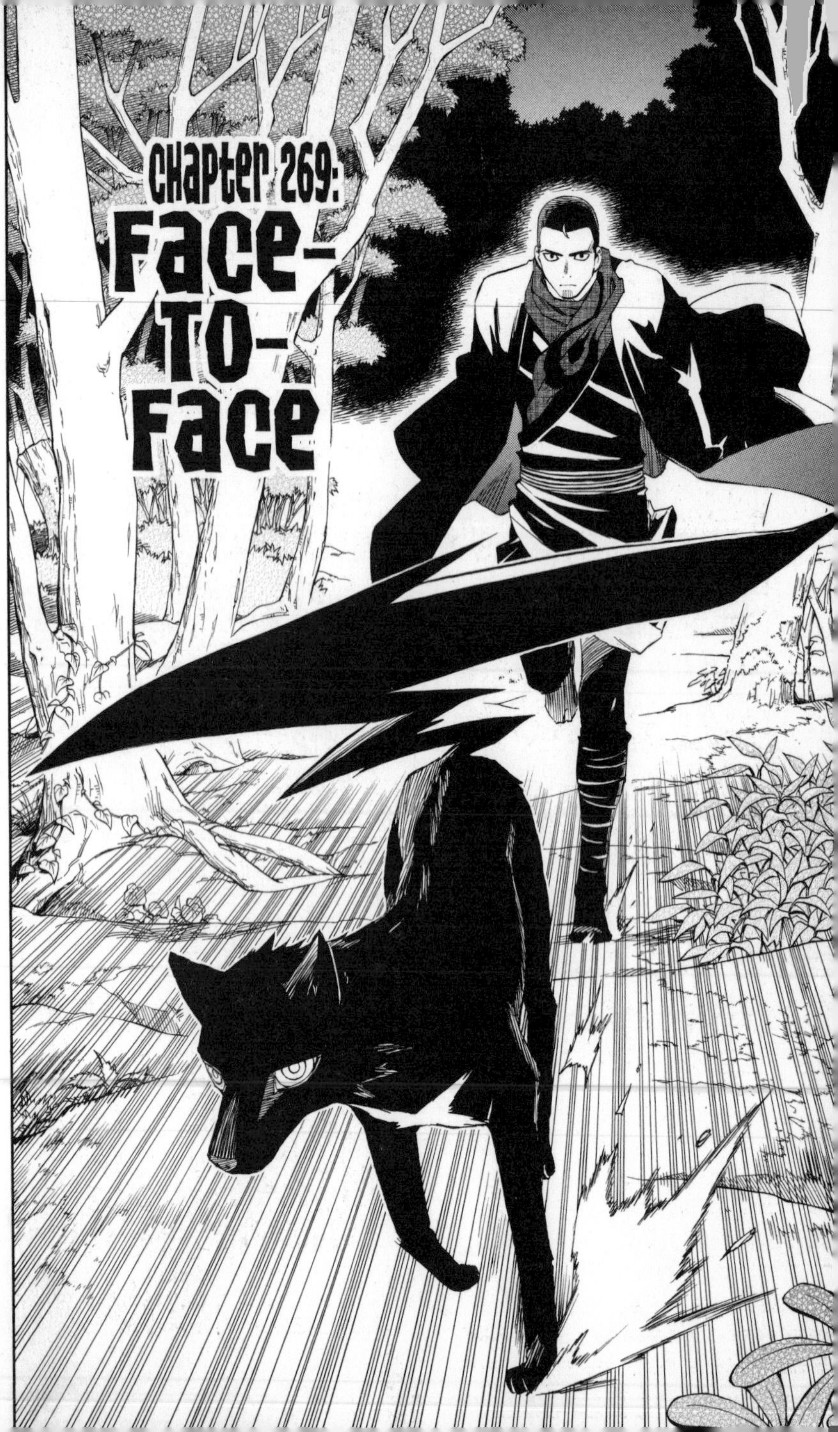
Chapter 269:
Face-To-Face

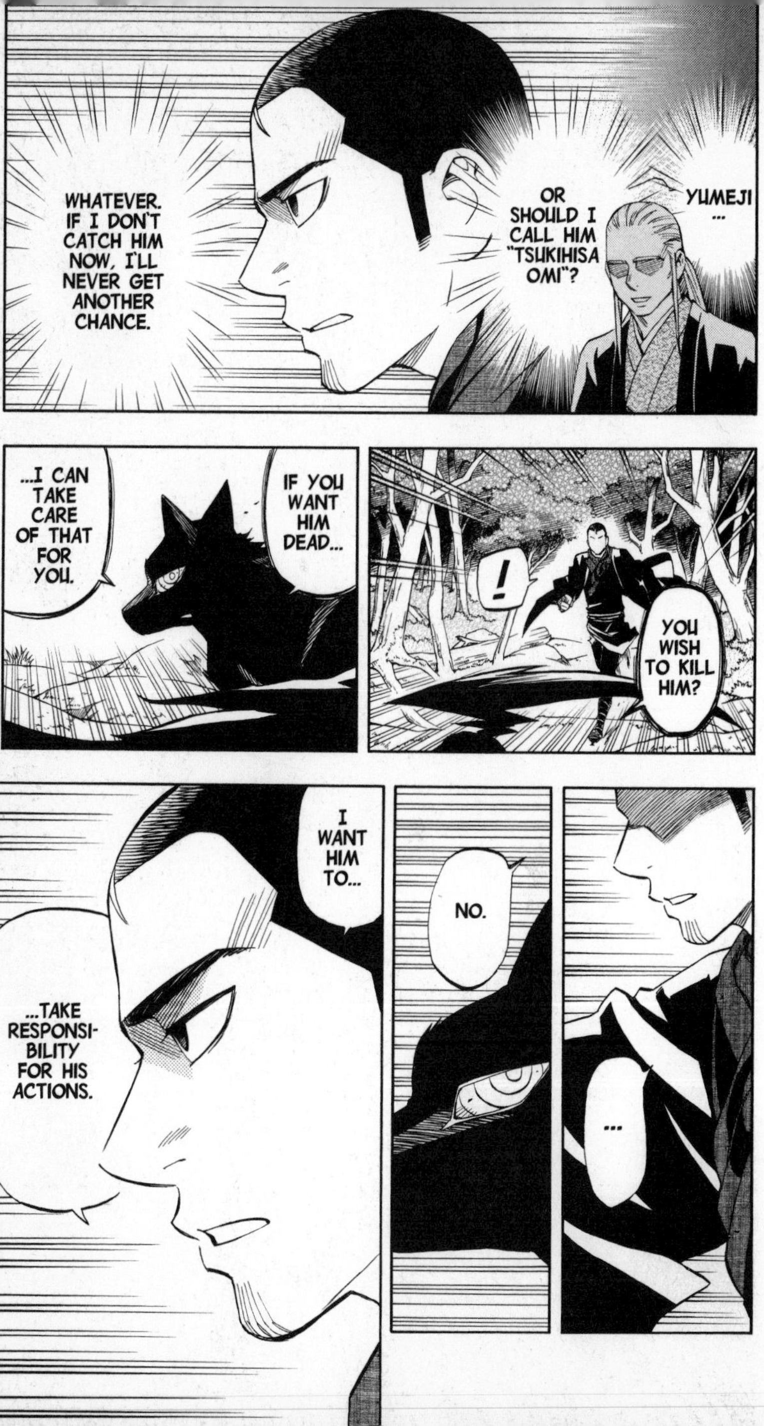
YUMEJI...
OR SHOULD I CALL HIM "TSUKIHISA OMI"?
WHATEVER. IF I DON'T CATCH HIM NOW, I'LL NEVER GET ANOTHER CHANCE.
!
YOU WISH TO KILL HIM?
IF YOU WANT HIM DEAD...
...I CAN TAKE CARE OF THAT FOR YOU.
...
NO.
I WANT HIM TO...
...TAKE RESPONSI-BILITY FOR HIS ACTIONS.

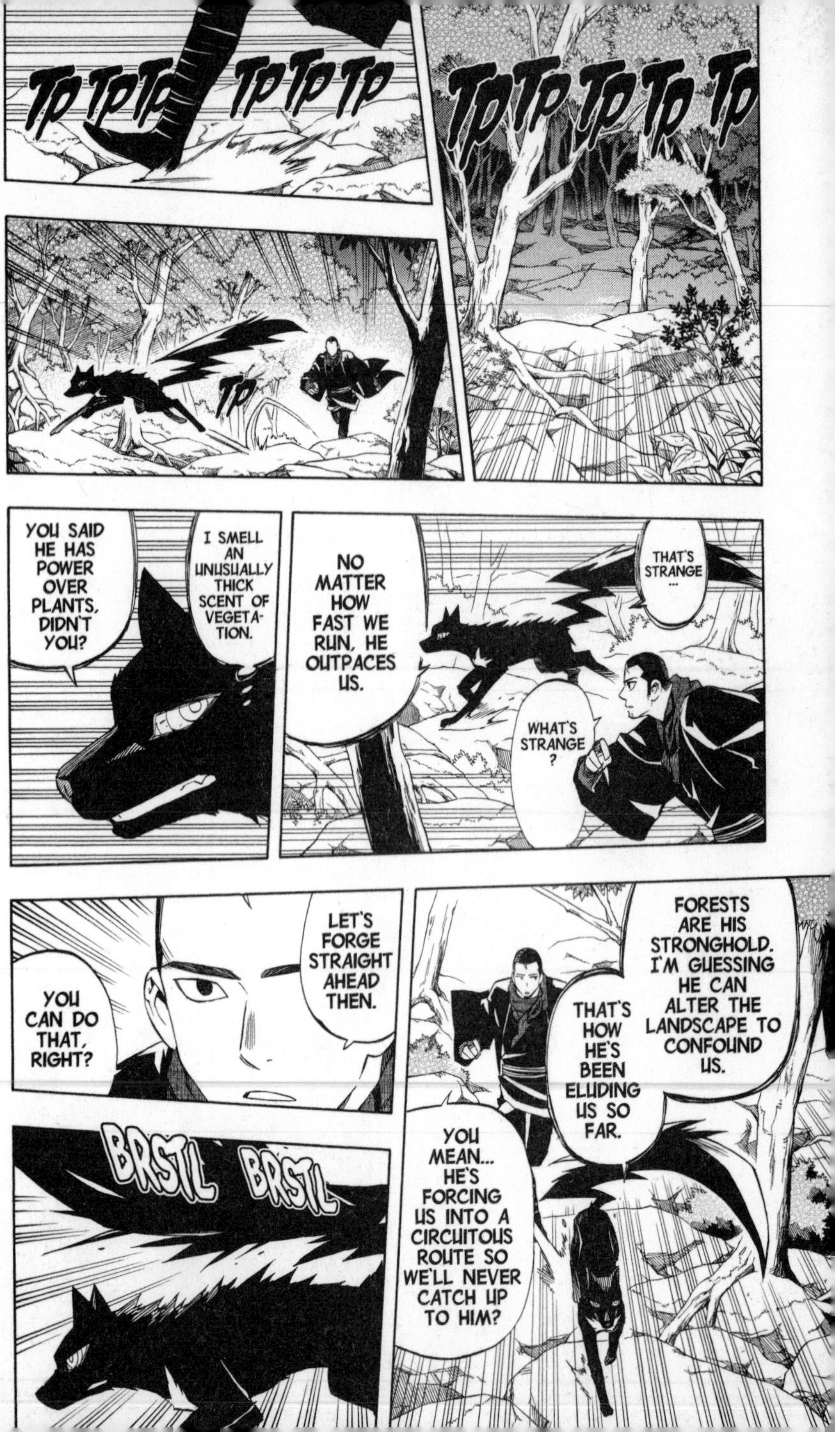
Tp Tp Tp Tp Tp
Tp Tp Tp Tp Tp Tp
Tp
THAT'S STRANGE...
WHAT'S STRANGE?
NO MATTER HOW FAST WE RUN, HE OUTPACES US.
I SMELL AN UNUSUALLY THICK SCENT OF VEGETATION.
YOU SAID HE HAS POWER OVER PLANTS, DIDN'T YOU?
FORESTS ARE HIS STRONGHOLD. I'M GUESSING HE CAN ALTER THE LANDSCAPE TO CONFOUND US.
THAT'S HOW HE'S BEEN ELUDING US SO FAR.
YOU MEAN... HE'S FORCING US INTO A CIRCUITOUS ROUTE SO WE'LL NEVER CATCH UP TO HIM?
LET'S FORGE STRAIGHT AHEAD THEN.
YOU CAN DO THAT, RIGHT?
BRSTL BRSTL

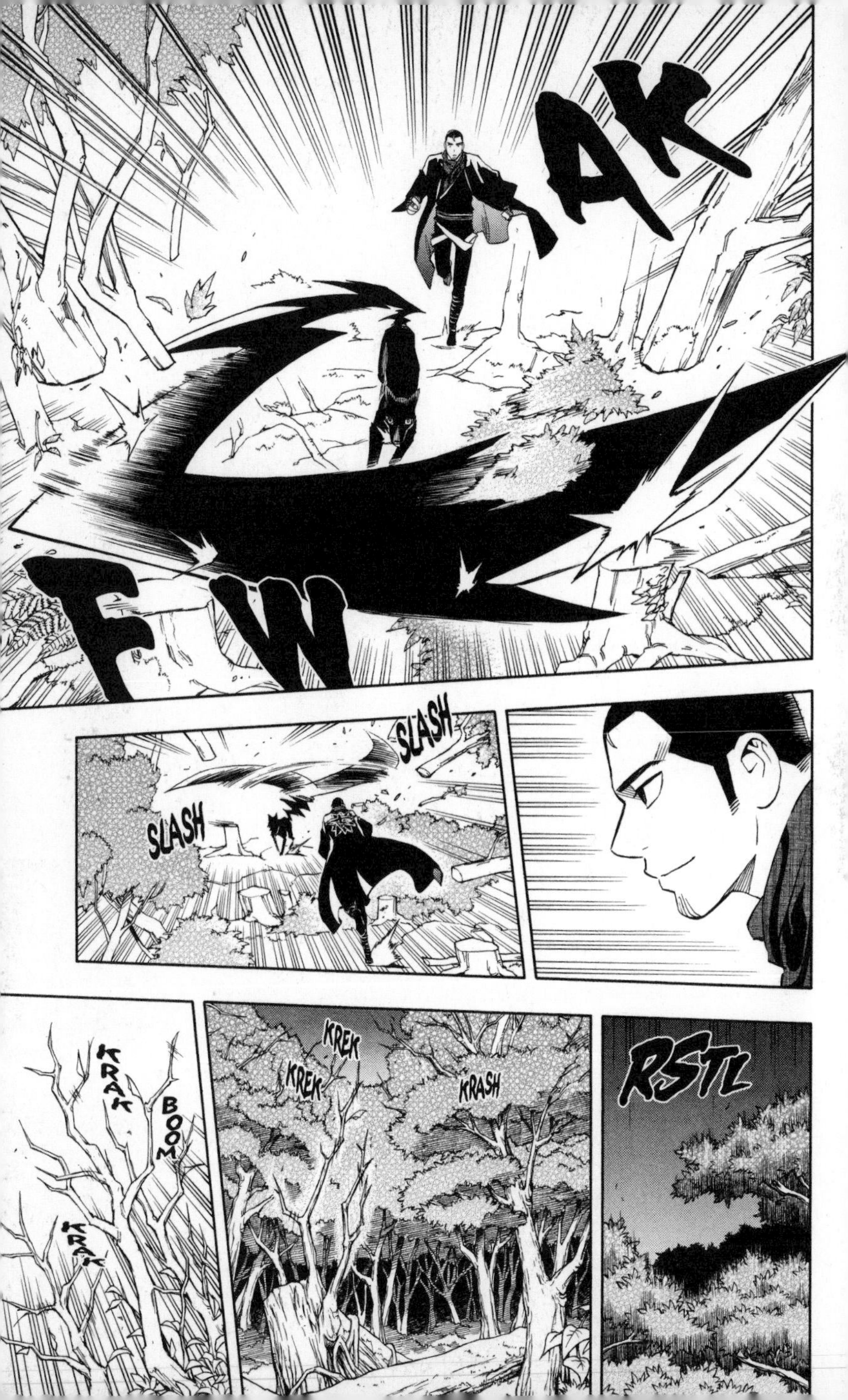
FW
AK
SLASH
SLASH
RSTL
KREK
KRASH
KREK
KRAK
BOOM
KRAK

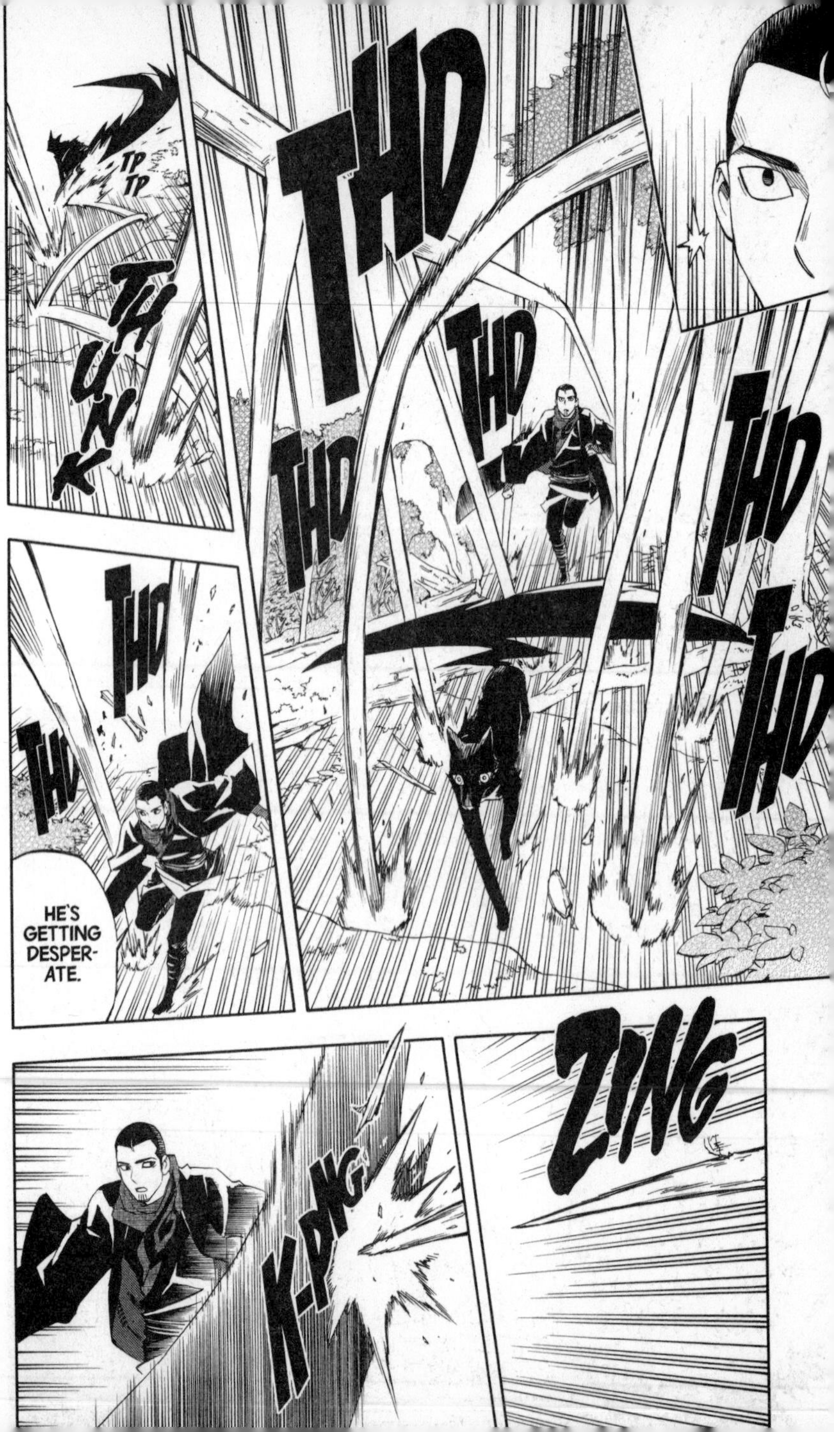
THD
THD
THD
THD
THD
THD
TP TP
THUNK
THD
THD
HE'S GETTING DESPER-ATE.
ZING
K-PNG

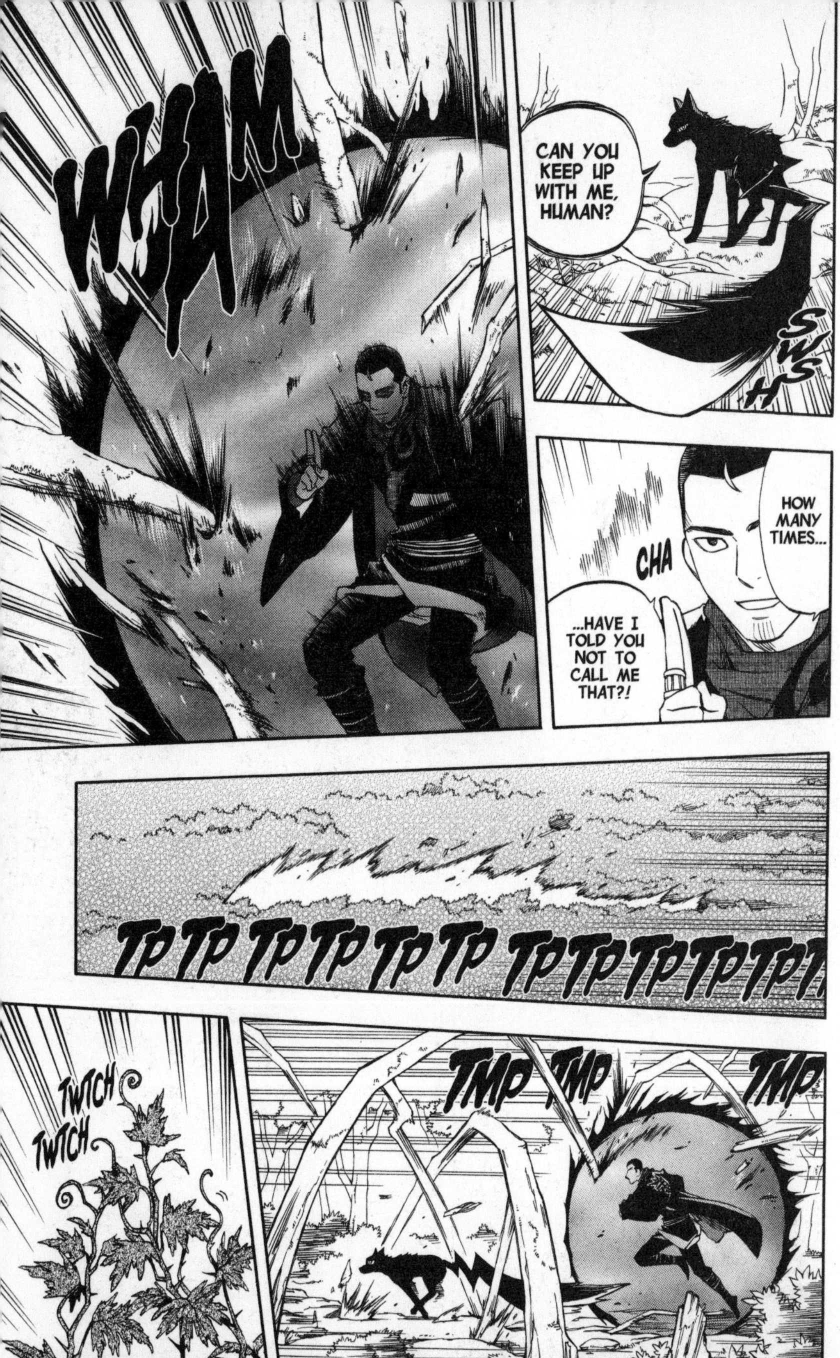
CAN YOU KEEP UP WITH ME, HUMAN?
SWSH
HOW MANY TIMES...
CHA
...HAVE I TOLD YOU NOT TO CALL ME THAT?!
WHAM
TP TP TP TP TP TP TP TP TP TP TP
TMP TMP TMP
TWITCH
TWITCH

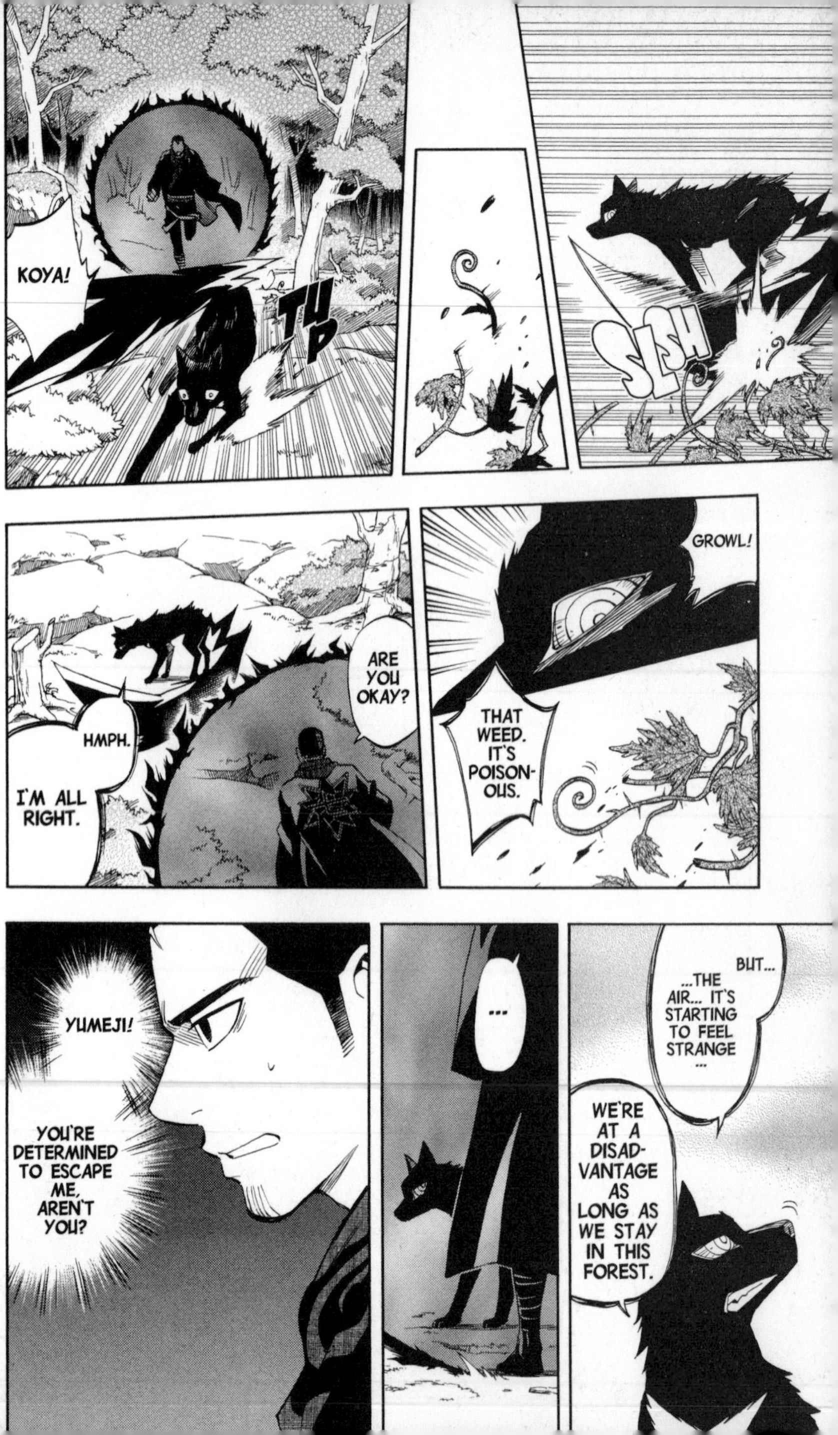
SLSH
KOYA!
TUP
GROWL!
THAT WEED. IT'S POISONOUS.
ARE YOU OKAY?
HMPH.
I'M ALL RIGHT.
BUT...
...THE AIR... IT'S STARTING TO FEEL STRANGE...
WE'RE AT A DISADVANTAGE AS LONG AS WE STAY IN THIS FOREST.
...
YUMEJI!
YOU'RE DETERMINED TO ESCAPE ME, AREN'T YOU?

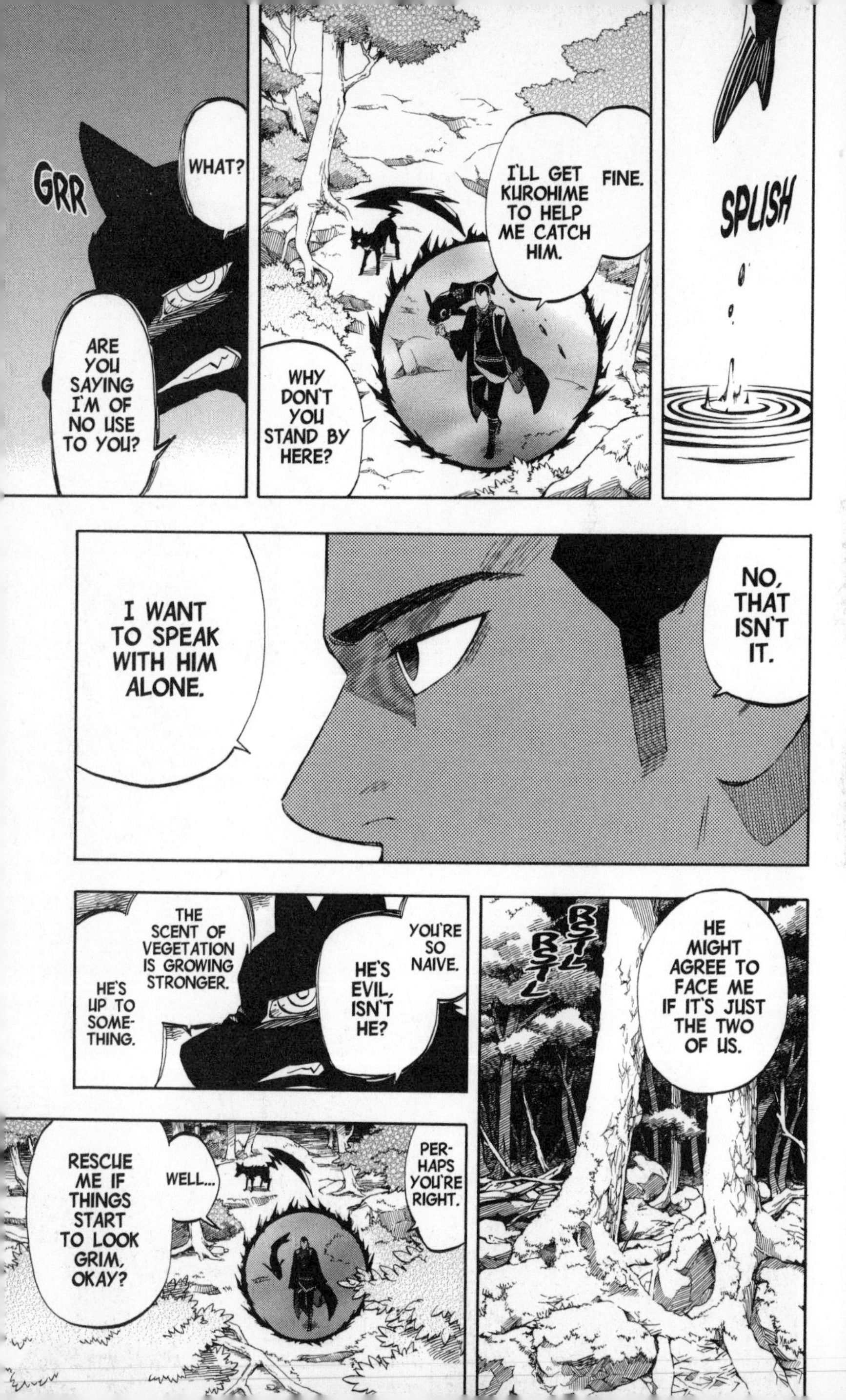
SPLISH
FINE.
I'LL GET KUROHIME TO HELP ME CATCH HIM.
WHY DON'T YOU STAND BY HERE?
WHAT?
GRR
ARE YOU SAYING I'M OF NO USE TO YOU?
NO, THAT ISN'T IT.
I WANT TO SPEAK WITH HIM ALONE.
RSTL RSTL
HE MIGHT AGREE TO FACE ME IF IT'S JUST THE TWO OF US.
YOU'RE SO NAIVE.
HE'S EVIL, ISN'T HE?
THE SCENT OF VEGETATION IS GROWING STRONGER.
HE'S UP TO SOME-THING.
PER-HAPS YOU'RE RIGHT.
WELL...
RESCUE ME IF THINGS START TO LOOK GRIM, OKAY?

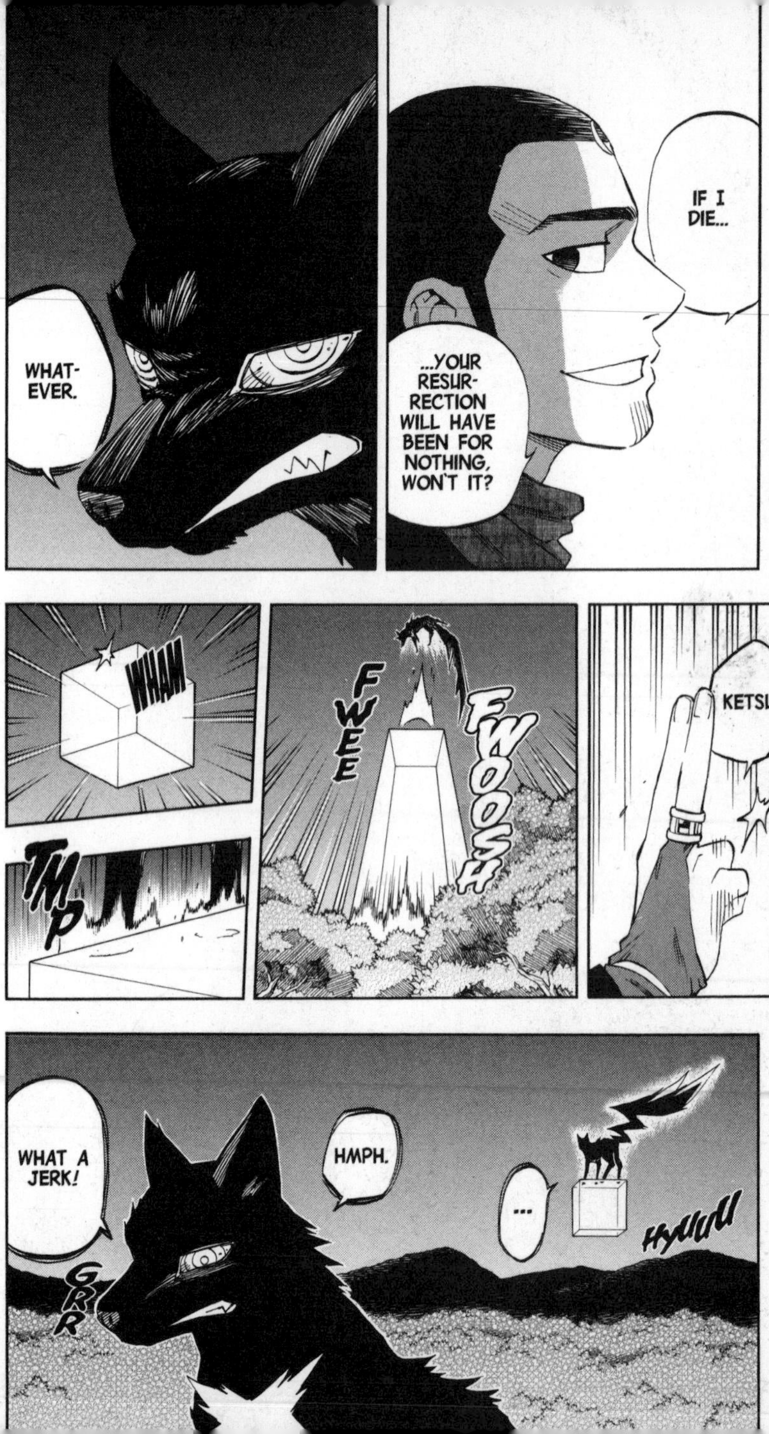
IF I DIE...
...YOUR RESURRECTION WILL HAVE BEEN FOR NOTHING, WON'T IT?
WHATEVER.
KETSU!
FWOOSH
FWEE
WHAM
TMP
HYUUU
...
HMPH.
WHAT A JERK!
GRR

KURO-
HIME...

HURRY.
WE HAVE
TO CATCH
YUMEJI.

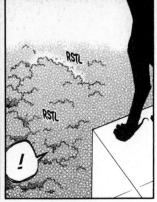

RSTL

RSTL

!

SCREE

SNAP SNAP

SNAP

SNAP

WO BBLE

!!

SNAP

SNAP SNAP

SNAP

SNAP

SNAP

SNAP

SNAP

SNAP

SNAP

SNAP

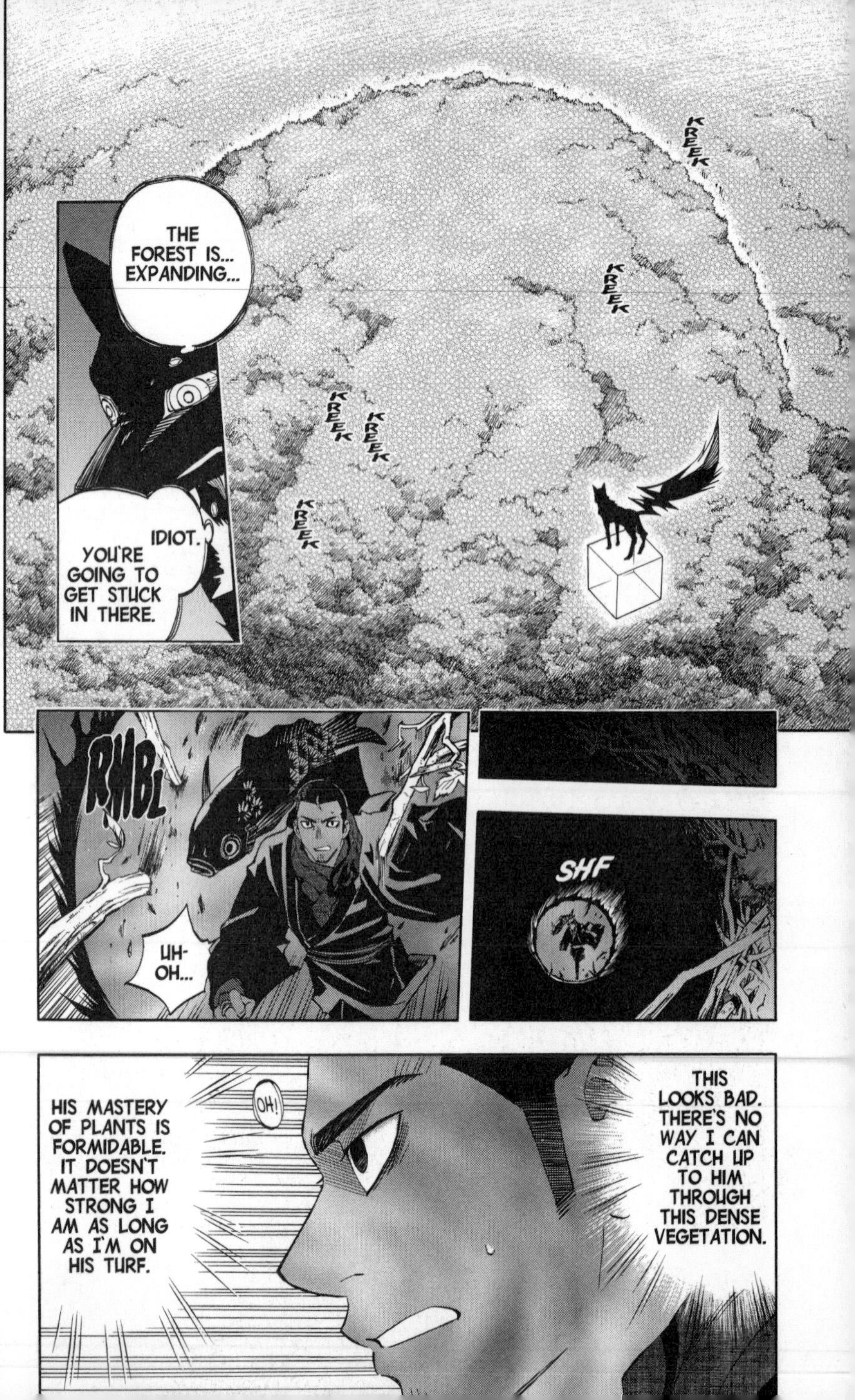

KREEK
KREEK
KREEK
KREEK
KREEK
THE FOREST IS... EXPANDING...
IDIOT. YOU'RE GOING TO GET STUCK IN THERE.
SHF
RMBL
UH-OH...
THIS LOOKS BAD. THERE'S NO WAY I CAN CATCH UP TO HIM THROUGH THIS DENSE VEGETATION.
OH!
HIS MASTERY OF PLANTS IS FORMIDABLE. IT DOESN'T MATTER HOW STRONG I AM AS LONG AS I'M ON HIS TURF.

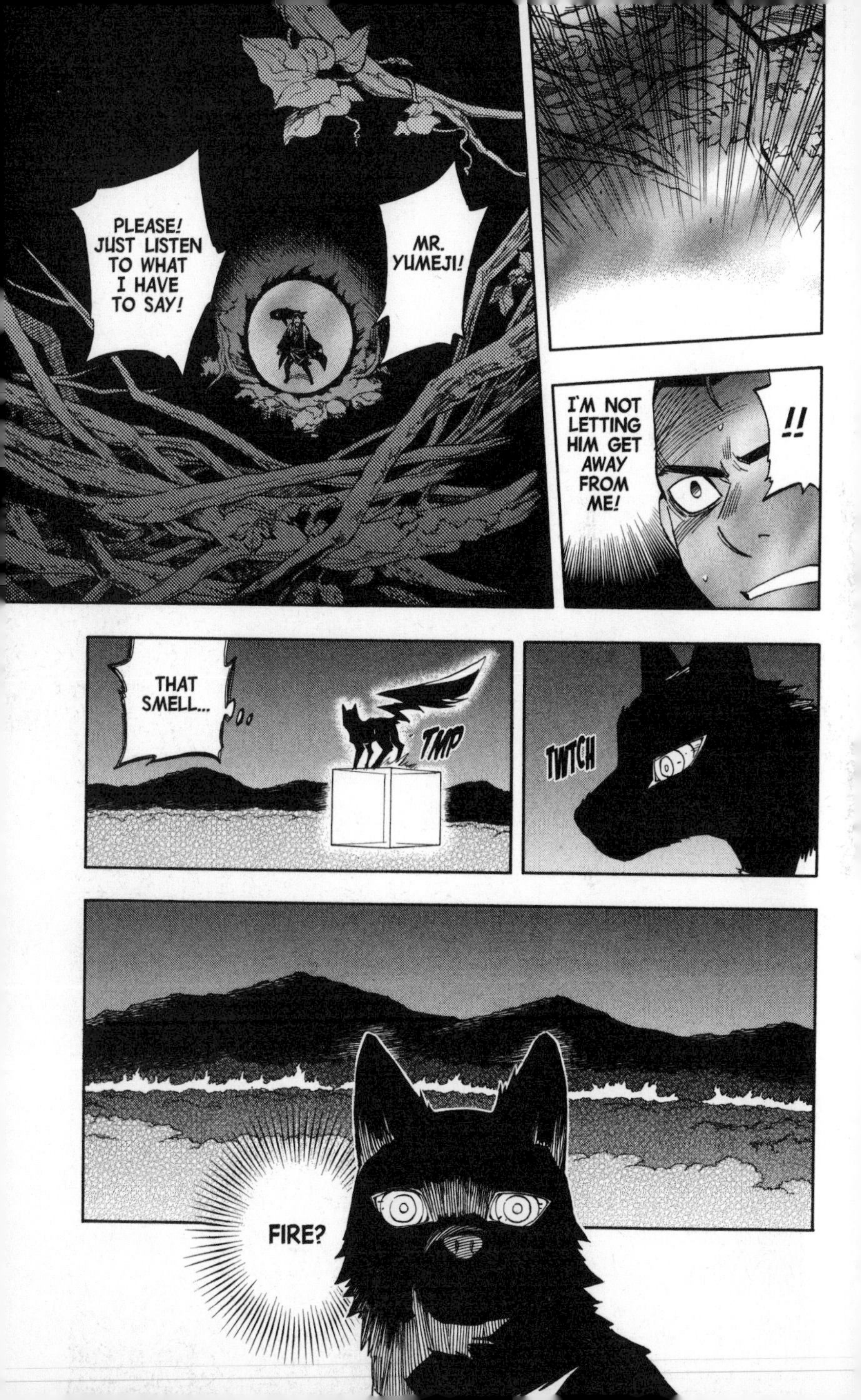
I'M NOT LETTING HIM GET AWAY FROM ME!
!!
MR. YUMEJI!
PLEASE! JUST LISTEN TO WHAT I HAVE TO SAY!
TWITCH
THAT SMELL...
TMP
FIRE?

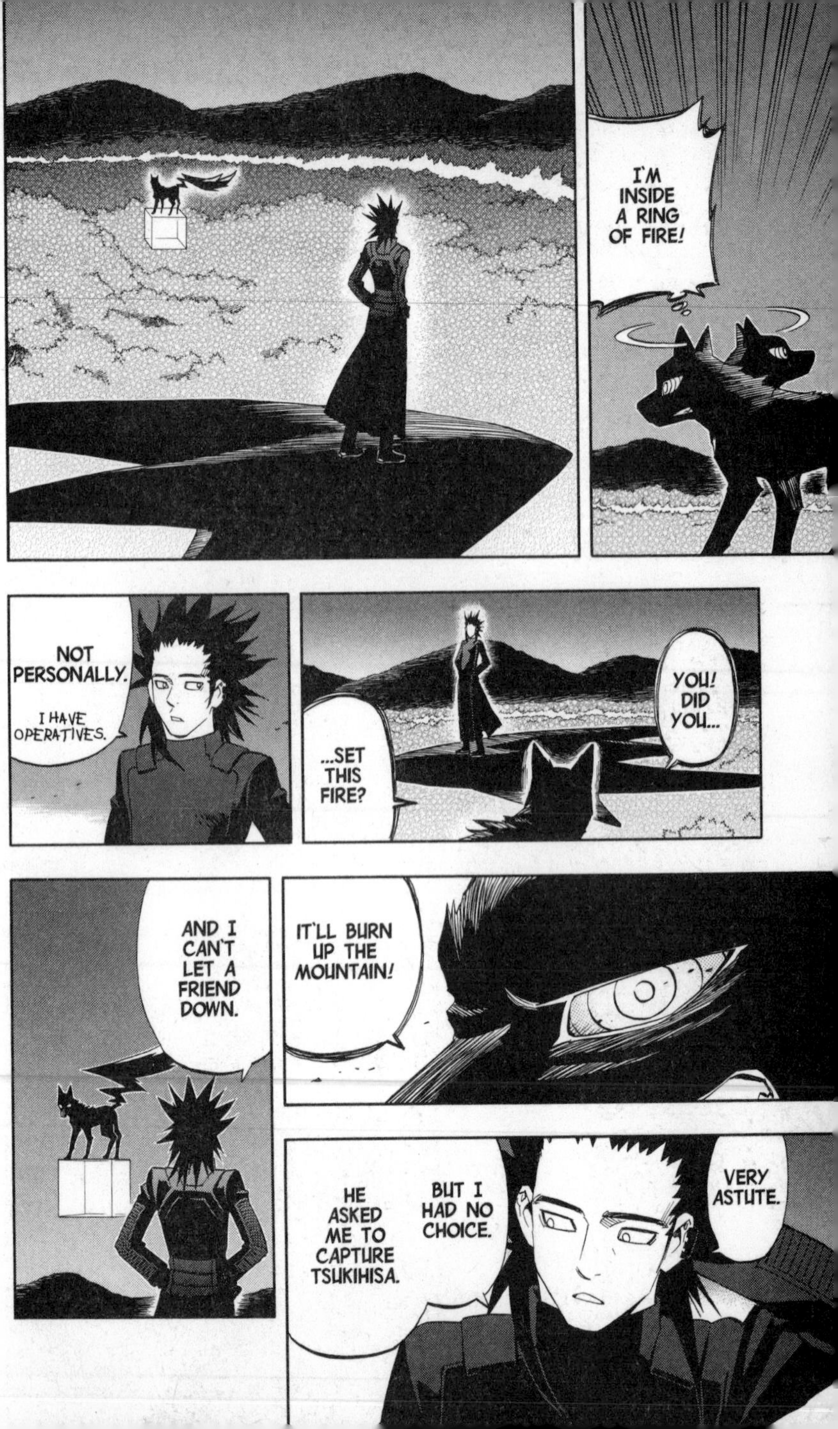
I'M INSIDE A RING OF FIRE!
YOU! DID YOU...
...SET THIS FIRE?
NOT PERSONALLY.
I HAVE OPERATIVES.
IT'LL BURN UP THE MOUNTAIN!
VERY ASTUTE.
BUT I HAD NO CHOICE.
HE ASKED ME TO CAPTURE TSUKIHISA.
AND I CAN'T LET A FRIEND DOWN.

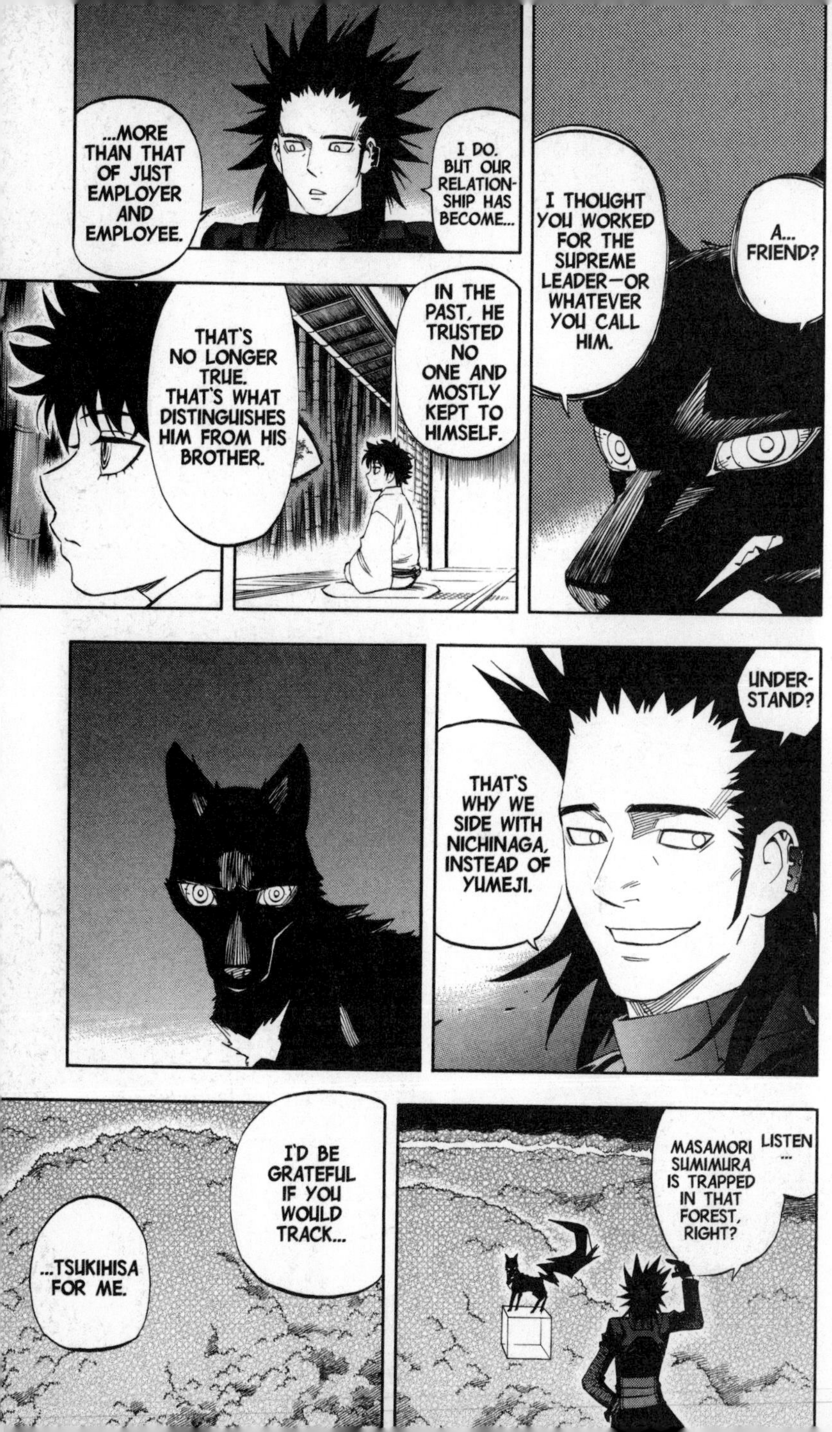
A... FRIEND?
I THOUGHT YOU WORKED FOR THE SUPREME LEADER—OR WHATEVER YOU CALL HIM.
I DO. BUT OUR RELATION-SHIP HAS BECOME...
...MORE THAN THAT OF JUST EMPLOYER AND EMPLOYEE.
IN THE PAST, HE TRUSTED NO ONE AND MOSTLY KEPT TO HIMSELF.
THAT'S NO LONGER TRUE. THAT'S WHAT DISTINGUISHES HIM FROM HIS BROTHER.
UNDER-STAND?
THAT'S WHY WE SIDE WITH NICHINAGA, INSTEAD OF YUMEJI.
LISTEN...
MASAMORI SUMIMURA IS TRAPPED IN THAT FOREST, RIGHT?
I'D BE GRATEFUL IF YOU WOULD TRACK...
...TSUKIHISA FOR ME.

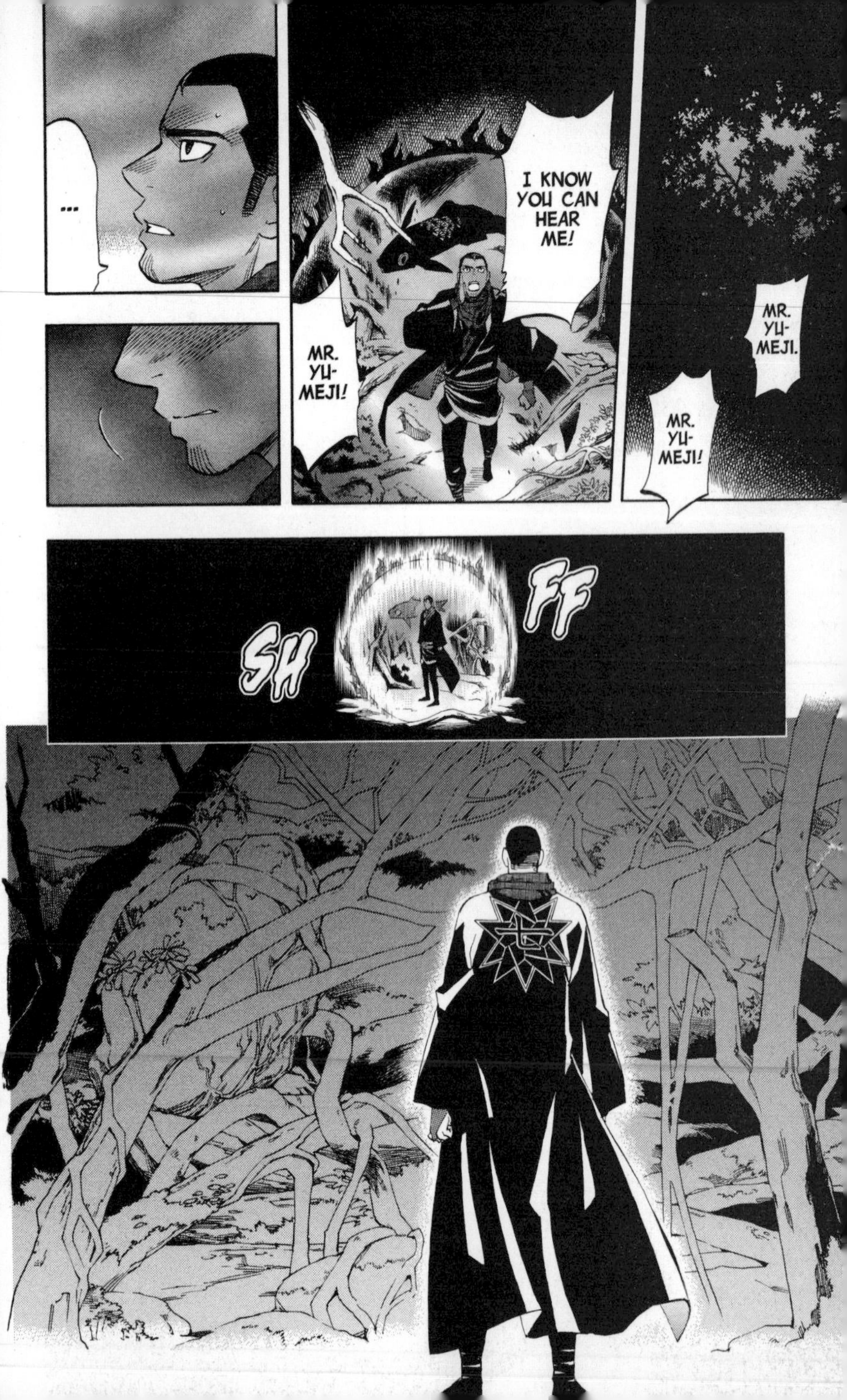
MR. YU-MEJI.
MR. YU-MEJI!
I KNOW YOU CAN HEAR ME!
MR. YU-MEJI!
...
SH FF

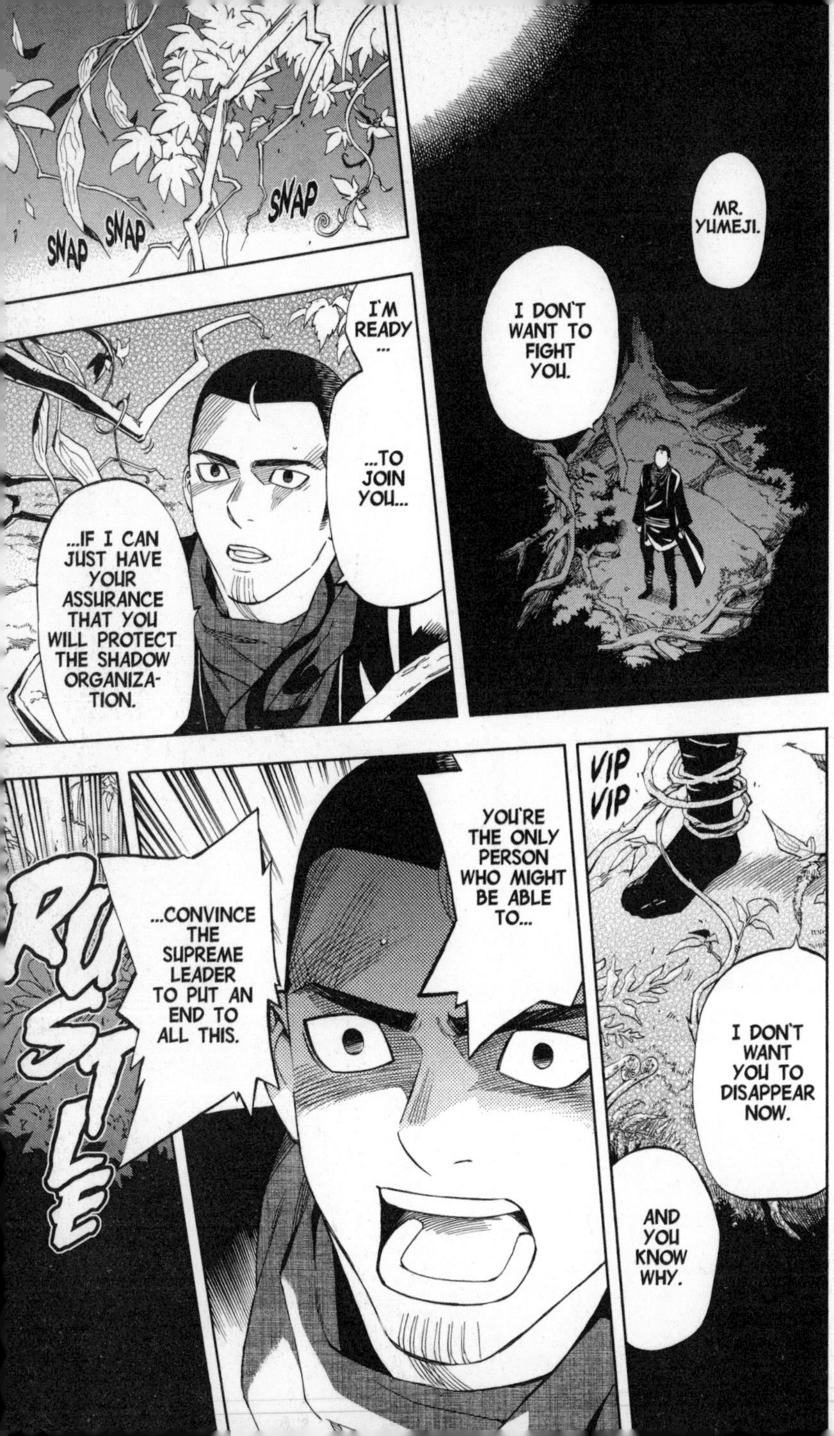
MR. YUMEJI.
I DON'T WANT TO FIGHT YOU.
SNAP
SNAP
SNAP
I'M READY...
...TO JOIN YOU...
...IF I CAN JUST HAVE YOUR ASSURANCE THAT YOU WILL PROTECT THE SHADOW ORGANIZATION.
VIP VIP
I DON'T WANT YOU TO DISAPPEAR NOW.
AND YOU KNOW WHY.
YOU'RE THE ONLY PERSON WHO MIGHT BE ABLE TO...
...CONVINCE THE SUPREME LEADER TO PUT AN END TO ALL THIS.
RUSTLE

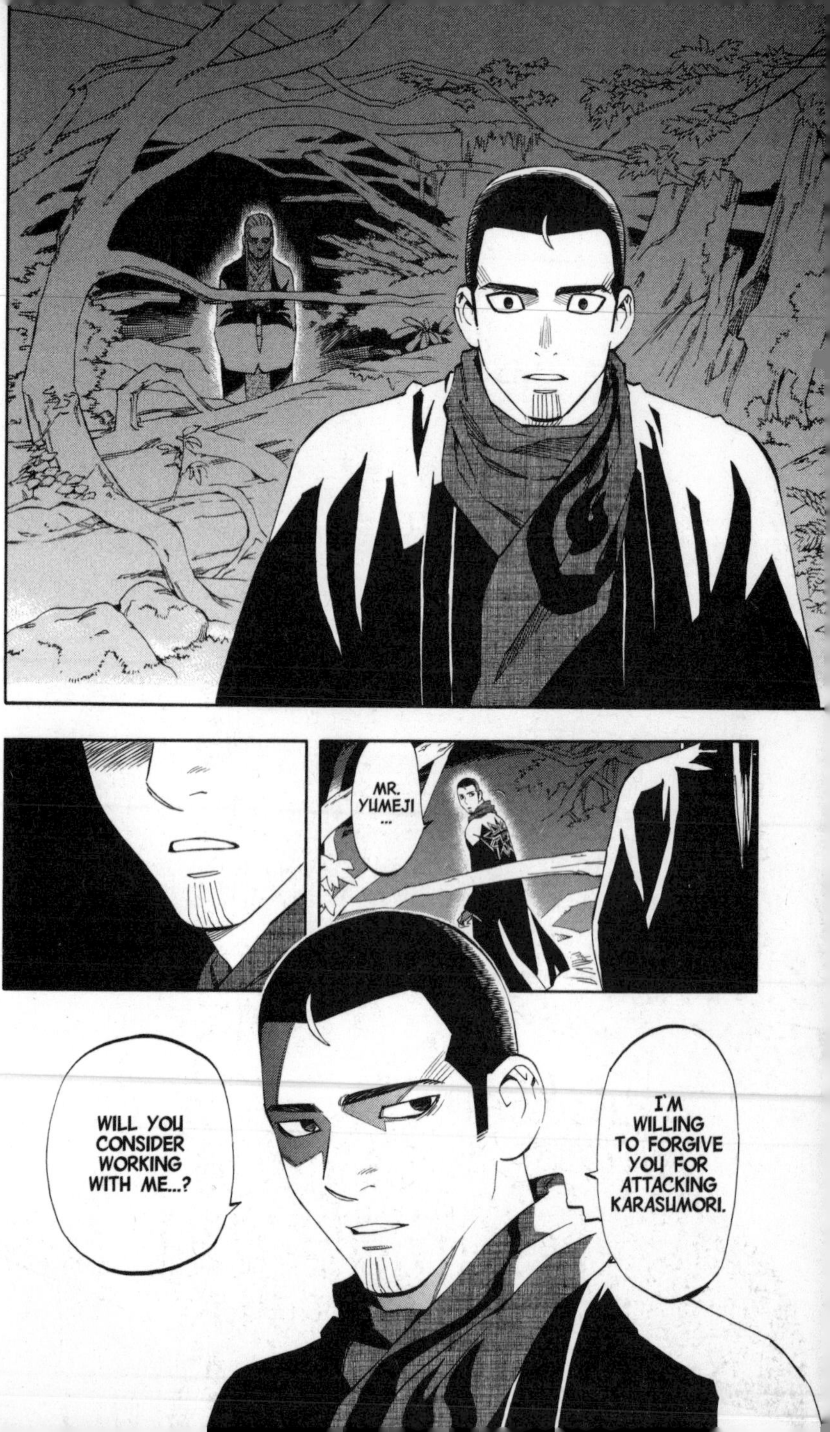
MR. YUMEJI ...
I'M WILLING TO FORGIVE YOU FOR ATTACKING KARASUMORI.
WILL YOU CONSIDER WORKING WITH ME...?

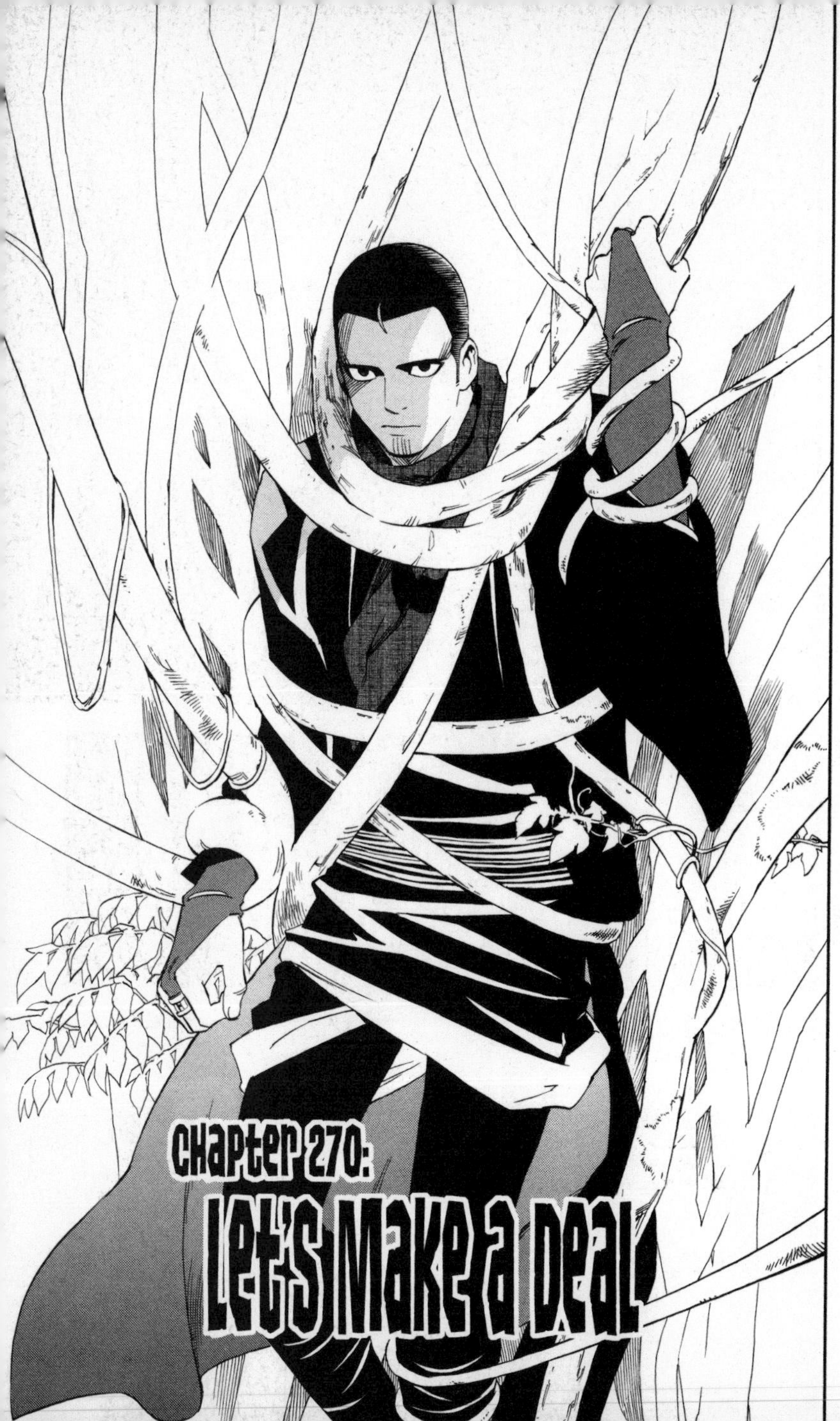
Chapter 270:
Let's Make a Deal

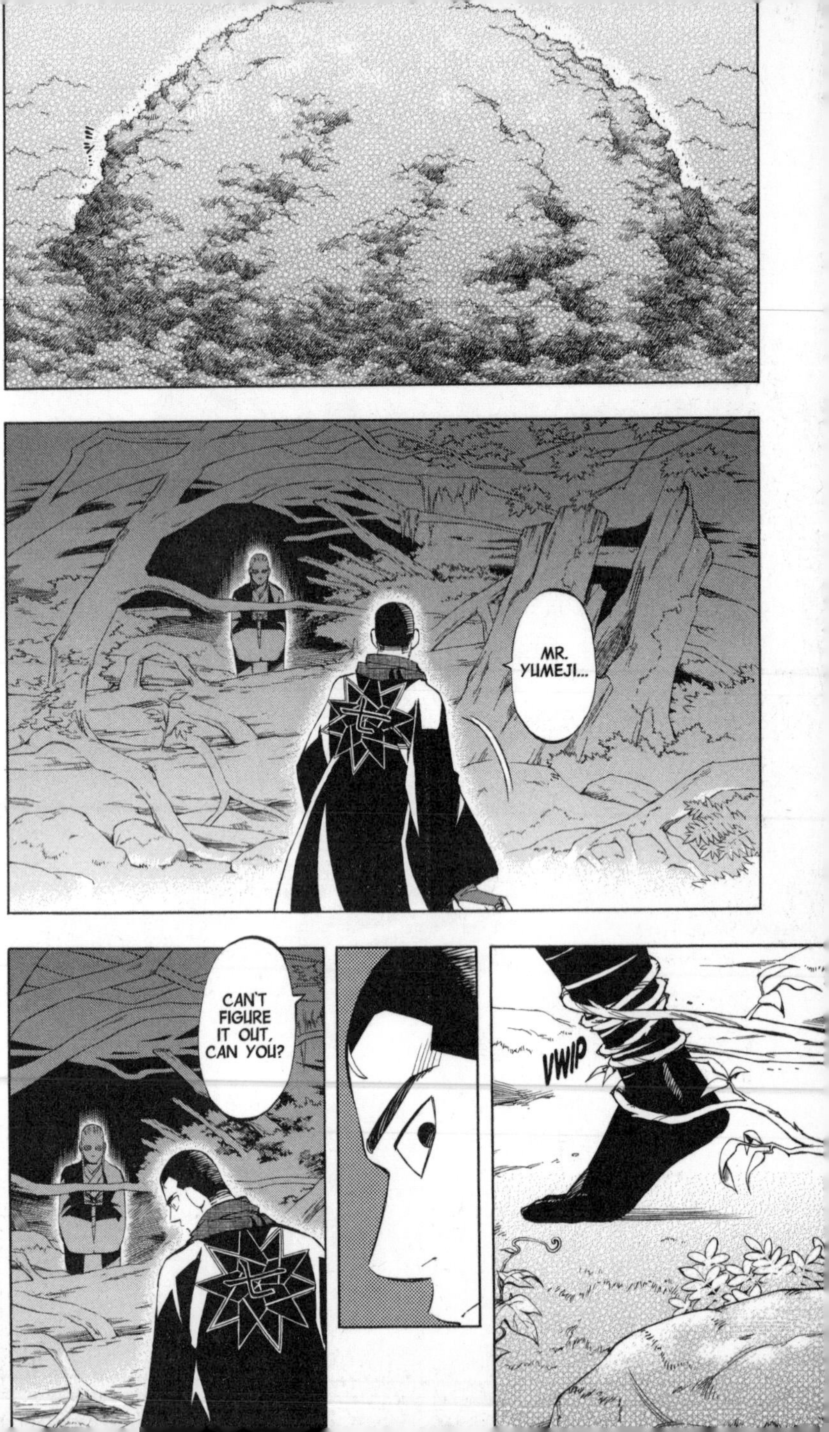
MR. YUMEJI...
VWIP
CAN'T FIGURE IT OUT, CAN YOU?

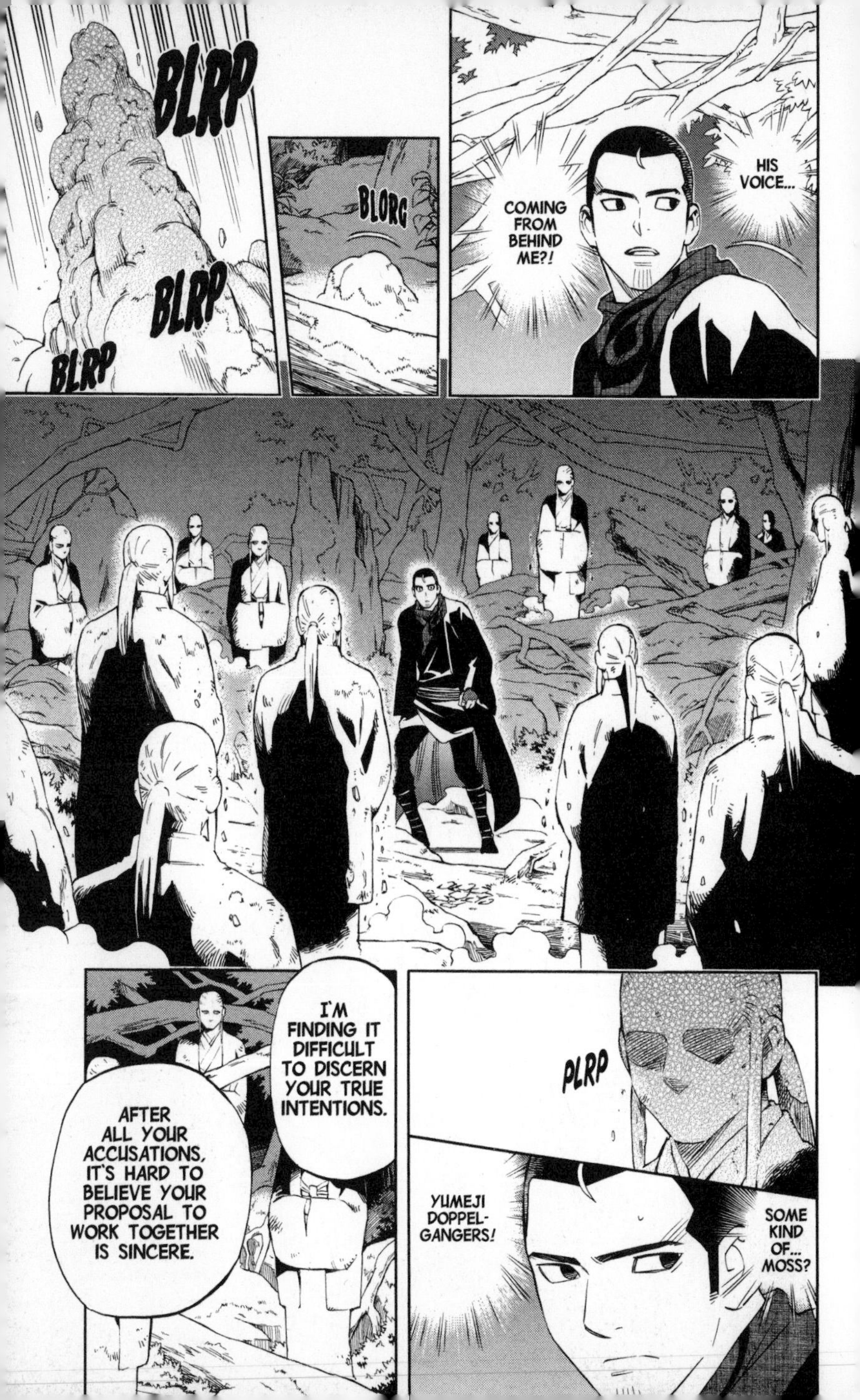
HIS VOICE...
COMING FROM BEHIND ME?!
BLORG
BLRP
BLRP
BLRP
PLRP
SOME KIND OF... MOSS?
YUMEJI DOPPEL-GANGERS!
I'M FINDING IT DIFFICULT TO DISCERN YOUR TRUE INTENTIONS.
AFTER ALL YOUR ACCUSATIONS, IT'S HARD TO BELIEVE YOUR PROPOSAL TO WORK TOGETHER IS SINCERE.

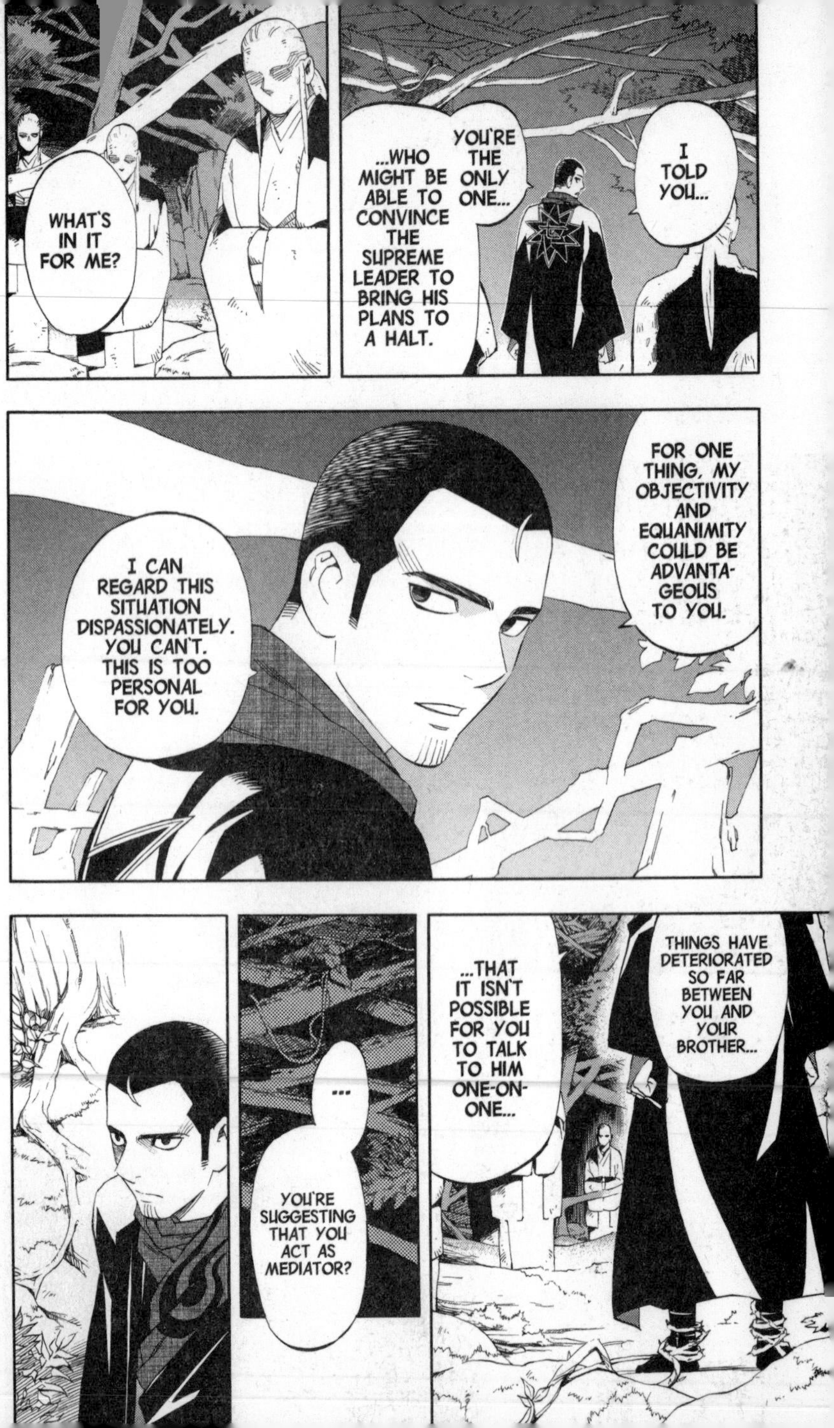
I TOLD YOU...
YOU'RE THE ONLY ONE...
...WHO MIGHT BE ABLE TO CONVINCE THE SUPREME LEADER TO BRING HIS PLANS TO A HALT.
WHAT'S IN IT FOR ME?
FOR ONE THING, MY OBJECTIVITY AND EQUANIMITY COULD BE ADVANTAGEOUS TO YOU.
I CAN REGARD THIS SITUATION DISPASSIONATELY. YOU CAN'T. THIS IS TOO PERSONAL FOR YOU.
THINGS HAVE DETERIORATED SO FAR BETWEEN YOU AND YOUR BROTHER...
...THAT IT ISN'T POSSIBLE FOR YOU TO TALK TO HIM ONE-ON-ONE...
...
YOU'RE SUGGESTING THAT YOU ACT AS MEDIATOR?

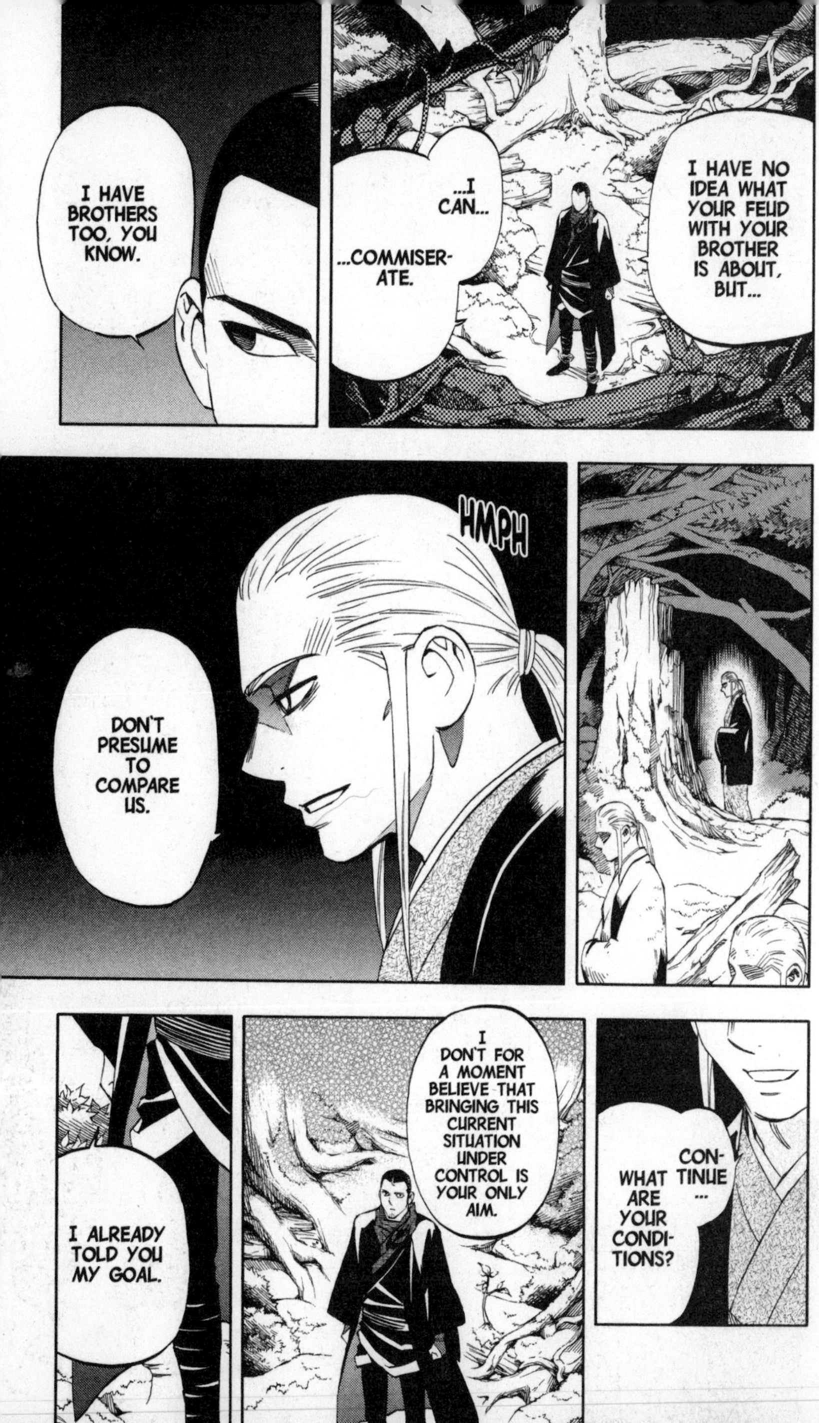
I HAVE NO IDEA WHAT YOUR FEUD WITH YOUR BROTHER IS ABOUT, BUT...
...I CAN...
...COMMISER-ATE.
I HAVE BROTHERS TOO, YOU KNOW.
HMPH
DON'T PRESUME TO COMPARE US.
CON-TINUE...
WHAT ARE YOUR CONDI-TIONS?
I DON'T FOR A MOMENT BELIEVE THAT BRINGING THIS CURRENT SITUATION UNDER CONTROL IS YOUR ONLY AIM.
I ALREADY TOLD YOU MY GOAL.

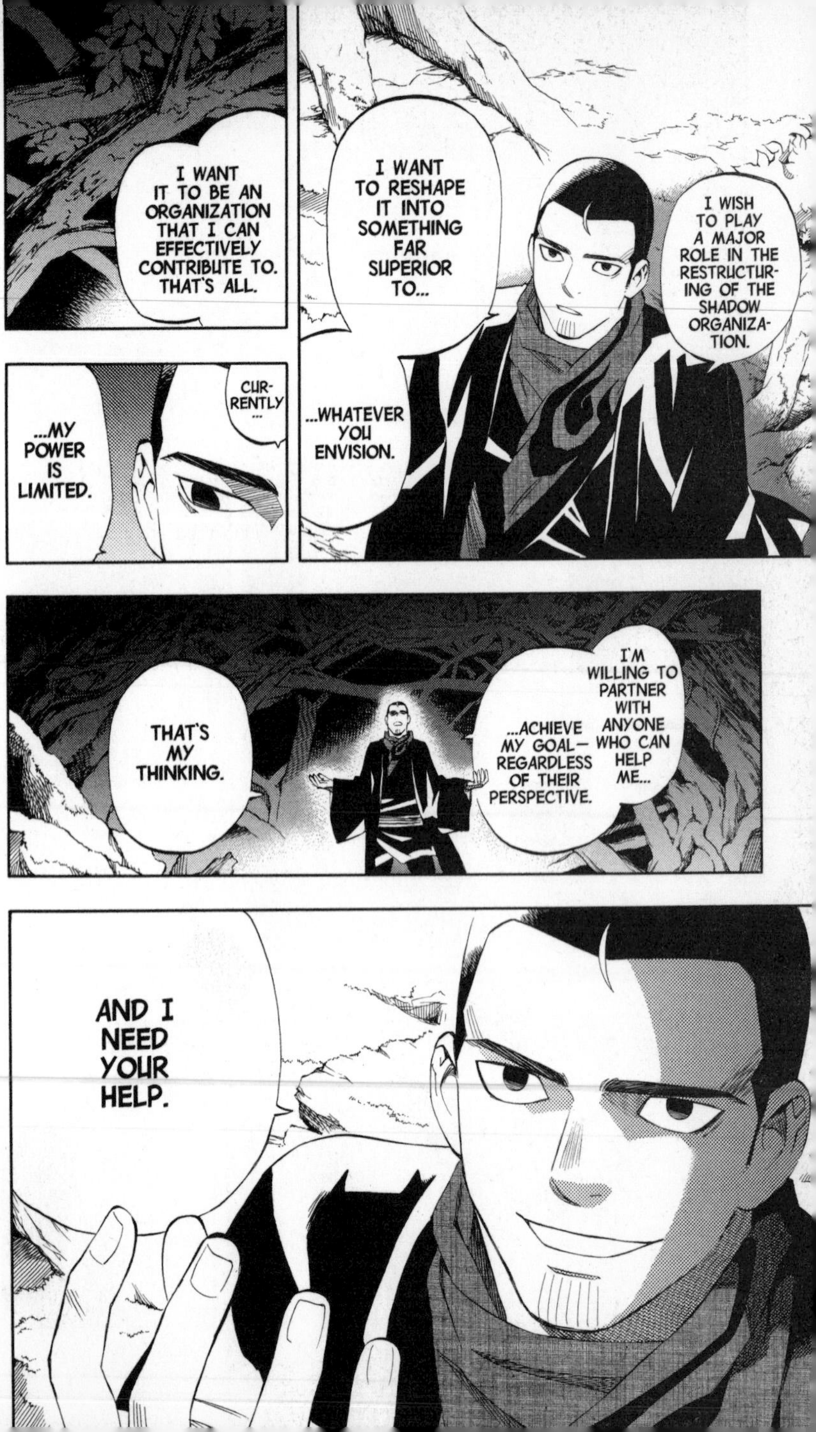
I WISH TO PLAY A MAJOR ROLE IN THE RESTRUCTURING OF THE SHADOW ORGANIZATION.
I WANT TO RESHAPE IT INTO SOMETHING FAR SUPERIOR TO...
...WHATEVER YOU ENVISION.
I WANT IT TO BE AN ORGANIZATION THAT I CAN EFFECTIVELY CONTRIBUTE TO. THAT'S ALL.
CURRENTLY...
...MY POWER IS LIMITED.
I'M WILLING TO PARTNER WITH ANYONE WHO CAN HELP ME...
...ACHIEVE MY GOAL— REGARDLESS OF THEIR PERSPECTIVE.
THAT'S MY THINKING.
AND I NEED YOUR HELP.

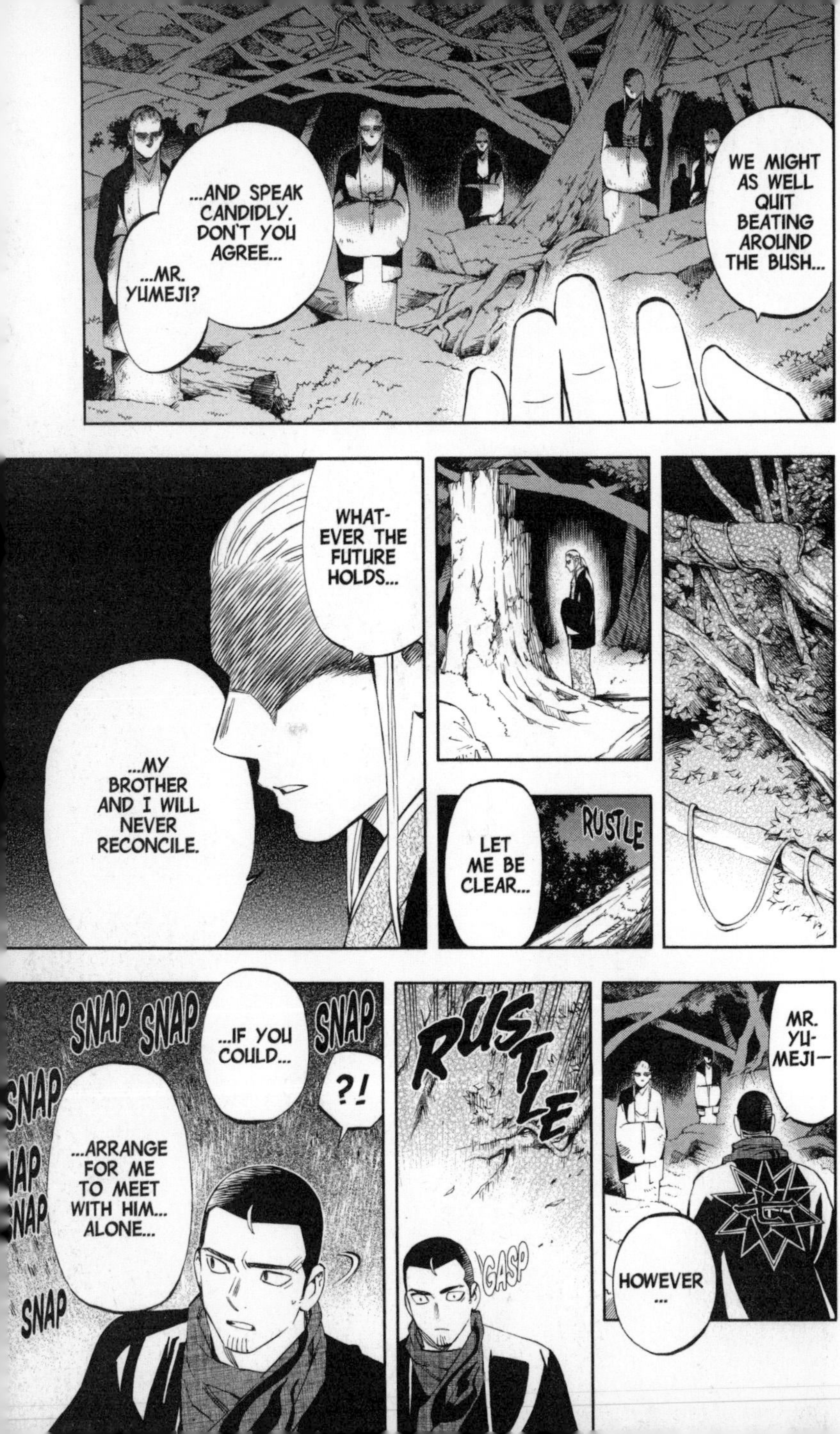
WE MIGHT AS WELL QUIT BEATING AROUND THE BUSH...
...AND SPEAK CANDIDLY. DON'T YOU AGREE...
...MR. YUMEJI?
RUSTLE
LET ME BE CLEAR...
WHAT-EVER THE FUTURE HOLDS...
...MY BROTHER AND I WILL NEVER RECONCILE.
MR. YU-MEJI—
HOWEVER ...
RUSTLE
GASP
SNAP
?!
...IF YOU COULD...
SNAP SNAP
SNAP
SNAP
SNAP
...ARRANGE FOR ME TO MEET WITH HIM... ALONE...
SNAP

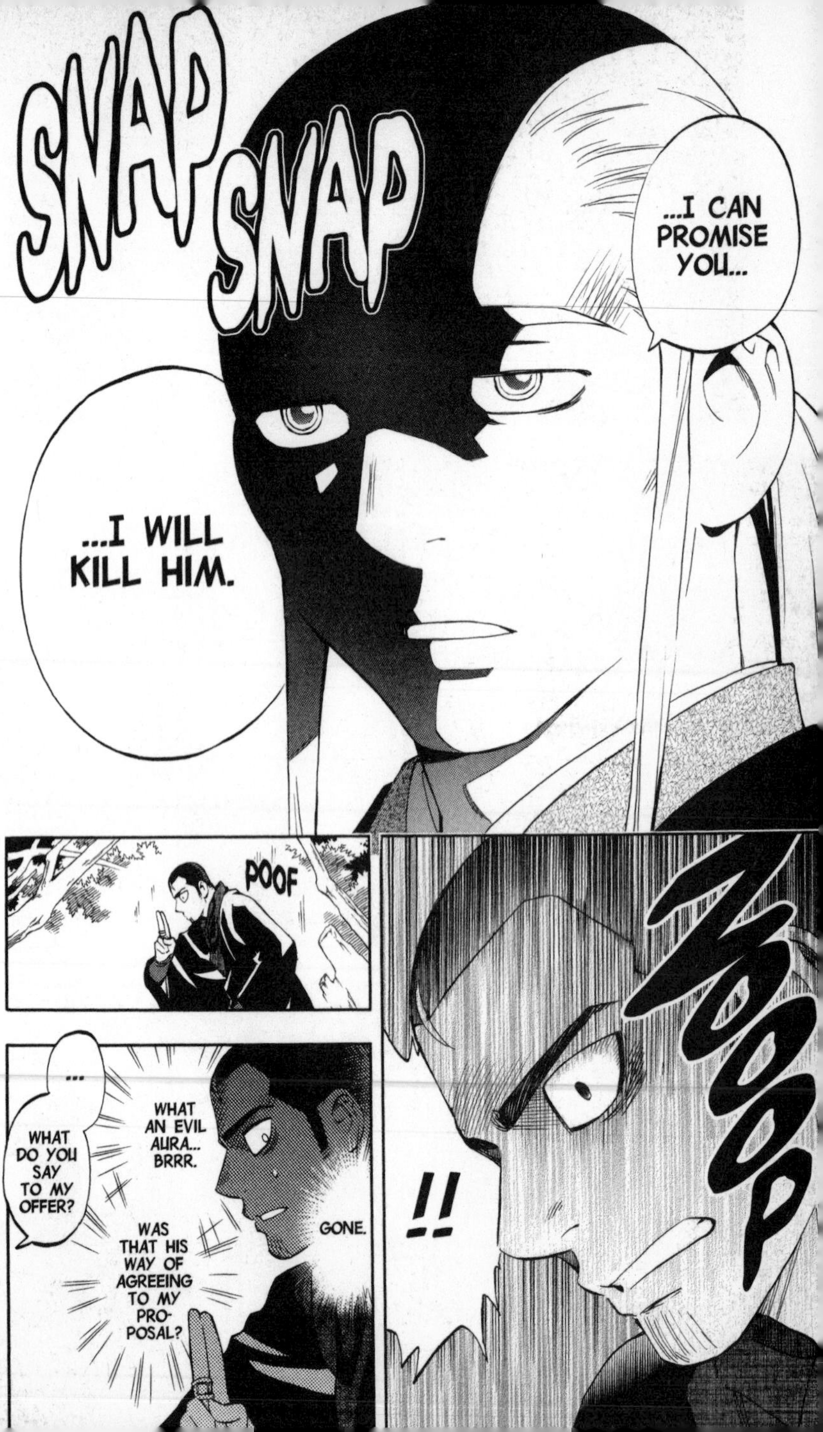
...I CAN PROMISE YOU...
SNAP SNAP
...I WILL KILL HIM.
WOOOP
!!
POOF
GONE.
WHAT AN EVIL AURA... BRRR.
WAS THAT HIS WAY OF AGREEING TO MY PRO-POSAL?
...
WHAT DO YOU SAY TO MY OFFER?

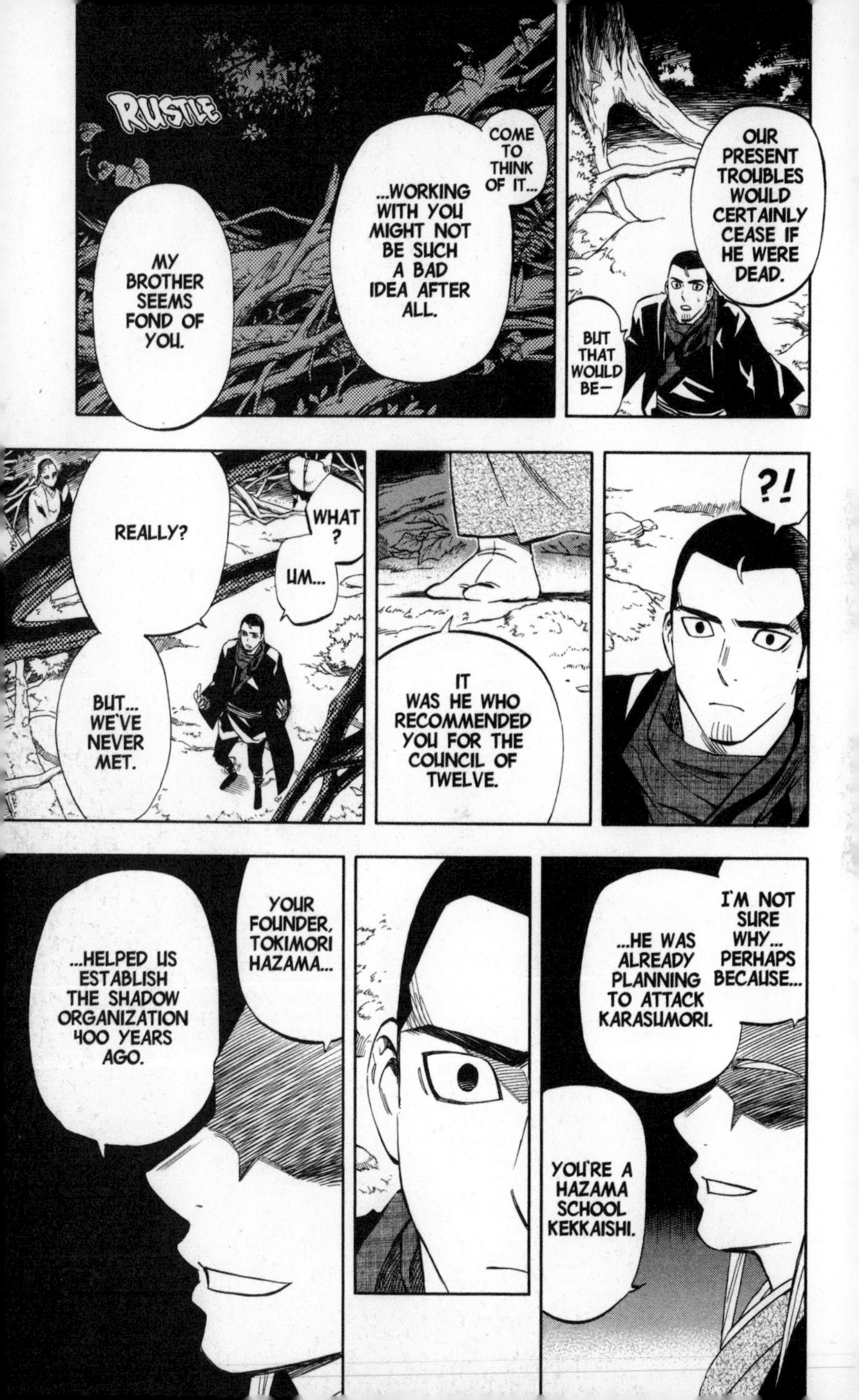
OUR PRESENT TROUBLES WOULD CERTAINLY CEASE IF HE WERE DEAD.
BUT THAT WOULD BE—
RUSTLE
COME TO THINK OF IT...
...WORKING WITH YOU MIGHT NOT BE SUCH A BAD IDEA AFTER ALL.
MY BROTHER SEEMS FOND OF YOU.
?!
IT WAS HE WHO RECOMMENDED YOU FOR THE COUNCIL OF TWELVE.
WHAT?
UM...
REALLY?
BUT... WE'VE NEVER MET.
I'M NOT SURE WHY... PERHAPS BECAUSE...
...HE WAS ALREADY PLANNING TO ATTACK KARASUMORI.
YOU'RE A HAZAMA SCHOOL KEKKAISHI.
YOUR FOUNDER, TOKIMORI HAZAMA...
...HELPED US ESTABLISH THE SHADOW ORGANIZATION 400 YEARS AGO.

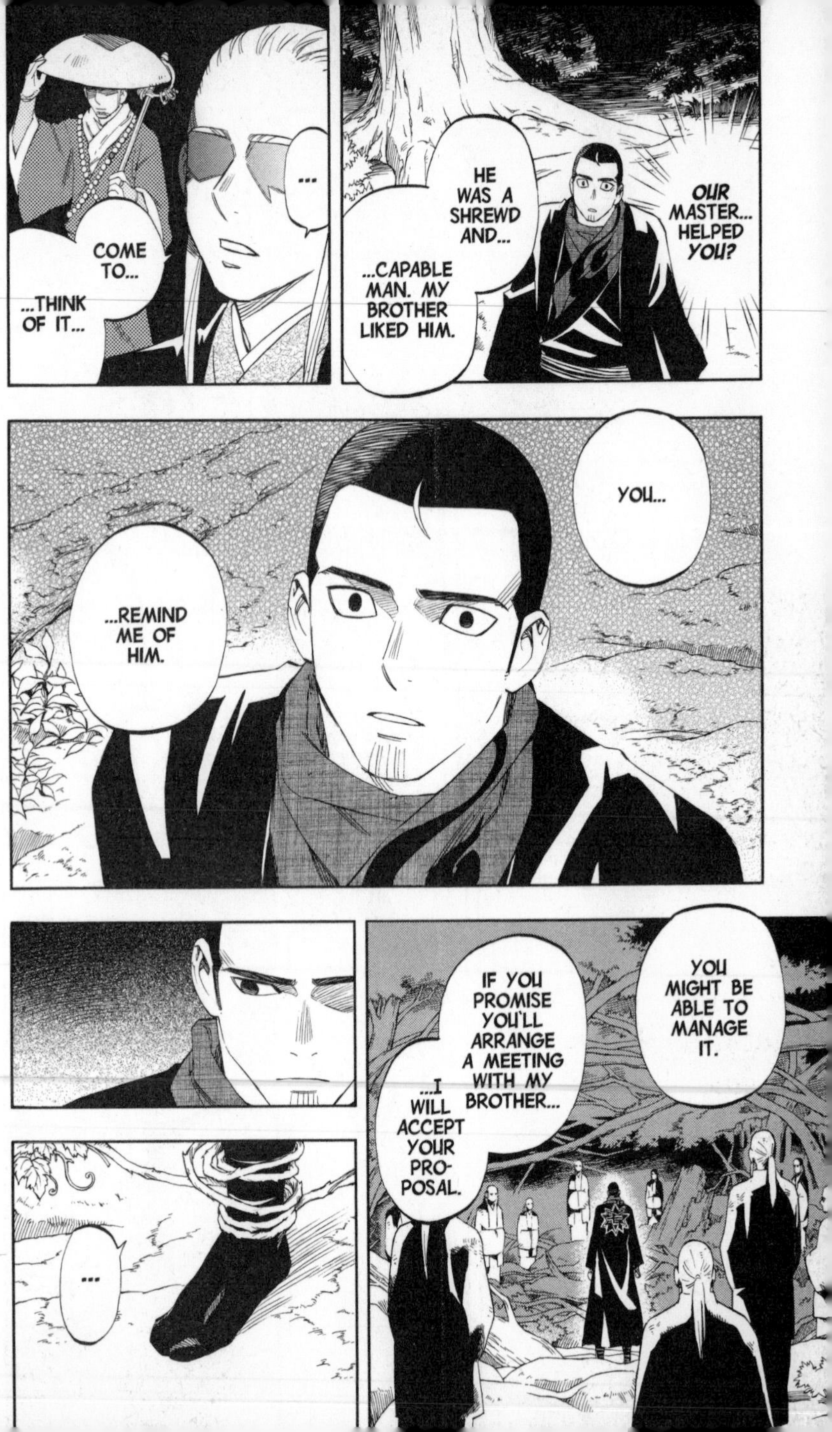
OUR MASTER... HELPED YOU?
HE WAS A SHREWD AND...
...CAPABLE MAN. MY BROTHER LIKED HIM.
...
COME TO...
...THINK OF IT...
YOU...
...REMIND ME OF HIM.
YOU MIGHT BE ABLE TO MANAGE IT.
IF YOU PROMISE YOU'LL ARRANGE A MEETING WITH MY BROTHER...
...I WILL ACCEPT YOUR PRO-POSAL.
...

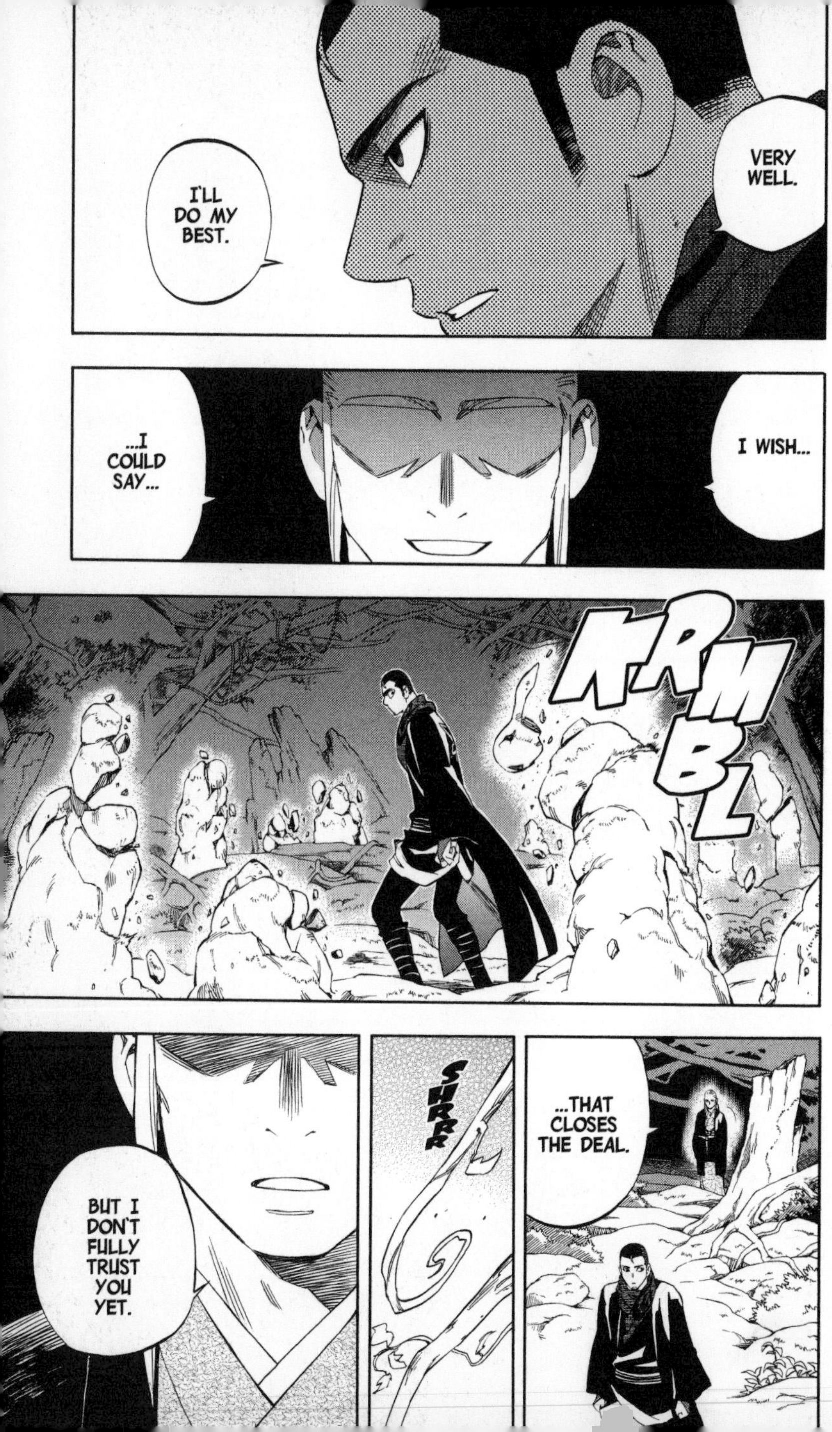

VERY WELL.
I'LL DO MY BEST.
I WISH...
...I COULD SAY...
KRMBL
...THAT CLOSES THE DEAL.
SHRRR
BUT I DON'T FULLY TRUST YOU YET.

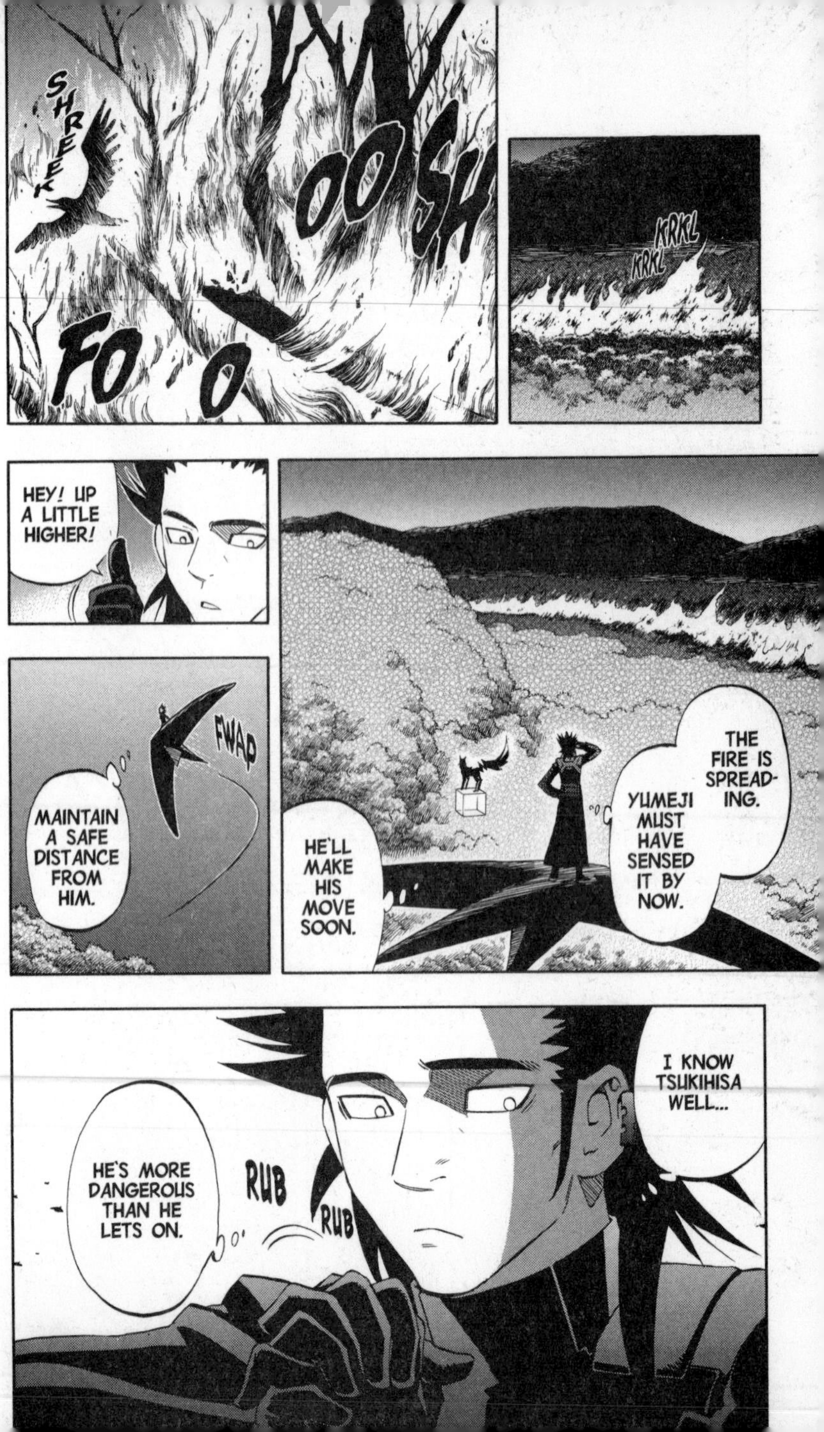
KRKL KRKL
SHREEK
FO O OOSH
THE FIRE IS SPREADING.
YUMEJI MUST HAVE SENSED IT BY NOW.
HE'LL MAKE HIS MOVE SOON.
HEY! UP A LITTLE HIGHER!
FWAP
MAINTAIN A SAFE DISTANCE FROM HIM.
I KNOW TSUKIHISA WELL...
RUB RUB
HE'S MORE DANGEROUS THAN HE LETS ON.

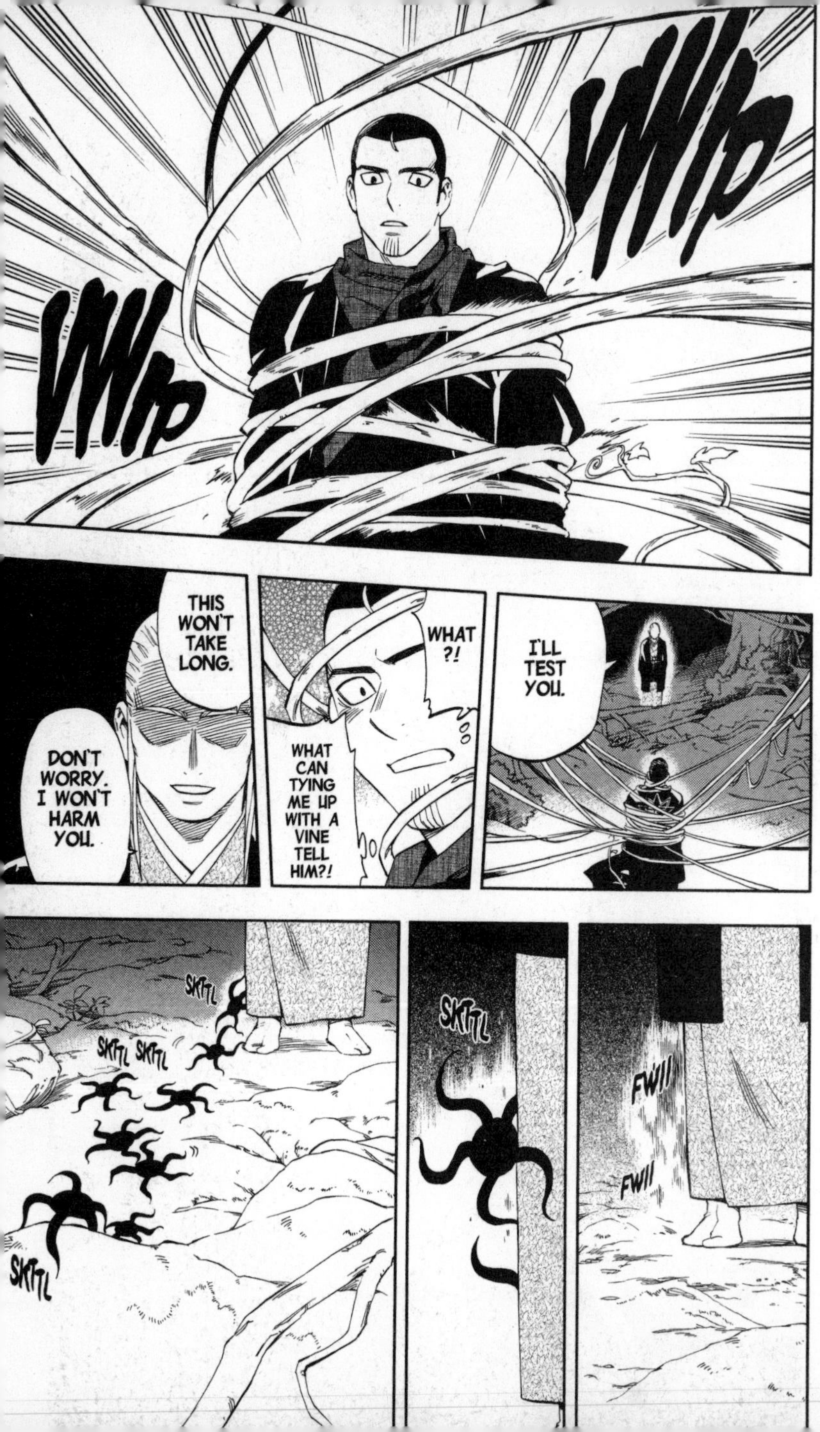
WHIP
WHIP
I'LL TEST YOU.
WHAT?!
WHAT CAN TYING ME UP WITH A VINE TELL HIM?!
THIS WON'T TAKE LONG.
DON'T WORRY. I WON'T HARM YOU.
FWII
FWII
SKITTL
SKITTL
SKITTL SKITTL
SKITTL

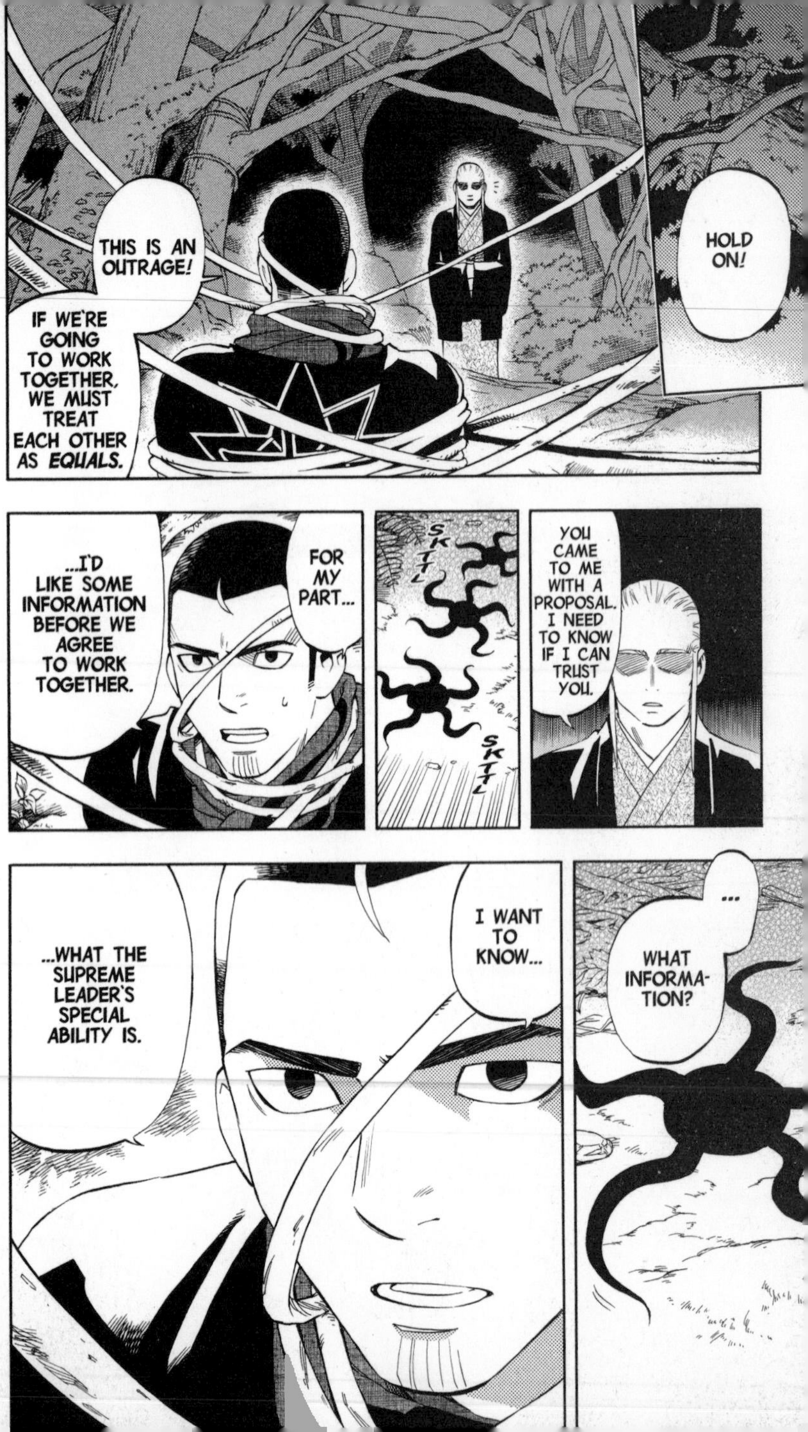
HOLD ON!
THIS IS AN OUTRAGE!
IF WE'RE GOING TO WORK TOGETHER, WE MUST TREAT EACH OTHER AS *EQUALS.*
YOU CAME TO ME WITH A PROPOSAL. I NEED TO KNOW IF I CAN TRUST YOU.
SKTTL
SKTTL
FOR MY PART...
...I'D LIKE SOME INFORMATION BEFORE WE AGREE TO WORK TOGETHER.
...
WHAT INFORMATION?
I WANT TO KNOW...
...WHAT THE SUPREME LEADER'S SPECIAL ABILITY IS.

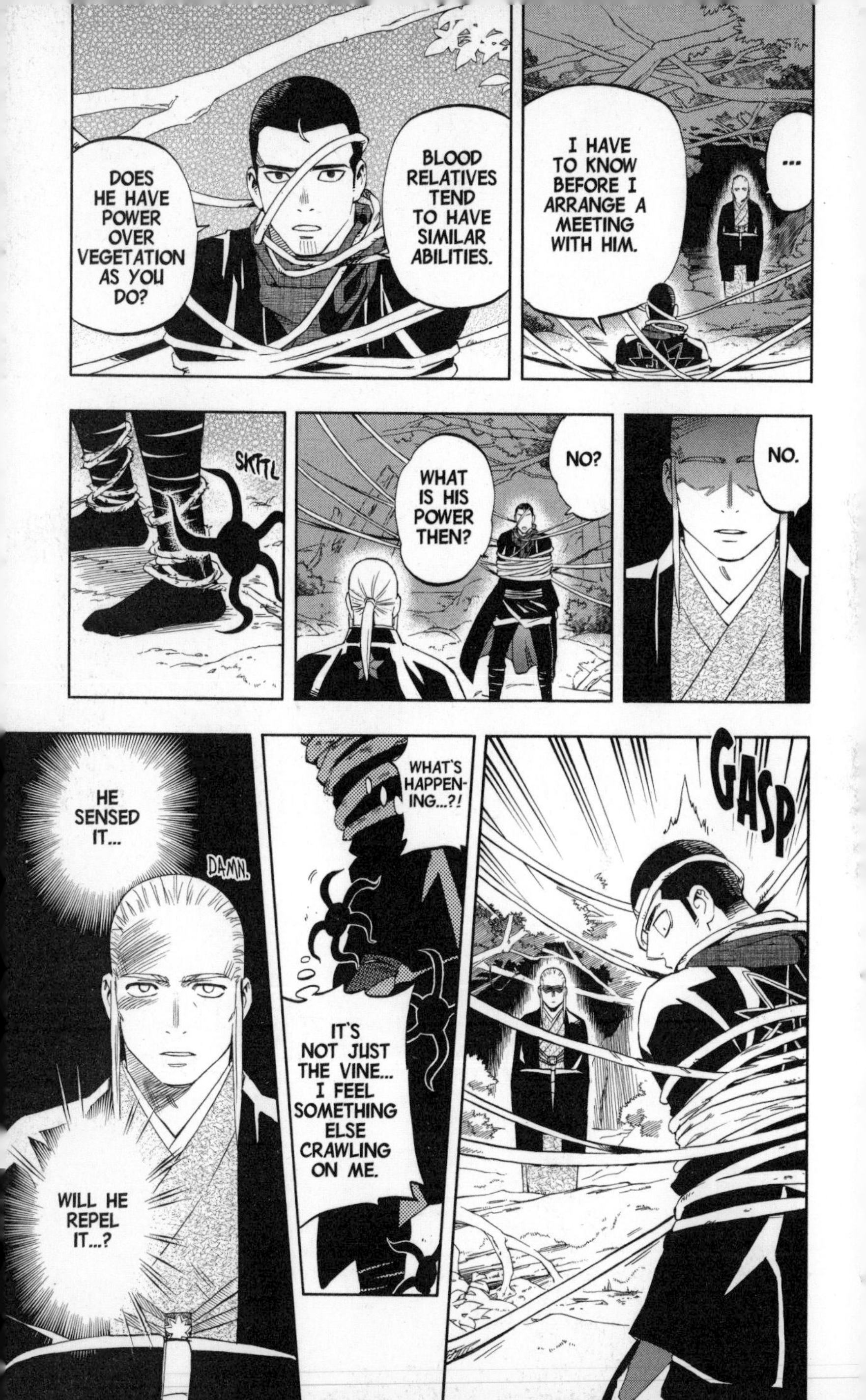
...
I HAVE TO KNOW BEFORE I ARRANGE A MEETING WITH HIM.
BLOOD RELATIVES TEND TO HAVE SIMILAR ABILITIES.
DOES HE HAVE POWER OVER VEGETATION AS YOU DO?
NO.
NO?
WHAT IS HIS POWER THEN?
SKTTL
GASP
WHAT'S HAPPEN-ING...?!
IT'S NOT JUST THE VINE... I FEEL SOMETHING ELSE CRAWLING ON ME.
HE SENSED IT...
DAMN.
WILL HE REPEL IT...?

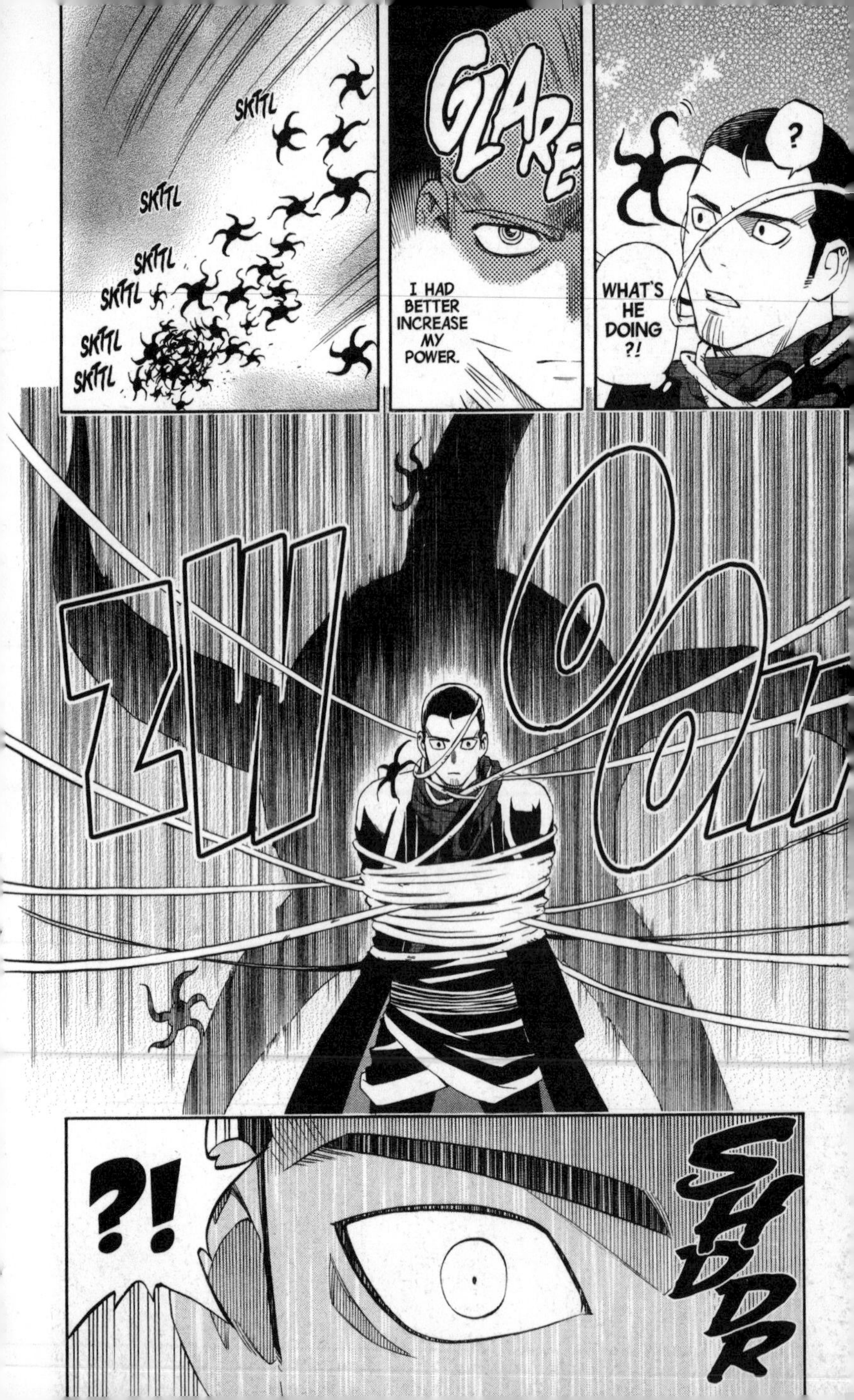
?
WHAT'S HE DOING ?!
GLARE
I HAD BETTER INCREASE MY POWER.
SKTTL
SKTTL
SKTTL
SKTTL
SKTTL
SKTTL
ZWOOM
SHDR
?!

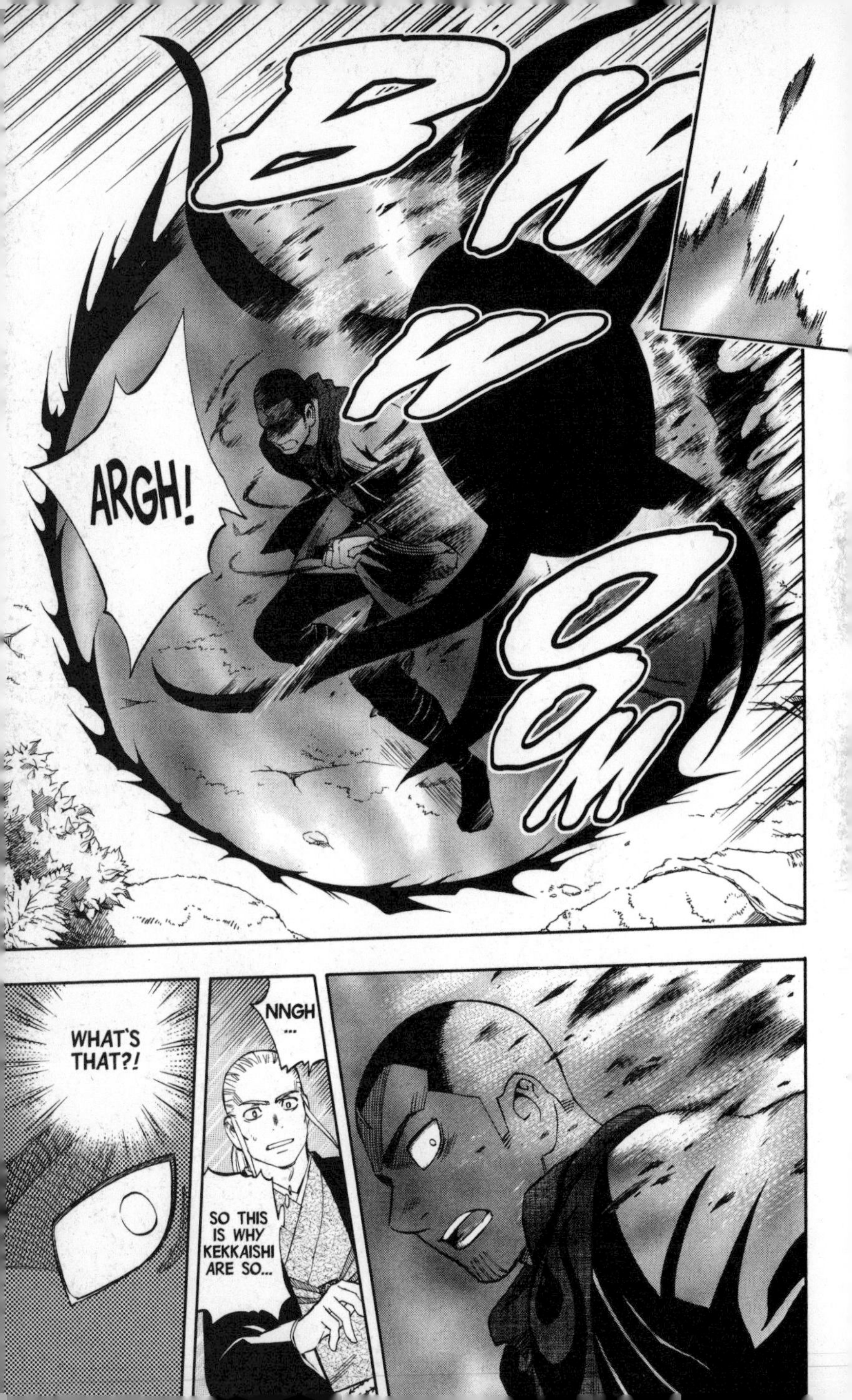
ARGH!
NNGH ...
SO THIS IS WHY KEKKAISHI ARE SO...
WHAT'S THAT?!

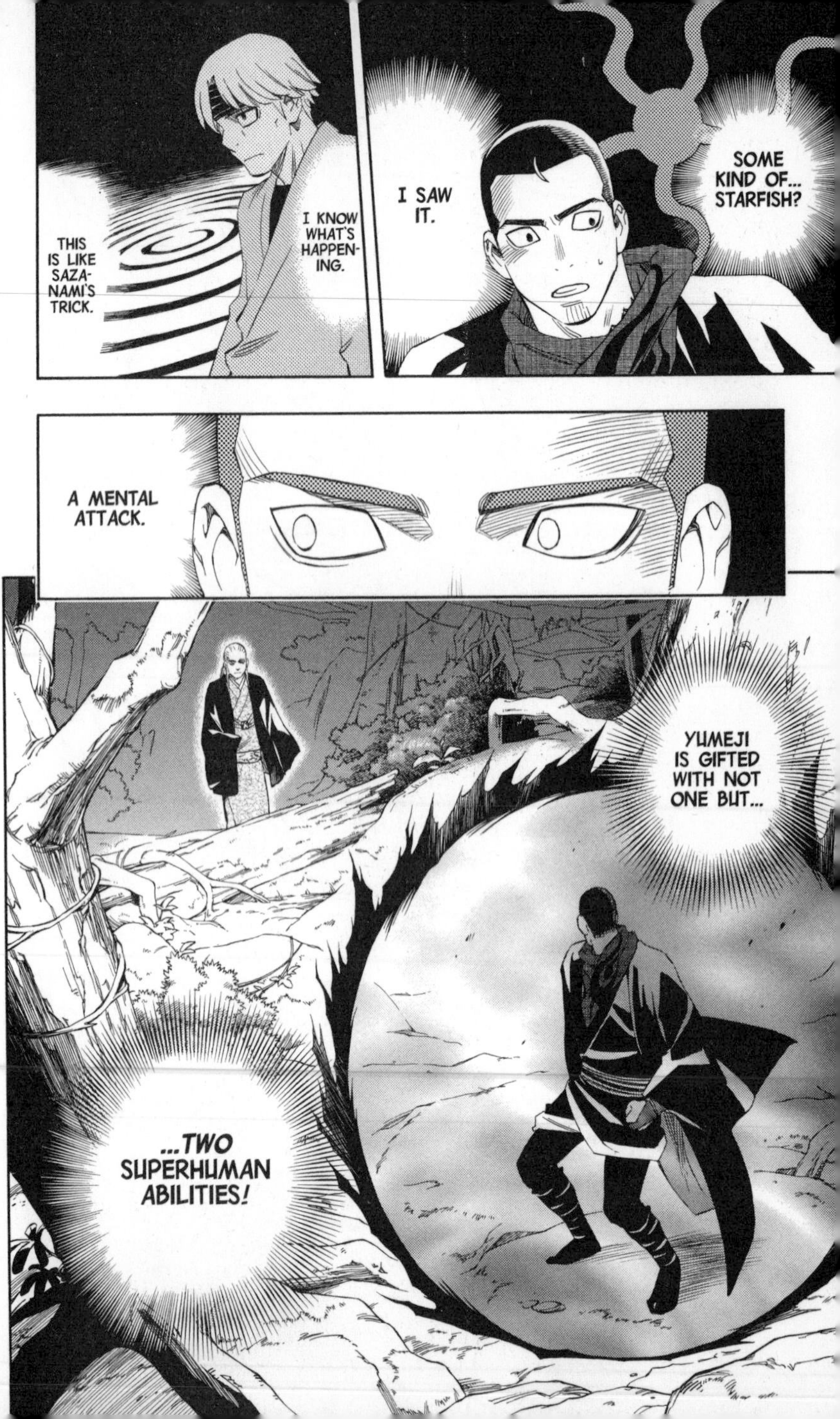
SOME KIND OF... STARFISH?
I SAW IT.
I KNOW WHAT'S HAPPENING.
THIS IS LIKE SAZANAMI'S TRICK.
A MENTAL ATTACK.
YUMEJI IS GIFTED WITH NOT ONE BUT...
...TWO SUPERHUMAN ABILITIES!

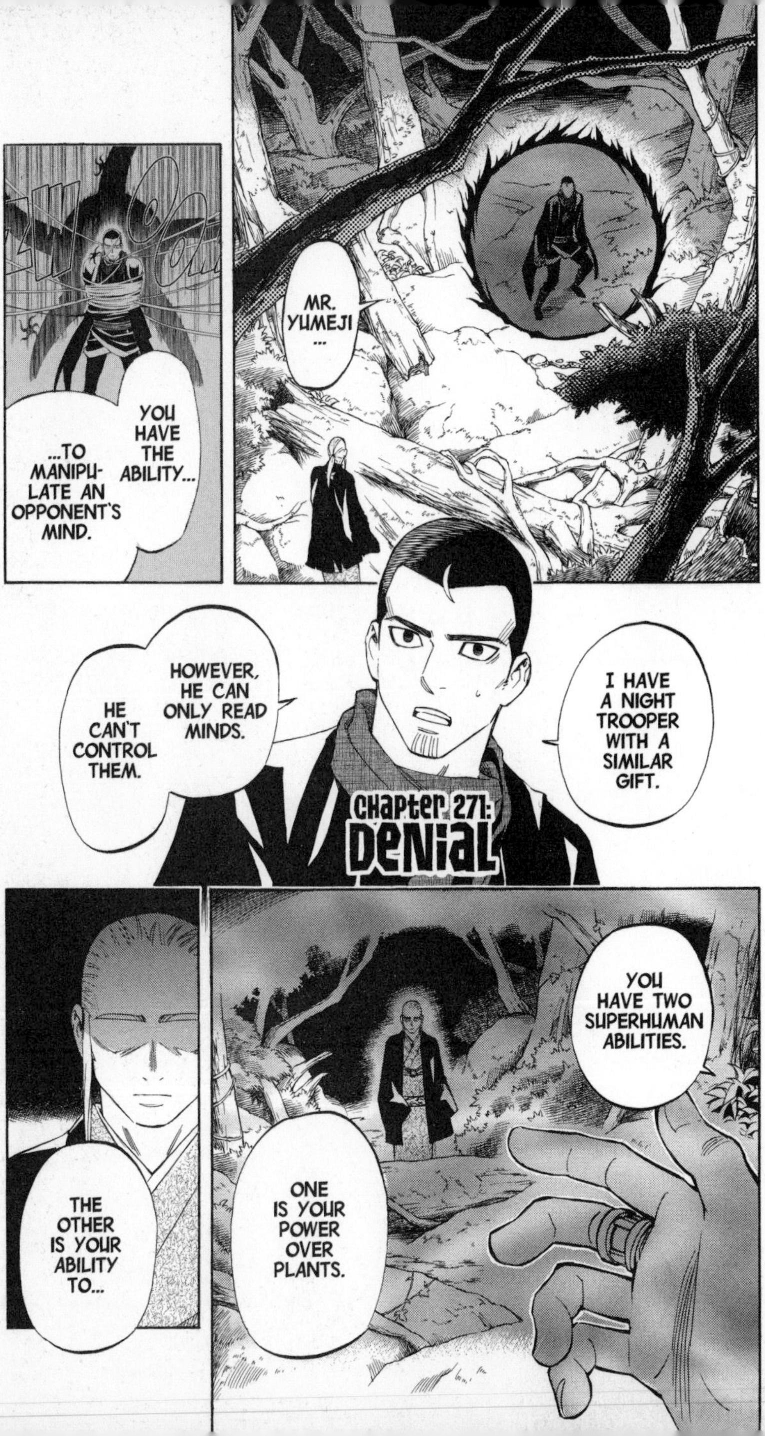
MR. YUMEJI ...
YOU HAVE THE ABILITY...
...TO MANIPU-LATE AN OPPONENT'S MIND.
I HAVE A NIGHT TROOPER WITH A SIMILAR GIFT.
HOWEVER, HE CAN ONLY READ MINDS.
HE CAN'T CONTROL THEM.
Chapter 271: Denial
YOU HAVE TWO SUPERHUMAN ABILITIES.
ONE IS YOUR POWER OVER PLANTS.
THE OTHER IS YOUR ABILITY TO...

Chapter 271: Denial

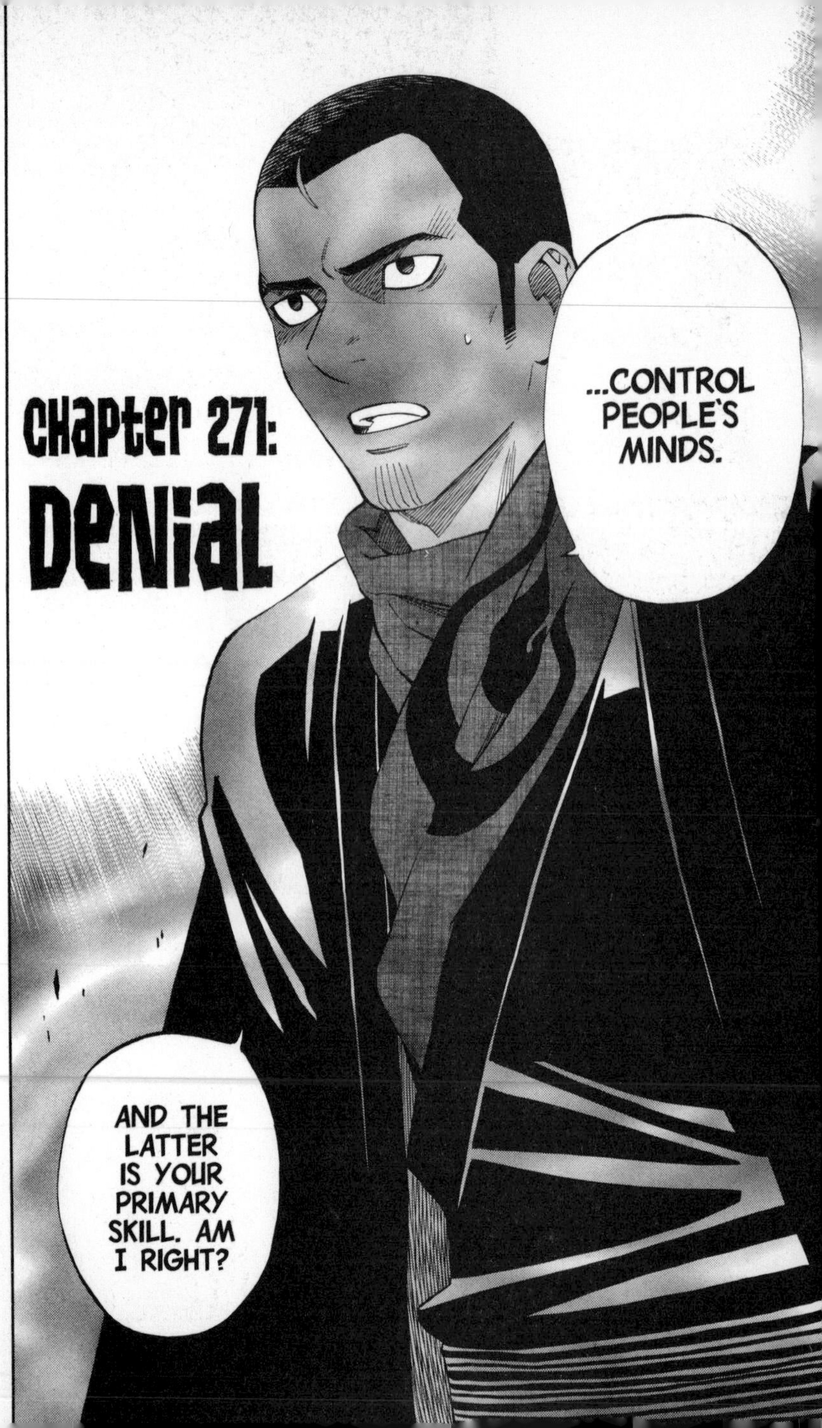
...CONTROL PEOPLE'S MINDS.
AND THE LATTER IS YOUR PRIMARY SKILL. AM I RIGHT?

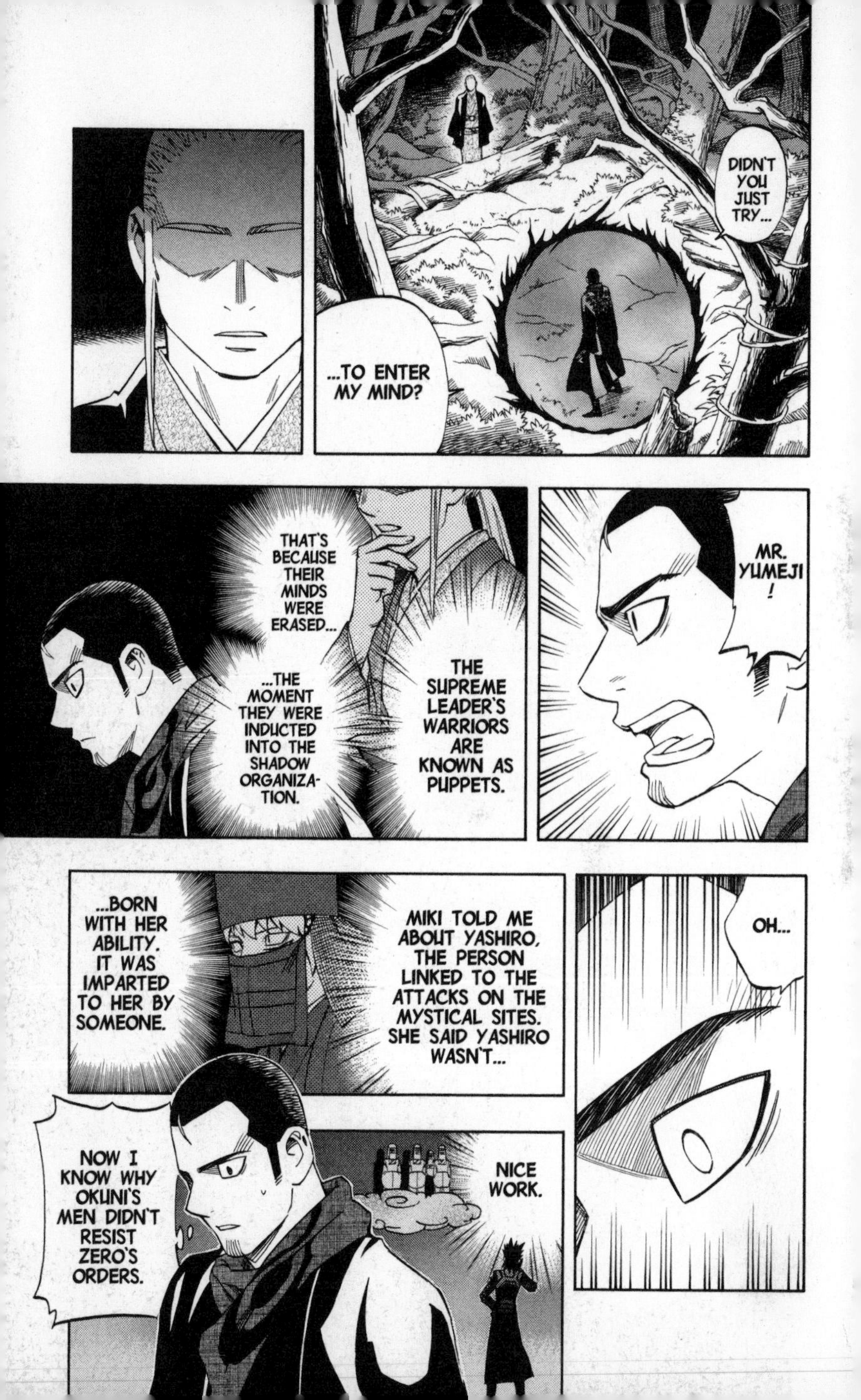
DIDN'T YOU JUST TRY...
...TO ENTER MY MIND?
MR. YUMEJI!
THE SUPREME LEADER'S WARRIORS ARE KNOWN AS PUPPETS.
THAT'S BECAUSE THEIR MINDS WERE ERASED...
...THE MOMENT THEY WERE INDUCTED INTO THE SHADOW ORGANIZATION.
OH...
MIKI TOLD ME ABOUT YASHIRO, THE PERSON LINKED TO THE ATTACKS ON THE MYSTICAL SITES. SHE SAID YASHIRO WASN'T...
...BORN WITH HER ABILITY. IT WAS IMPARTED TO HER BY SOMEONE.
NICE WORK.
NOW I KNOW WHY OKUNI'S MEN DIDN'T RESIST ZERO'S ORDERS.

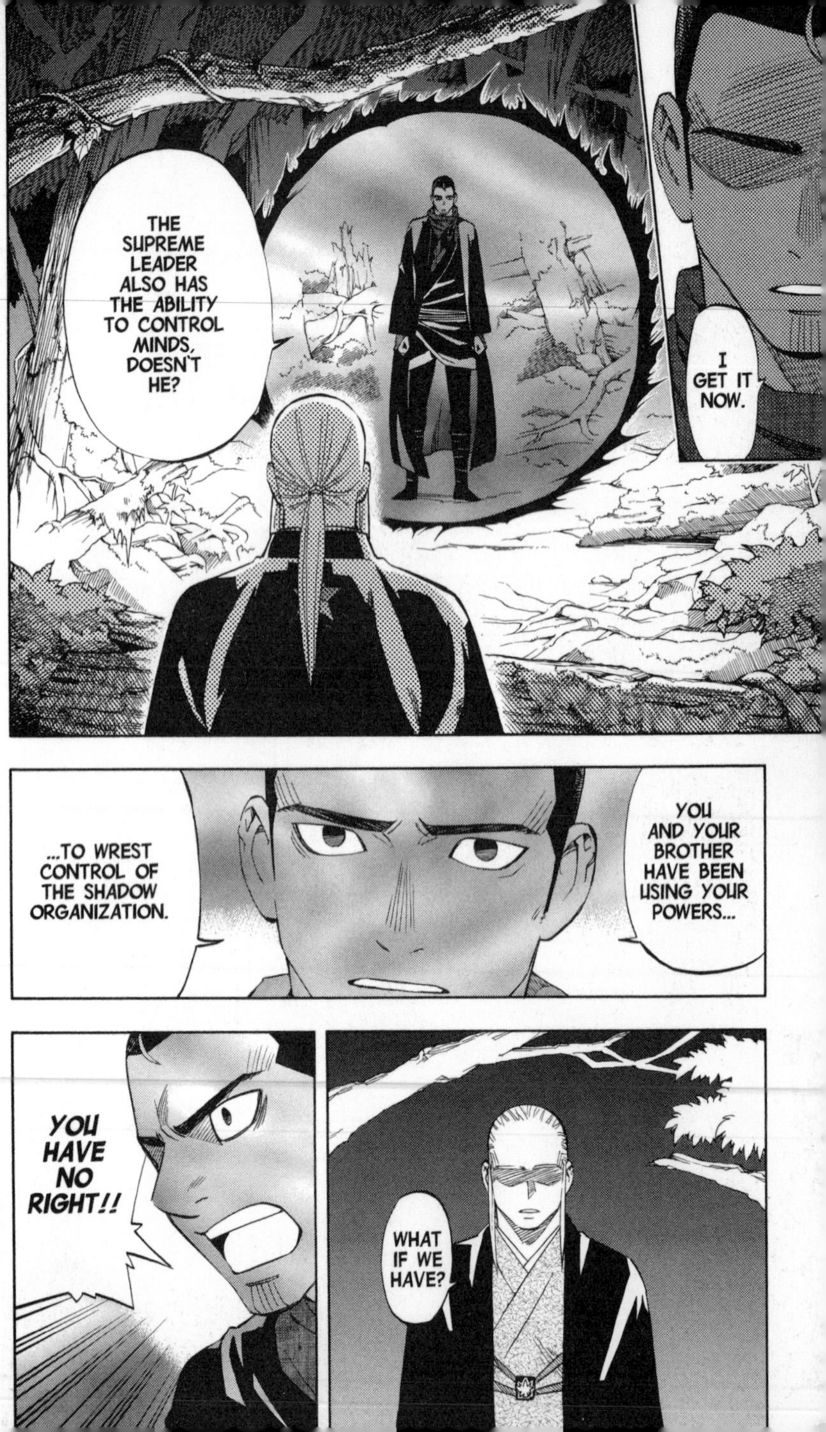
I GET IT NOW.
THE SUPREME LEADER ALSO HAS THE ABILITY TO CONTROL MINDS, DOESN'T HE?
YOU AND YOUR BROTHER HAVE BEEN USING YOUR POWERS...
...TO WREST CONTROL OF THE SHADOW ORGANIZATION.
WHAT IF WE HAVE?
YOU HAVE NO RIGHT!!

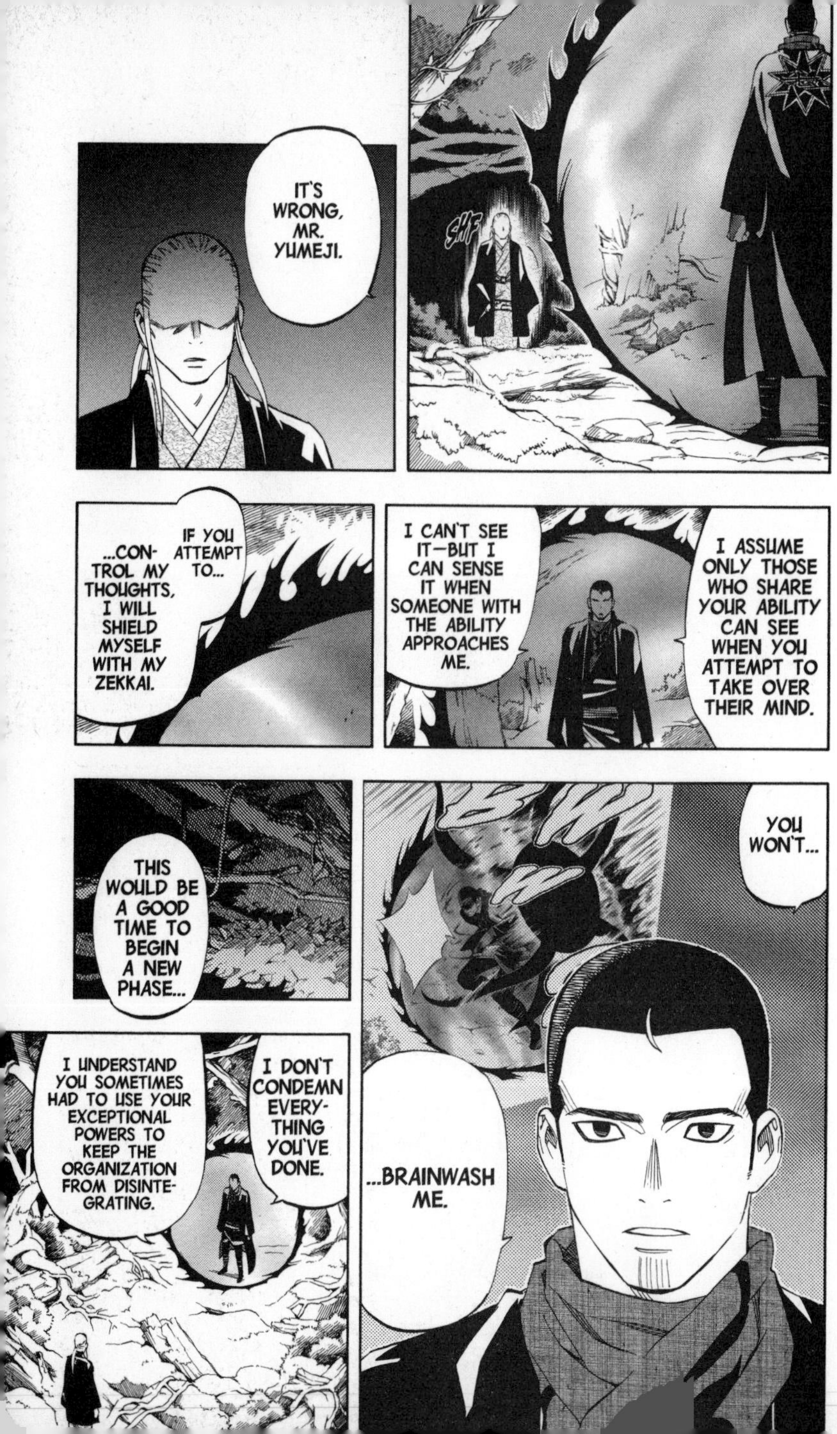
SHF
IT'S WRONG, MR. YUMEJI.
I ASSUME ONLY THOSE WHO SHARE YOUR ABILITY CAN SEE WHEN YOU ATTEMPT TO TAKE OVER THEIR MIND.
I CAN'T SEE IT—BUT I CAN SENSE IT WHEN SOMEONE WITH THE ABILITY APPROACHES ME.
IF YOU ATTEMPT TO...
...CONTROL MY THOUGHTS, I WILL SHIELD MYSELF WITH MY ZEKKAI.
YOU WON'T...
...BRAINWASH ME.
THIS WOULD BE A GOOD TIME TO BEGIN A NEW PHASE...
I DON'T CONDEMN EVERYTHING YOU'VE DONE.
I UNDERSTAND YOU SOMETIMES HAD TO USE YOUR EXCEPTIONAL POWERS TO KEEP THE ORGANIZATION FROM DISINTEGRATING.

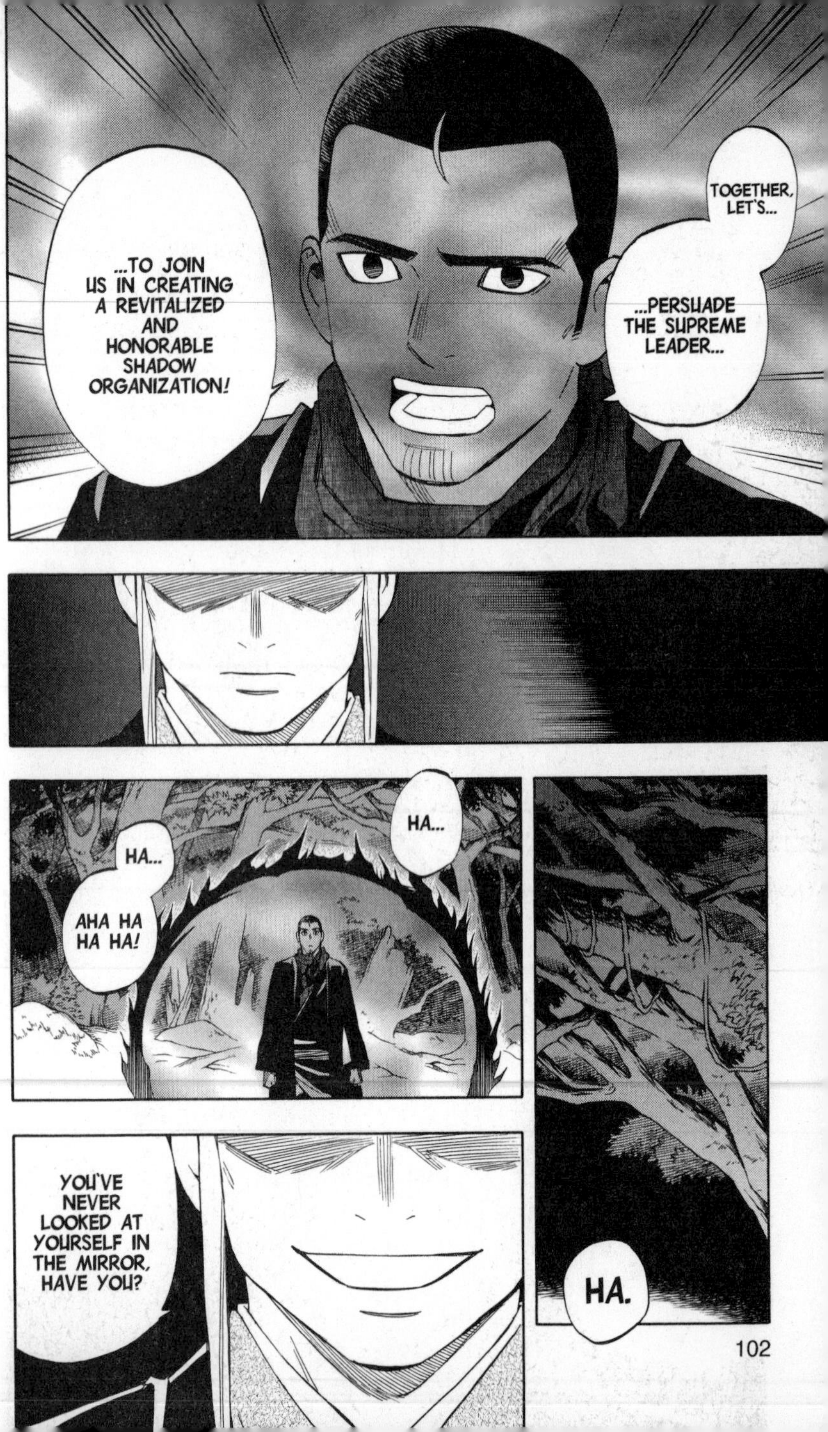
TOGETHER, LET'S...
...PERSUADE THE SUPREME LEADER...
...TO JOIN US IN CREATING A REVITALIZED AND HONORABLE SHADOW ORGANIZATION!
HA.
HA...
HA...
AHA HA HA HA!
YOU'VE NEVER LOOKED AT YOURSELF IN THE MIRROR, HAVE YOU?

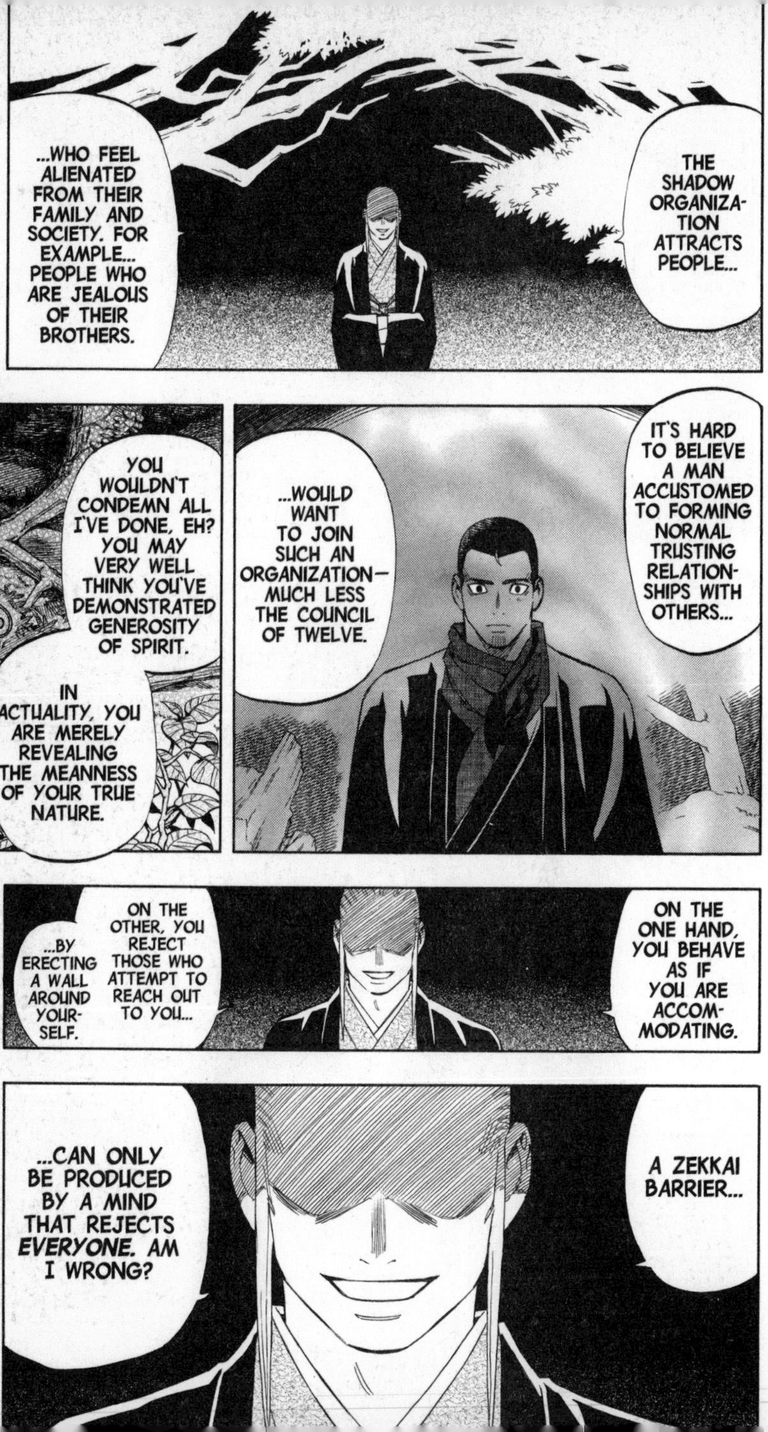
THE SHADOW ORGANIZATION ATTRACTS PEOPLE...
...WHO FEEL ALIENATED FROM THEIR FAMILY AND SOCIETY. FOR EXAMPLE... PEOPLE WHO ARE JEALOUS OF THEIR BROTHERS.
IT'S HARD TO BELIEVE A MAN ACCUSTOMED TO FORMING NORMAL TRUSTING RELATIONSHIPS WITH OTHERS...
...WOULD WANT TO JOIN SUCH AN ORGANIZATION—MUCH LESS THE COUNCIL OF TWELVE.
YOU WOULDN'T CONDEMN ALL I'VE DONE, EH? YOU MAY VERY WELL THINK YOU'VE DEMONSTRATED GENEROSITY OF SPIRIT.
IN ACTUALITY, YOU ARE MERELY REVEALING THE MEANNESS OF YOUR TRUE NATURE.
ON THE ONE HAND, YOU BEHAVE AS IF YOU ARE ACCOMMODATING.
ON THE OTHER, YOU REJECT THOSE WHO ATTEMPT TO REACH OUT TO YOU...
...BY ERECTING A WALL AROUND YOURSELF.
A ZEKKAI BARRIER...
...CAN ONLY BE PRODUCED BY A MIND THAT REJECTS *EVERYONE*. AM I WRONG?

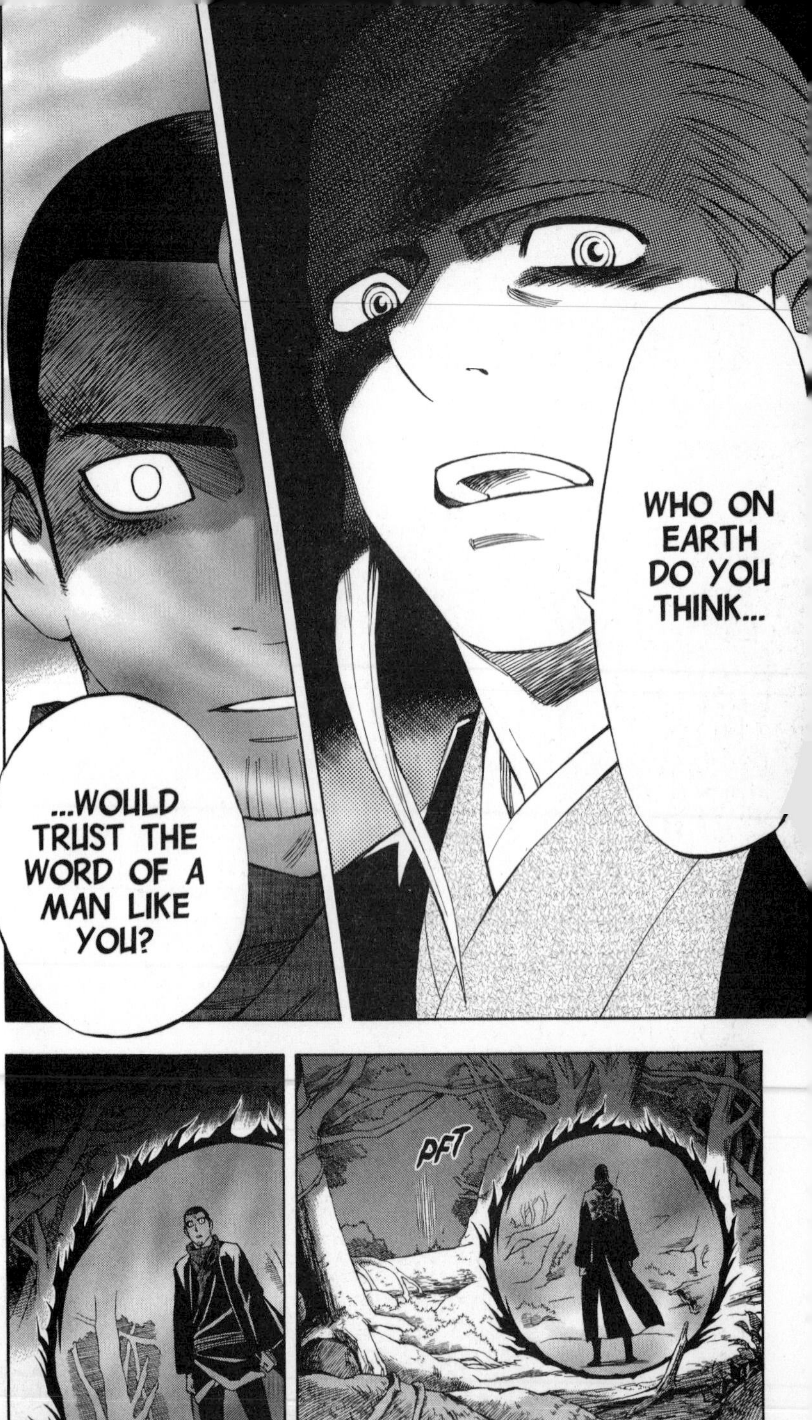
WHO ON EARTH DO YOU THINK...
...WOULD TRUST THE WORD OF A MAN LIKE YOU?
PFT

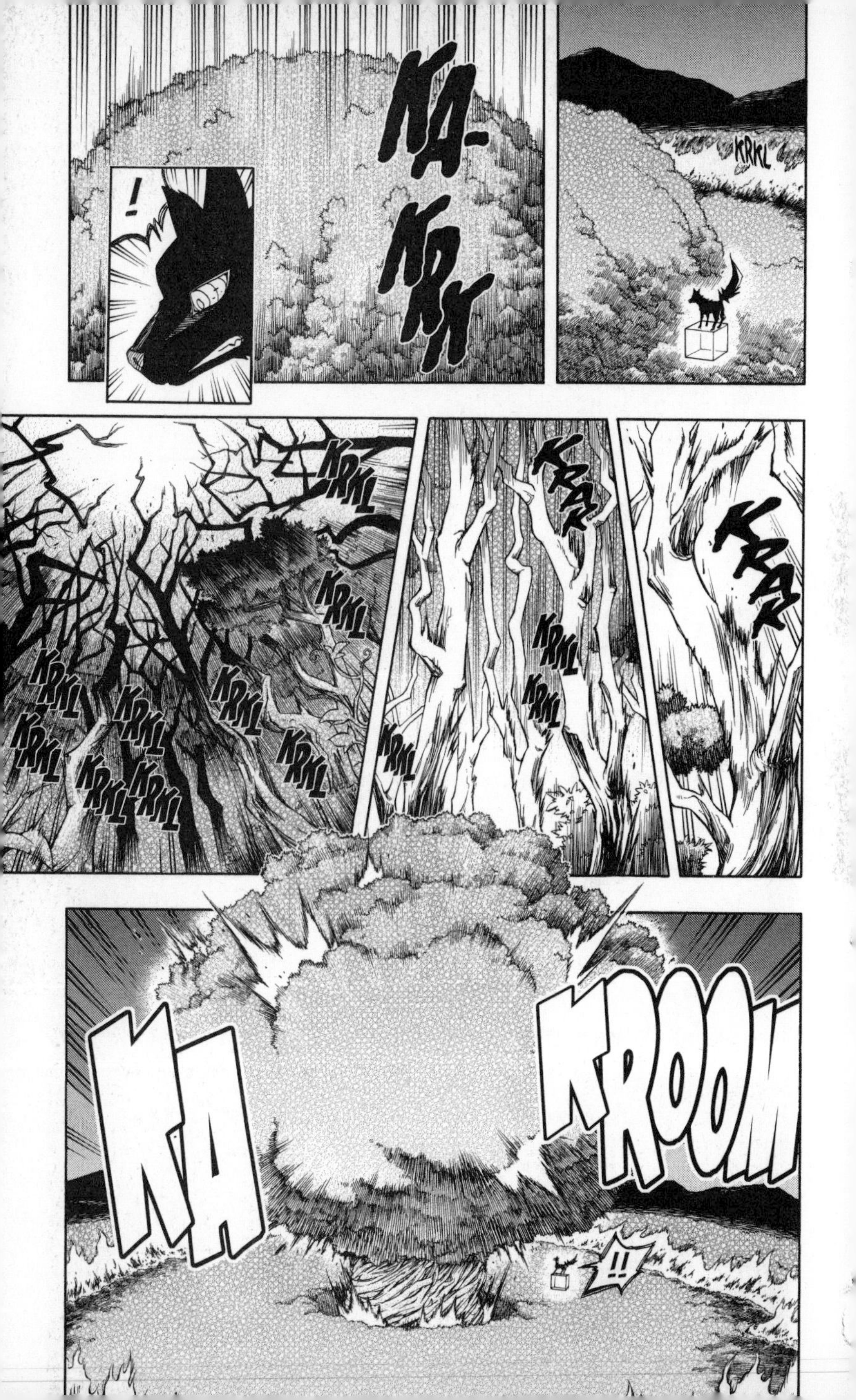

KRKL
KA-
KRKK
!
KRAK
KRAK
KRKL
KRKL
KRKL
KRKL
KRKL
KRKL
KRKL
KRKL
KRKL
KRKL
KRKL
KA
KROOM
!!

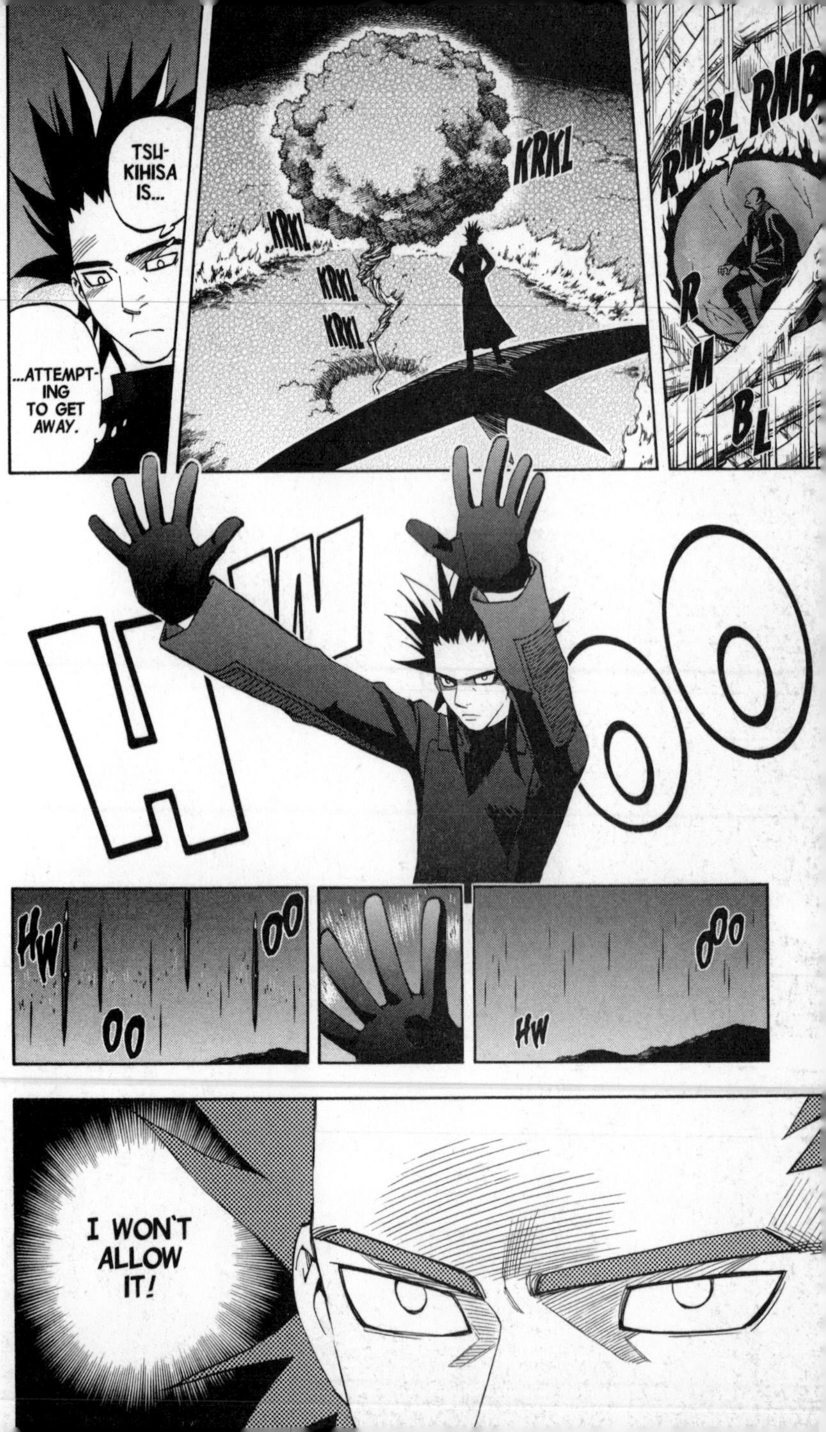
RMBL RMB
RMBL
KRKL
KRKL
KRKL
KRKL
TSU-KIHISA IS...
...ATTEMPT-ING TO GET AWAY.
HWOOO
OOO
HW
HW
OO
OO
I WON'T ALLOW IT!

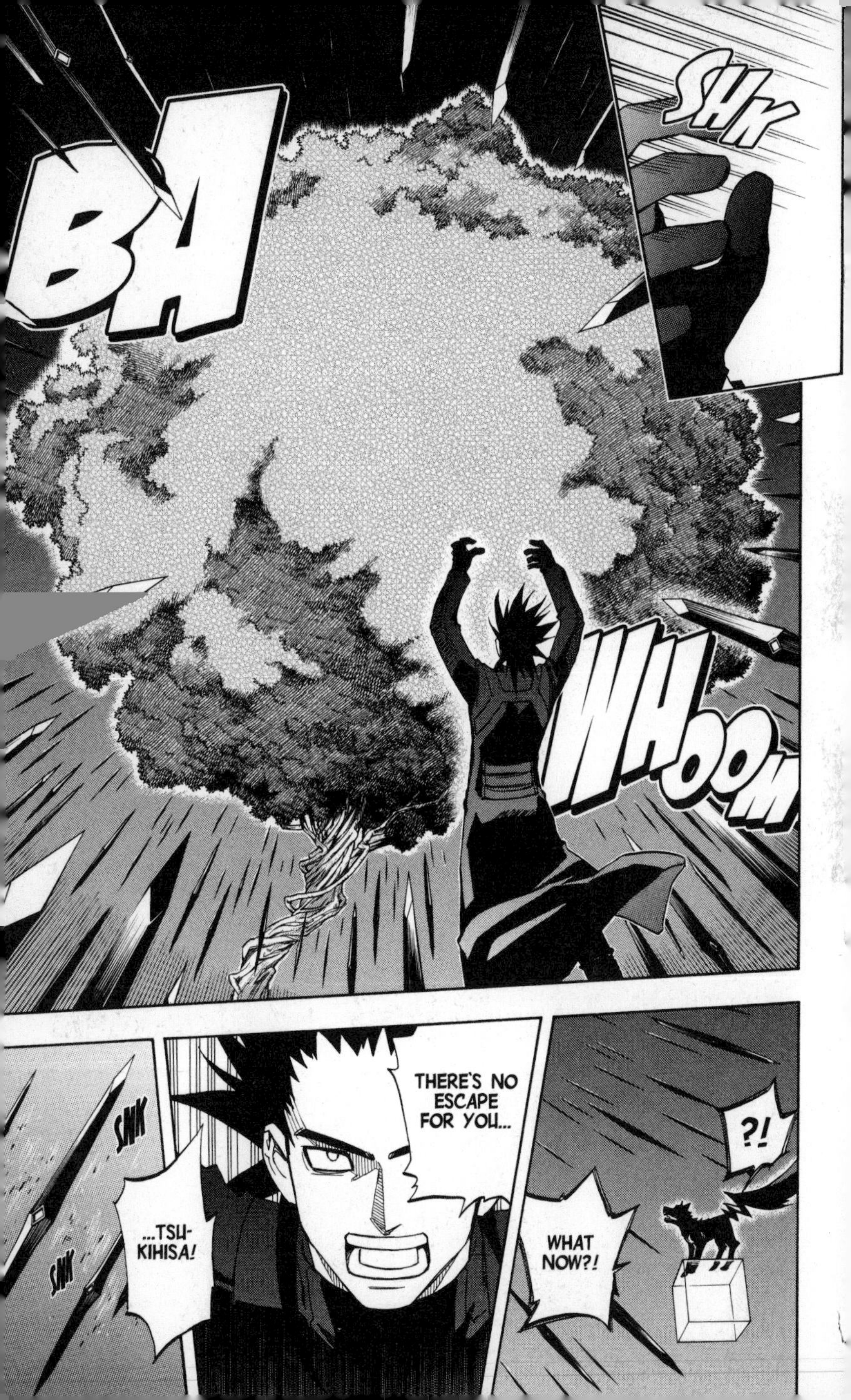
SHK
BA
WHOOM
?!
WHAT NOW?!
THERE'S NO ESCAPE FOR YOU...
...TSU-KIHISA!
SNK
SNK

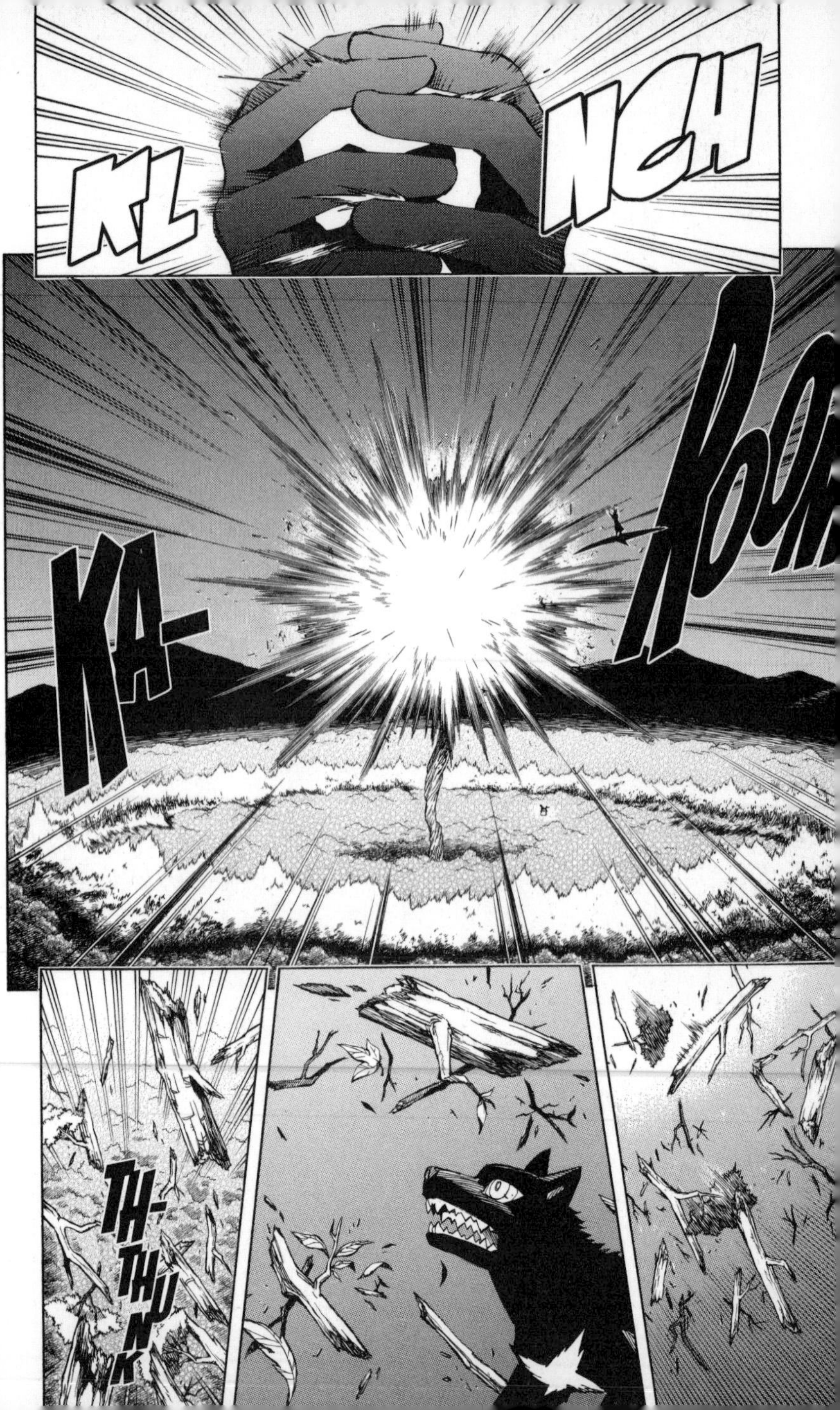
KL NCH
KA-
BOOM
TH-THUNK

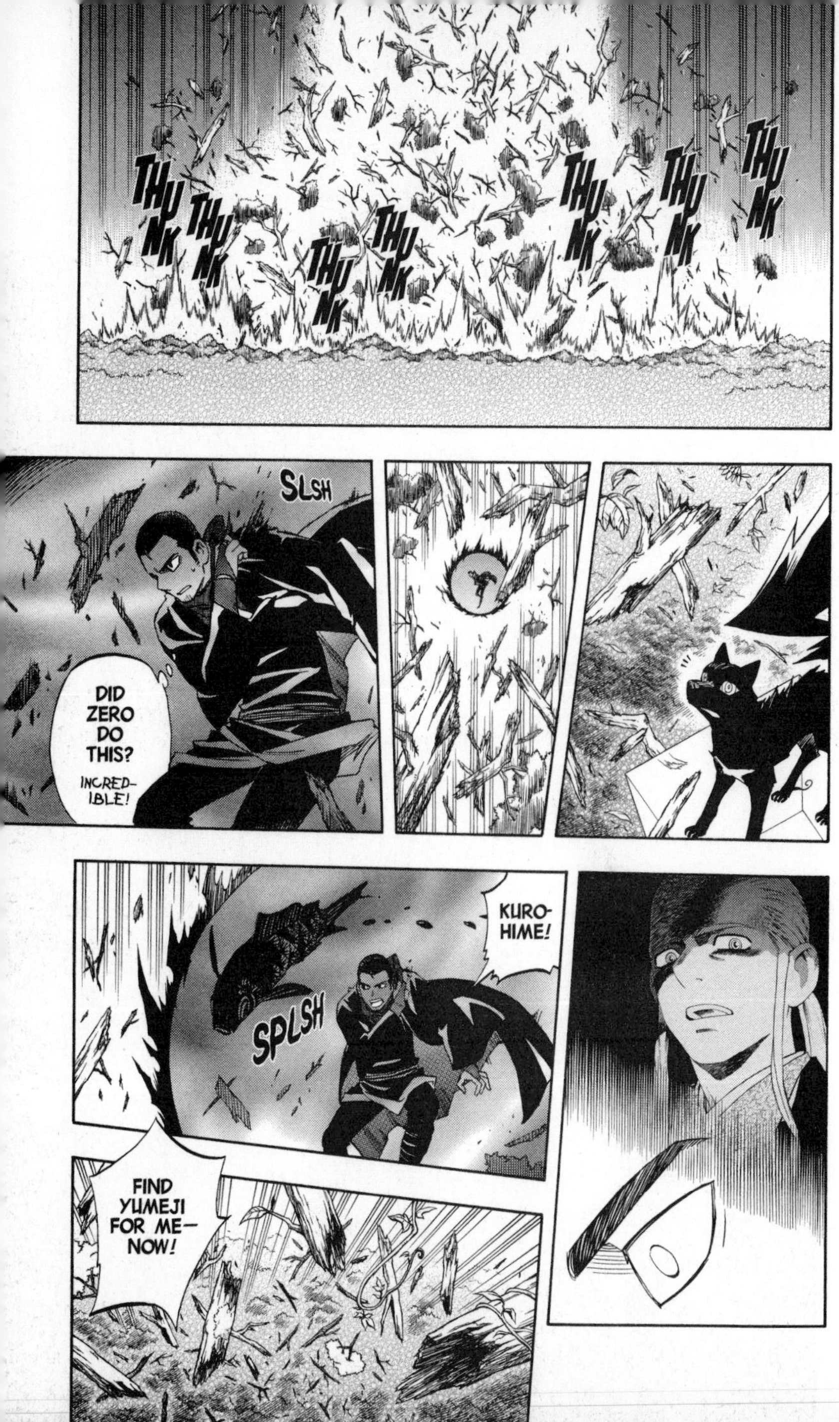
THUNK
THUNK
THUNK
THUNK
THUNK
THUNK
THUNK
SLSH
DID ZERO DO THIS?
INCRED-IBLE!
KURO-HIME!
SPLSH
FIND YUMEJI FOR ME— NOW!

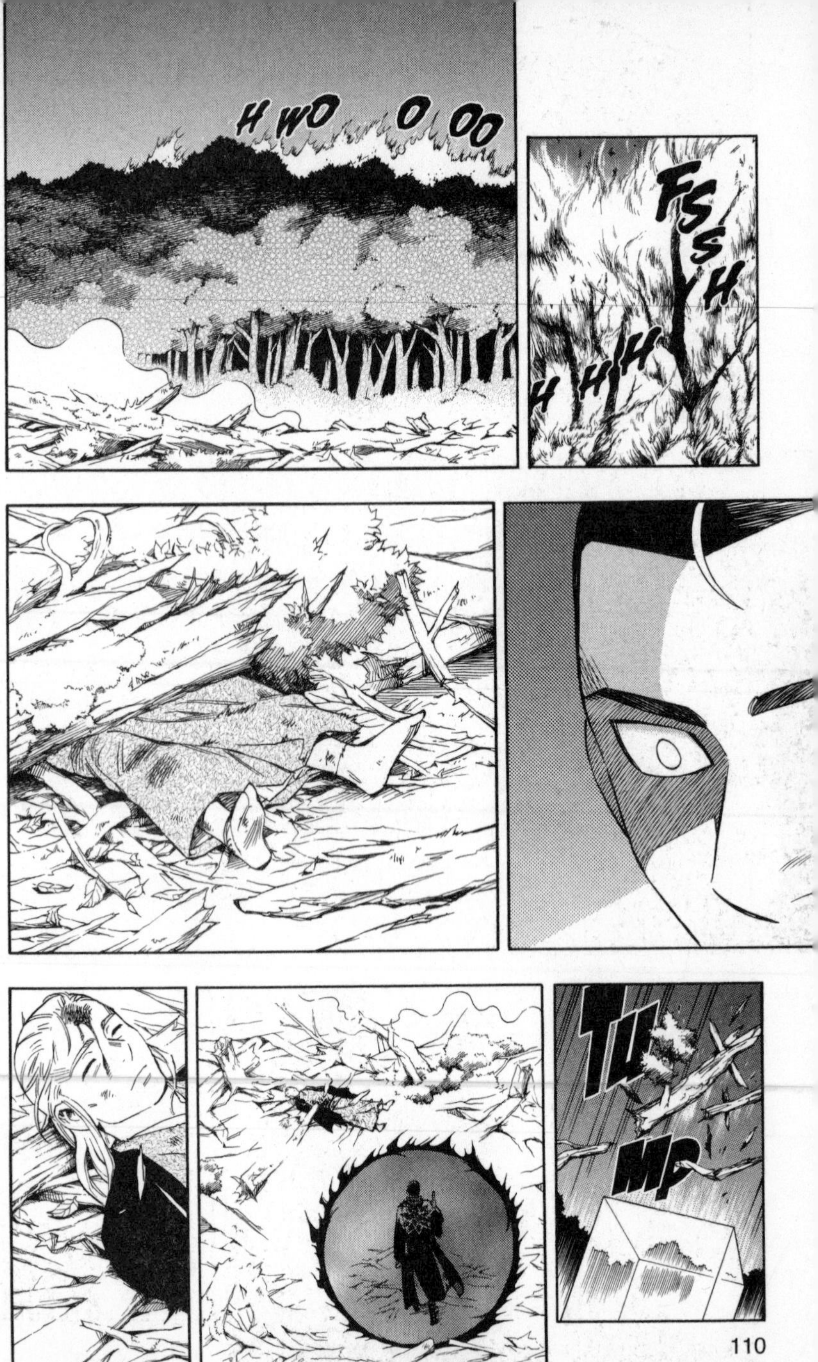
FSSH
HHHH
HWO O OO
TH
MP

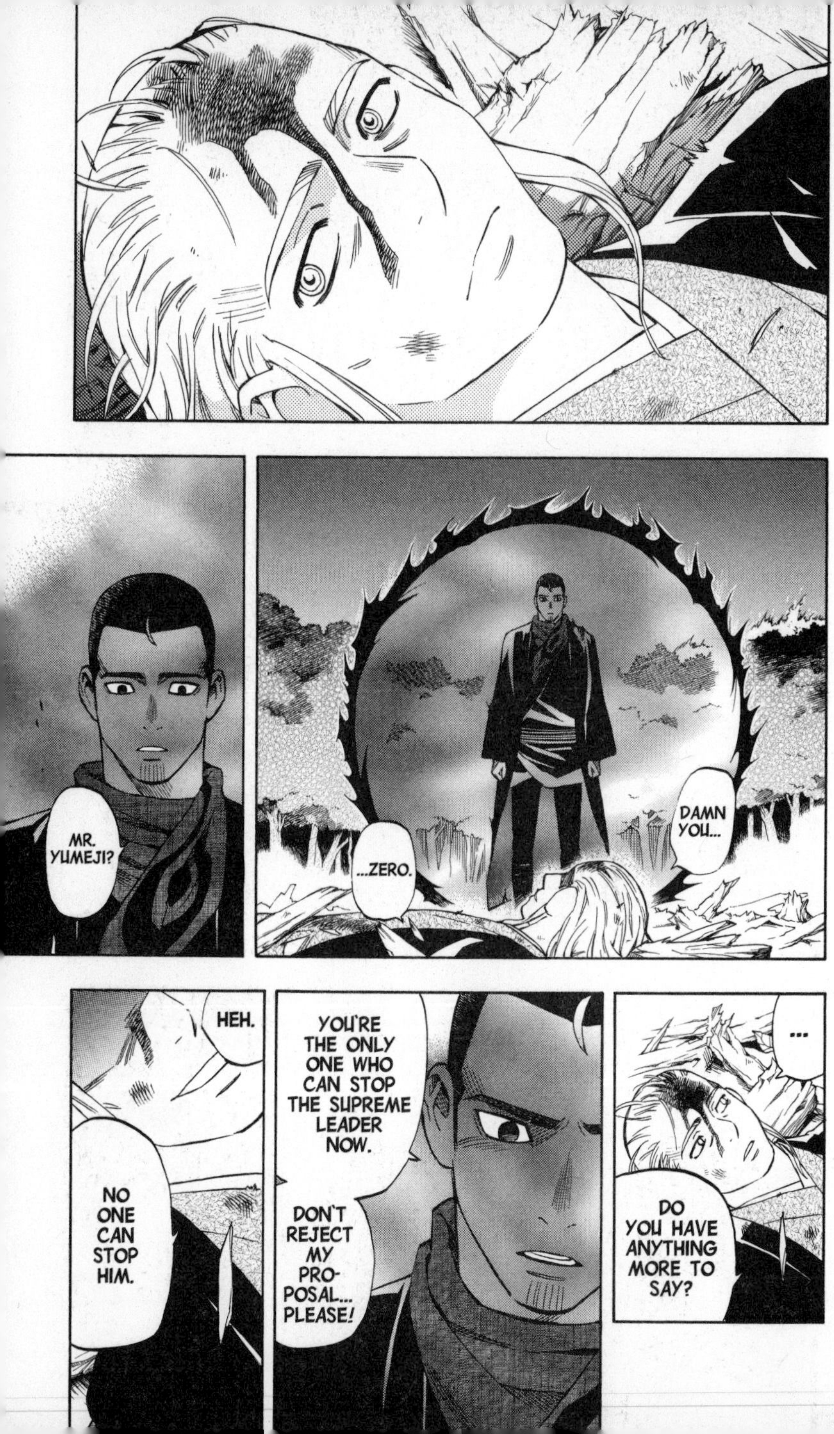
DAMN YOU...
...ZERO.
MR. YUMEJI?
...
DO YOU HAVE ANYTHING MORE TO SAY?
YOU'RE THE ONLY ONE WHO CAN STOP THE SUPREME LEADER NOW.
DON'T REJECT MY PRO-POSAL... PLEASE!
HEH.
NO ONE CAN STOP HIM.

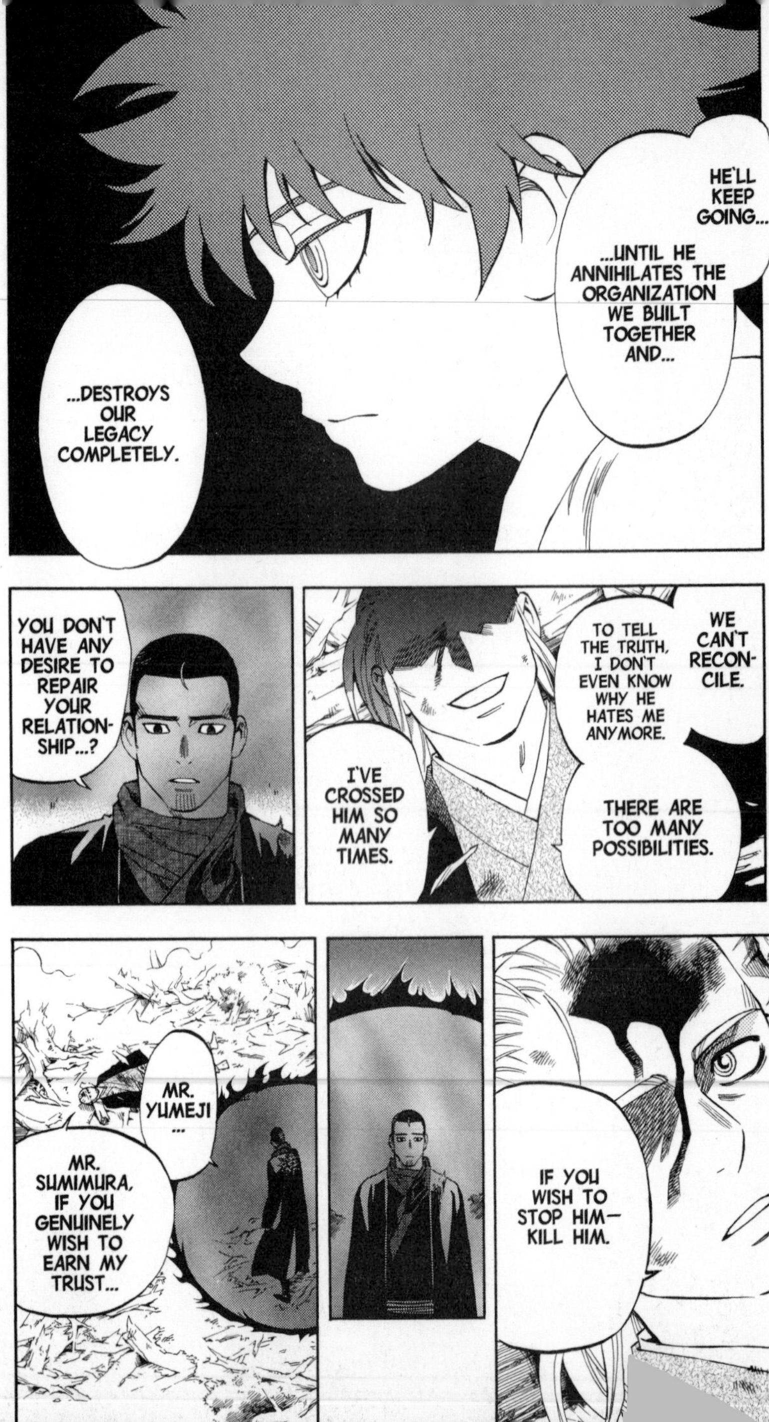
HE'LL KEEP GOING...
...UNTIL HE ANNIHILATES THE ORGANIZATION WE BUILT TOGETHER AND...
...DESTROYS OUR LEGACY COMPLETELY.
WE CAN'T RECONCILE.
TO TELL THE TRUTH, I DON'T EVEN KNOW WHY HE HATES ME ANYMORE.
THERE ARE TOO MANY POSSIBILITIES.
I'VE CROSSED HIM SO MANY TIMES.
YOU DON'T HAVE ANY DESIRE TO REPAIR YOUR RELATIONSHIP...?
IF YOU WISH TO STOP HIM— KILL HIM.
MR. YUMEJI...
MR. SUMIMURA, IF YOU GENUINELY WISH TO EARN MY TRUST...

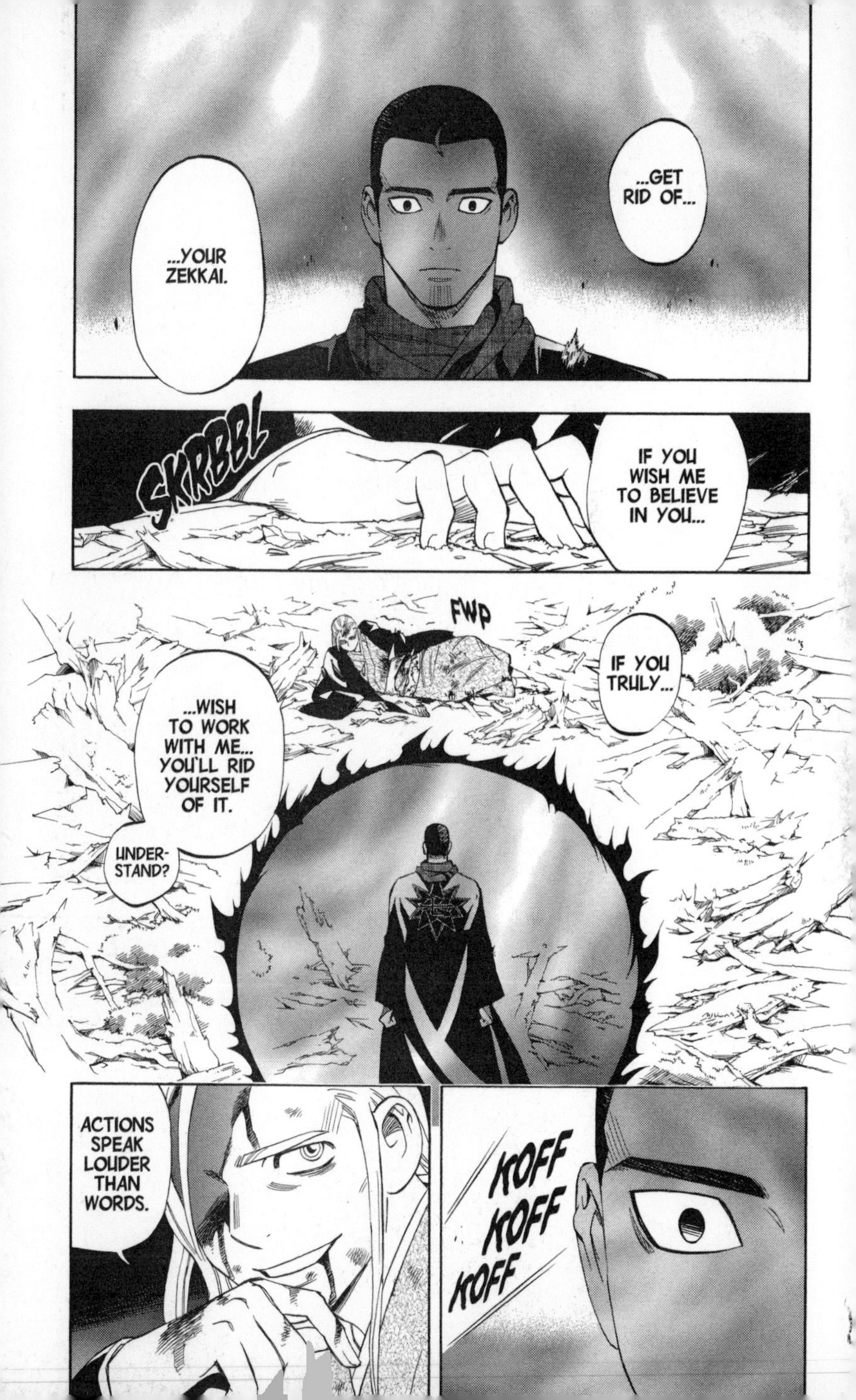
...GET RID OF...
...YOUR ZEKKAI.
IF YOU WISH ME TO BELIEVE IN YOU...
SKRBBL
FWP
IF YOU TRULY...
...WISH TO WORK WITH ME... YOU'LL RID YOURSELF OF IT.
UNDER-STAND?
KOFF KOFF KOFF
ACTIONS SPEAK LOUDER THAN WORDS.

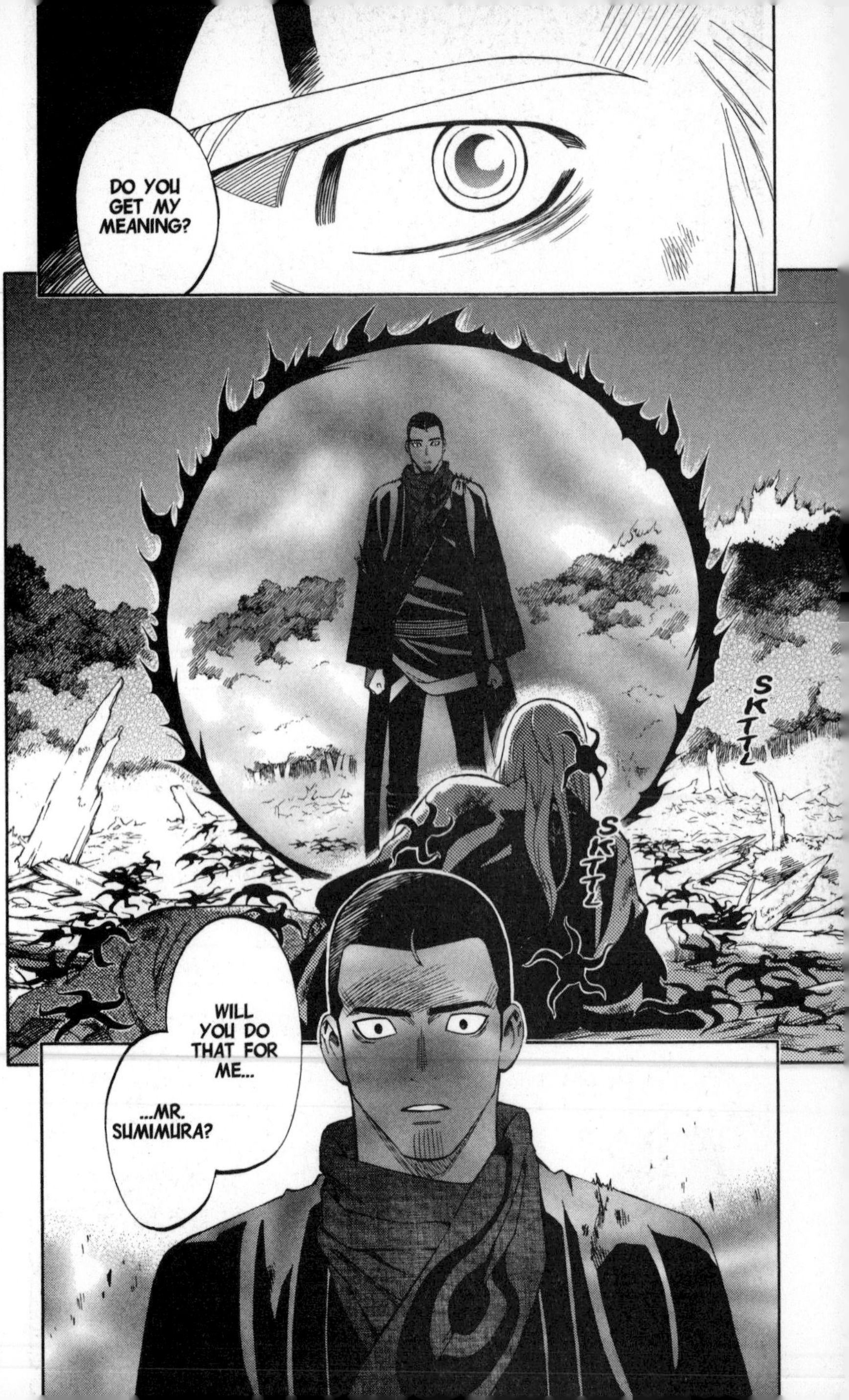
DO YOU GET MY MEANING?
SKTTL
SKTTL
WILL YOU DO THAT FOR ME...
...MR. SUMIMURA?

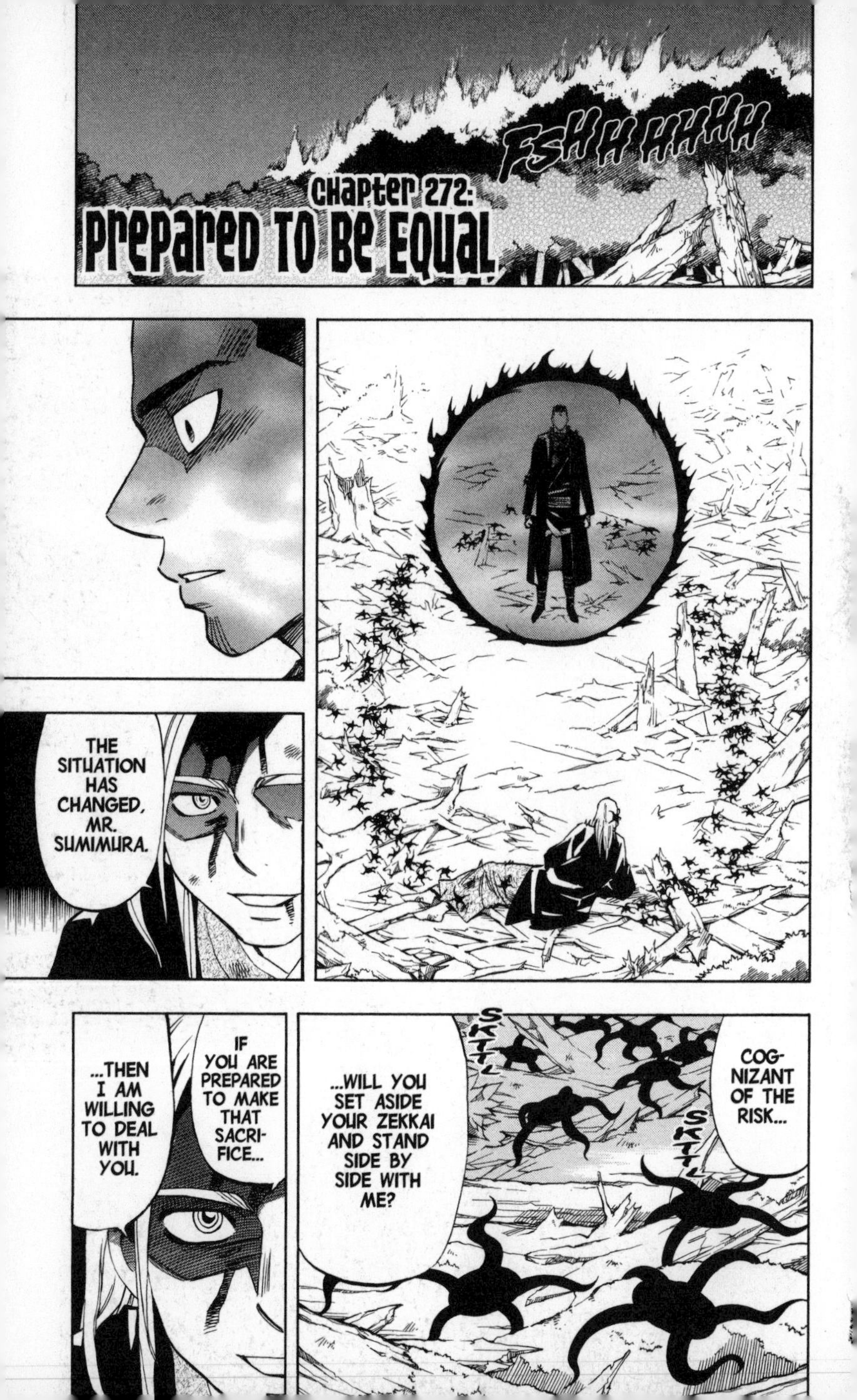
FSHHHHHH
Chapter 272:
Prepared to Be Equal
THE SITUATION HAS CHANGED, MR. SUMIMURA.
COG-NIZANT OF THE RISK...
SKTTL
SKTTL
...WILL YOU SET ASIDE YOUR ZEKKAI AND STAND SIDE BY SIDE WITH ME?
IF YOU ARE PREPARED TO MAKE THAT SACRI-FICE...
...THEN I AM WILLING TO DEAL WITH YOU.

Chapter 272: Prepared to Be Equal

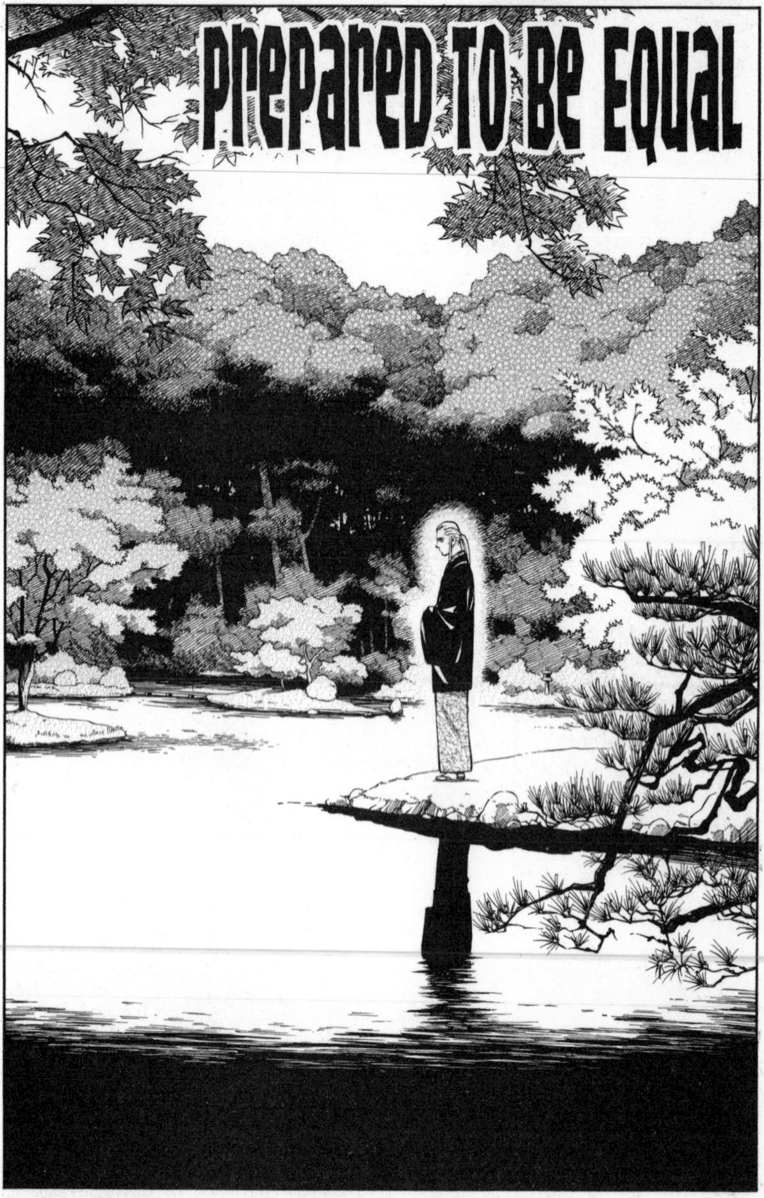

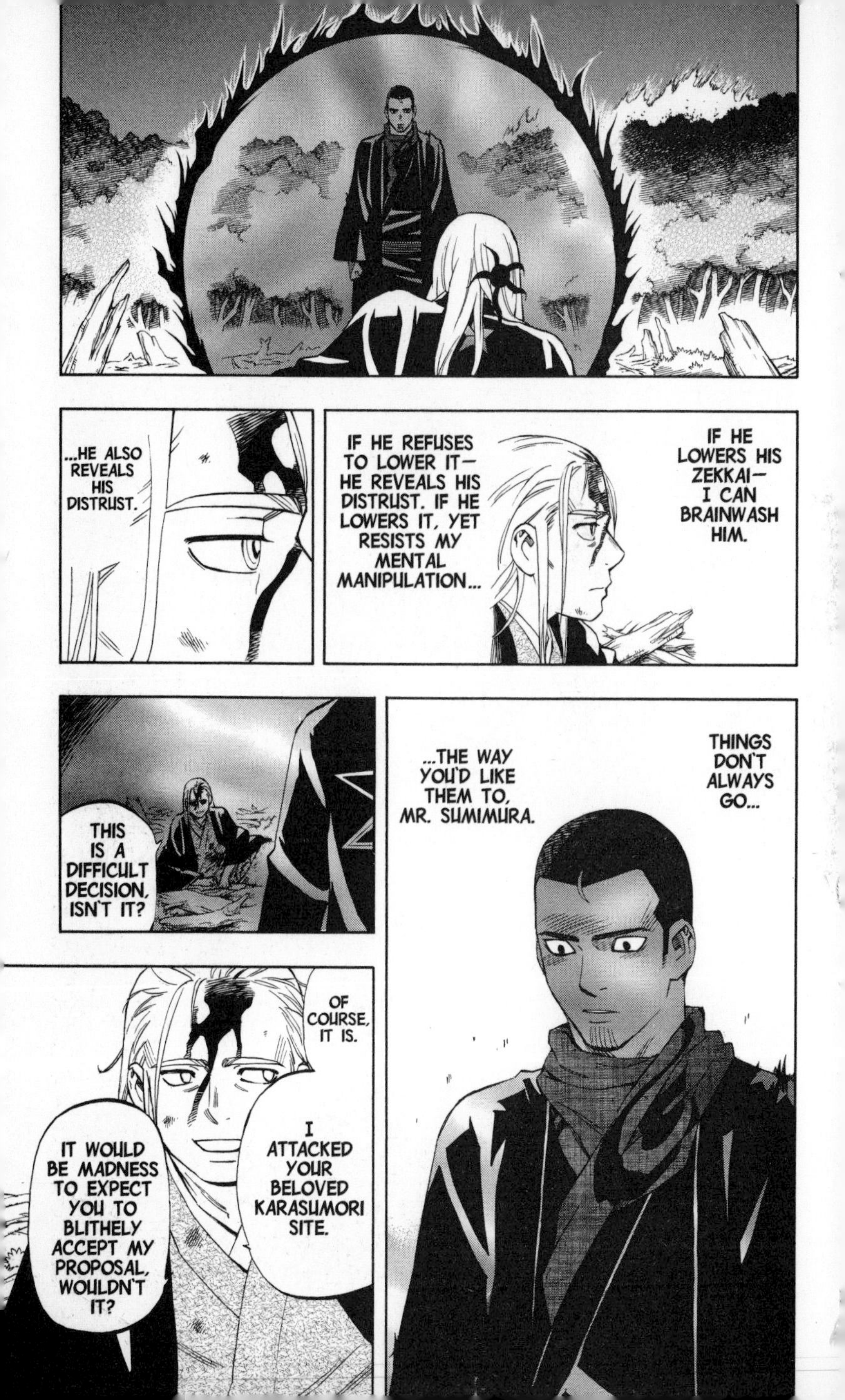
IF HE LOWERS HIS ZEKKAI— I CAN BRAINWASH HIM.
IF HE REFUSES TO LOWER IT— HE REVEALS HIS DISTRUST. IF HE LOWERS IT, YET RESISTS MY MENTAL MANIPULATION...
...HE ALSO REVEALS HIS DISTRUST.
THINGS DON'T ALWAYS GO...
...THE WAY YOU'D LIKE THEM TO, MR. SUMIMURA.
THIS IS A DIFFICULT DECISION, ISN'T IT?
OF COURSE, IT IS.
I ATTACKED YOUR BELOVED KARASUMORI SITE.
IT WOULD BE MADNESS TO EXPECT YOU TO BLITHELY ACCEPT MY PROPOSAL, WOULDN'T IT?

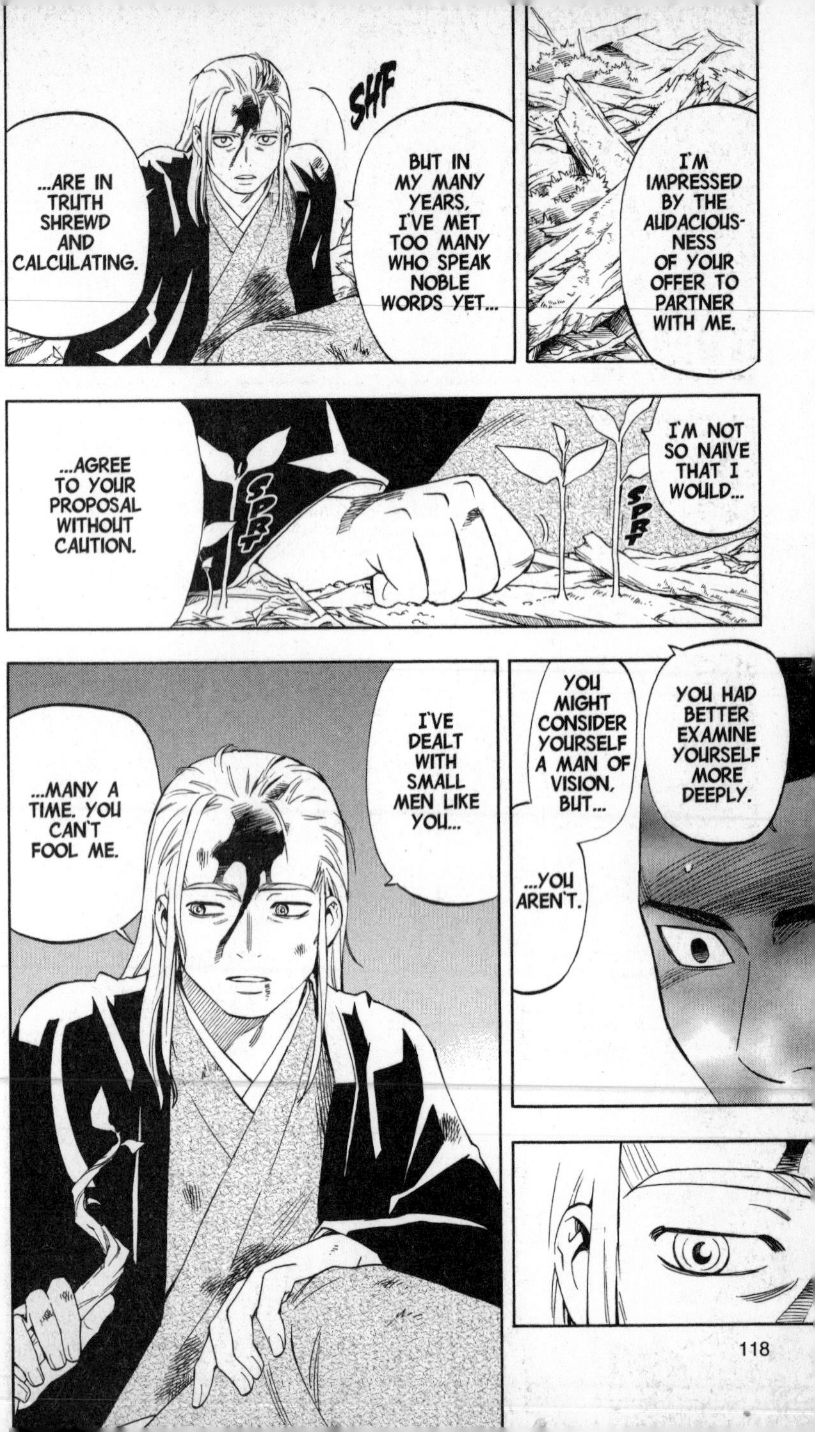
I'M IMPRESSED BY THE AUDACIOUSNESS OF YOUR OFFER TO PARTNER WITH ME.
SHF
BUT IN MY MANY YEARS, I'VE MET TOO MANY WHO SPEAK NOBLE WORDS YET...
...ARE IN TRUTH SHREWD AND CALCULATING.
I'M NOT SO NAIVE THAT I WOULD...
SPRT
SPRT
...AGREE TO YOUR PROPOSAL WITHOUT CAUTION.
YOU HAD BETTER EXAMINE YOURSELF MORE DEEPLY.
YOU MIGHT CONSIDER YOURSELF A MAN OF VISION, BUT...
...YOU AREN'T.
I'VE DEALT WITH SMALL MEN LIKE YOU...
...MANY A TIME. YOU CAN'T FOOL ME.

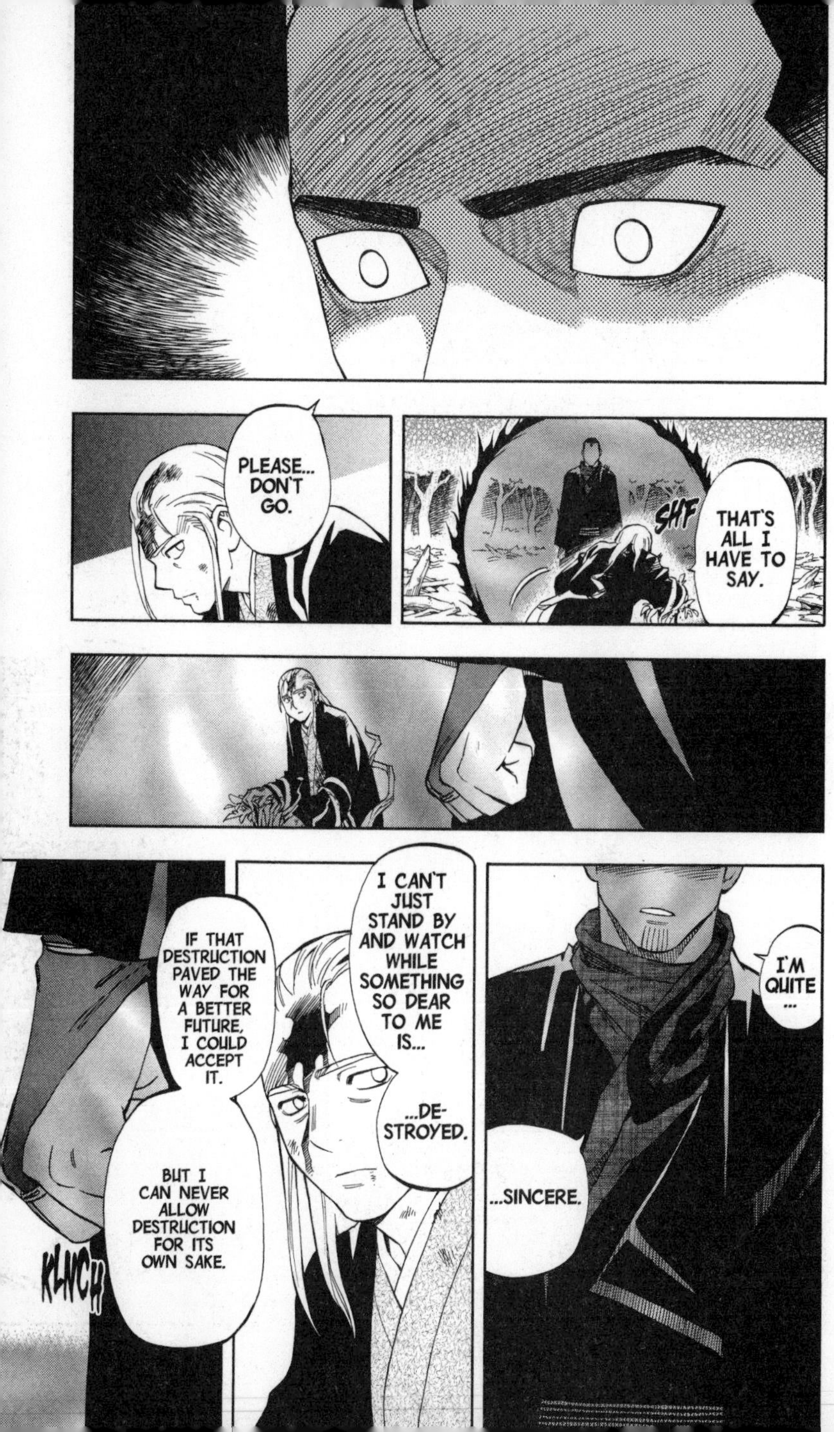
SHF
THAT'S ALL I HAVE TO SAY.
PLEASE... DON'T GO.
I'M QUITE ...
...SINCERE.
I CAN'T JUST STAND BY AND WATCH WHILE SOMETHING SO DEAR TO ME IS...
...DE-STROYED.
IF THAT DESTRUCTION PAVED THE WAY FOR A BETTER FUTURE, I COULD ACCEPT IT.
BUT I CAN NEVER ALLOW DESTRUCTION FOR ITS OWN SAKE.
KLNCH

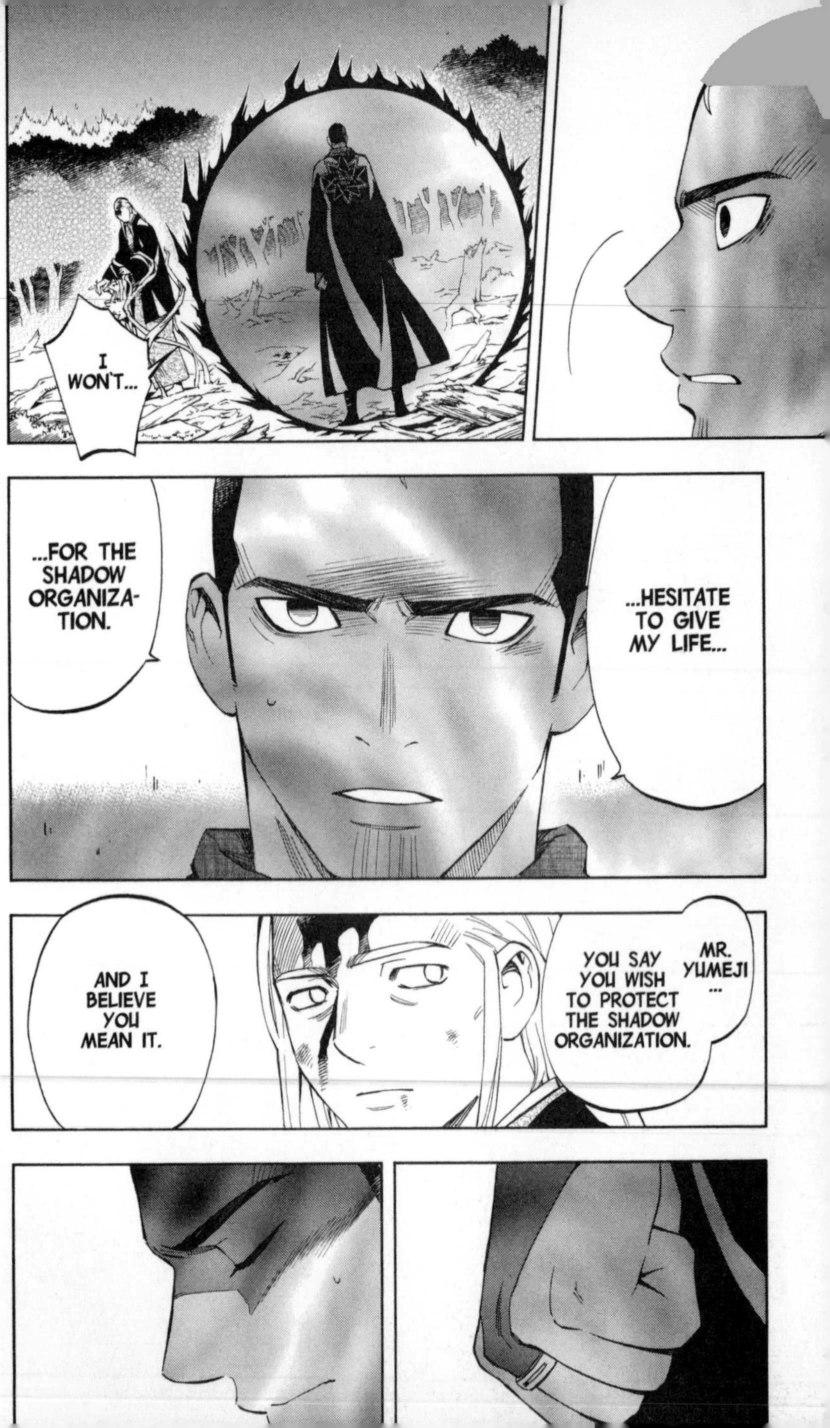
I WON'T...
...HESITATE TO GIVE MY LIFE...
...FOR THE SHADOW ORGANIZATION.
MR. YUMEJI...
YOU SAY YOU WISH TO PROTECT THE SHADOW ORGANIZATION.
AND I BELIEVE YOU MEAN IT.

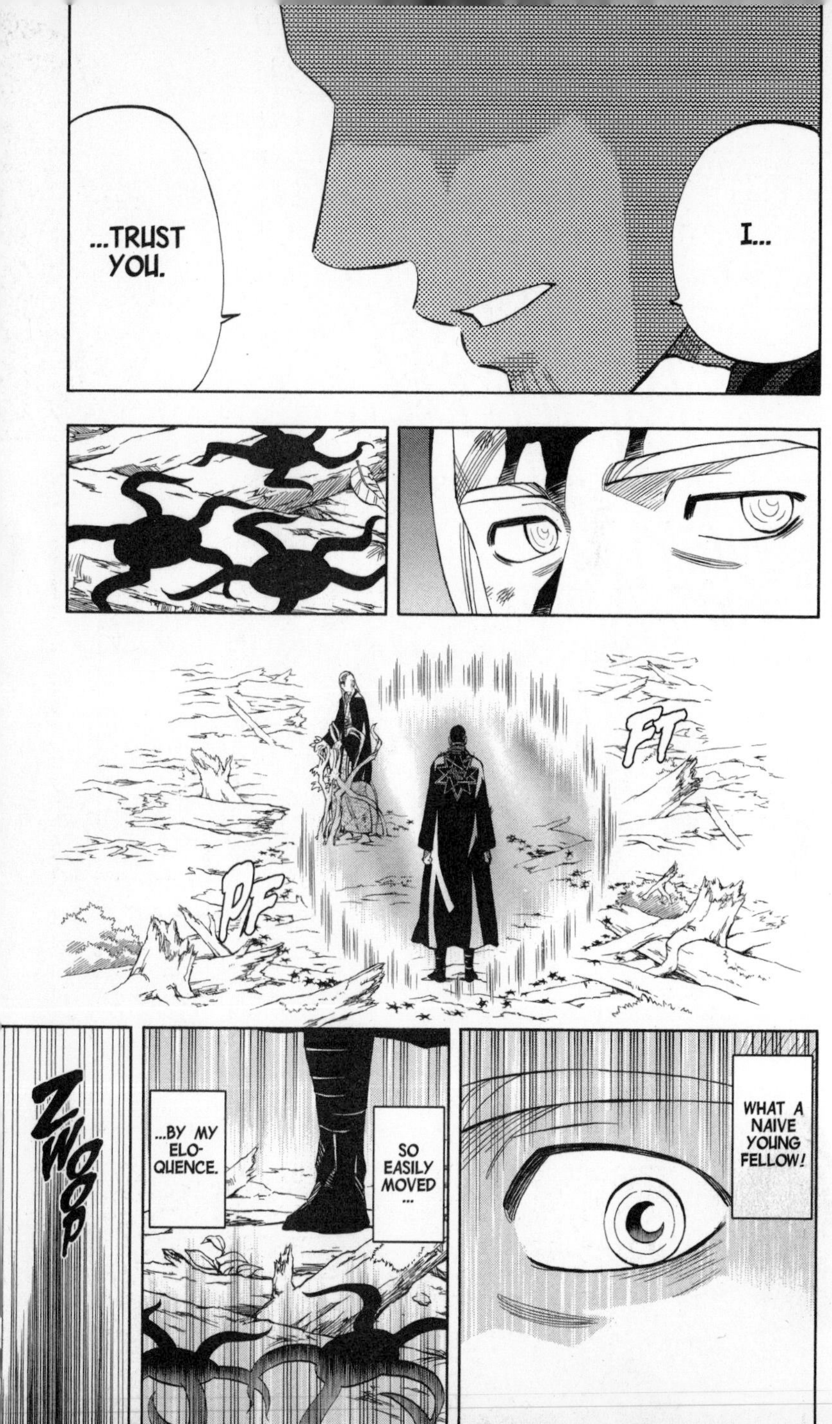
I...
...TRUST YOU.
FT
PF
WHAT A NAIVE YOUNG FELLOW!
SO EASILY MOVED ...
...BY MY ELO-QUENCE.
ZWOOP

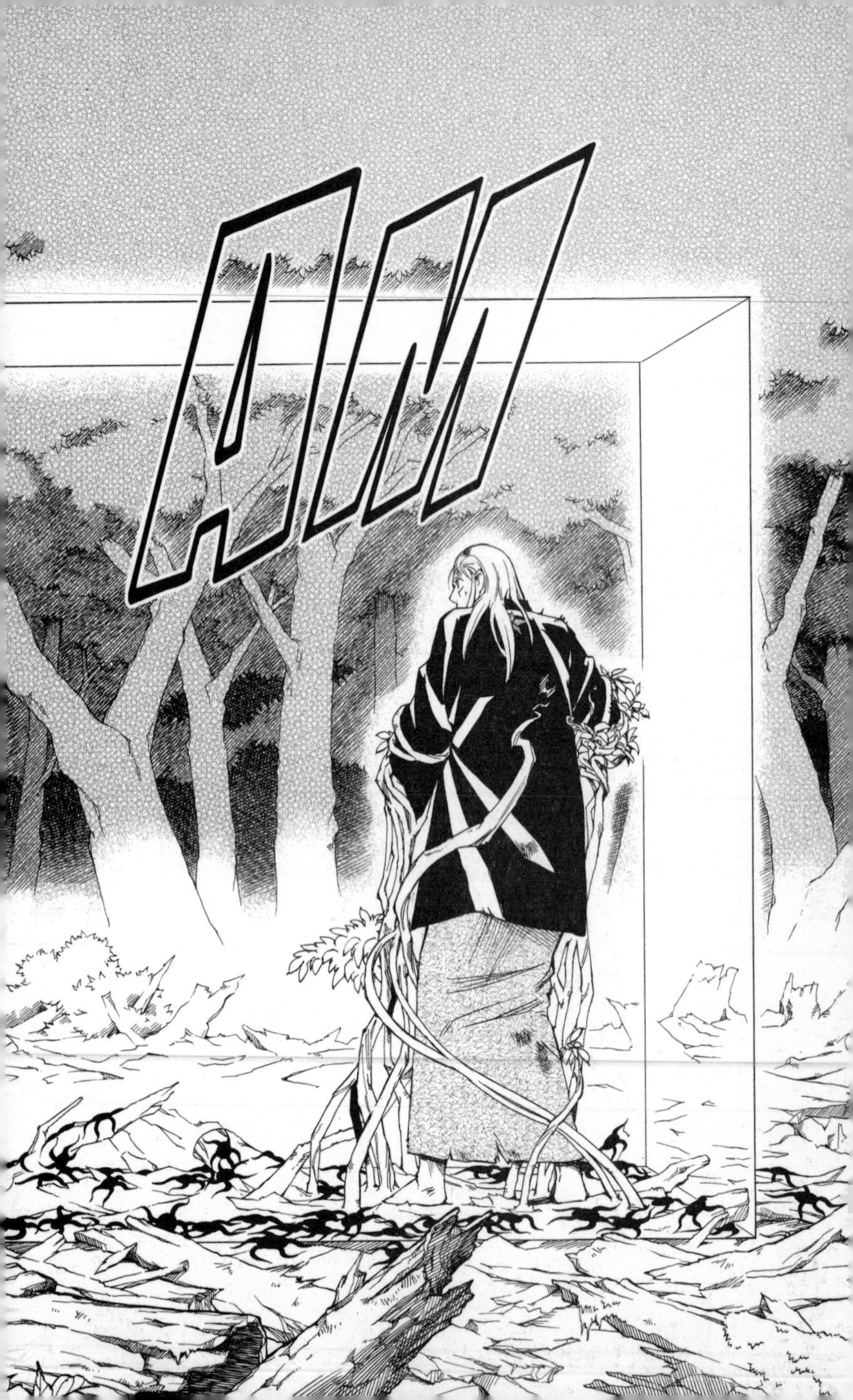

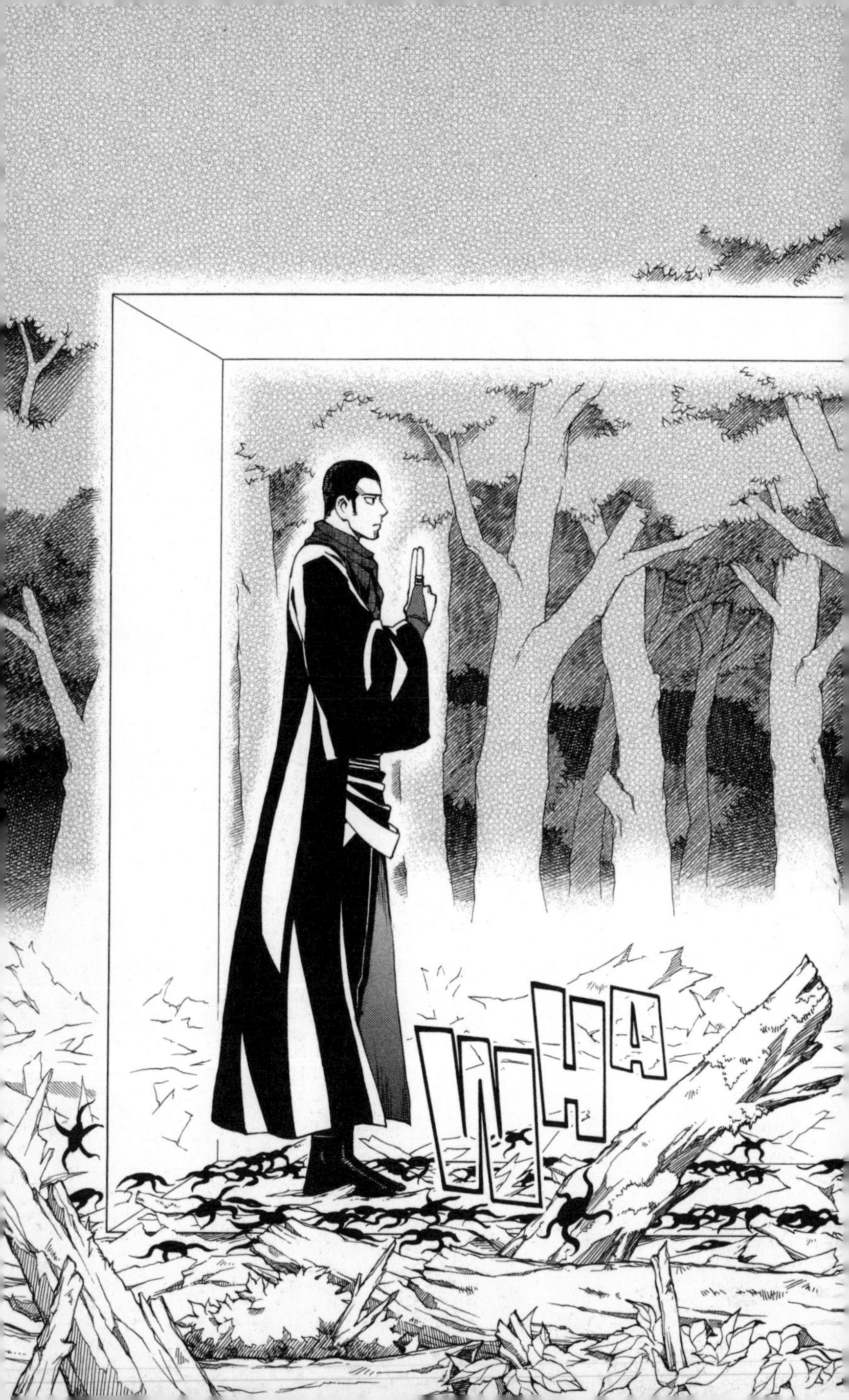
WHA

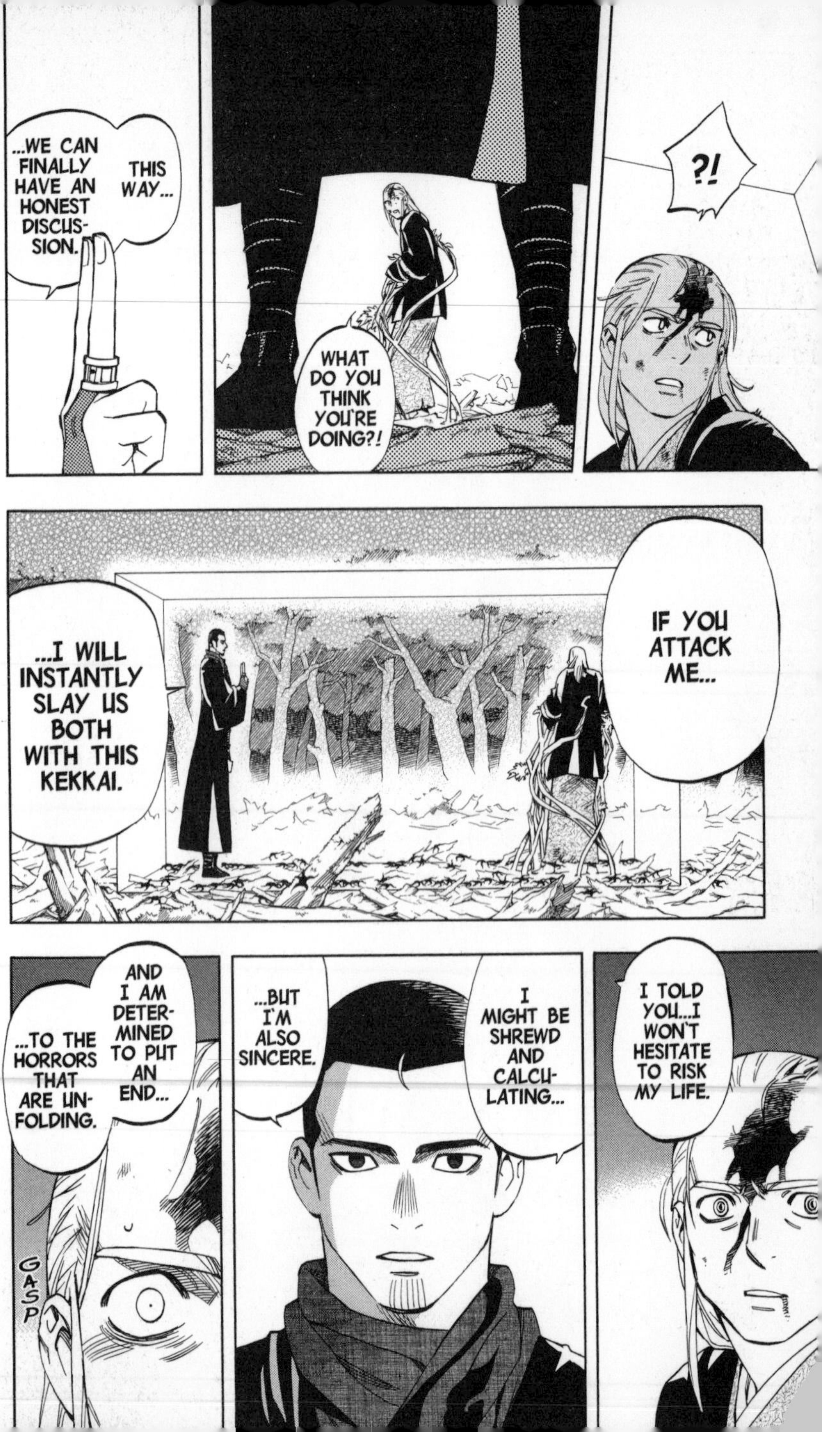
?!
WHAT DO YOU THINK YOU'RE DOING?!
THIS WAY...
...WE CAN FINALLY HAVE AN HONEST DISCUSSION.
IF YOU ATTACK ME...
...I WILL INSTANTLY SLAY US BOTH WITH THIS KEKKAI.
I TOLD YOU...I WON'T HESITATE TO RISK MY LIFE.
I MIGHT BE SHREWD AND CALCULATING...
...BUT I'M ALSO SINCERE.
AND I AM DETERMINED TO PUT AN END...
...TO THE HORRORS THAT ARE UNFOLDING.
GASP

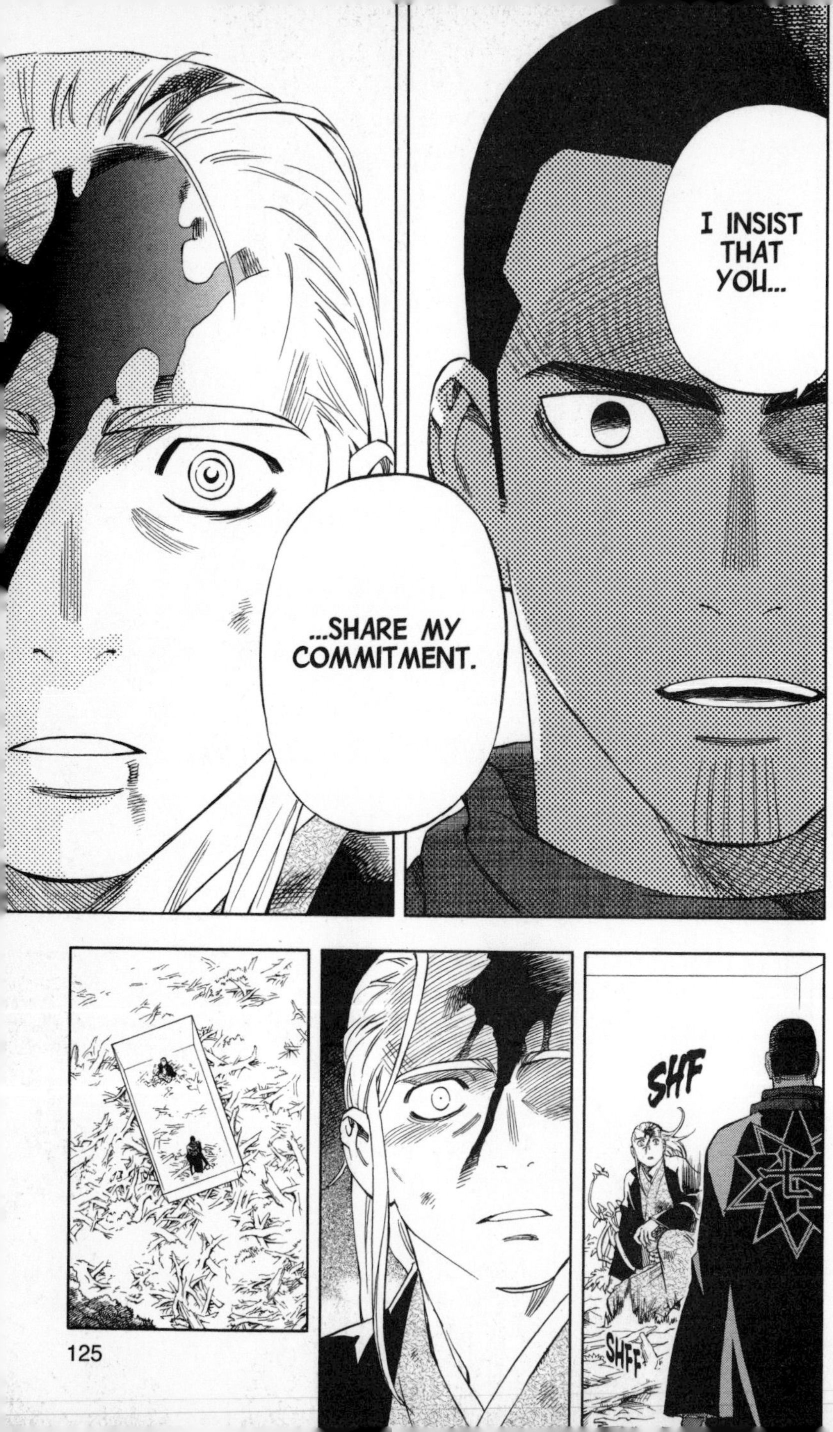
I INSIST THAT YOU...
...SHARE MY COMMITMENT.
SHF
SHFF

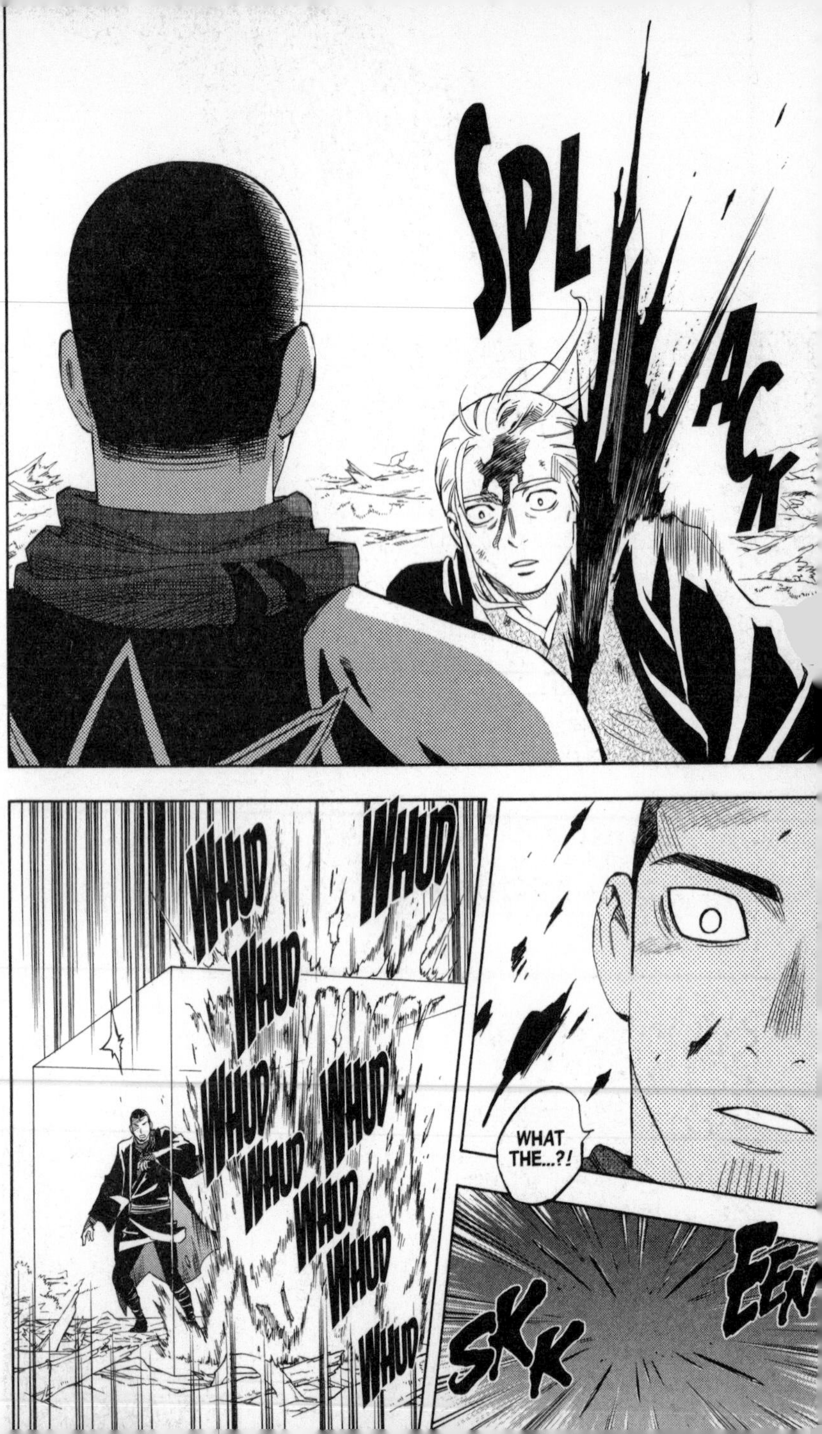
SPLACK
WHAT THE...?!
SKK
EEN
WHUD
WHUD
WHUD
WHUD
WHUD
WHUD
WHUD
WHUD
WHUD

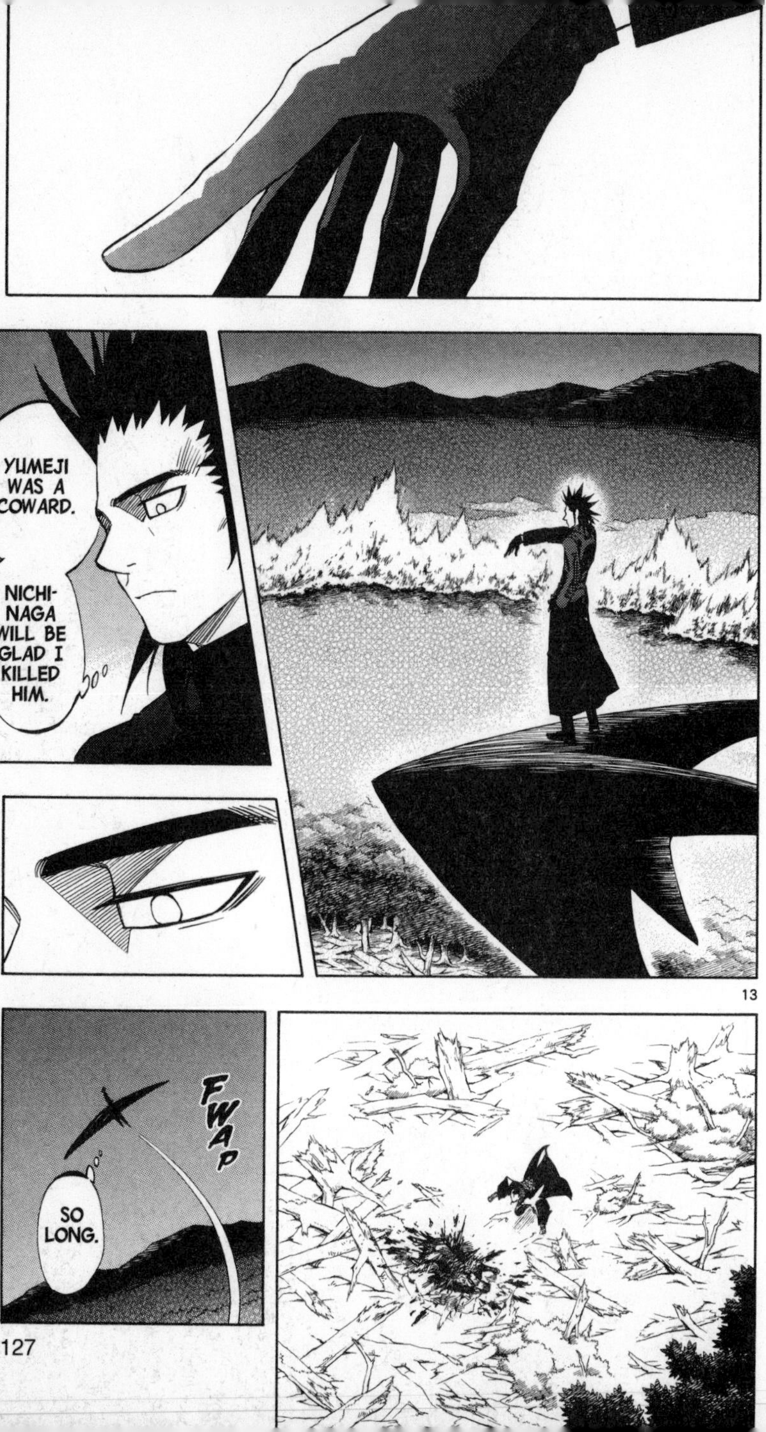
YUMEJI WAS A COWARD.
NICHI-NAGA WILL BE GLAD I KILLED HIM.
FWAP
SO LONG.

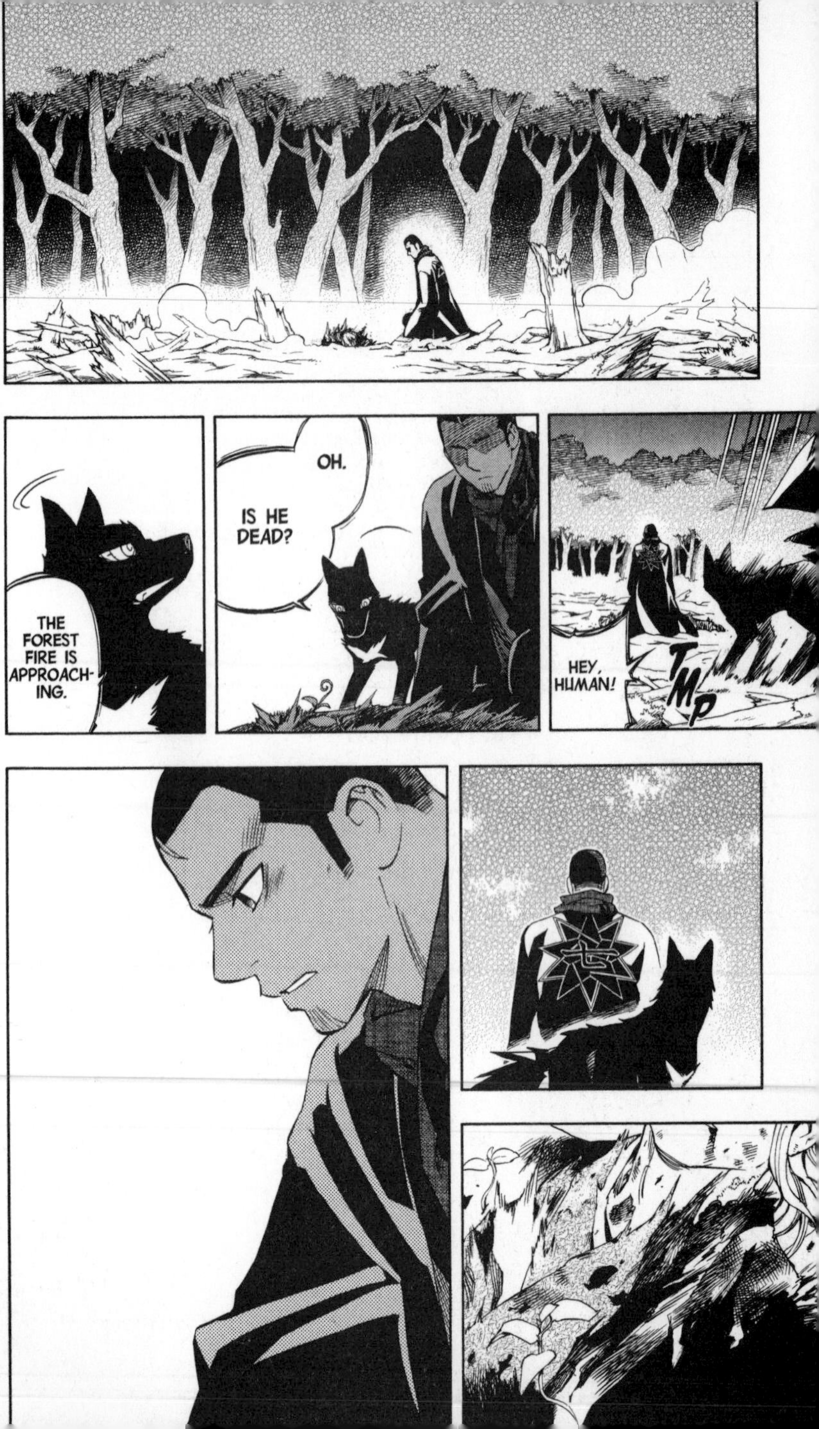
HEY, HUMAN!
TMP
OH.
IS HE DEAD?
THE FOREST FIRE IS APPROACHING.

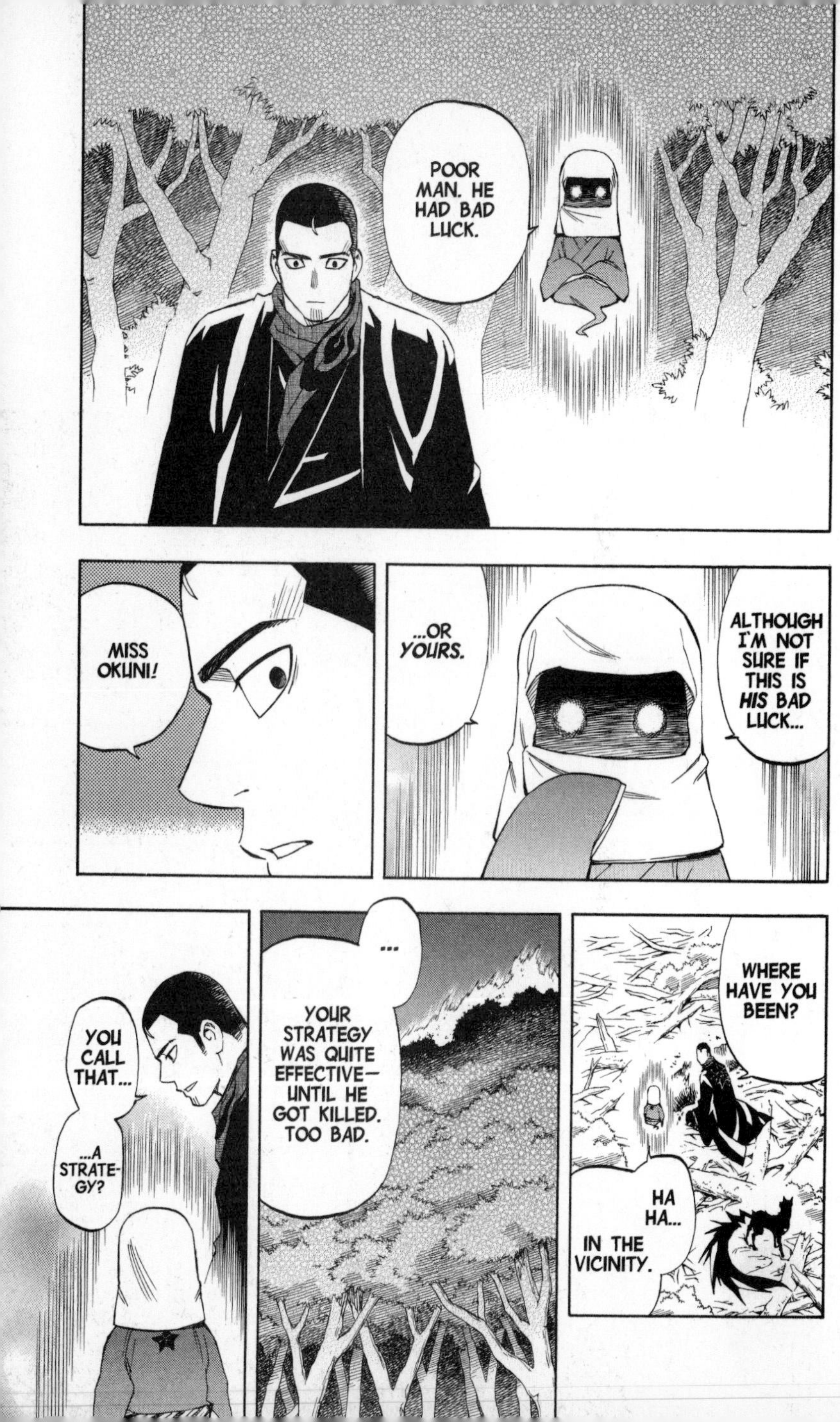
POOR MAN. HE HAD BAD LUCK.
ALTHOUGH I'M NOT SURE IF THIS IS *HIS* BAD LUCK...
...OR *YOURS*.
MISS OKUNI!
WHERE HAVE YOU BEEN?
HA HA...
IN THE VICINITY.
...
YOUR STRATEGY WAS QUITE EFFECTIVE—UNTIL HE GOT KILLED. TOO BAD.
YOU CALL THAT...
...A STRATE-GY?

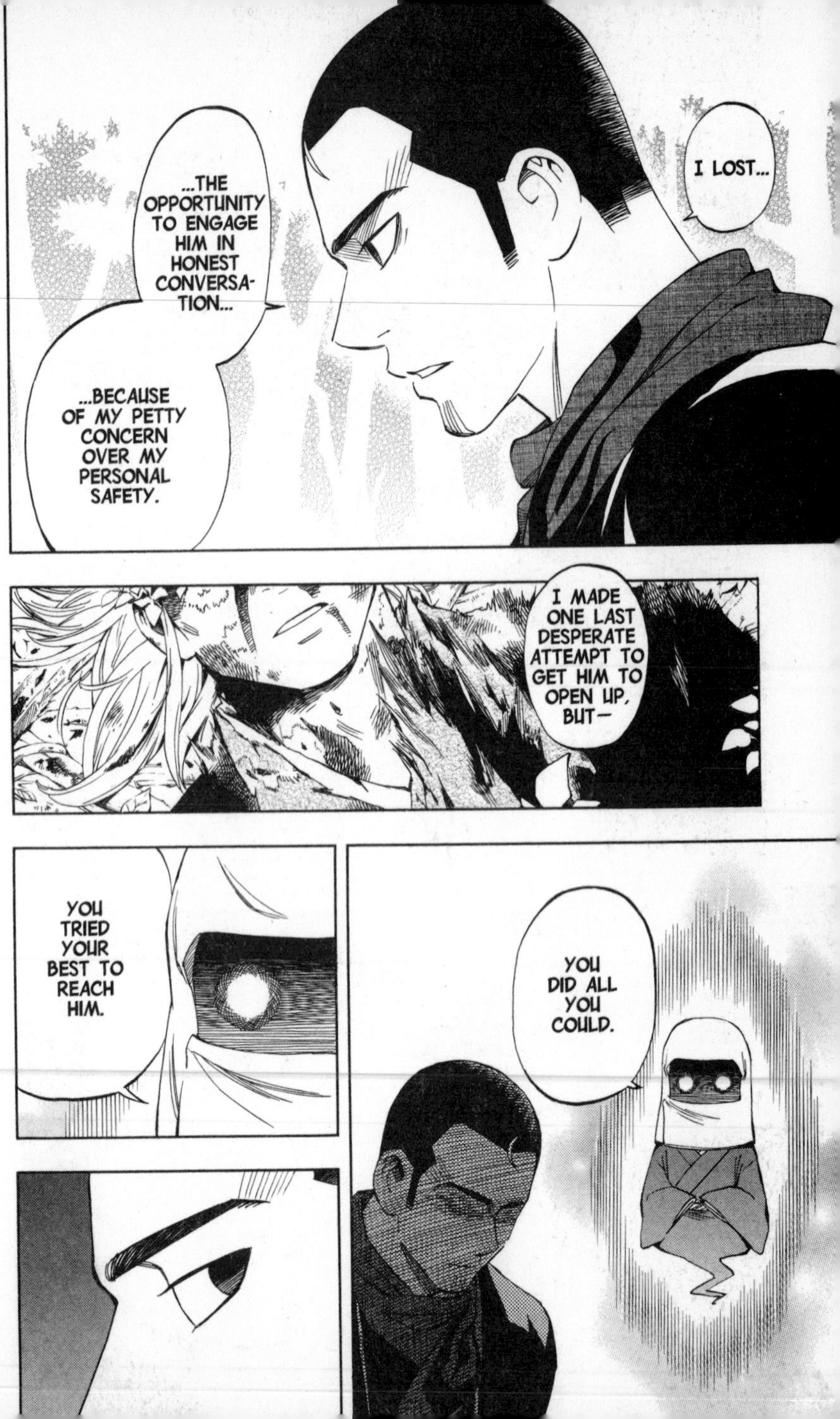
I LOST...
...THE OPPORTUNITY TO ENGAGE HIM IN HONEST CONVERSA-TION...
...BECAUSE OF MY PETTY CONCERN OVER MY PERSONAL SAFETY.
I MADE ONE LAST DESPERATE ATTEMPT TO GET HIM TO OPEN UP, BUT—
YOU DID ALL YOU COULD.
YOU TRIED YOUR BEST TO REACH HIM.

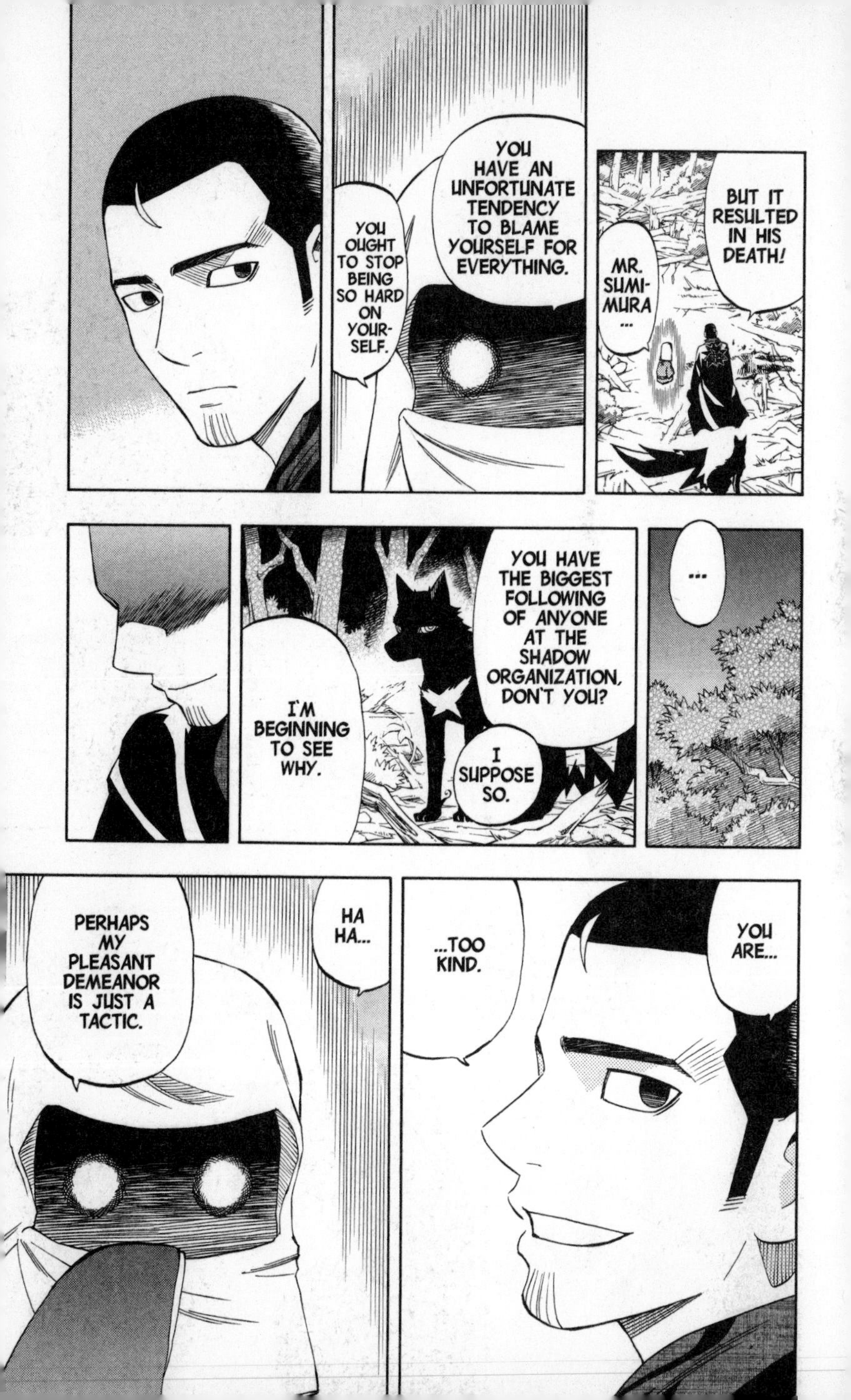
BUT IT RESULTED IN HIS DEATH!
MR. SUMIMURA...
YOU HAVE AN UNFORTUNATE TENDENCY TO BLAME YOURSELF FOR EVERYTHING.
YOU OUGHT TO STOP BEING SO HARD ON YOURSELF.
...
YOU HAVE THE BIGGEST FOLLOWING OF ANYONE AT THE SHADOW ORGANIZATION, DON'T YOU?
I SUPPOSE SO.
I'M BEGINNING TO SEE WHY.
YOU ARE...
...TOO KIND.
HA HA...
PERHAPS MY PLEASANT DEMEANOR IS JUST A TACTIC.

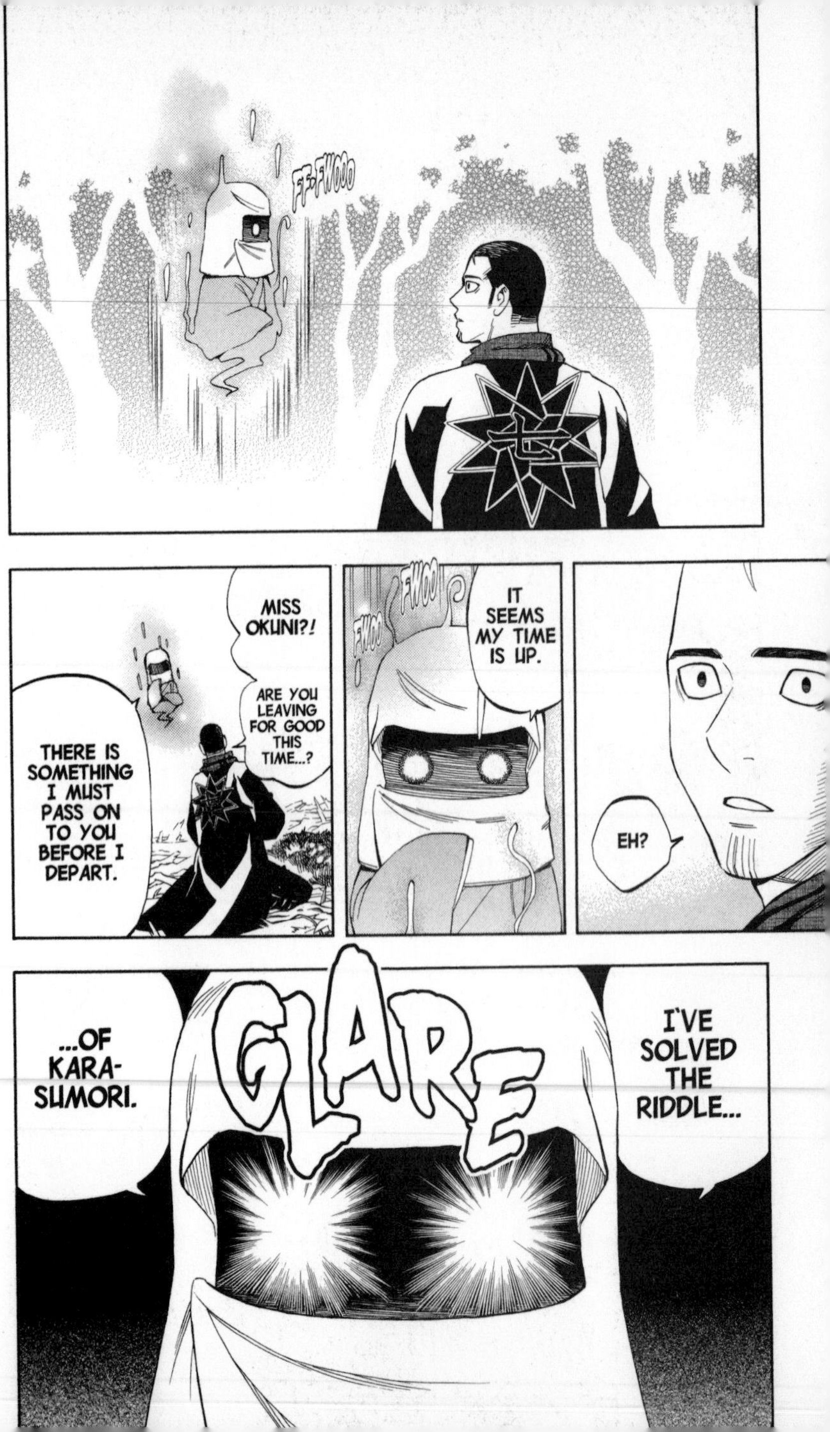
FF-FWOOO
EH?
FWOO
FWOO
IT SEEMS MY TIME IS UP.
MISS OKUNI?!
ARE YOU LEAVING FOR GOOD THIS TIME...?
THERE IS SOMETHING I MUST PASS ON TO YOU BEFORE I DEPART.
I'VE SOLVED THE RIDDLE...
GLARE
...OF KARA-SUMORI.

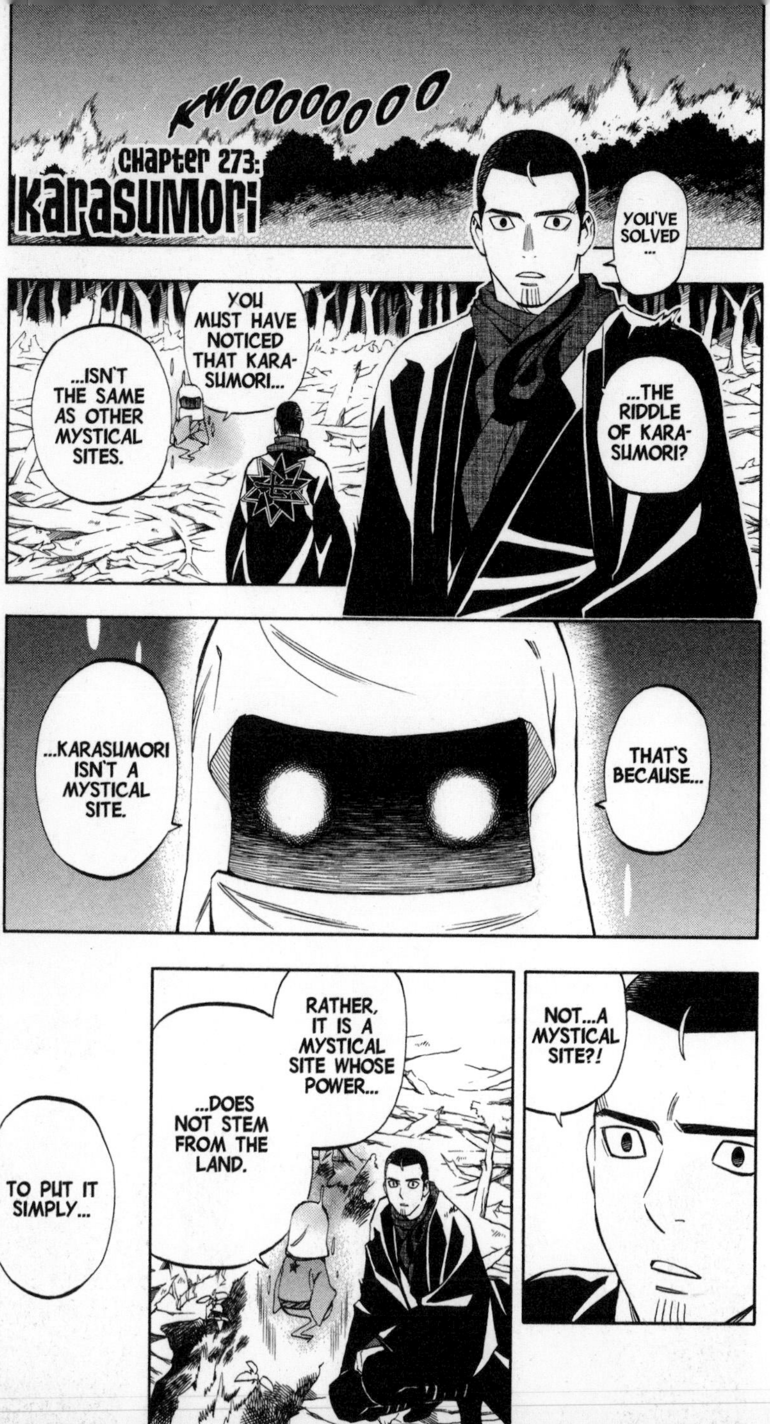
KWOOOOOOOOO
Chapter 273: Karasumori
YOU'VE SOLVED ...
...THE RIDDLE OF KARA-SUMORI?
YOU MUST HAVE NOTICED THAT KARA-SUMORI...
...ISN'T THE SAME AS OTHER MYSTICAL SITES.
THAT'S BECAUSE...
...KARASUMORI ISN'T A MYSTICAL SITE.
NOT...A MYSTICAL SITE?!
RATHER, IT IS A MYSTICAL SITE WHOSE POWER...
...DOES NOT STEM FROM THE LAND.
TO PUT IT SIMPLY...

Chapter 273
Karasumori

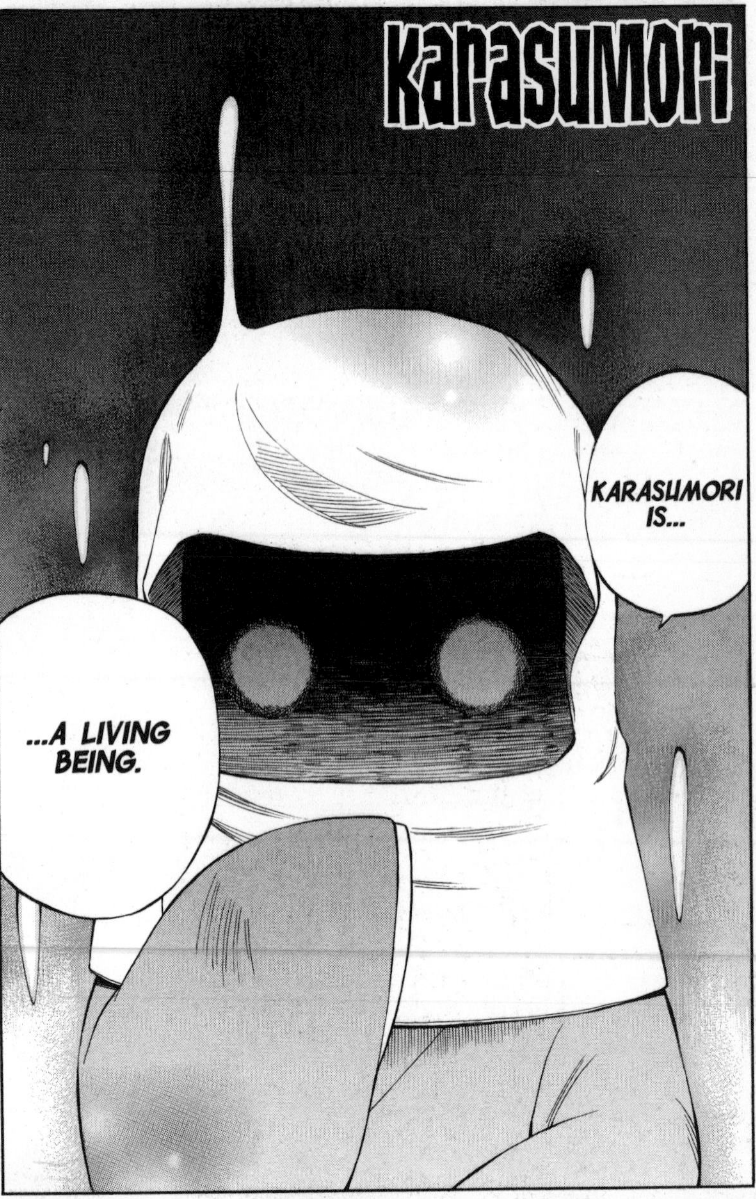
KARASUMORI IS...
...A LIVING BEING.

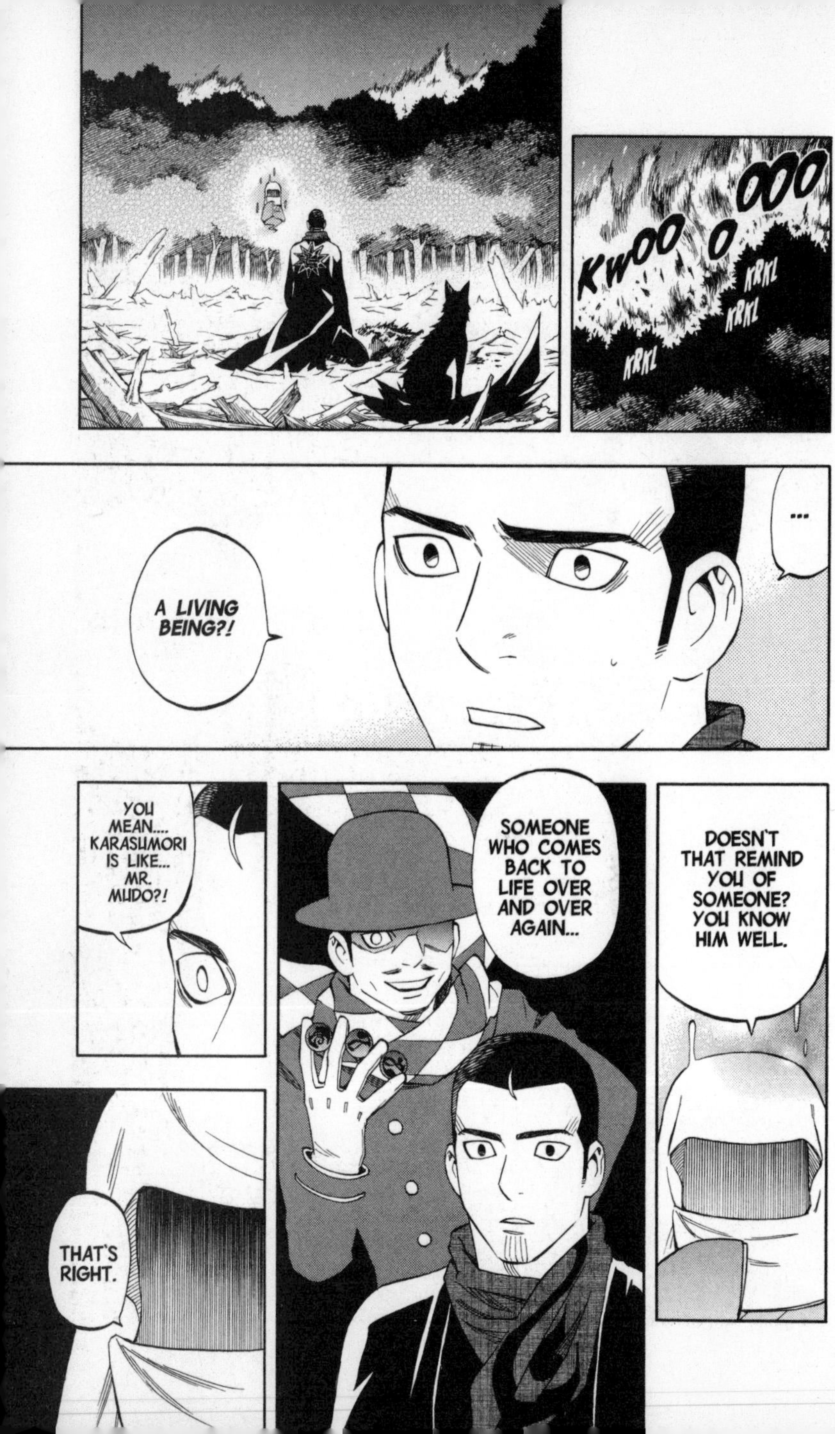
KWOO O OOO
KRKL
KRKL
KRKL
...
A LIVING BEING?!
DOESN'T THAT REMIND YOU OF SOMEONE? YOU KNOW HIM WELL.
SOMEONE WHO COMES BACK TO LIFE OVER AND OVER AGAIN...
YOU MEAN.... KARASUMORI IS LIKE... MR. MUDO?!
THAT'S RIGHT.

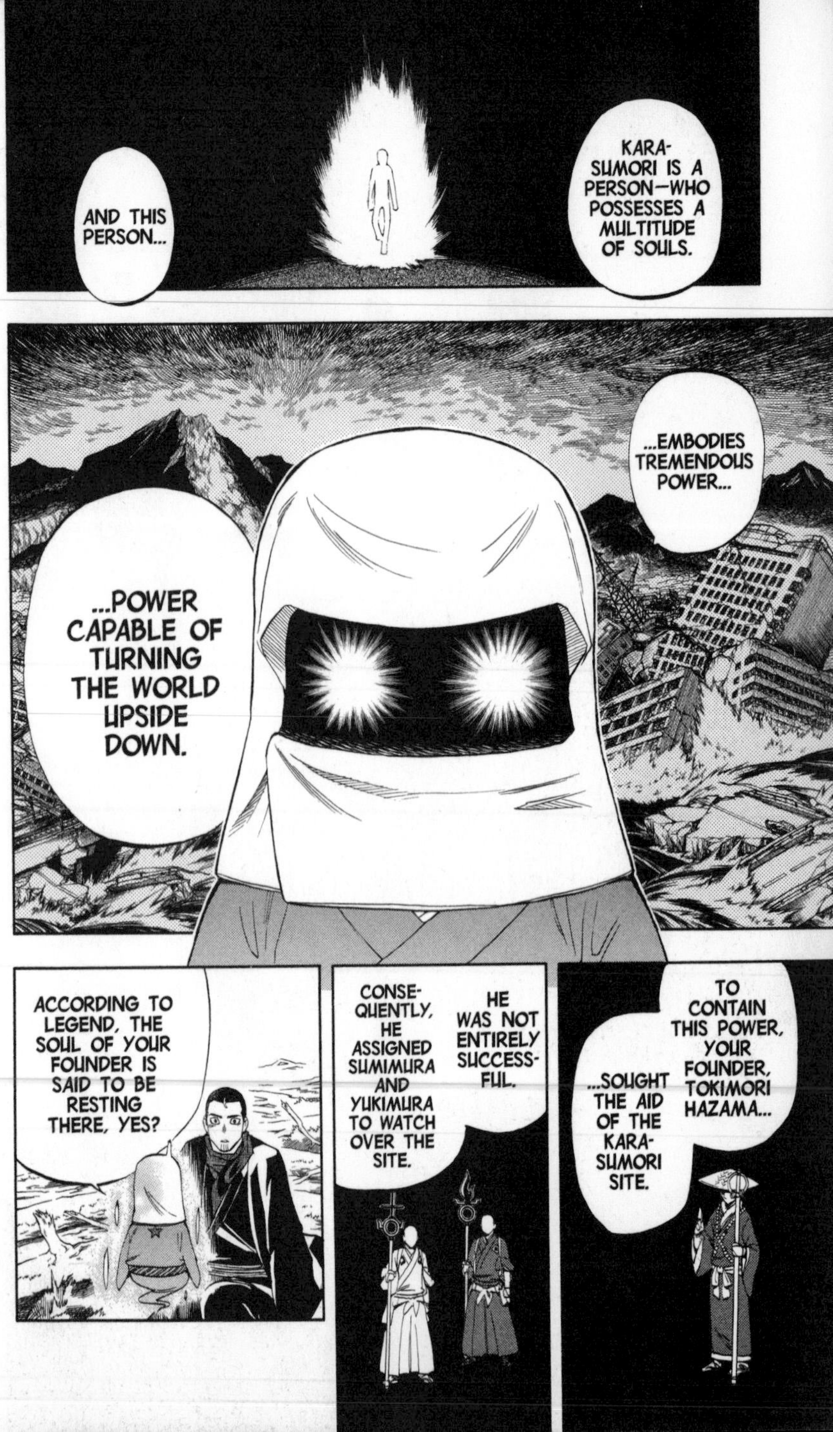
KARA-SUMORI IS A PERSON—WHO POSSESSES A MULTITUDE OF SOULS.
AND THIS PERSON...
...EMBODIES TREMENDOUS POWER...
...POWER CAPABLE OF TURNING THE WORLD UPSIDE DOWN.
TO CONTAIN THIS POWER, YOUR FOUNDER, TOKIMORI HAZAMA...
...SOUGHT THE AID OF THE KARA-SUMORI SITE.
HE WAS NOT ENTIRELY SUCCESSFUL.
CONSEQUENTLY, HE ASSIGNED SUMIMURA AND YUKIMURA TO WATCH OVER THE SITE.
ACCORDING TO LEGEND, THE SOUL OF YOUR FOUNDER IS SAID TO BE RESTING THERE, YES?

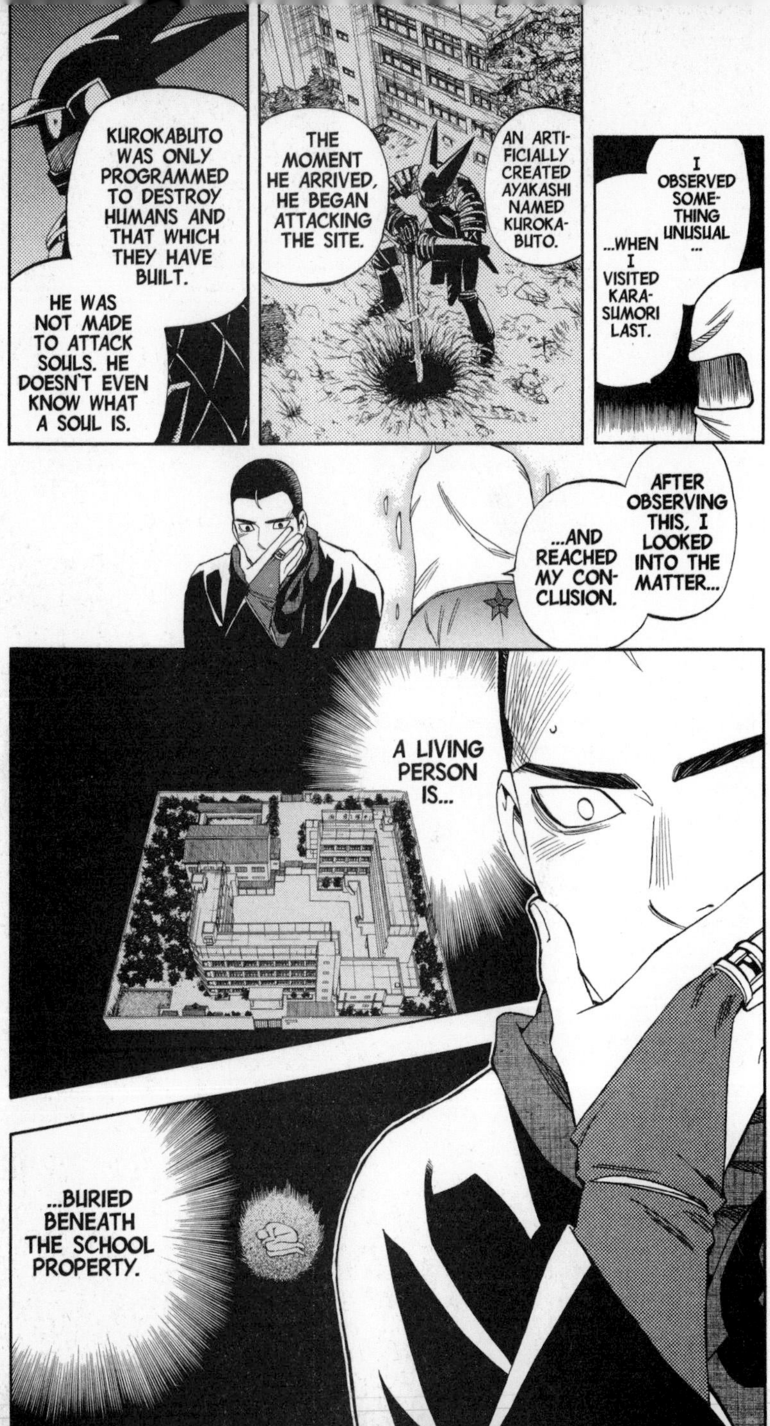
I OBSERVED SOMETHING UNUSUAL...
...WHEN I VISITED KARASUMORI LAST.
AN ARTIFICIALLY CREATED AYAKASHI NAMED KUROKABUTO.
THE MOMENT HE ARRIVED, HE BEGAN ATTACKING THE SITE.
KUROKABUTO WAS ONLY PROGRAMMED TO DESTROY HUMANS AND THAT WHICH THEY HAVE BUILT.
HE WAS NOT MADE TO ATTACK SOULS. HE DOESN'T EVEN KNOW WHAT A SOUL IS.
AFTER OBSERVING THIS, I LOOKED INTO THE MATTER...
...AND REACHED MY CONCLUSION.
A LIVING PERSON IS...
...BURIED BENEATH THE SCHOOL PROPERTY.

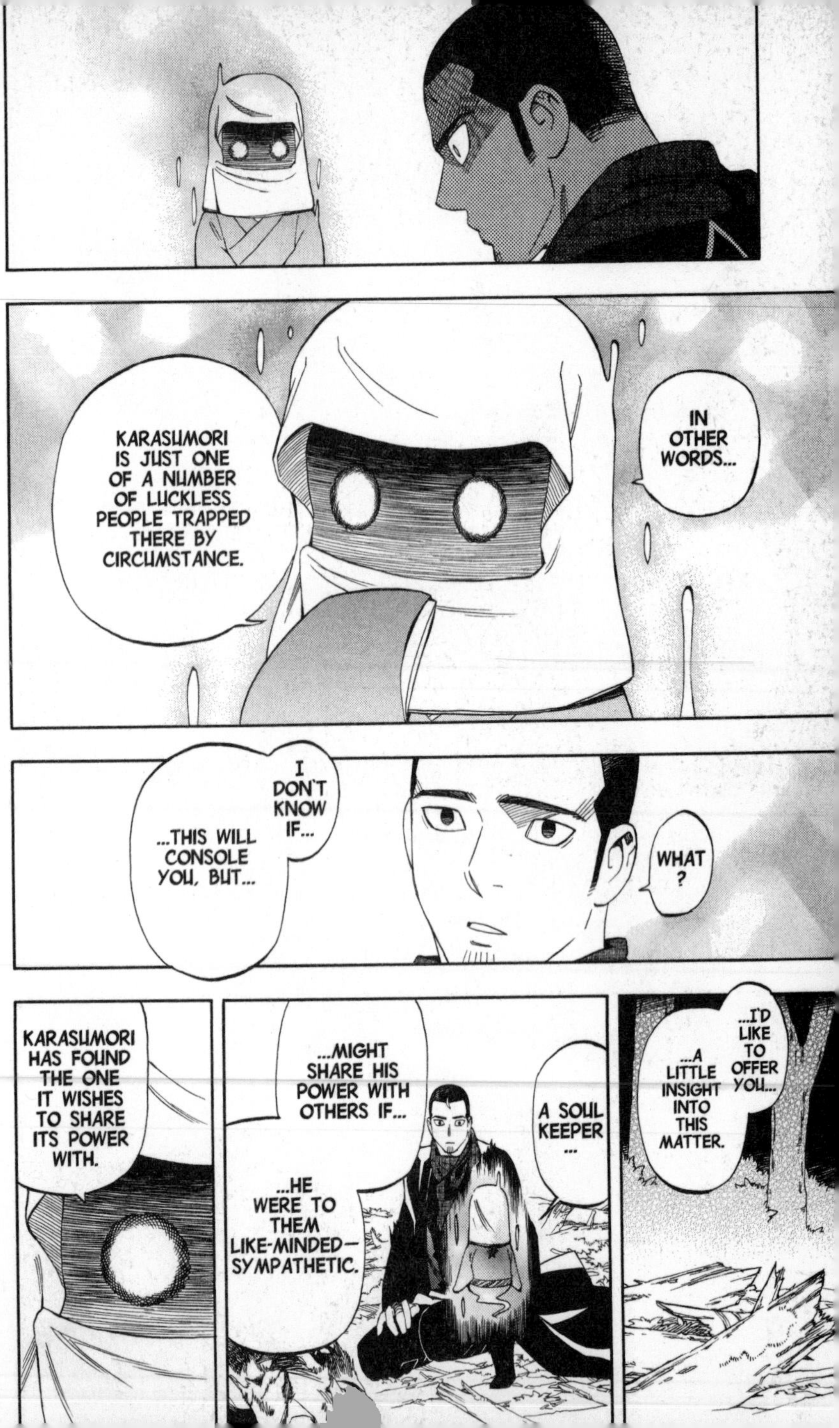
IN OTHER WORDS...
KARASUMORI IS JUST ONE OF A NUMBER OF LUCKLESS PEOPLE TRAPPED THERE BY CIRCUMSTANCE.
WHAT?
I DON'T KNOW IF...
...THIS WILL CONSOLE YOU, BUT...
...I'D LIKE TO OFFER YOU...
...A LITTLE INSIGHT INTO THIS MATTER.
A SOUL KEEPER...
...MIGHT SHARE HIS POWER WITH OTHERS IF...
...HE WERE TO THEM LIKE-MINDED—SYMPATHETIC.
KARASUMORI HAS FOUND THE ONE IT WISHES TO SHARE ITS POWER WITH.

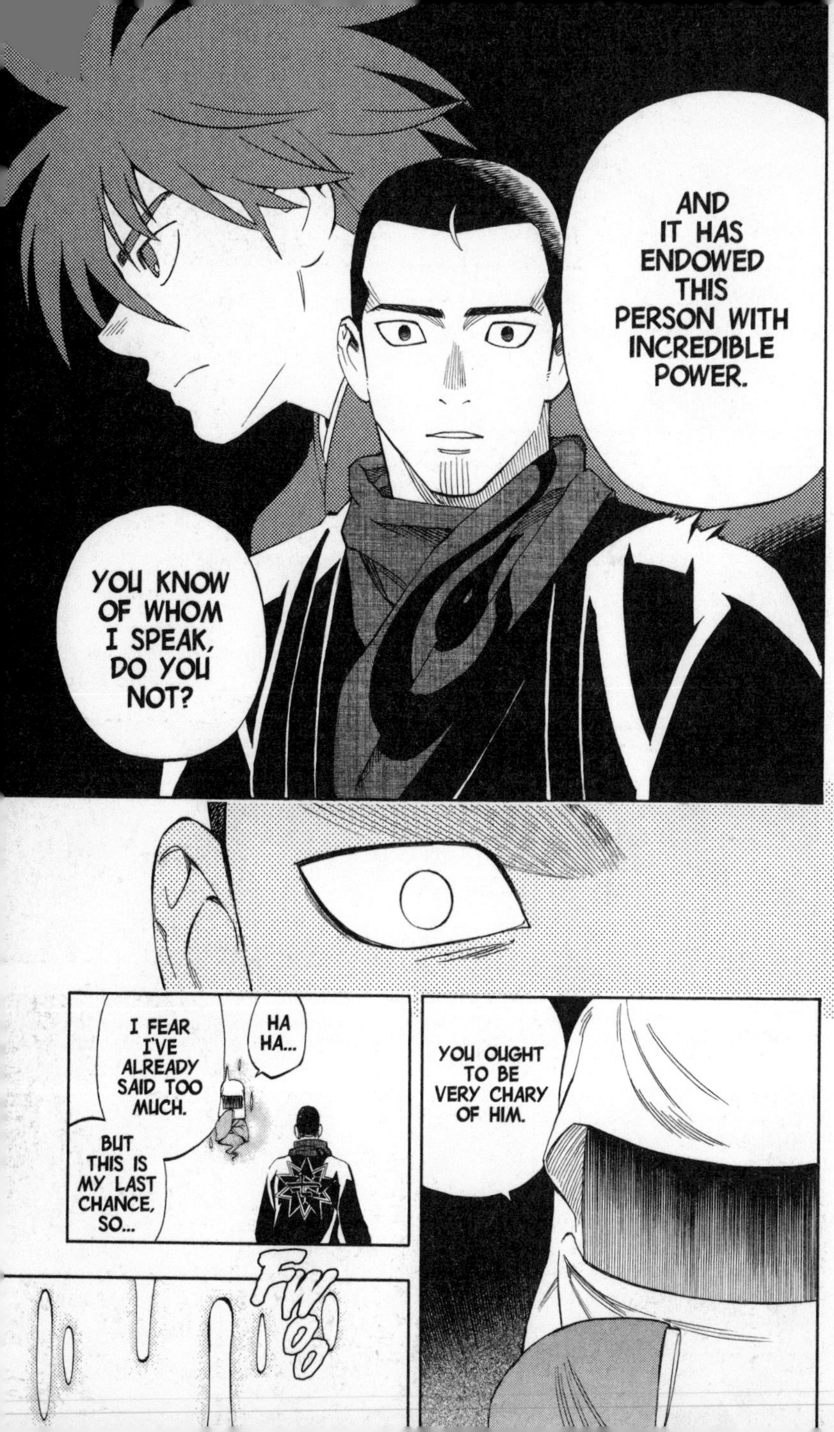
AND IT HAS ENDOWED THIS PERSON WITH INCREDIBLE POWER.
YOU KNOW OF WHOM I SPEAK, DO YOU NOT?
YOU OUGHT TO BE VERY CHARY OF HIM.
HA HA...
I FEAR I'VE ALREADY SAID TOO MUCH.
BUT THIS IS MY LAST CHANCE, SO...
FWOO

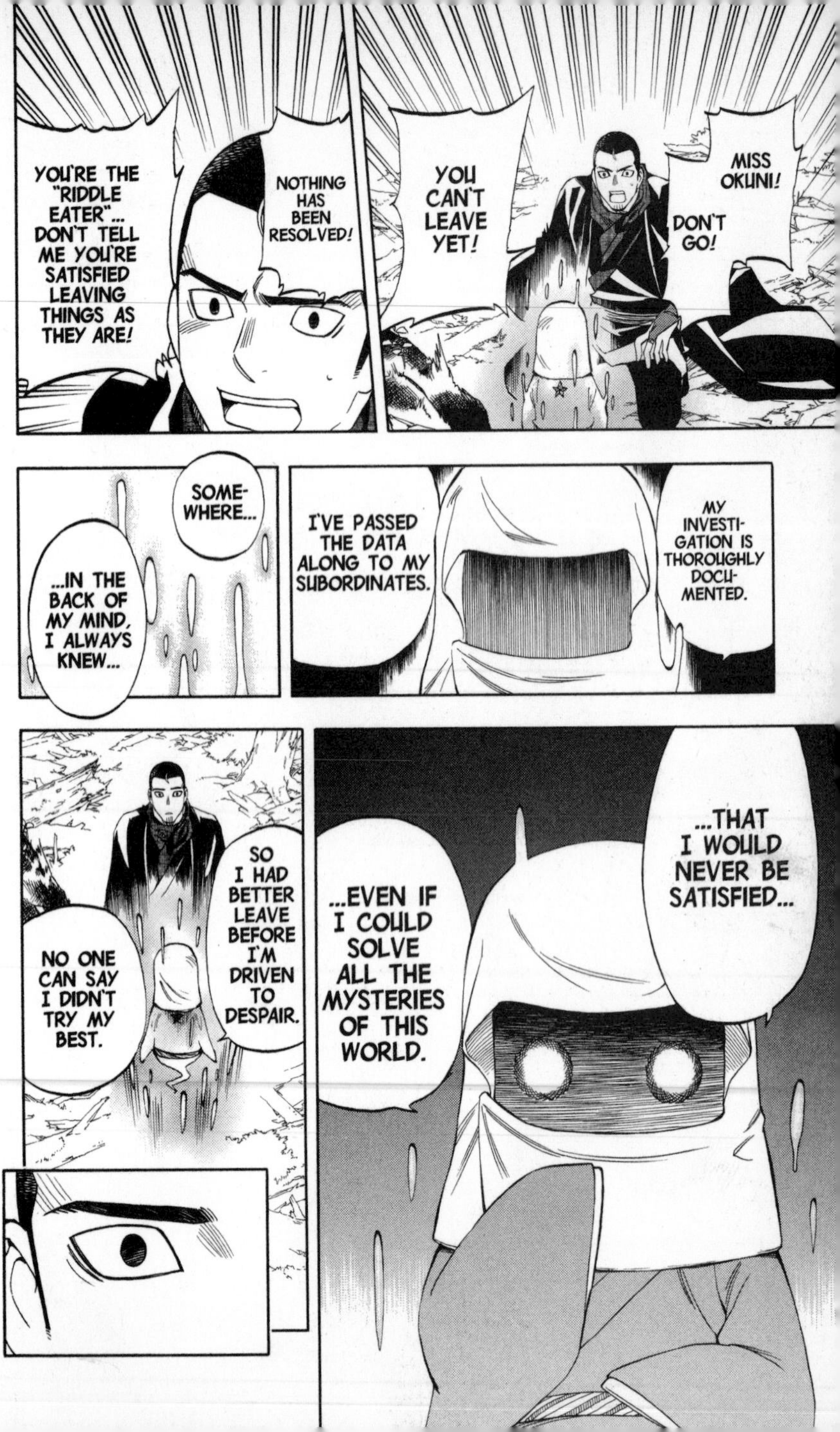
MISS OKUNI!
DON'T GO!
YOU CAN'T LEAVE YET!
NOTHING HAS BEEN RESOLVED!
YOU'RE THE "RIDDLE EATER"... DON'T TELL ME YOU'RE SATISFIED LEAVING THINGS AS THEY ARE!
MY INVESTIGATION IS THOROUGHLY DOCUMENTED.
I'VE PASSED THE DATA ALONG TO MY SUBORDINATES.
SOMEWHERE...
...IN THE BACK OF MY MIND, I ALWAYS KNEW...
...THAT I WOULD NEVER BE SATISFIED...
...EVEN IF I COULD SOLVE ALL THE MYSTERIES OF THIS WORLD.
SO I HAD BETTER LEAVE BEFORE I'M DRIVEN TO DESPAIR.
NO ONE CAN SAY I DIDN'T TRY MY BEST.

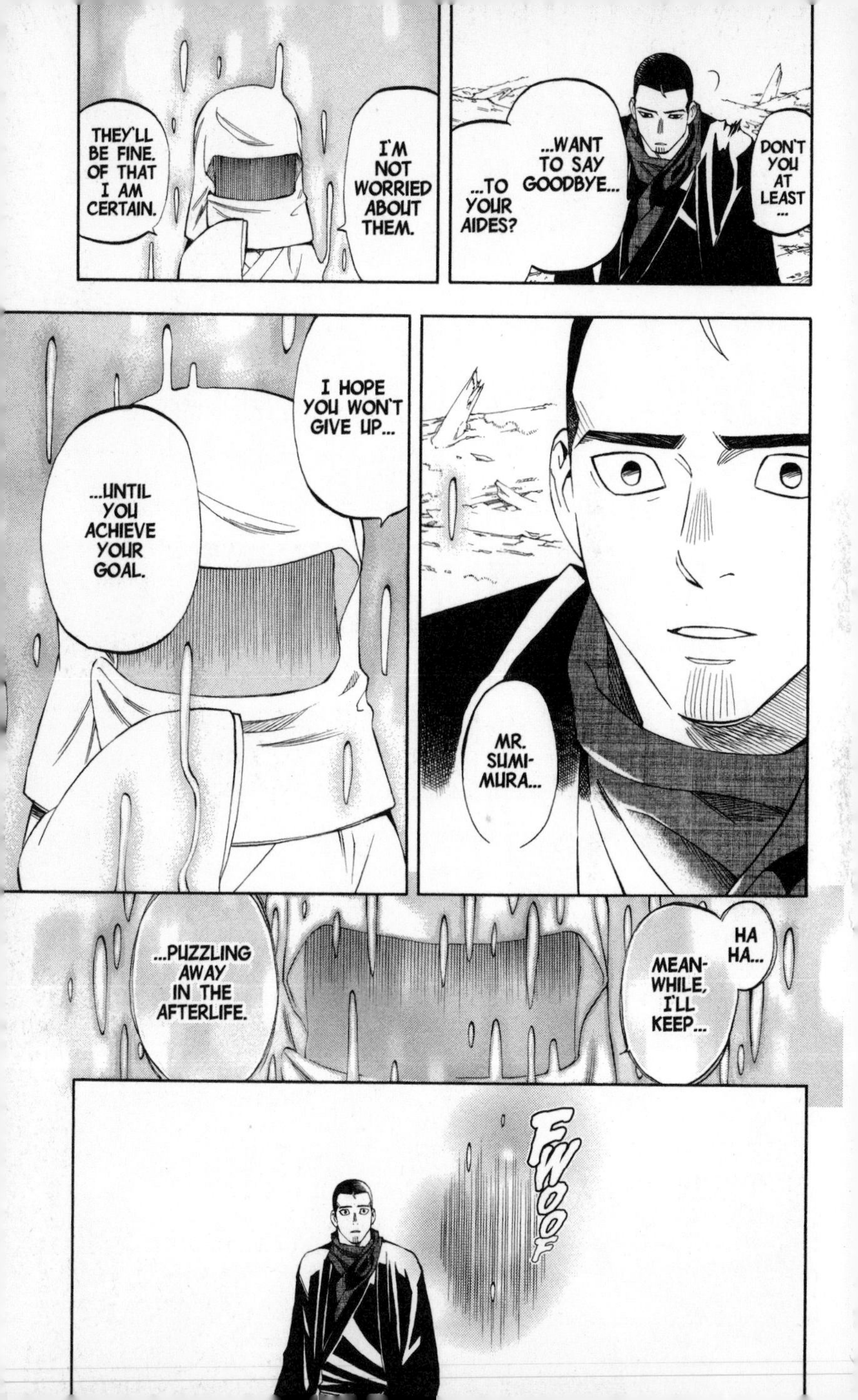
DON'T YOU AT LEAST ...
...WANT TO SAY GOODBYE...
...TO YOUR AIDES?
I'M NOT WORRIED ABOUT THEM.
THEY'LL BE FINE. OF THAT I AM CERTAIN.
MR. SUMI-MURA...
I HOPE YOU WON'T GIVE UP...
...UNTIL YOU ACHIEVE YOUR GOAL.
HA HA...
MEAN-WHILE, I'LL KEEP...
...PUZZLING AWAY IN THE AFTERLIFE.
FWOOF

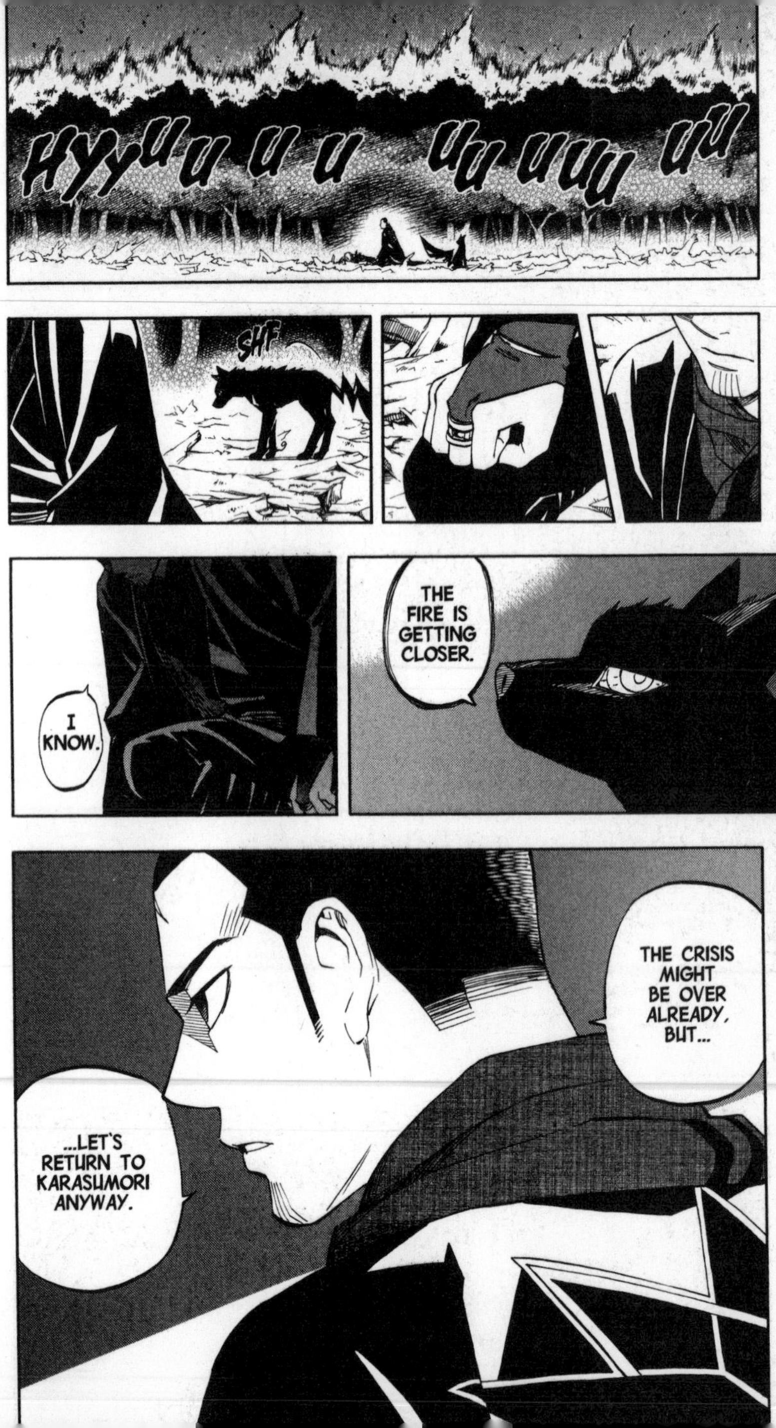
HYYUUUU UUUUUUUU
SHF
THE FIRE IS GETTING CLOSER.
I KNOW.
THE CRISIS MIGHT BE OVER ALREADY, BUT...
...LET'S RETURN TO KARASUMORI ANYWAY.

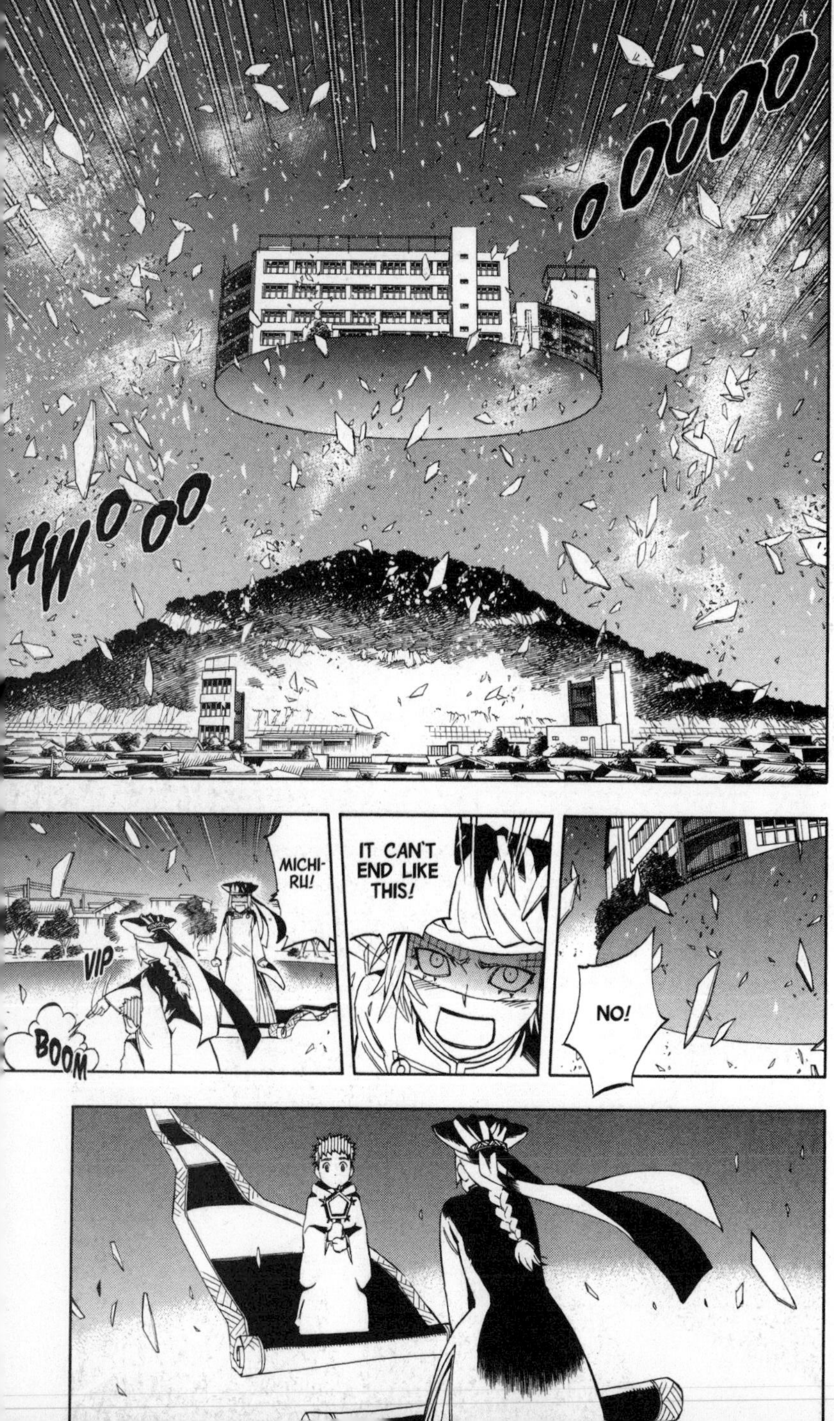
HWOOO
O OOOOO
NO!
IT CAN'T END LIKE THIS!
MICHI-RU!
VIP
BOOM

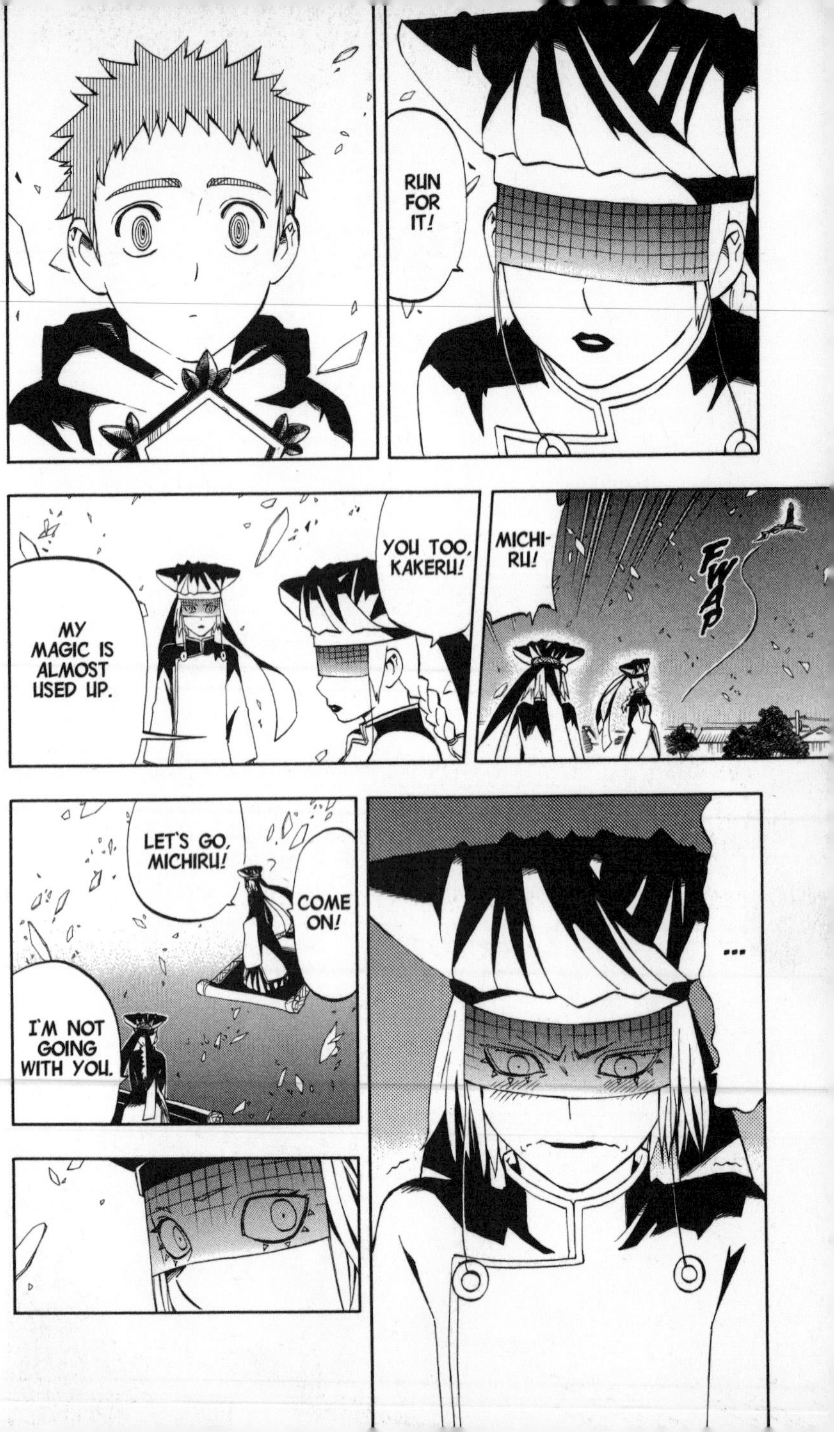
RUN FOR IT!
MICHIRU!
FWAP
YOU TOO, KAKERU!
MY MAGIC IS ALMOST USED UP.
...
LET'S GO, MICHIRU!
COME ON!
I'M NOT GOING WITH YOU.

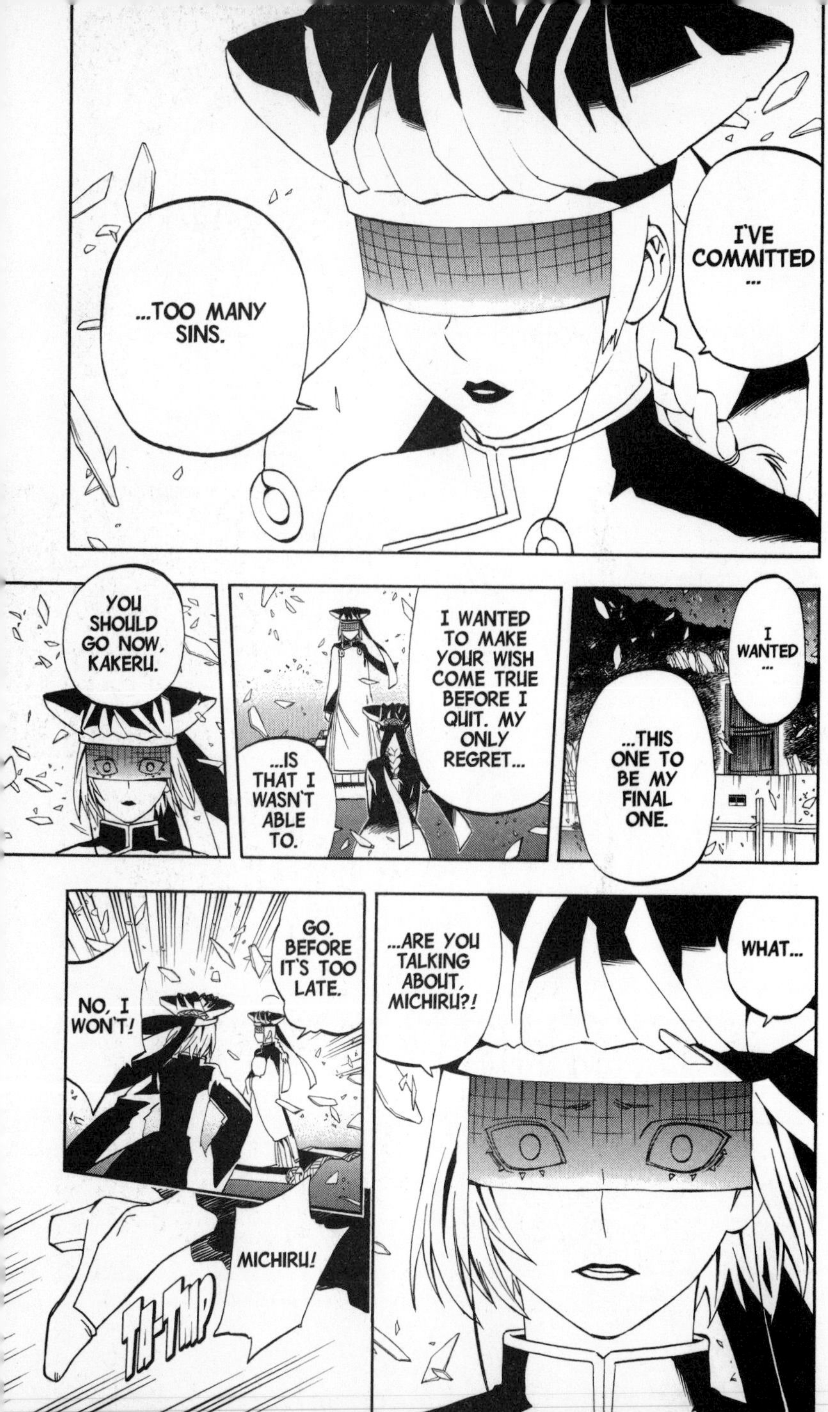
I'VE COMMITTED...
...TOO MANY SINS.
I WANTED...
...THIS ONE TO BE MY FINAL ONE.
I WANTED TO MAKE YOUR WISH COME TRUE BEFORE I QUIT. MY ONLY REGRET...
...IS THAT I WASN'T ABLE TO.
YOU SHOULD GO NOW, KAKERU.
WHAT...
...ARE YOU TALKING ABOUT, MICHIRU?!
GO. BEFORE IT'S TOO LATE.
NO, I WON'T!
MICHIRU!
TA-TMP

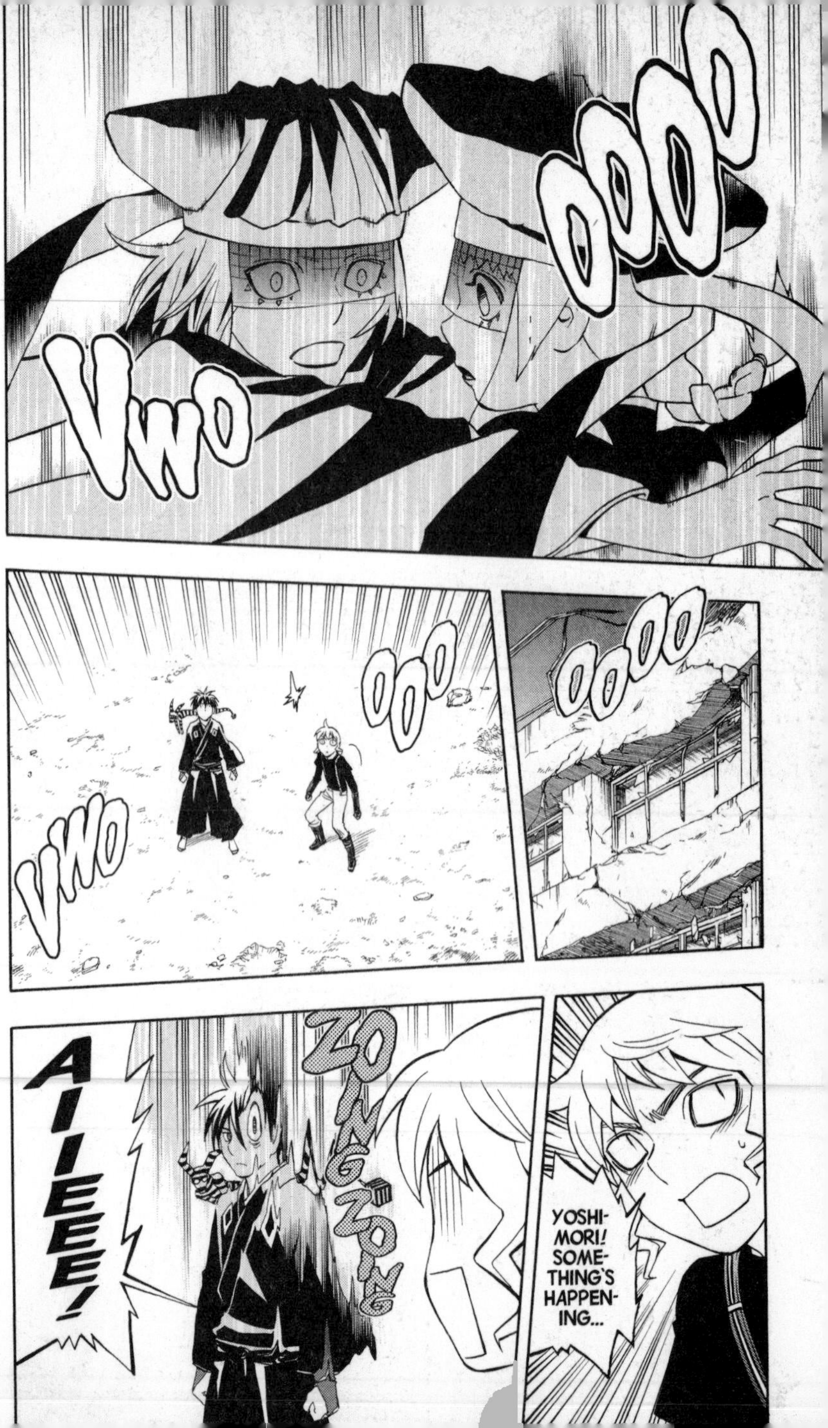
OOOOO
VWO
OOOOO
OOO
VWO
YOSHI-MORI! SOME-THING'S HAPPEN-ING...
ZOING ZOING
AIIEEE!

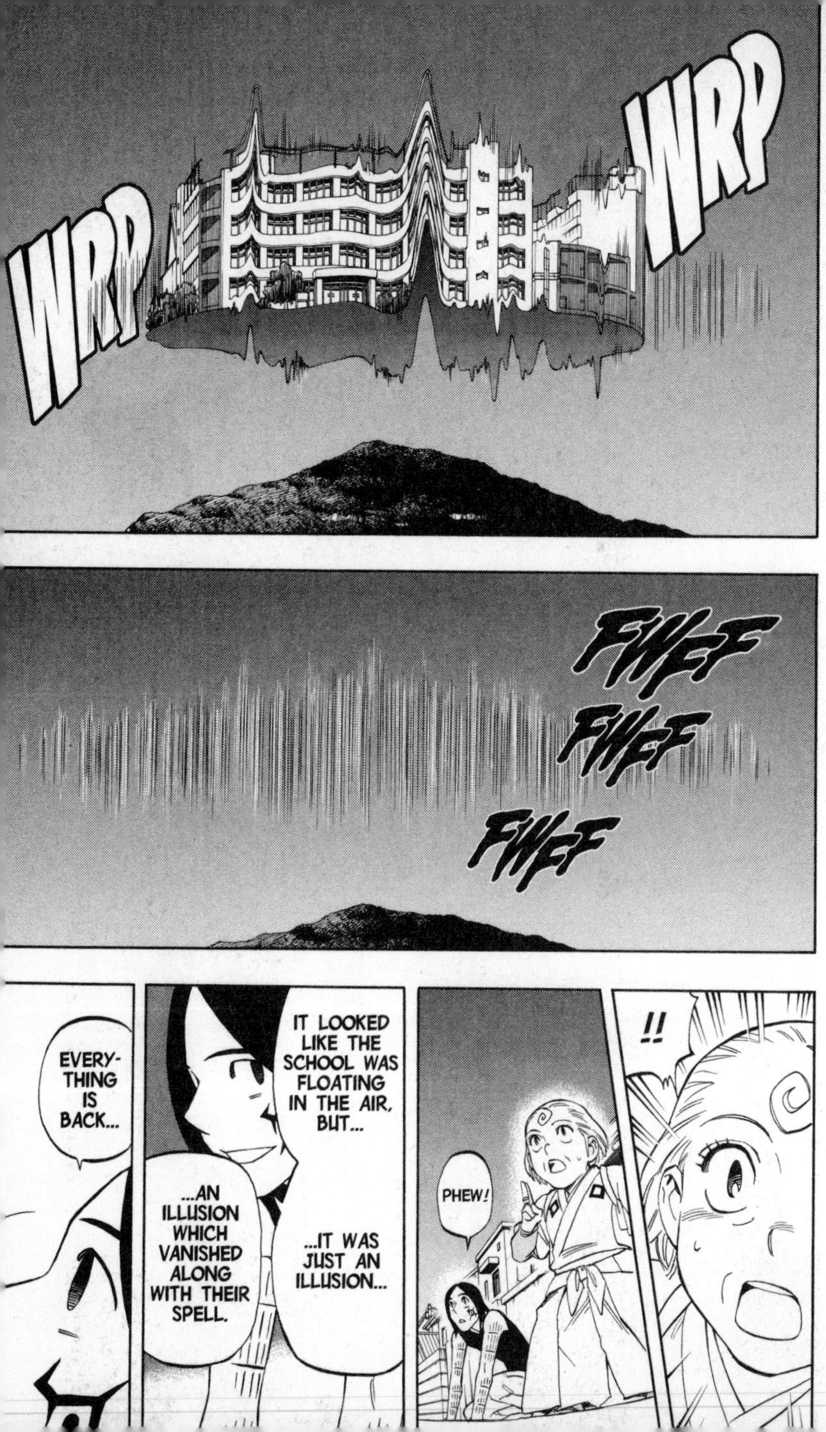
WRP
WRP
FWFF
FWFF
FWFF
!!
PHEW!
IT LOOKED LIKE THE SCHOOL WAS FLOATING IN THE AIR, BUT...
...IT WAS JUST AN ILLUSION...
...AN ILLUSION WHICH VANISHED ALONG WITH THEIR SPELL.
EVERY-THING IS BACK...

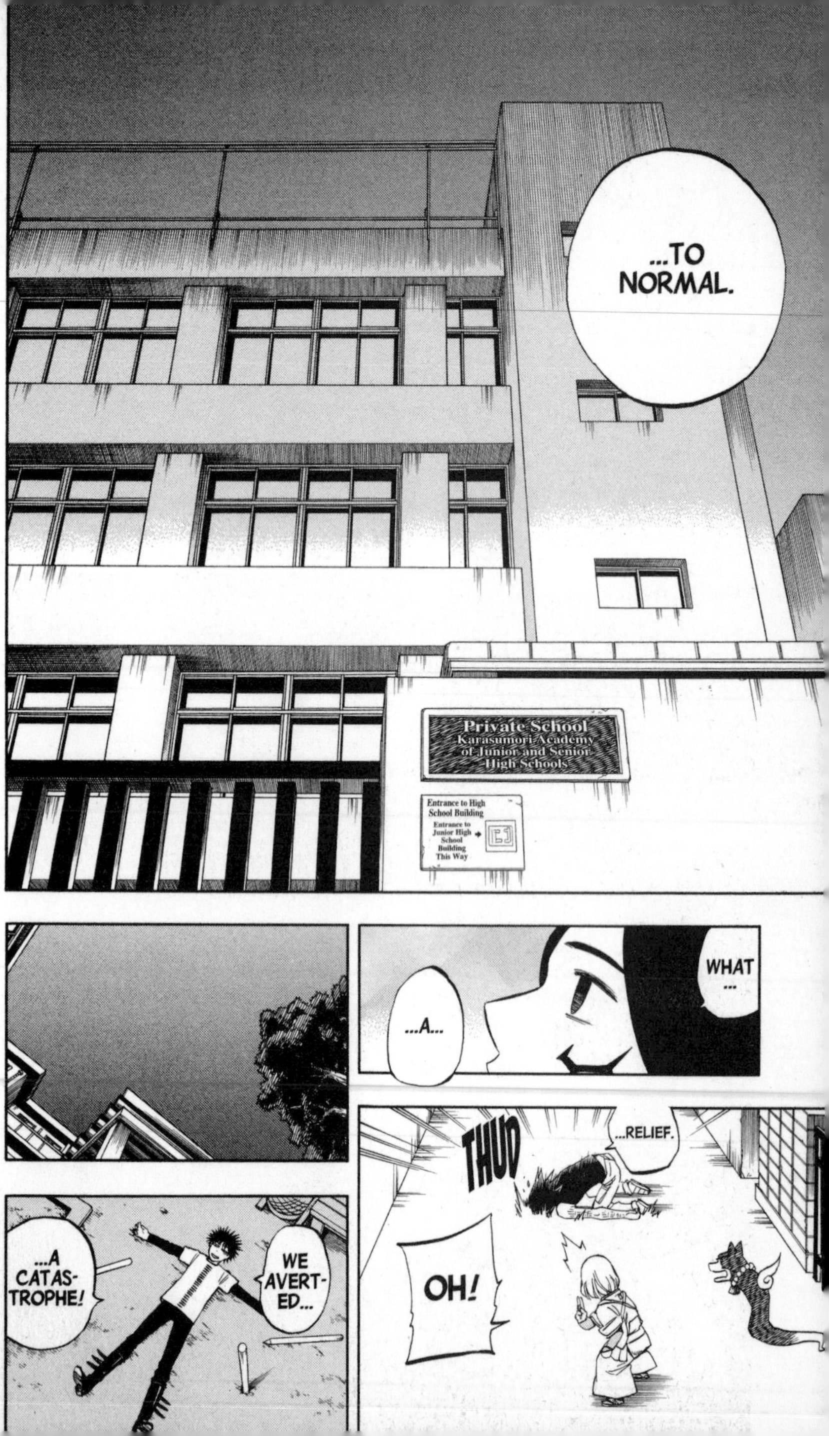
...TO NORMAL.
Private School Karasumori Academy of Junior and Senior High Schools
Entrance to High School Building
Entrance to Junior High School Building This Way
WHAT ...
...A...
...RELIEF.
THUD
OH!
WE AVERT-ED...
...A CATAS-TROPHE!

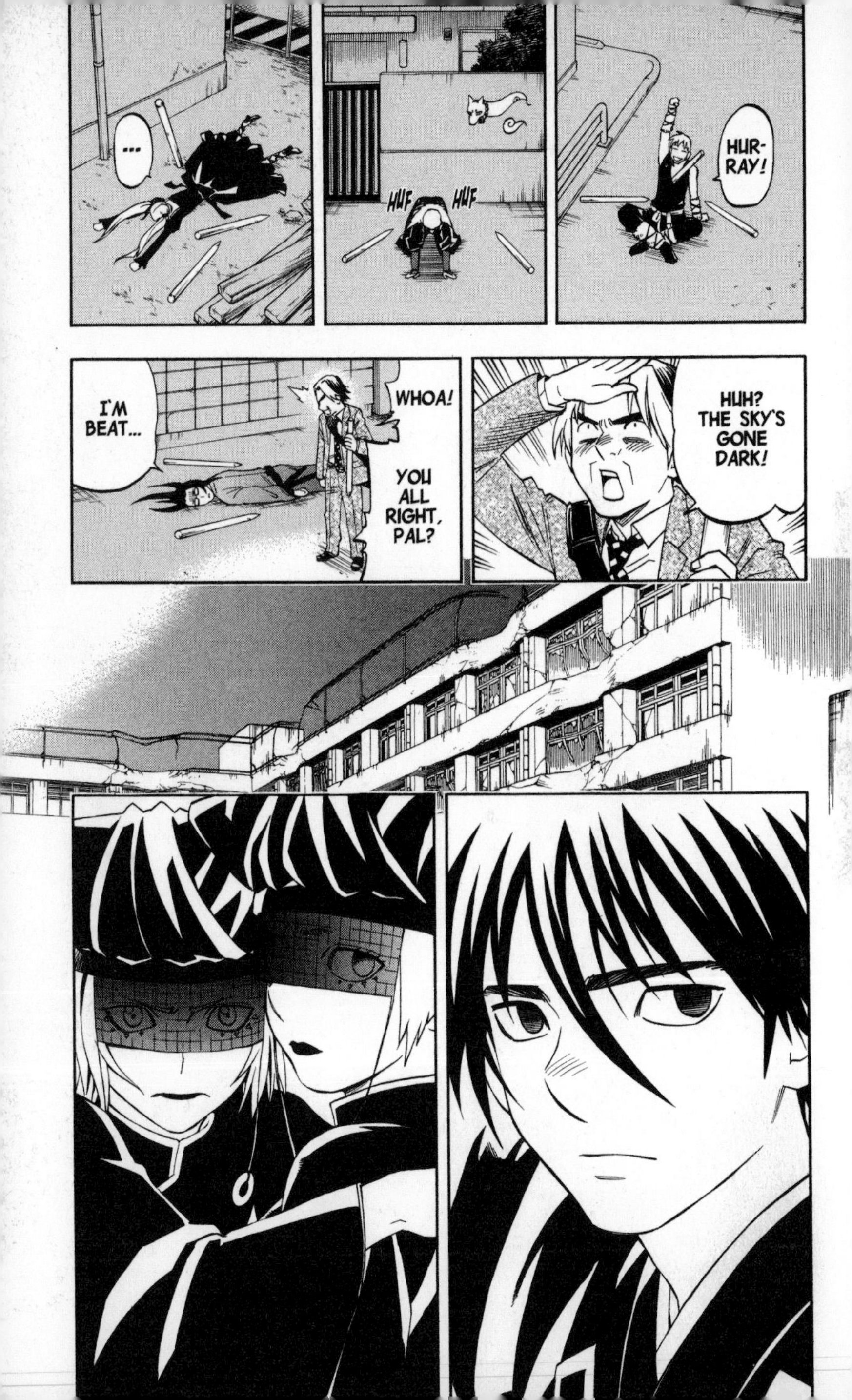
HUR-RAY!
HUF HUF
...
HUH? THE SKY'S GONE DARK!
WHOA!
YOU ALL RIGHT, PAL?
I'M BEAT...

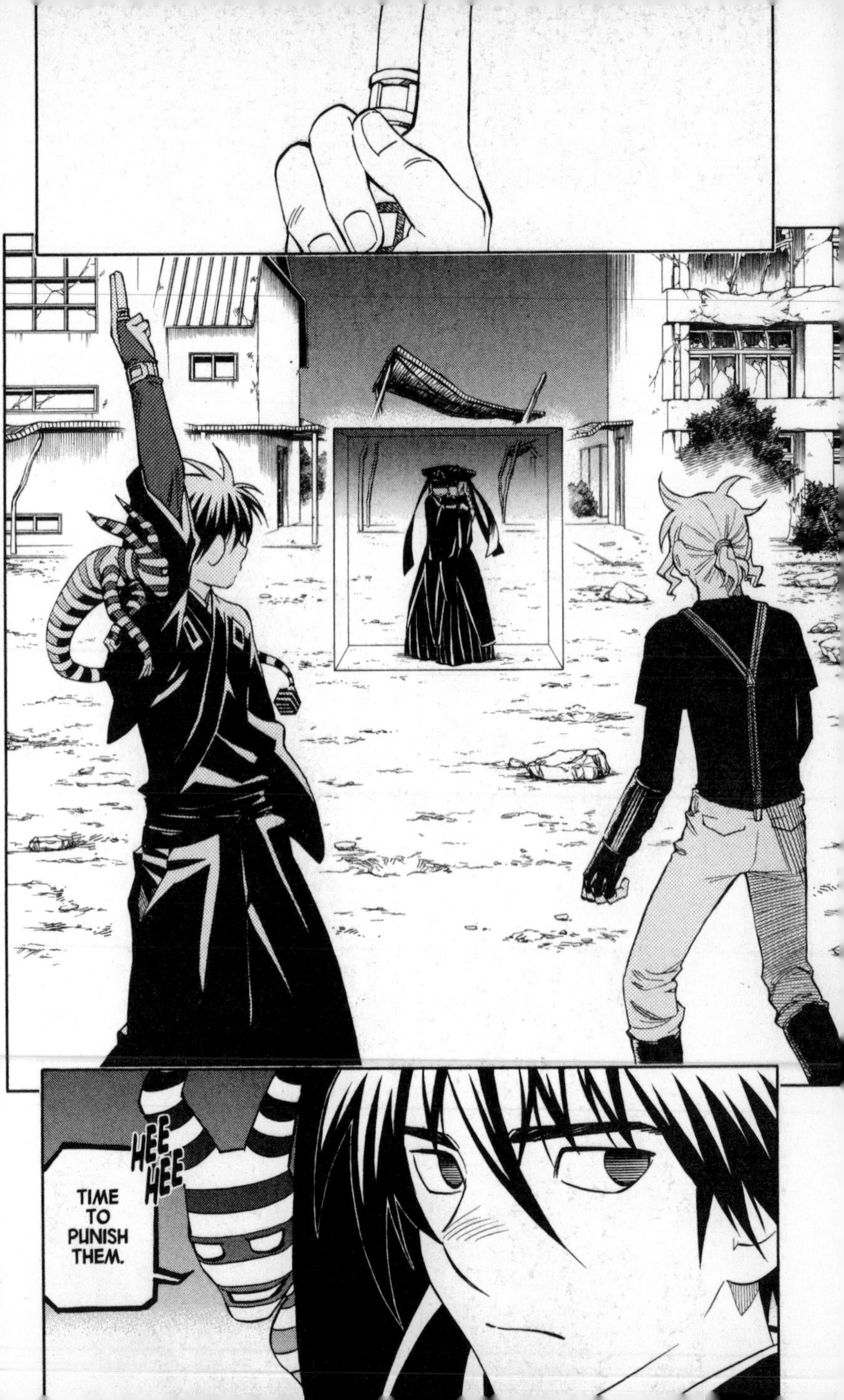
HEE HEE
TIME TO PUNISH THEM.

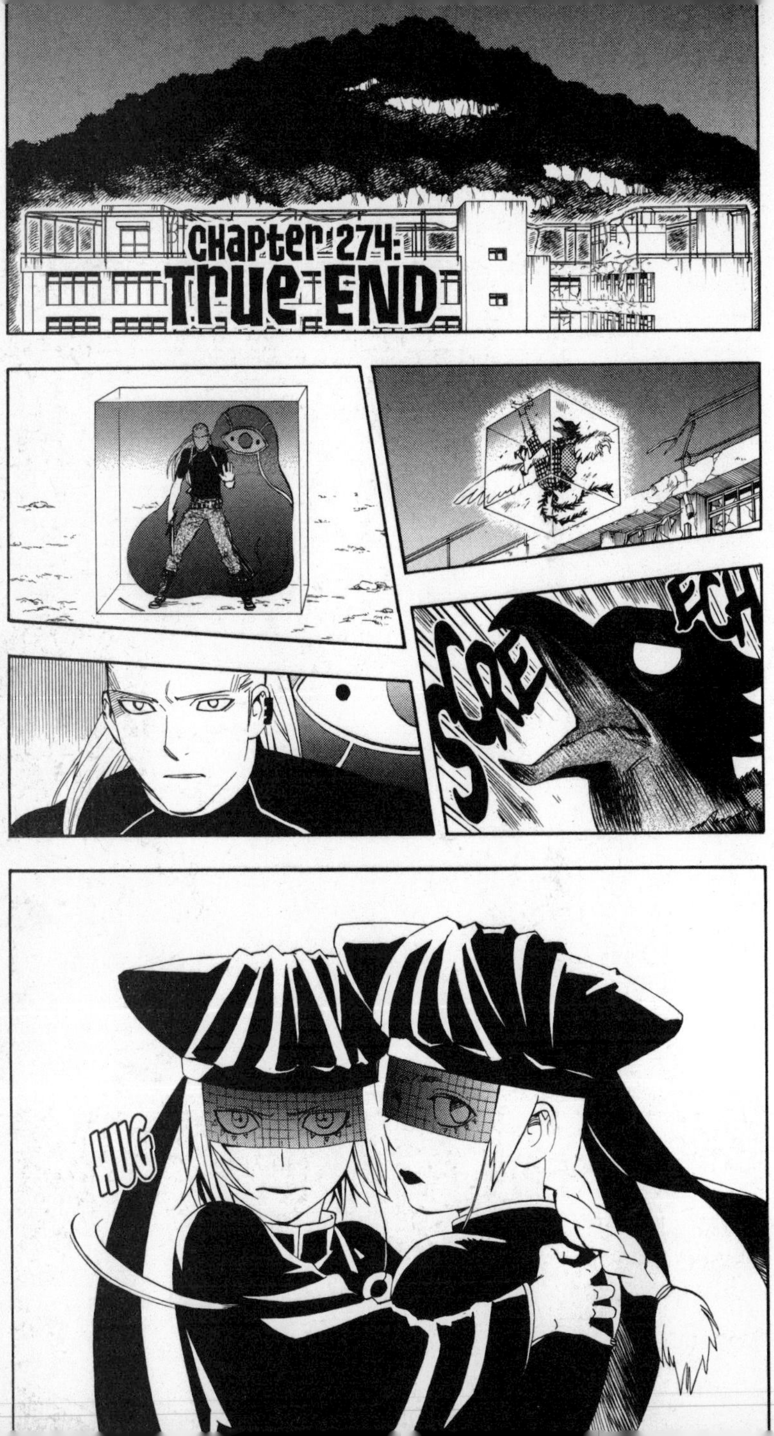
Chapter 274:
True End
SCRE
ECH
HUG

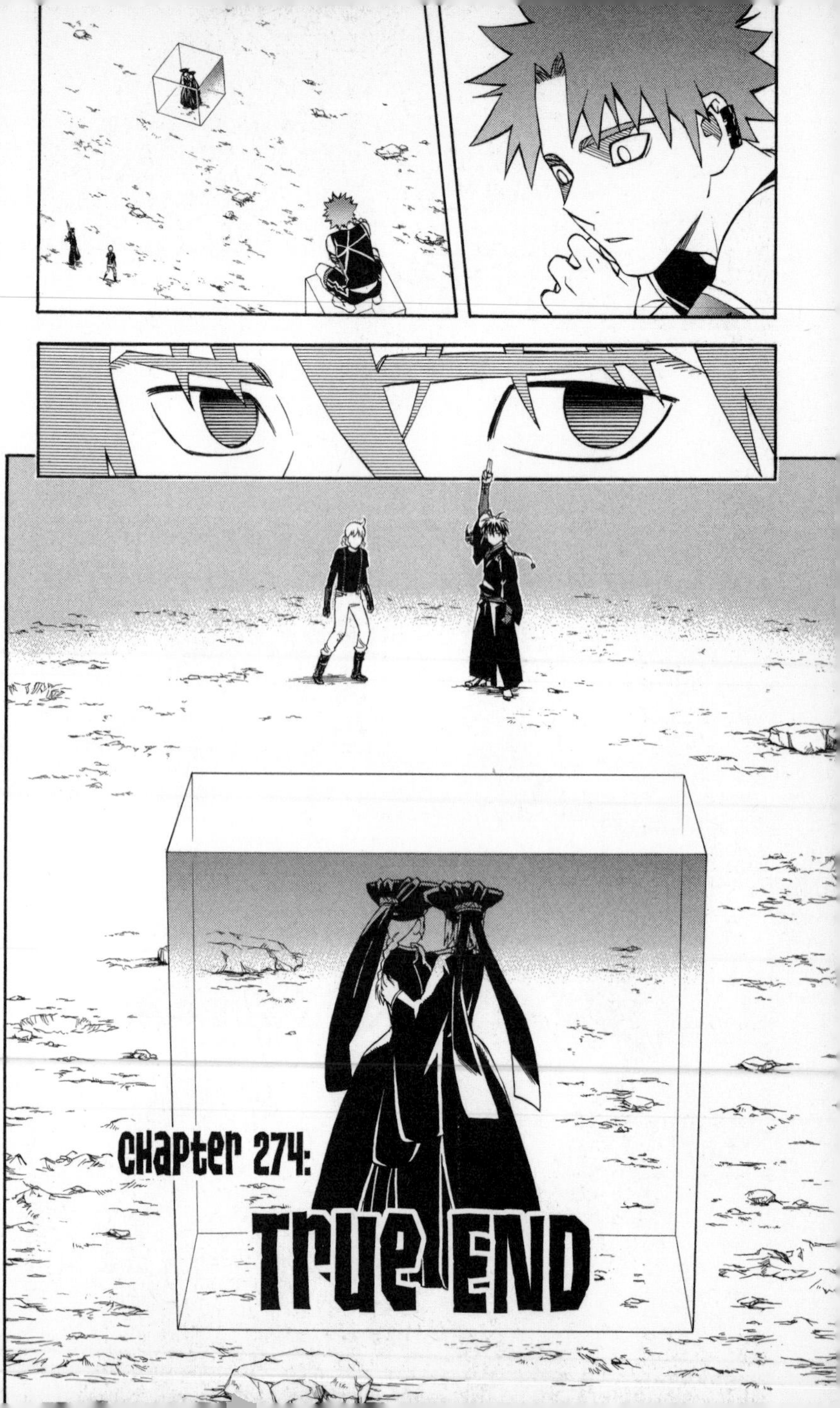
Chapter 274:
True End

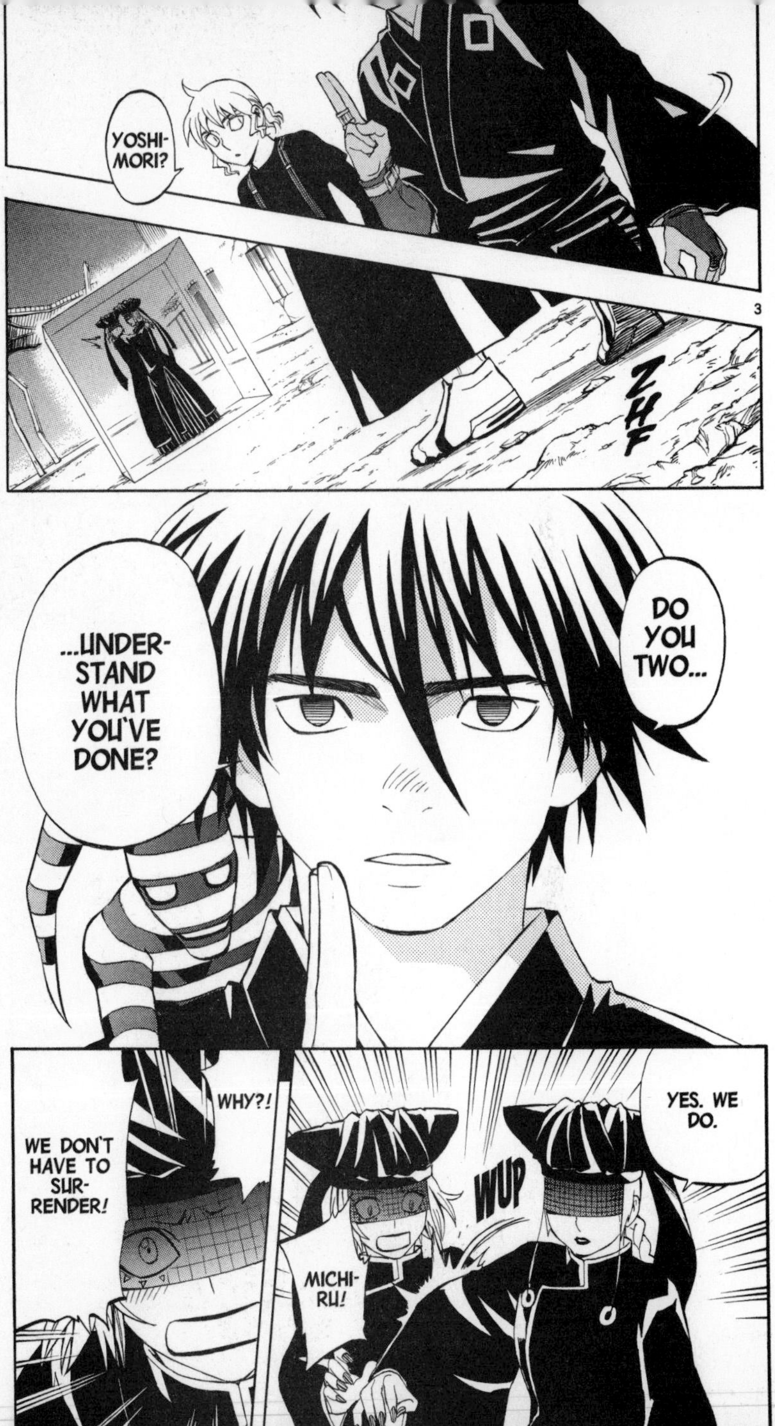
YOSHI-MORI?
ZHF
DO YOU TWO...
...UNDER-STAND WHAT YOU'VE DONE?
YES. WE DO.
WUP
WHY?!
MICHI-RU!
WE DON'T HAVE TO SUR-RENDER!

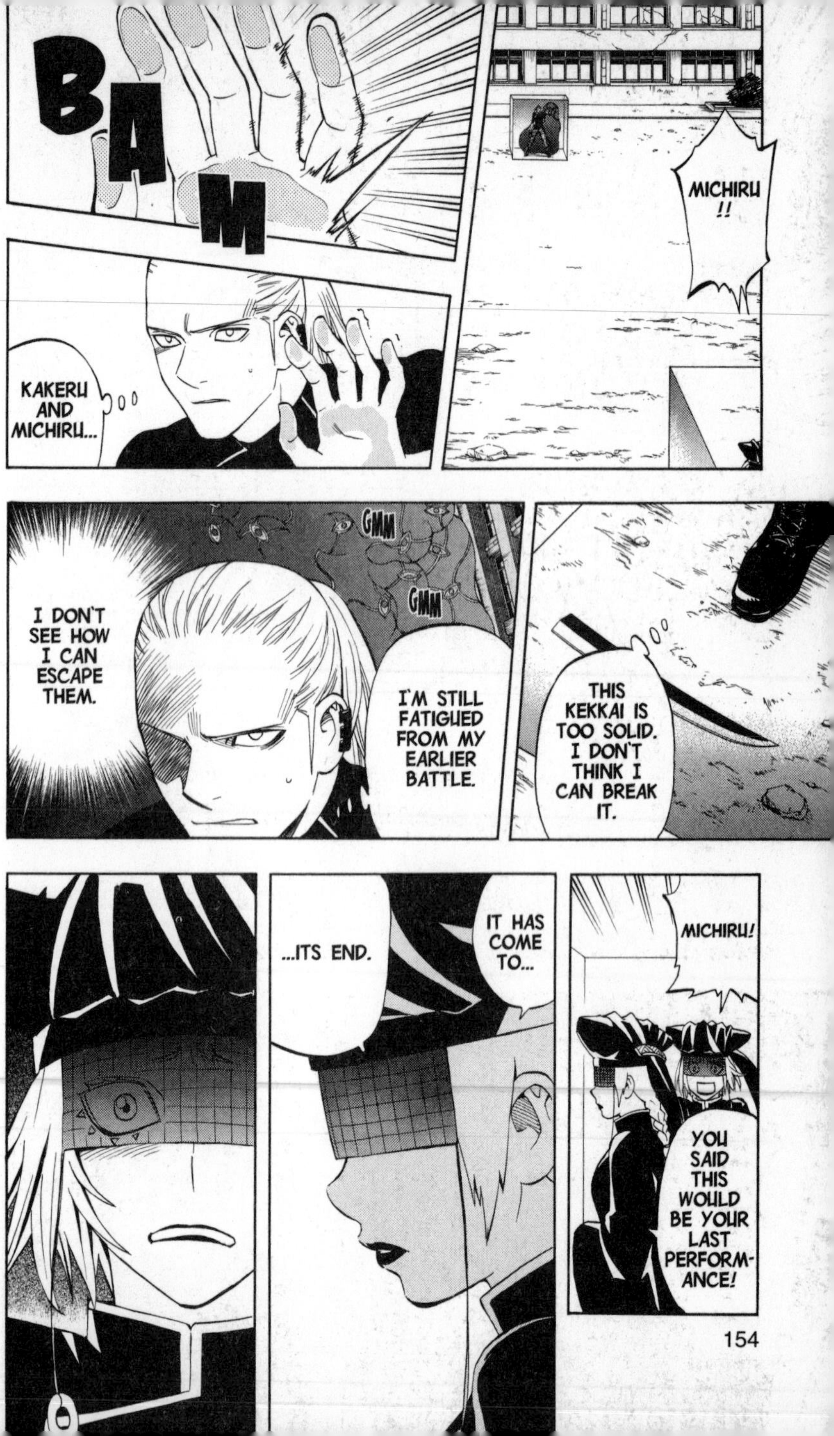
MICHIRU !!
BAM
KAKERU AND MICHIRU...
THIS KEKKAI IS TOO SOLID. I DON'T THINK I CAN BREAK IT.
GMM
GMM
I'M STILL FATIGUED FROM MY EARLIER BATTLE.
I DON'T SEE HOW I CAN ESCAPE THEM.
MICHIRU!
YOU SAID THIS WOULD BE YOUR LAST PERFORM-ANCE!
IT HAS COME TO...
...ITS END.

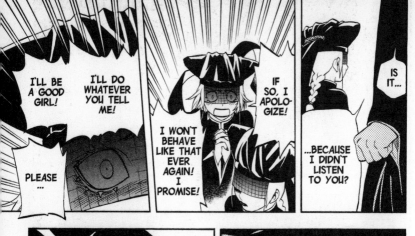

IS IT...
...BECAUSE I DIDN'T LISTEN TO YOU?
IF SO, I APOLOGIZE!
I WON'T BEHAVE LIKE THAT EVER AGAIN! I PROMISE!
I'LL DO WHATEVER YOU TELL ME!
I'LL BE A GOOD GIRL!
PLEASE...
MICHIRU!
WAAAAAAA!!
NO!
SOB
NOOOO!
SOB
PLIP
PLIP
SOB
SOB
SOB
PLIP

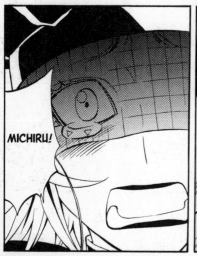

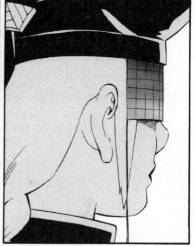

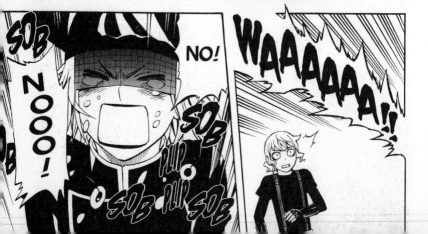

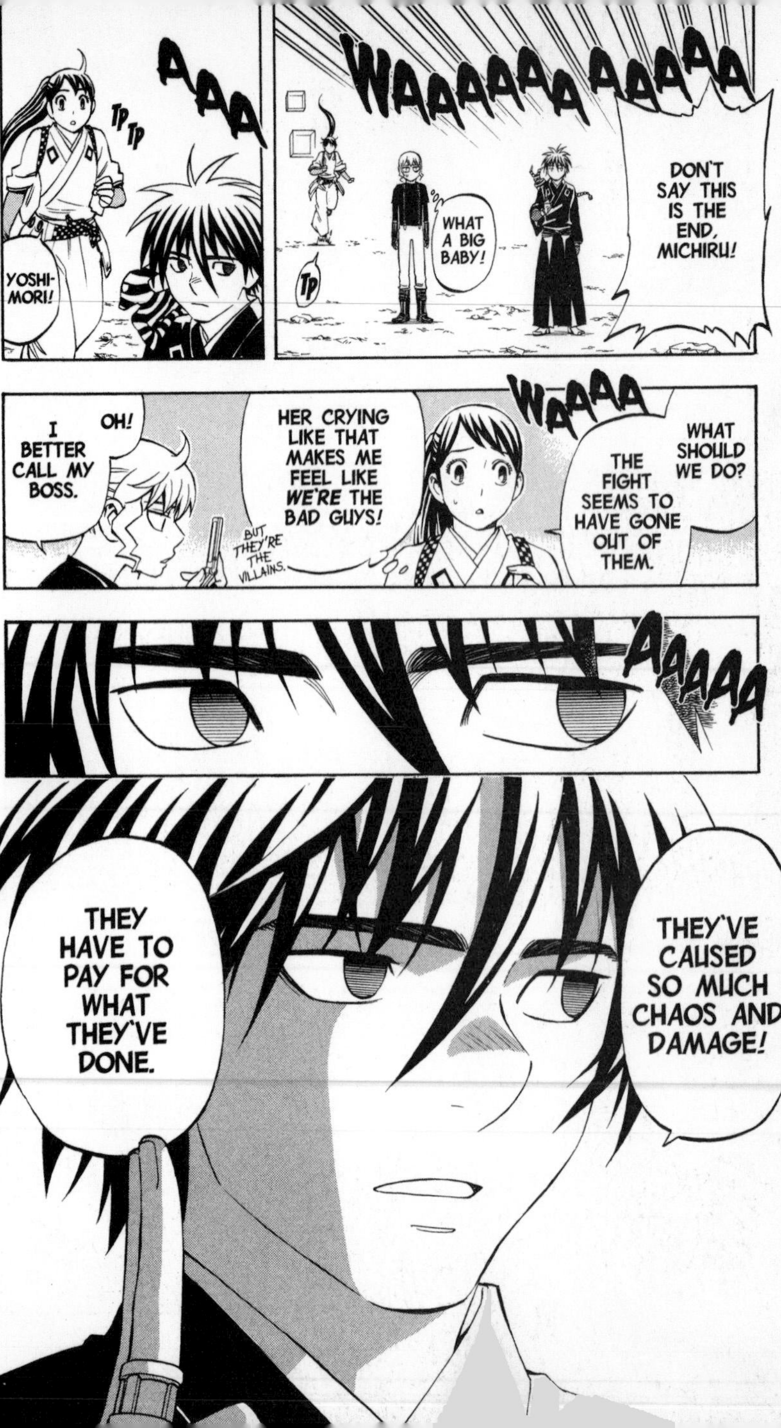
WAAAAAAA AAAAA
DON'T SAY THIS IS THE END, MICHIRU!
WHAT A BIG BABY!
TP
AAA
TP TP
YOSHI-MORI!
WAAAA
WHAT SHOULD WE DO?
THE FIGHT SEEMS TO HAVE GONE OUT OF THEM.
HER CRYING LIKE THAT MAKES ME FEEL LIKE *WE'RE* THE BAD GUYS!
BUT THEY'RE THE VILLAINS.
OH!
I BETTER CALL MY BOSS.
AAAAA
THEY'VE CAUSED SO MUCH CHAOS AND DAMAGE!
THEY HAVE TO PAY FOR WHAT THEY'VE DONE.

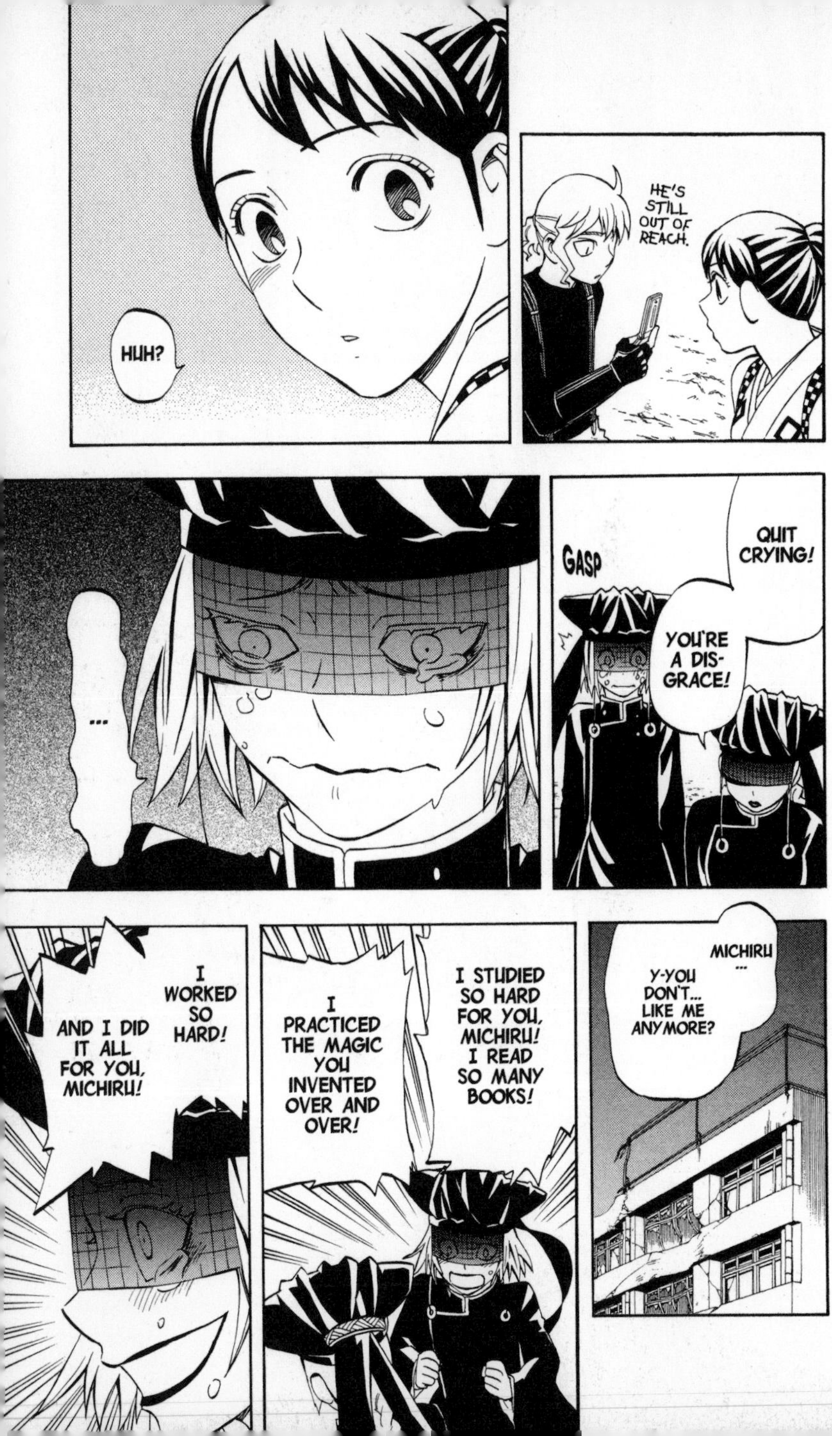

HE'S STILL OUT OF REACH.
HUH?
QUIT CRYING!
YOU'RE A DIS-GRACE!
GASP
...
MICHIRU ...
Y-YOU DON'T... LIKE ME ANYMORE?
I STUDIED SO HARD FOR YOU, MICHIRU! I READ SO MANY BOOKS!
I PRACTICED THE MAGIC YOU INVENTED OVER AND OVER!
I WORKED SO HARD!
AND I DID IT ALL FOR YOU, MICHIRU!

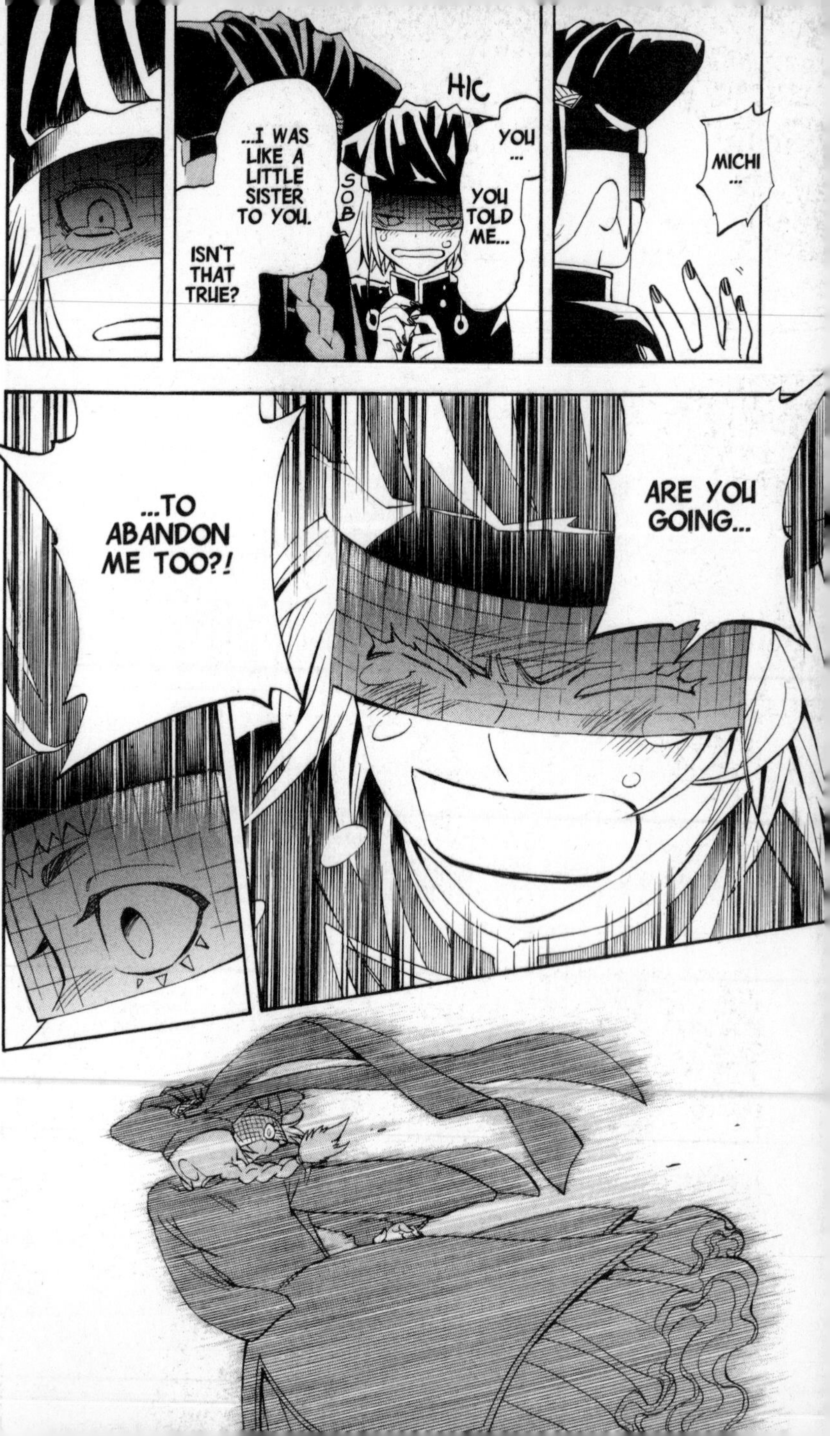
MICHI...
HIC
YOU... YOU TOLD ME...
SOB
...I WAS LIKE A LITTLE SISTER TO YOU.
ISN'T THAT TRUE?
ARE YOU GOING...
...TO ABANDON ME TOO?!

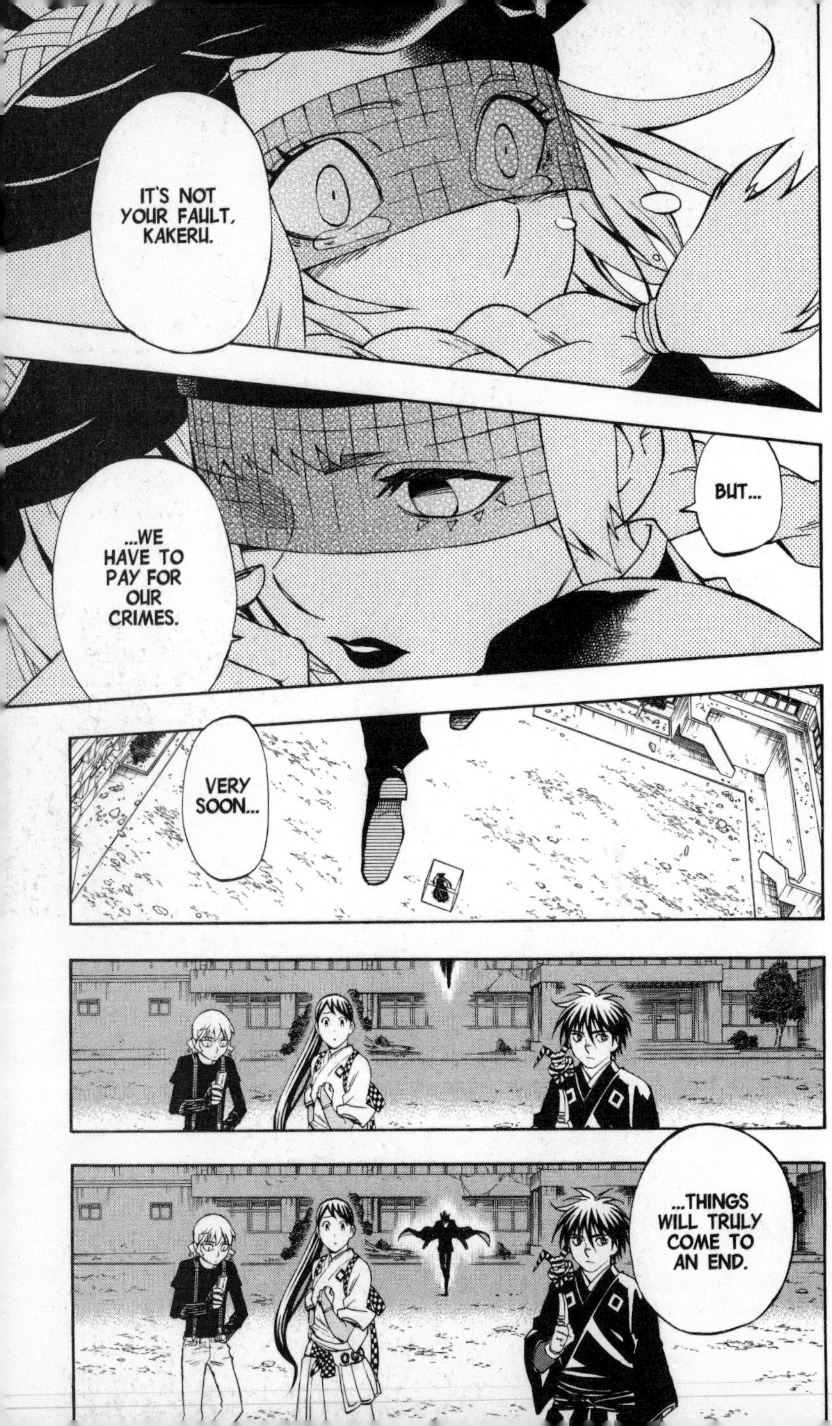
IT'S NOT YOUR FAULT, KAKERU.
BUT...
...WE HAVE TO PAY FOR OUR CRIMES.
VERY SOON...
...THINGS WILL TRULY COME TO AN END.

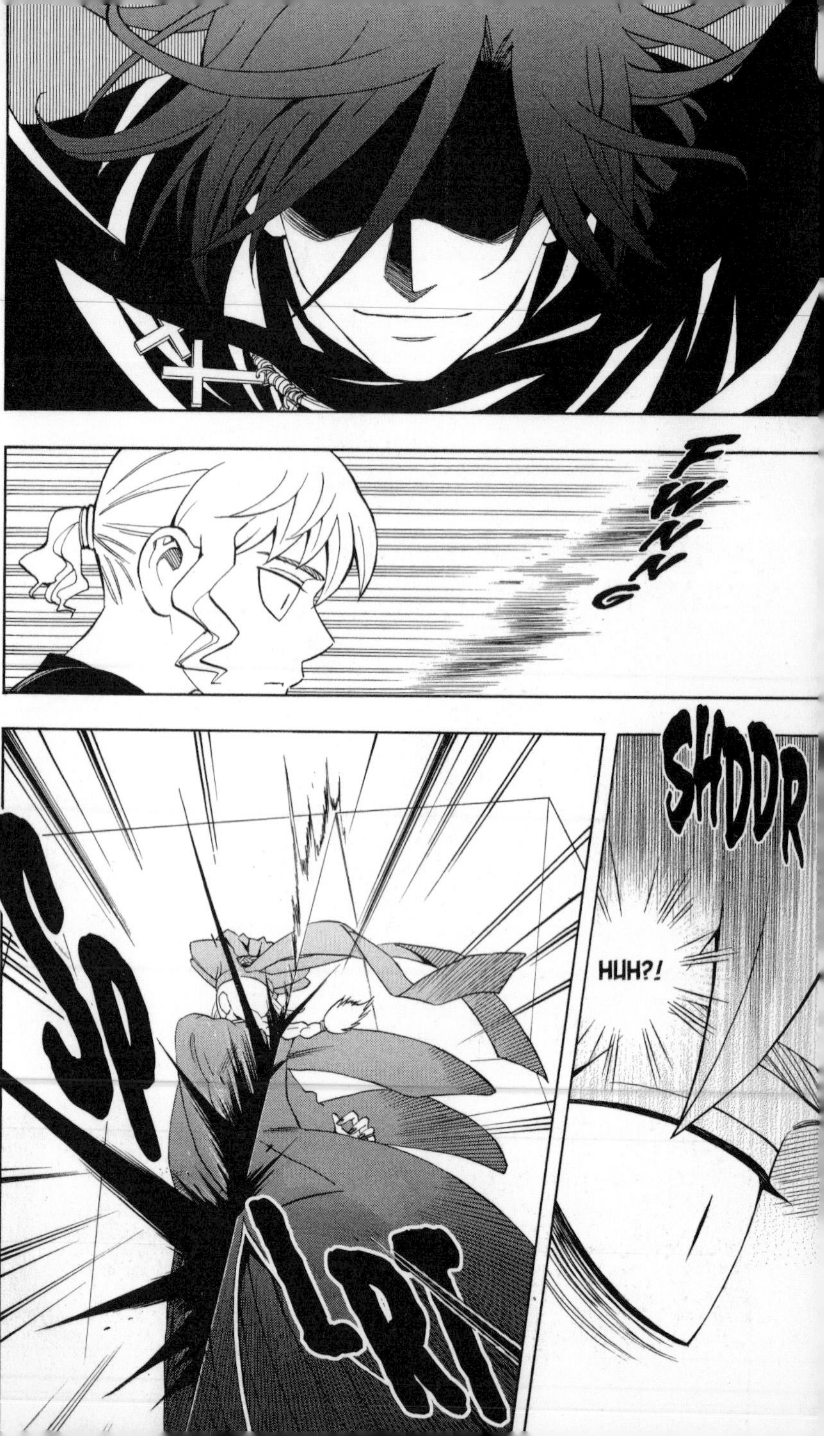
FWNNG
SHDDR
HUH?!
SPLRT

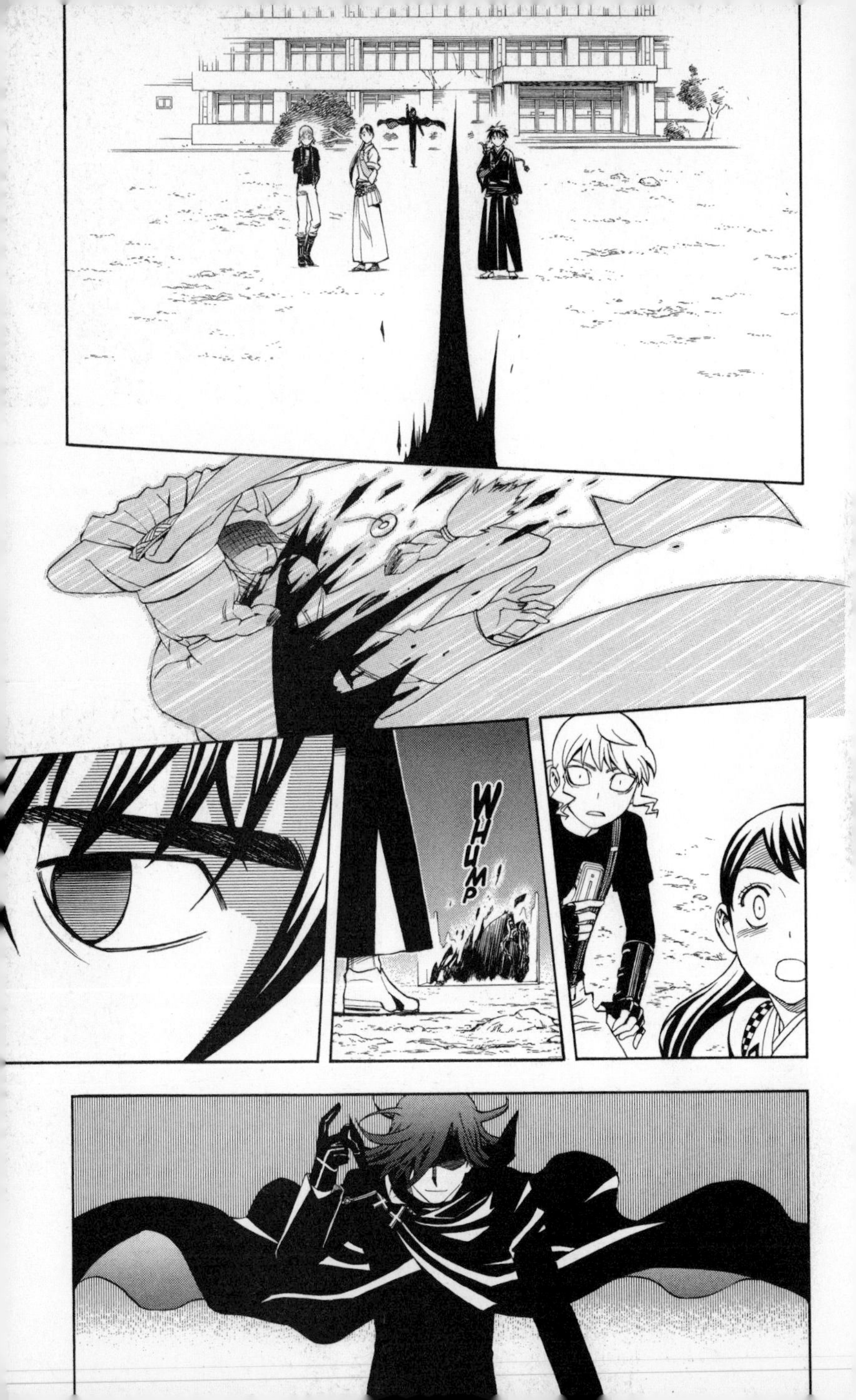
WHUMP

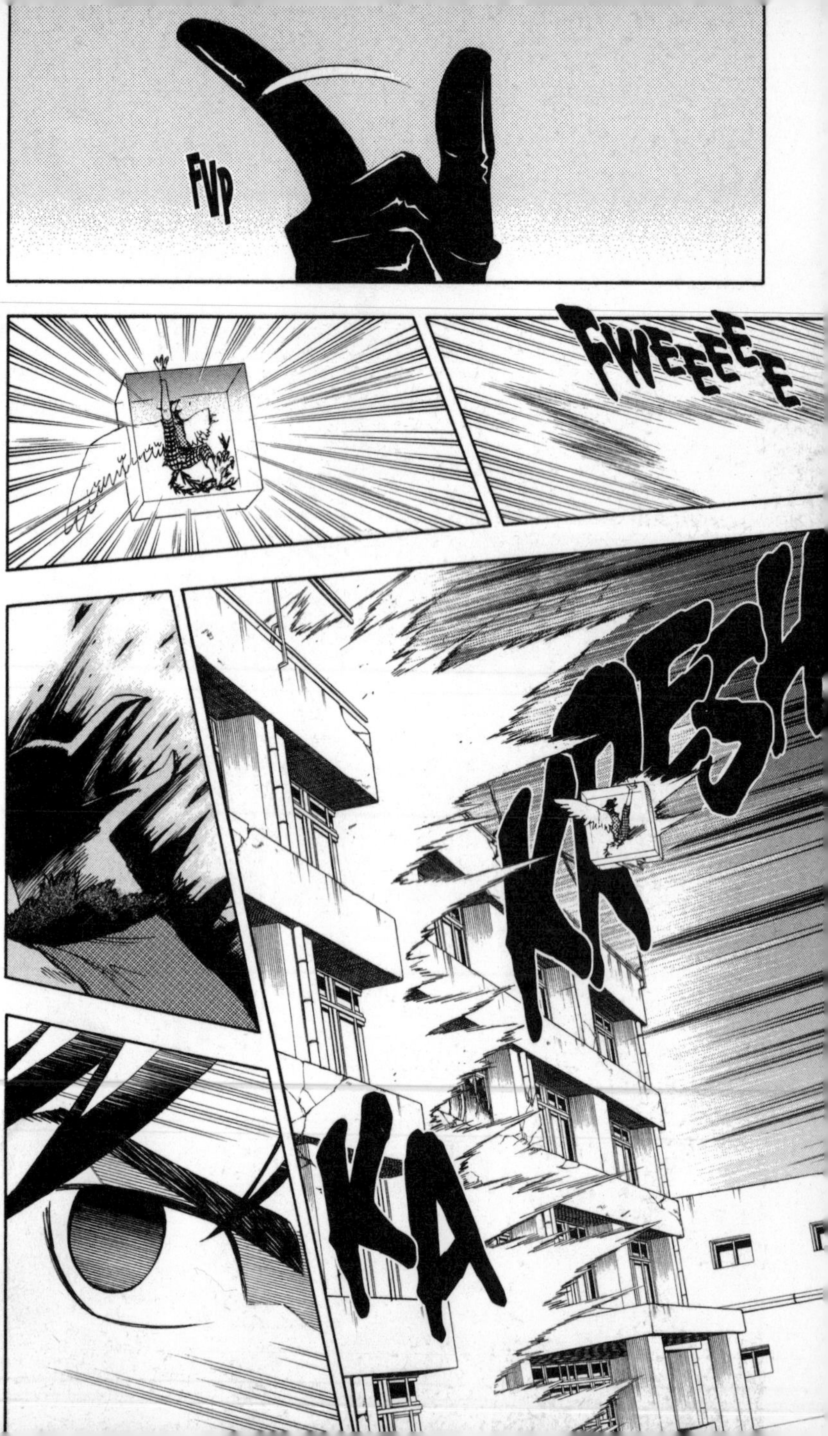
FVP
FWEEEEEEE
KRESH
KA

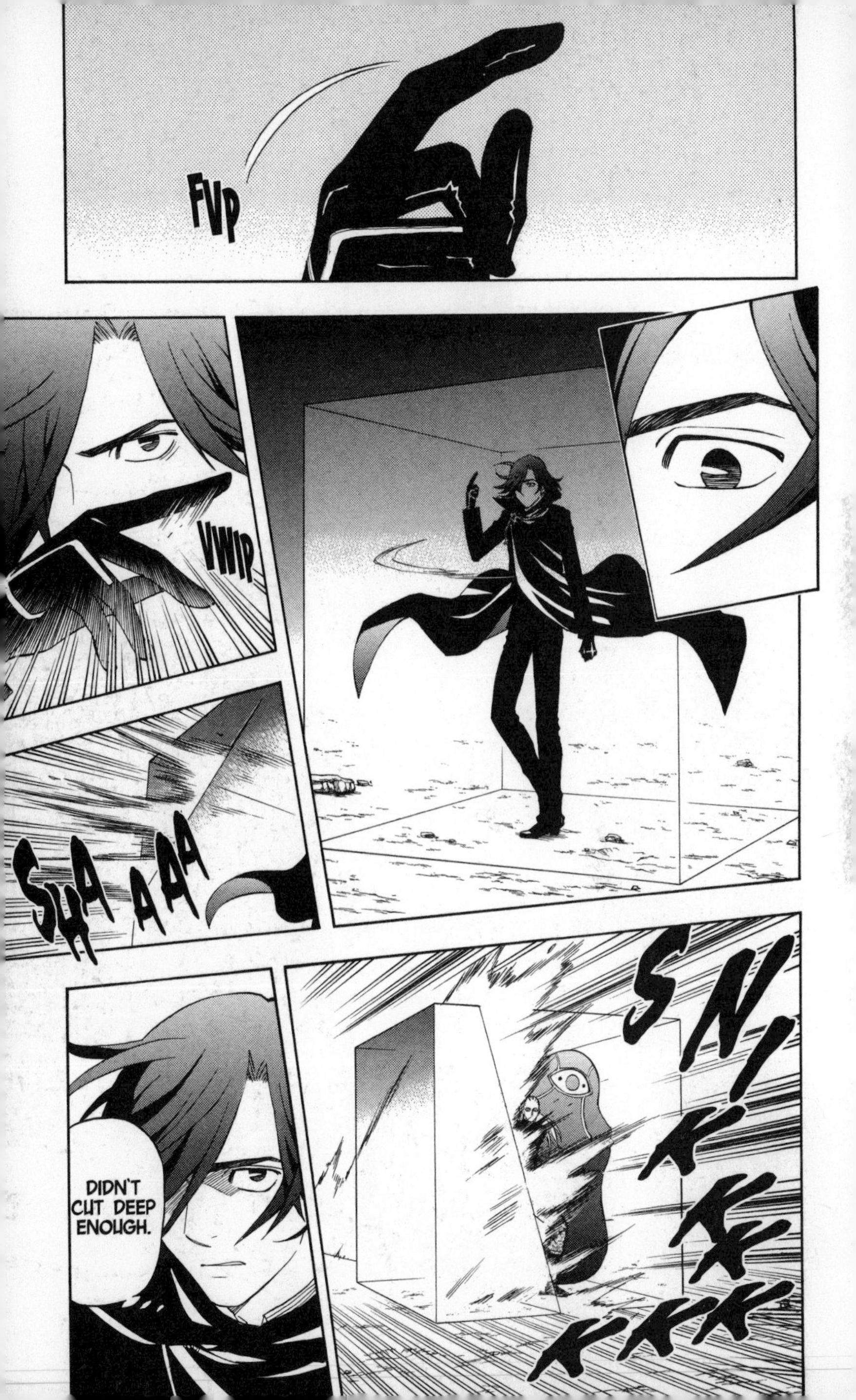
FVP
VWIP
SHAAAA
SNIKKKKK
DIDN'T CUT DEEP ENOUGH.

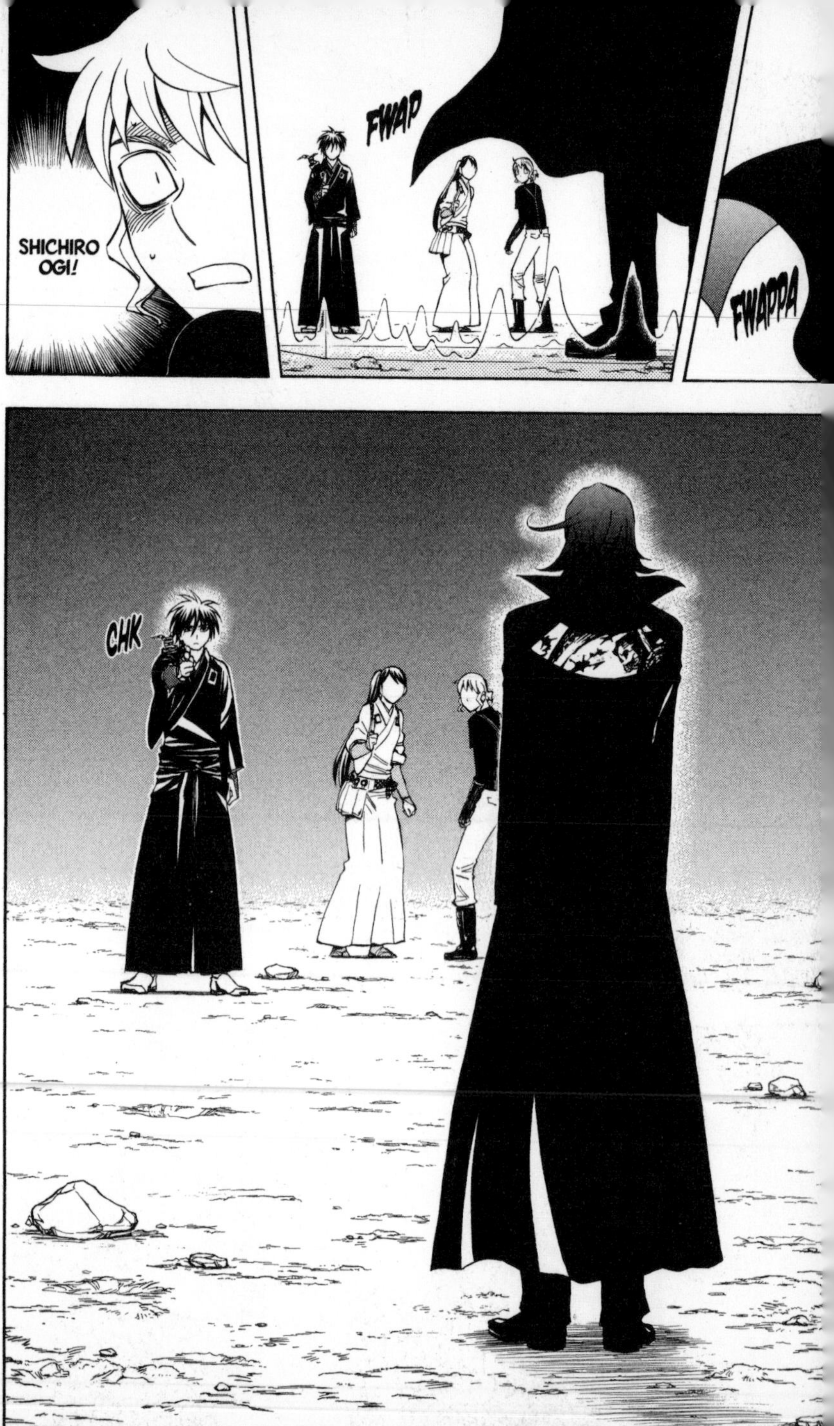
FWAPPA
FWAP
SHICHIRO OGI!
CHK

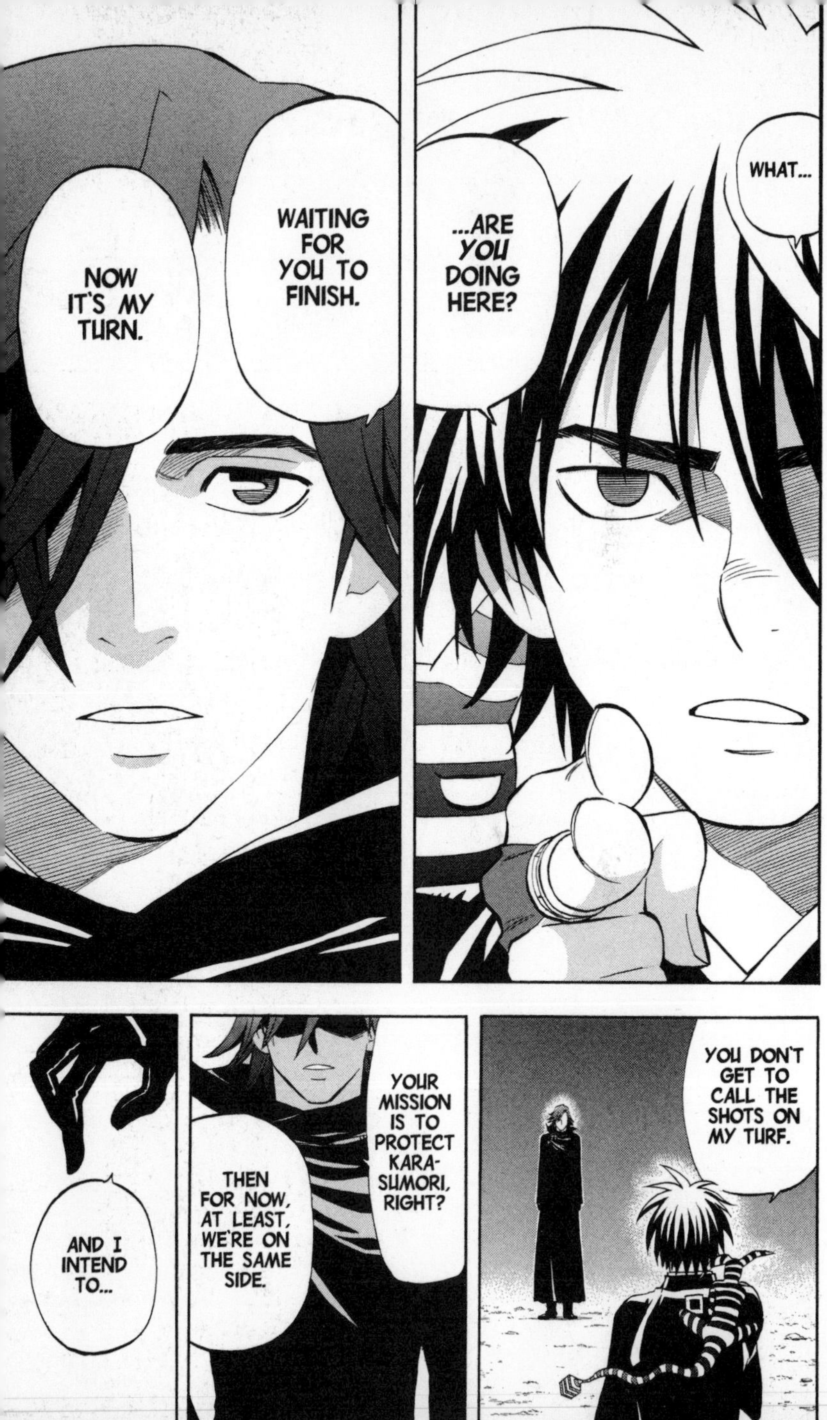
WHAT...
...ARE *YOU* DOING HERE?
WAITING FOR YOU TO FINISH.
NOW IT'S MY TURN.
YOU DON'T GET TO CALL THE SHOTS ON MY TURF.
YOUR MISSION IS TO PROTECT KARA-SUMORI, RIGHT?
THEN FOR NOW, AT LEAST, WE'RE ON THE SAME SIDE.
AND I INTEND TO...

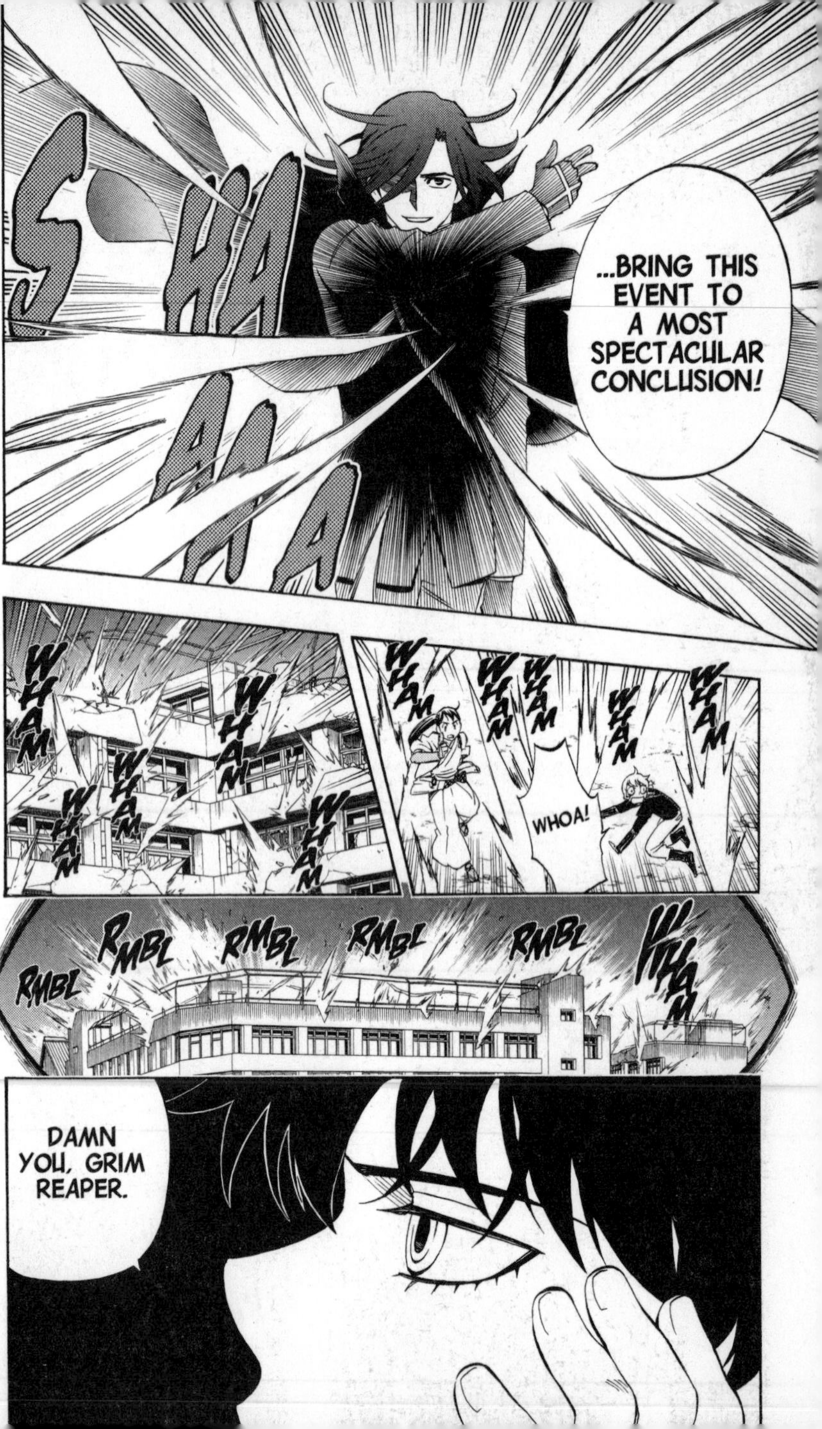
SHAAAA
...BRING THIS EVENT TO A MOST SPECTACULAR CONCLUSION!
WHAM WHAM WHAM WHAM WHAM
WHOA!
WHAM WHAM WHAM WHAM WHAM WHAM
WHAM
RMBL RMBL RMBL RMBL RMBL
DAMN YOU, GRIM REAPER.

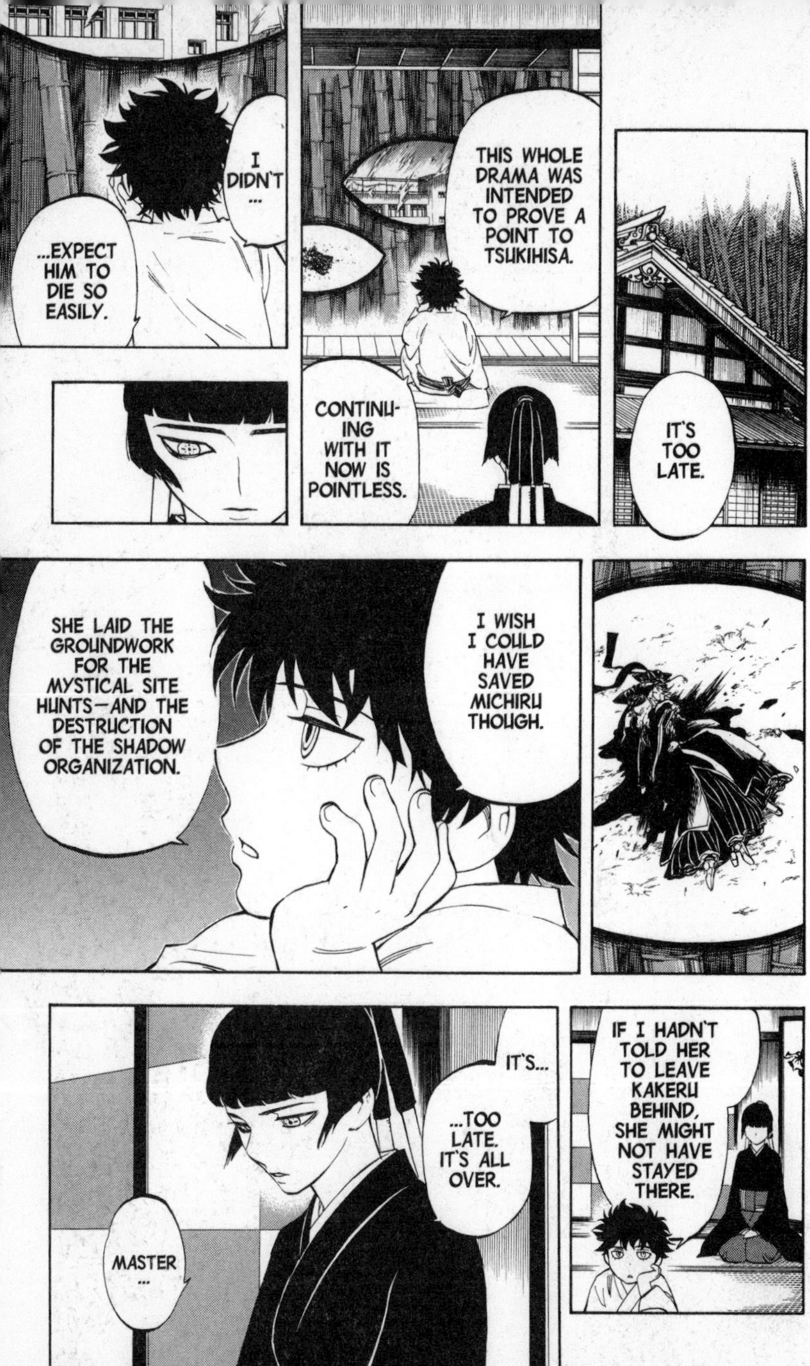
IT'S TOO LATE.
THIS WHOLE DRAMA WAS INTENDED TO PROVE A POINT TO TSUKIHISA.
CONTINUING WITH IT NOW IS POINTLESS.
I DIDN'T ...
...EXPECT HIM TO DIE SO EASILY.
I WISH I COULD HAVE SAVED MICHIRU THOUGH.
SHE LAID THE GROUNDWORK FOR THE MYSTICAL SITE HUNTS—AND THE DESTRUCTION OF THE SHADOW ORGANIZATION.
IF I HADN'T TOLD HER TO LEAVE KAKERU BEHIND, SHE MIGHT NOT HAVE STAYED THERE.
IT'S...
...TOO LATE. IT'S ALL OVER.
MASTER ...

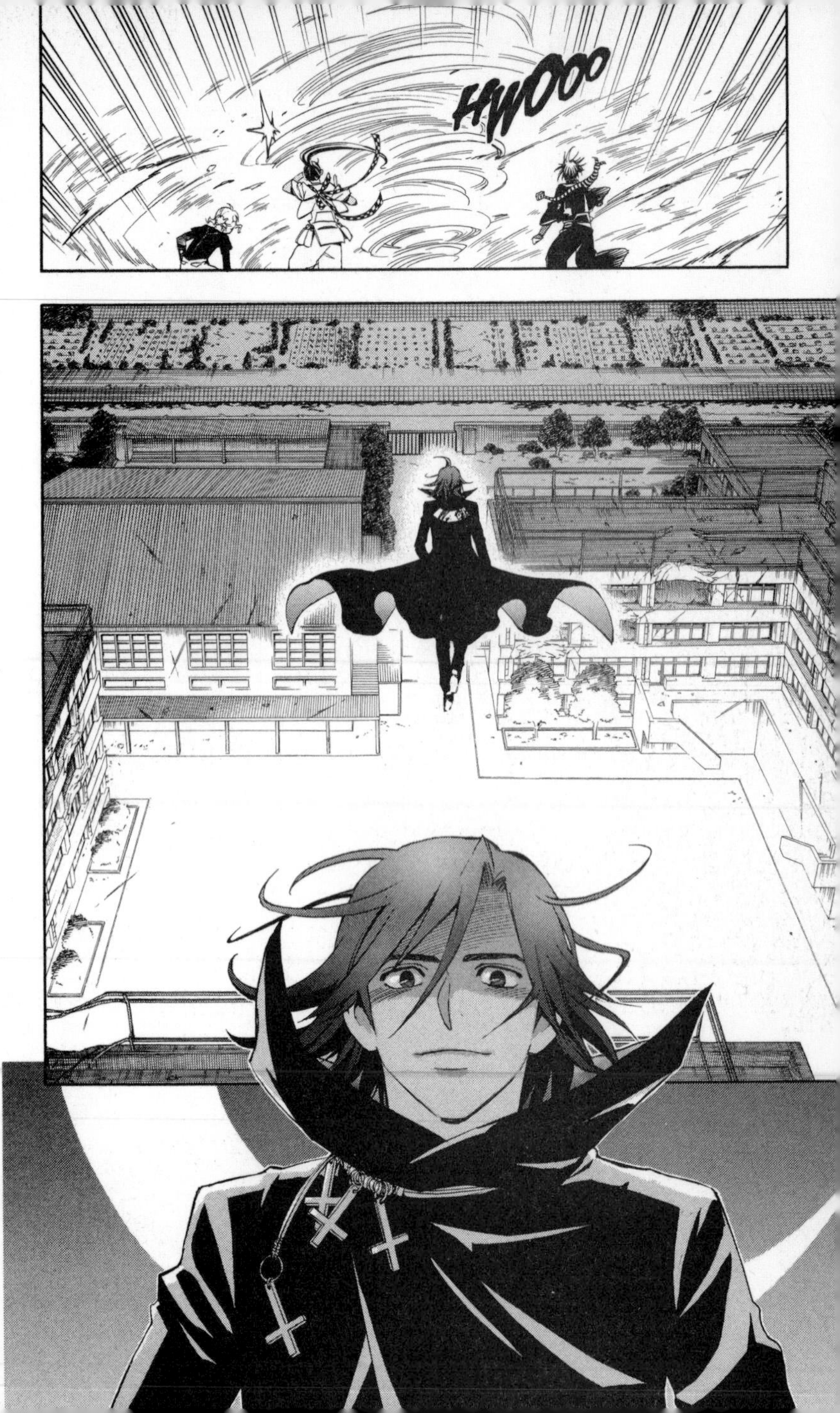
HWOOO

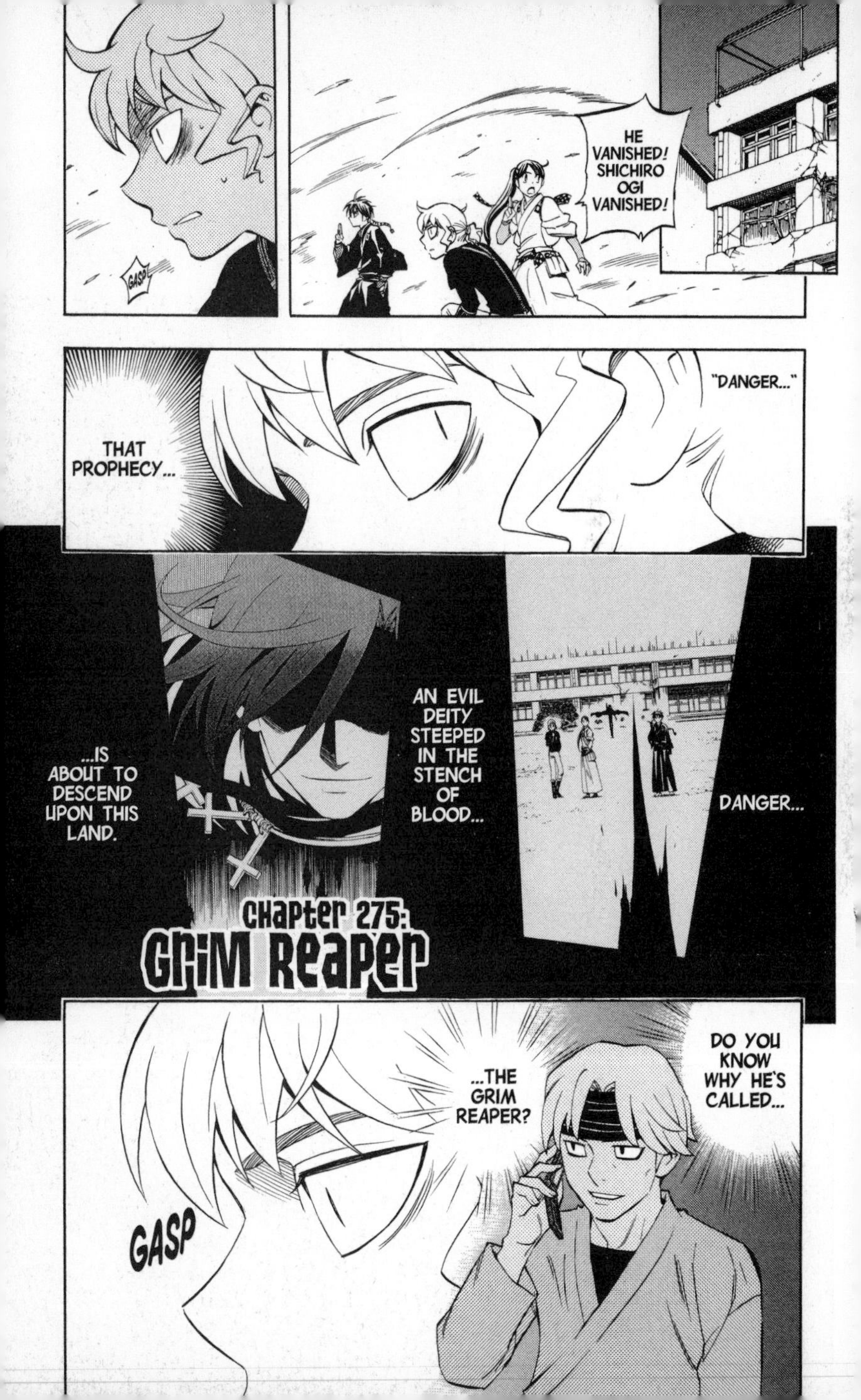
HE VANISHED! SHICHIRO OGI VANISHED!
GASP
"DANGER..."
THAT PROPHECY...
DANGER...
AN EVIL DEITY STEEPED IN THE STENCH OF BLOOD...
...IS ABOUT TO DESCEND UPON THIS LAND.
Chapter 275:
Grim Reaper
DO YOU KNOW WHY HE'S CALLED...
...THE GRIM REAPER?
GASP

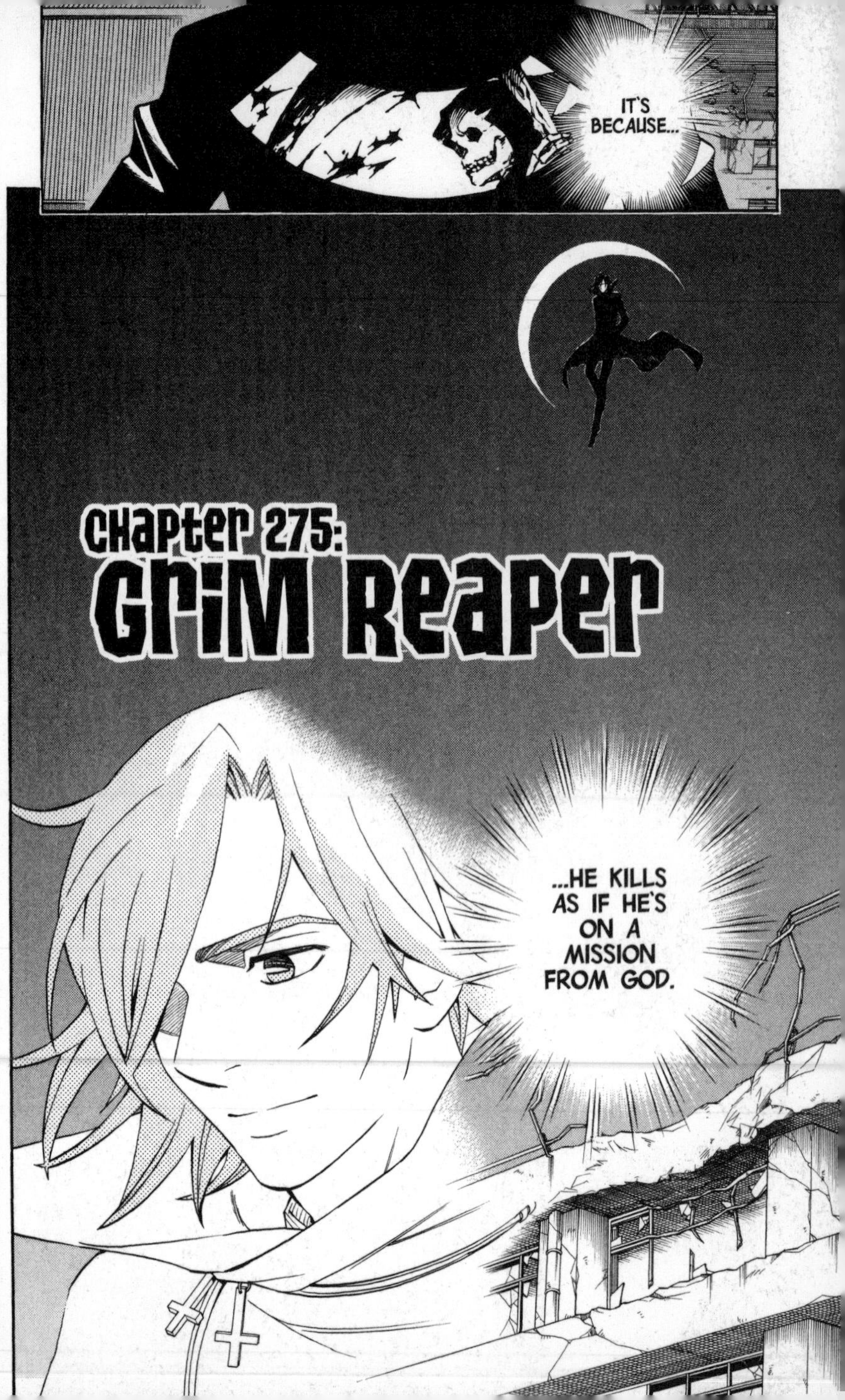
IT'S BECAUSE...
CHAPTER 275: GRIM REAPER
...HE KILLS AS IF HE'S ON A MISSION FROM GOD.

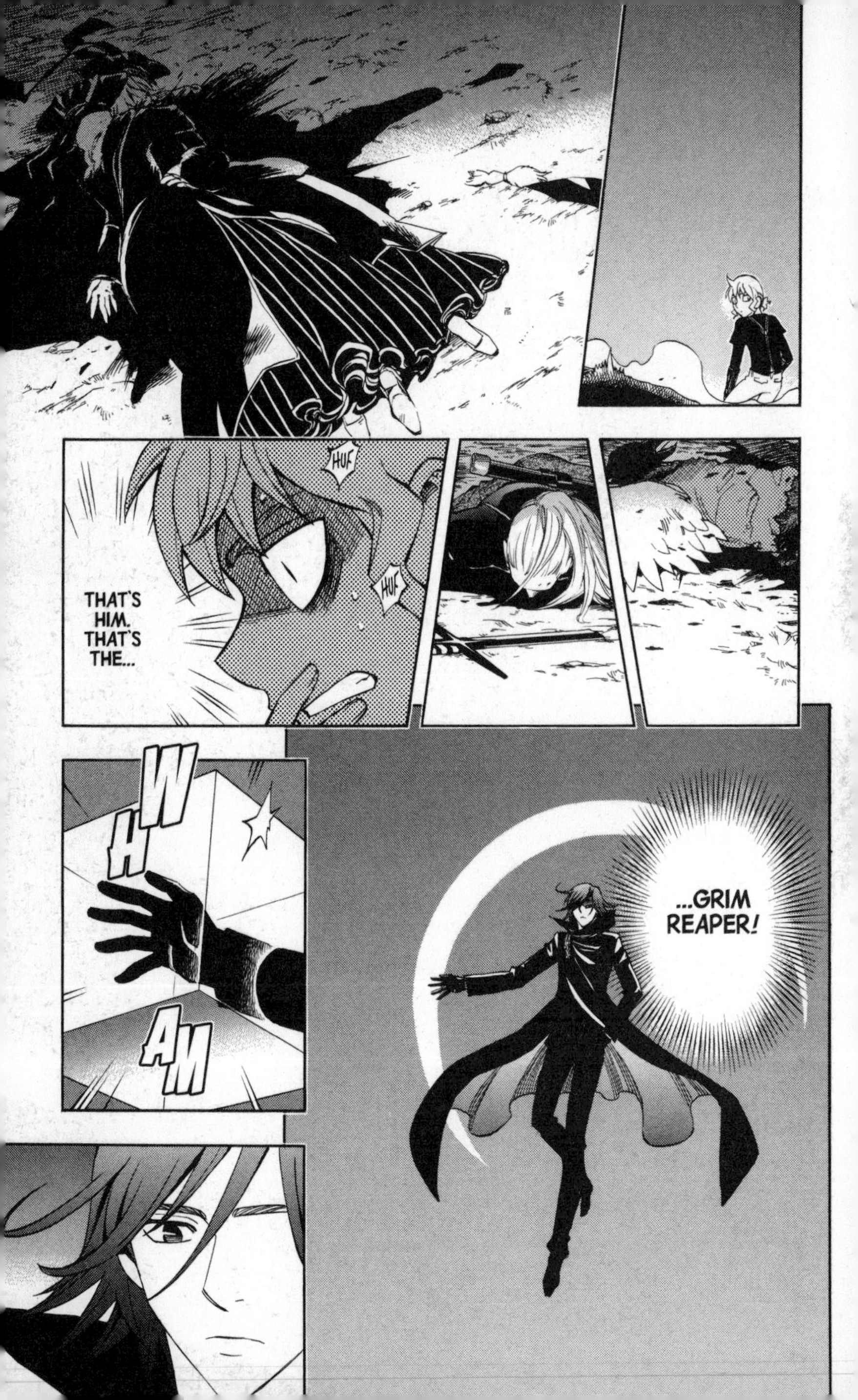
HUF
HUF
THAT'S HIM. THAT'S THE...
...GRIM REAPER!
WHAM

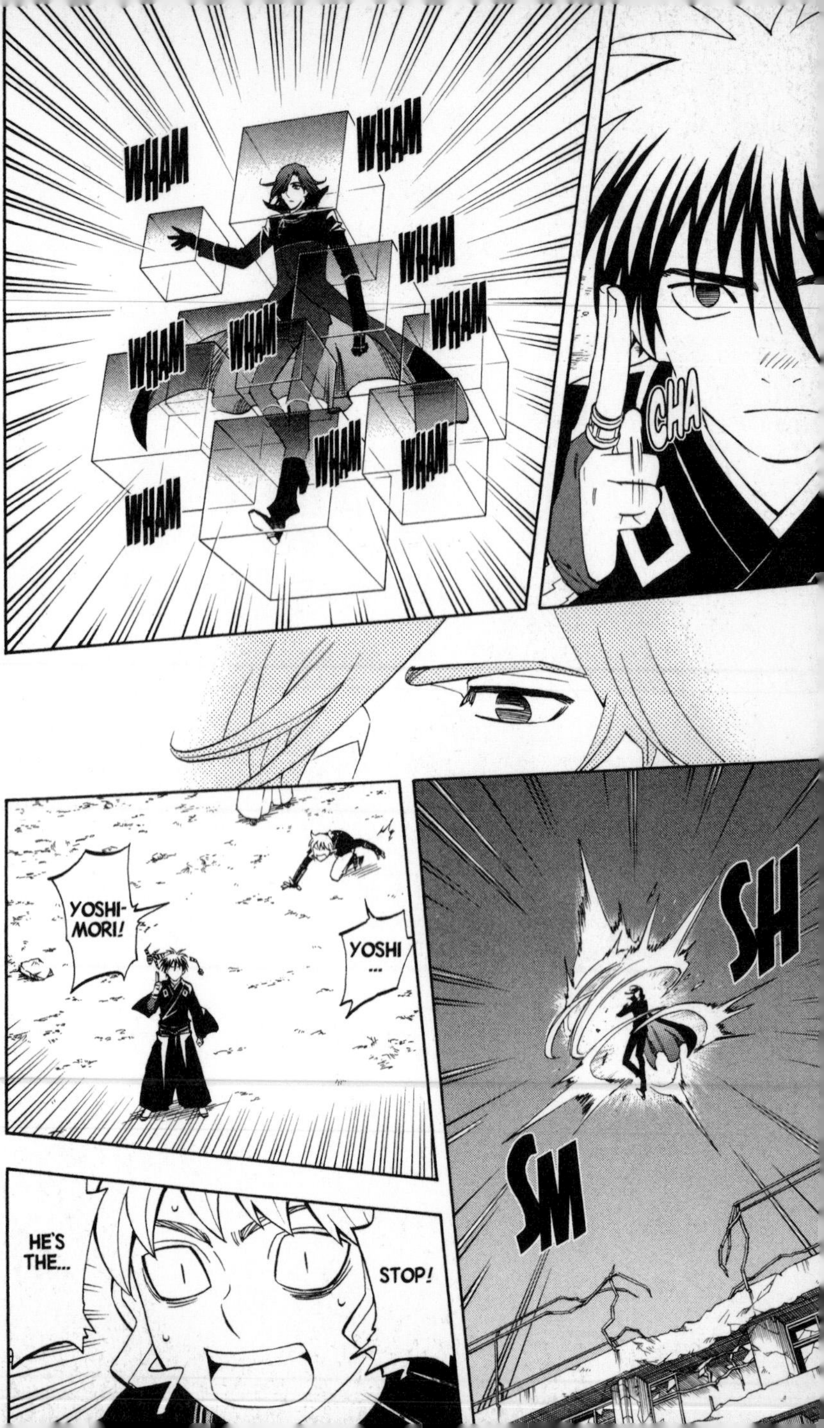
CHA
WHAM
WHAM
WHAM
WHAM
WHAM
WHAM
WHAM
WHAM
WHAM
SH
SM
YOSHI...
YOSHI-MORI!
STOP!
HE'S THE...

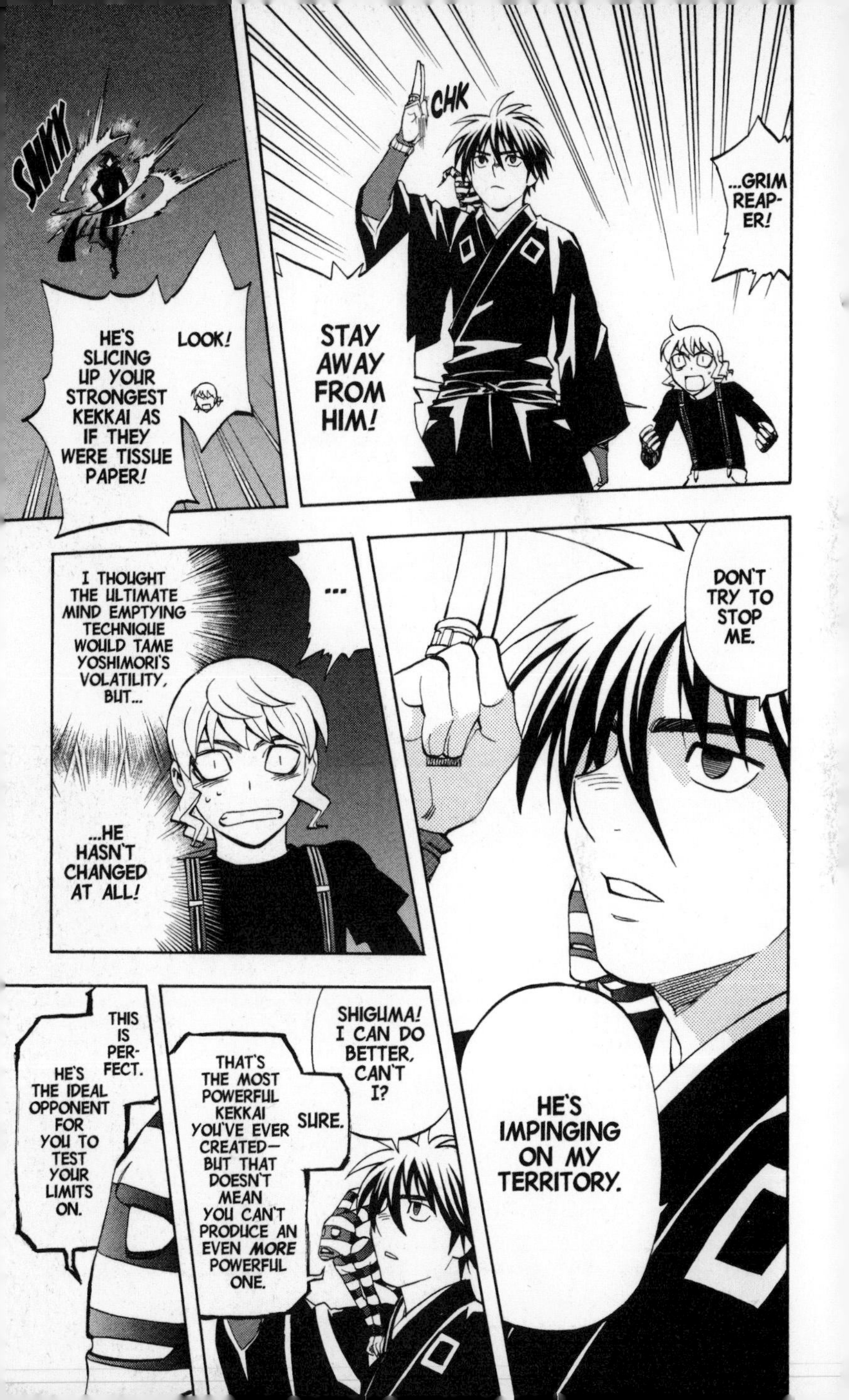
...GRIM REAPER!
CHK
STAY AWAY FROM HIM!
SNKK
LOOK!
HE'S SLICING UP YOUR STRONGEST KEKKAI AS IF THEY WERE TISSUE PAPER!
DON'T TRY TO STOP ME.
HE'S IMPINGING ON MY TERRITORY.
...
I THOUGHT THE ULTIMATE MIND EMPTYING TECHNIQUE WOULD TAME YOSHIMORI'S VOLATILITY, BUT...
...HE HASN'T CHANGED AT ALL!
SHIGUMA! I CAN DO BETTER, CAN'T I?
SURE.
THAT'S THE MOST POWERFUL KEKKAI YOU'VE EVER CREATED—BUT THAT DOESN'T MEAN YOU CAN'T PRODUCE AN EVEN *MORE* POWERFUL ONE.
THIS IS PERFECT.
HE'S THE IDEAL OPPONENT FOR YOU TO TEST YOUR LIMITS ON.

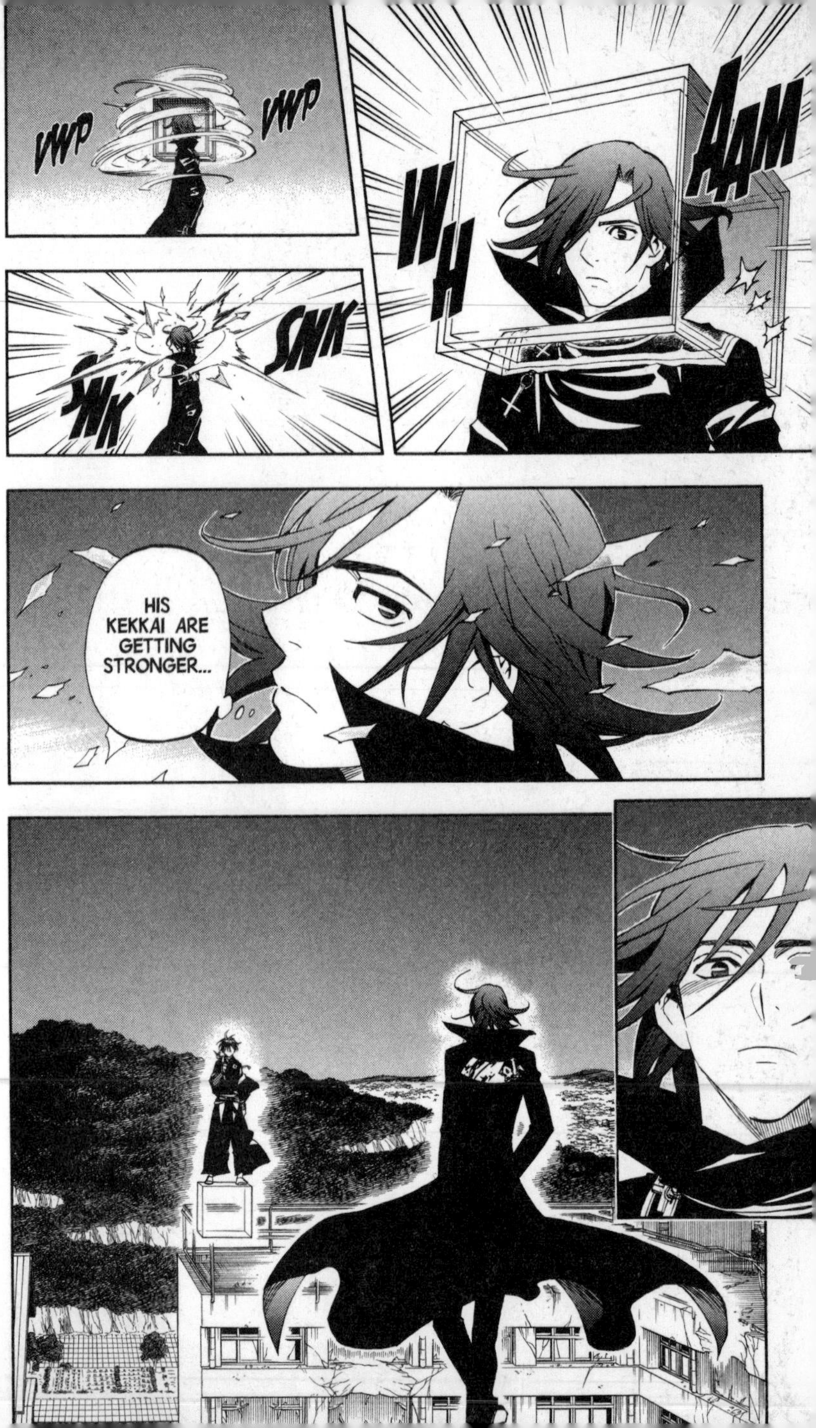
WHAAM
VWP
VWP
SNK
SNK
HIS KEKKAI ARE GETTING STRONGER...

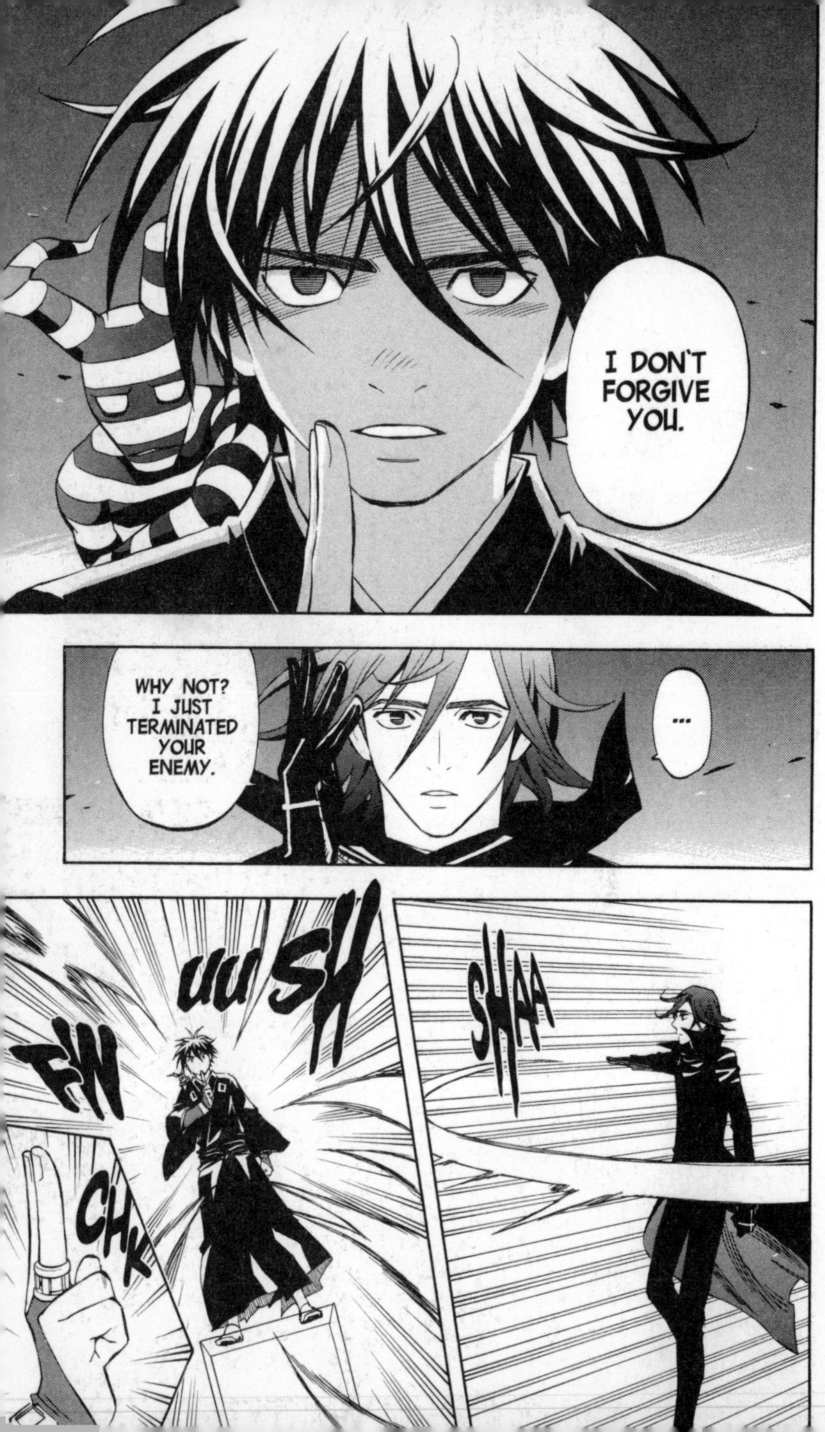
I DON'T FORGIVE YOU.
...
WHY NOT? I JUST TERMINATED YOUR ENEMY.
SHAA
FW
UUUSH
CHK

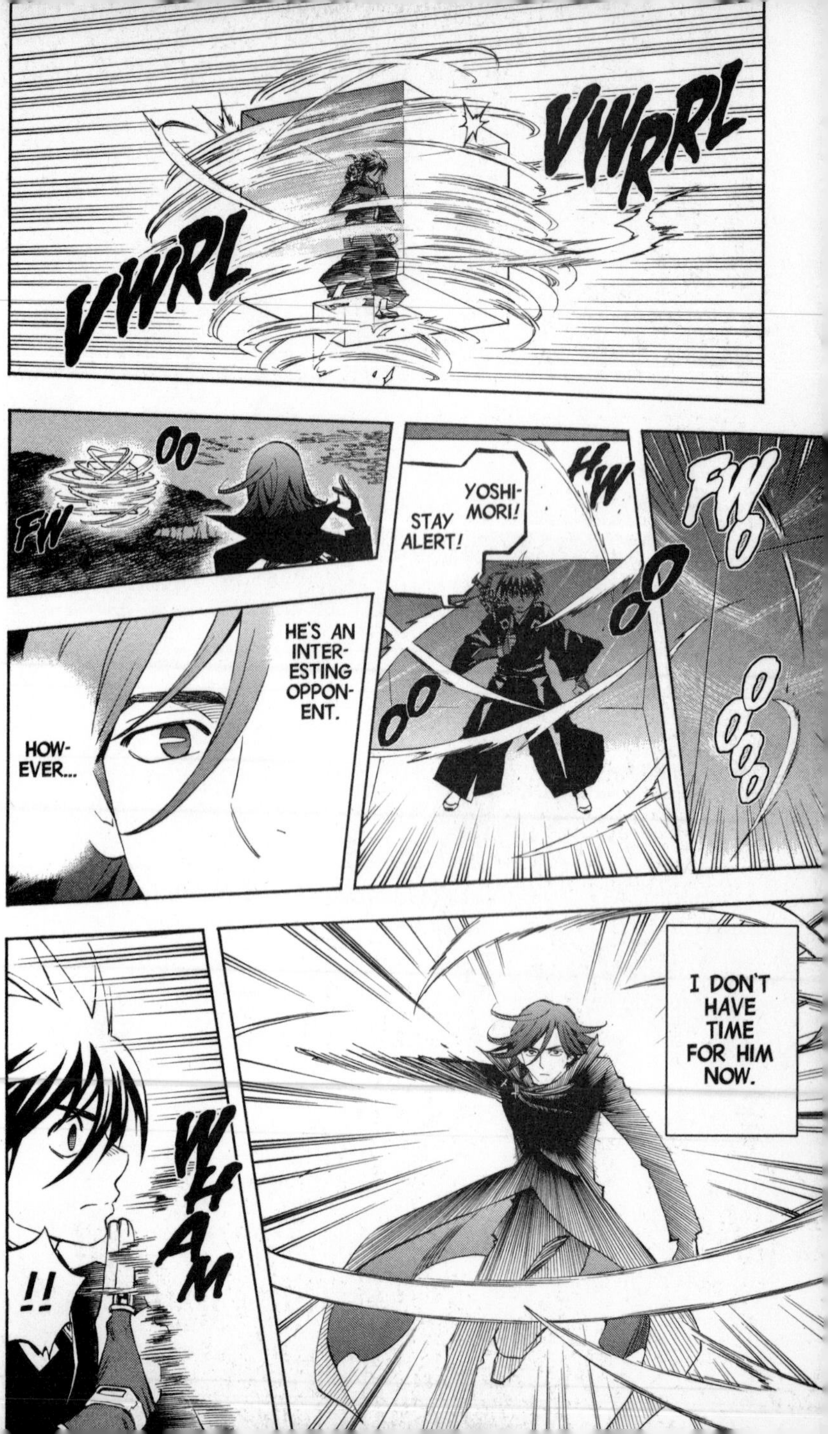

VWRRL
VWRL
FWOOOOO
YOSHI-MORI! STAY ALERT!
HW
OO
OO
OO
FW
HE'S AN INTER-ESTING OPPON-ENT.
HOW-EVER...
I DON'T HAVE TIME FOR HIM NOW.
WHAM
!!

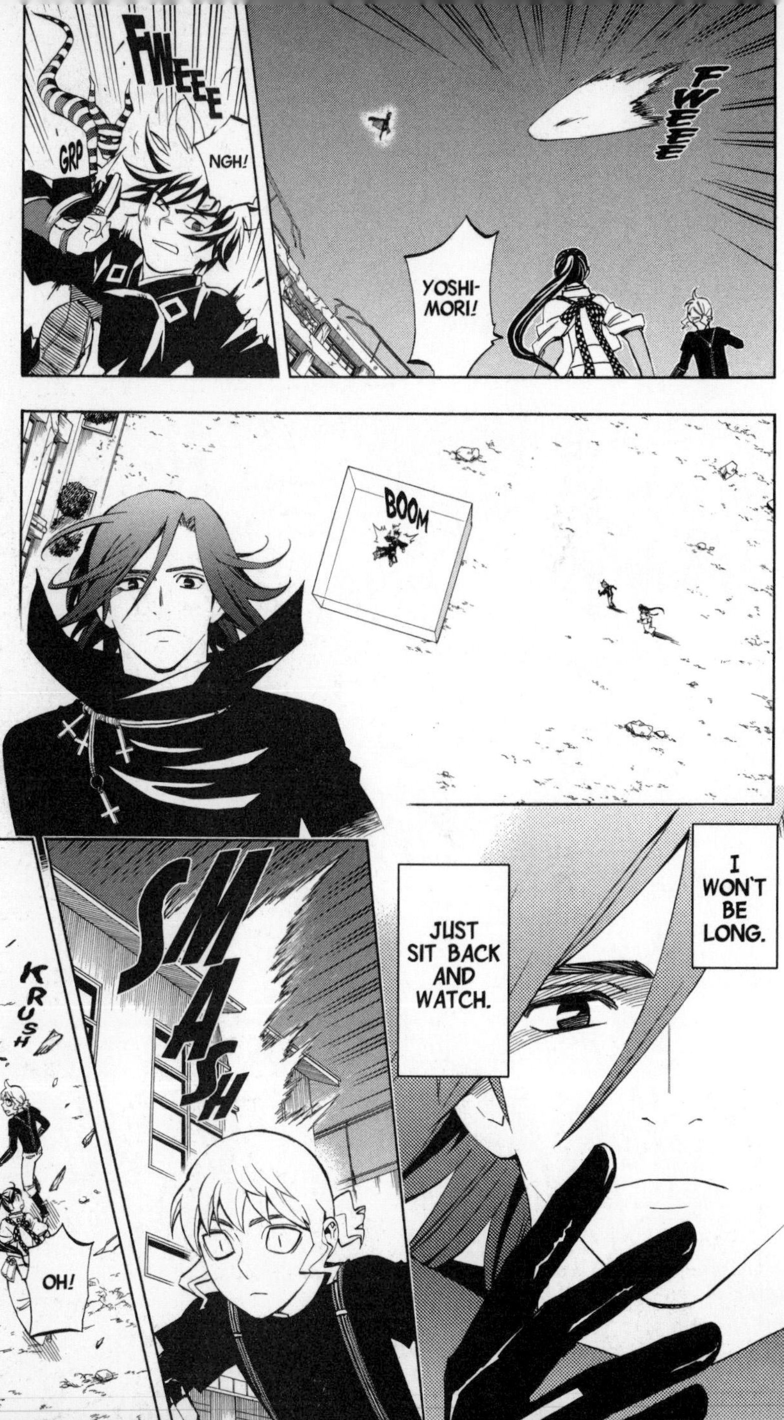
FWEEEE
YOSHI-MORI!
FWEEEE
GRP
NGH!
BOOM
I WON'T BE LONG.
JUST SIT BACK AND WATCH.
SMASH
KRUSH
OH!

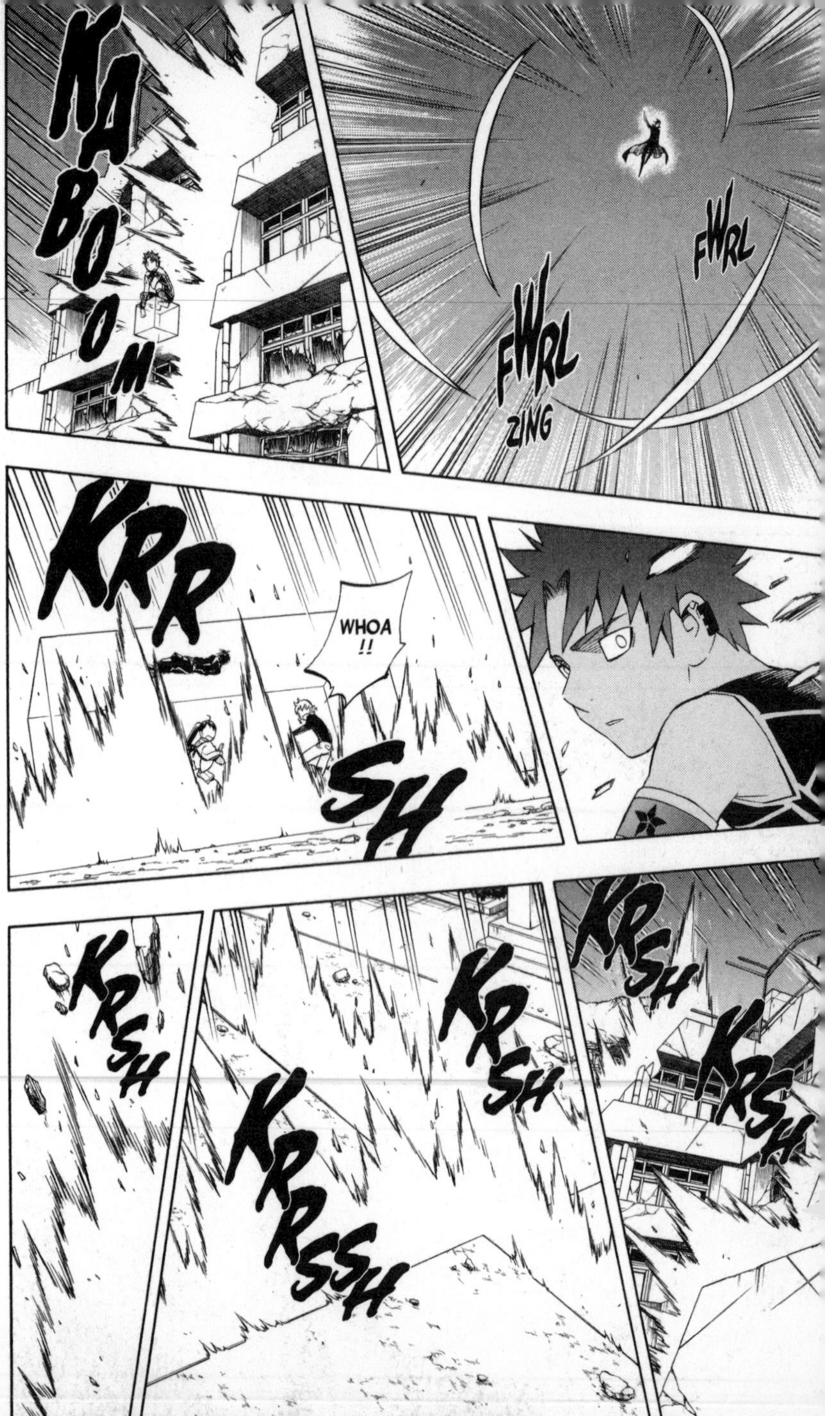
FWRL
FWRL
ZING
KABOOM
KRR
WHOA !!
SH
KRSH
KRSH
KRSH
KRRSSH
KRSH

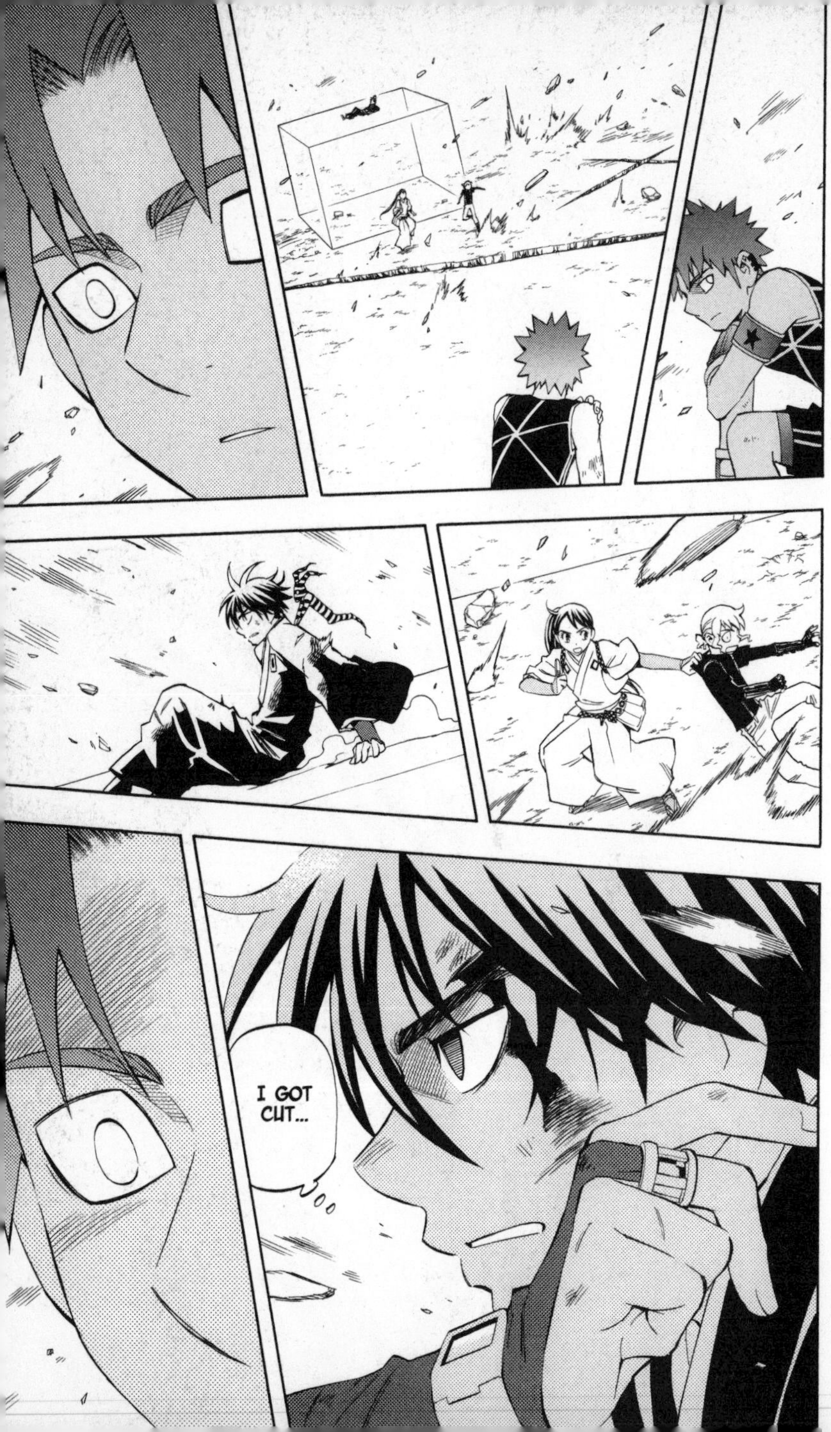
I GOT CUT...

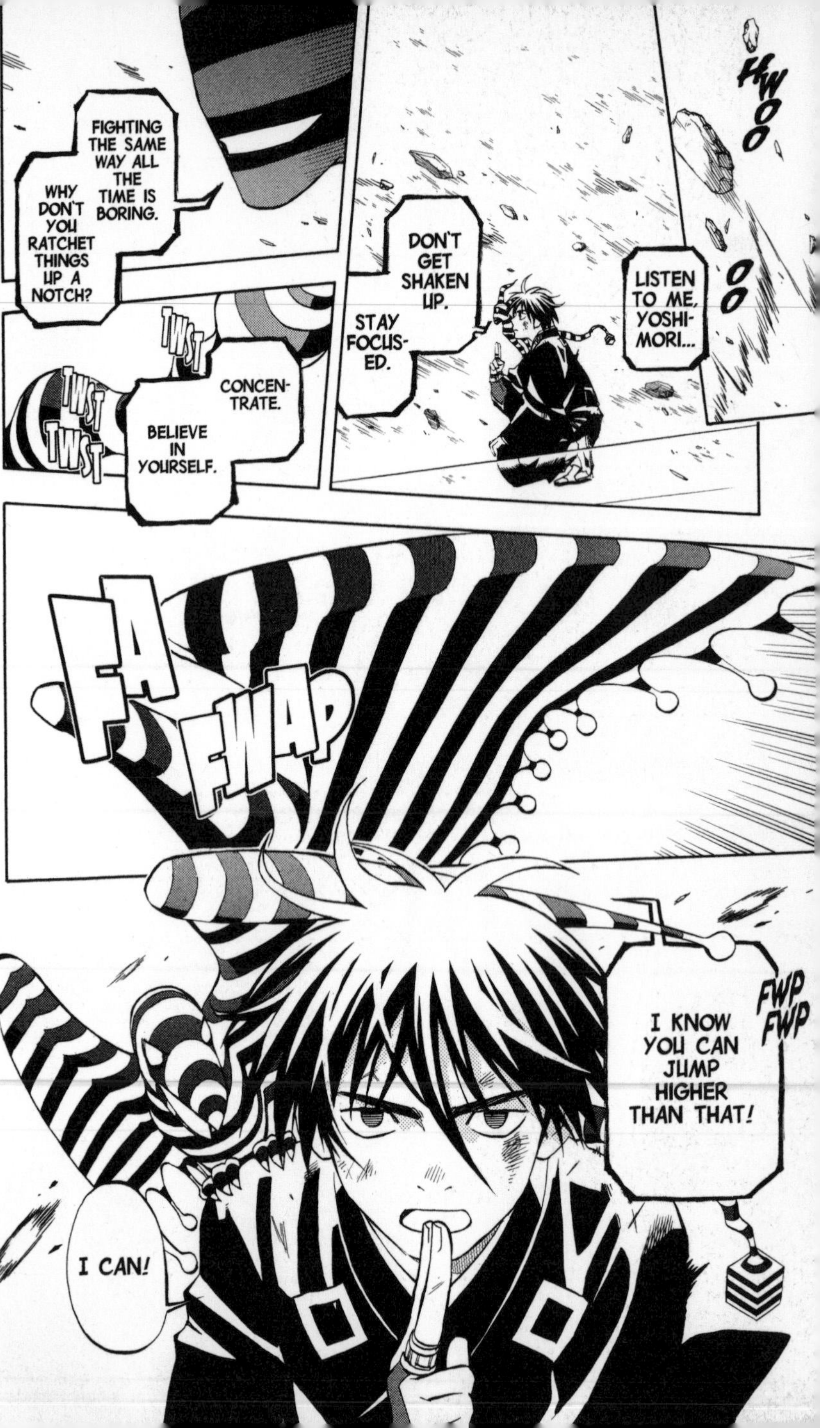
FWOOO
OO
LISTEN TO ME, YOSHIMORI...
DON'T GET SHAKEN UP.
STAY FOCUSED.
FIGHTING THE SAME WAY ALL THE TIME IS BORING.
WHY DON'T YOU RATCHET THINGS UP A NOTCH?
TWST
TWST
TWST
CONCENTRATE.
BELIEVE IN YOURSELF.
FA
FWAP
FWP
FWP
I KNOW YOU CAN JUMP HIGHER THAN THAT!
I CAN!

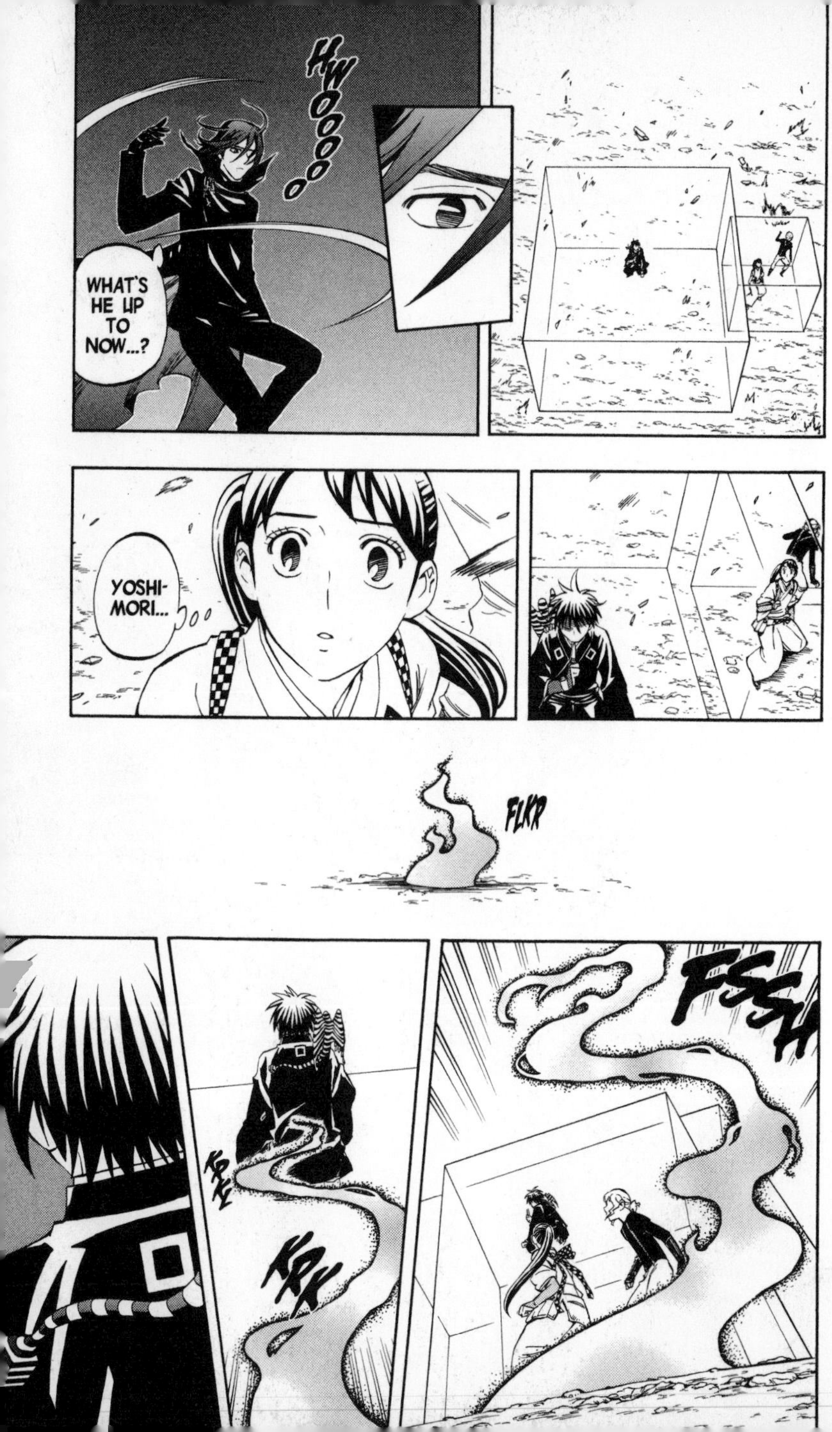
HWOOOOOO
WHAT'S HE UP TO NOW...?
YOSHIMORI...
FLKR
FSSH
KRK
KRK

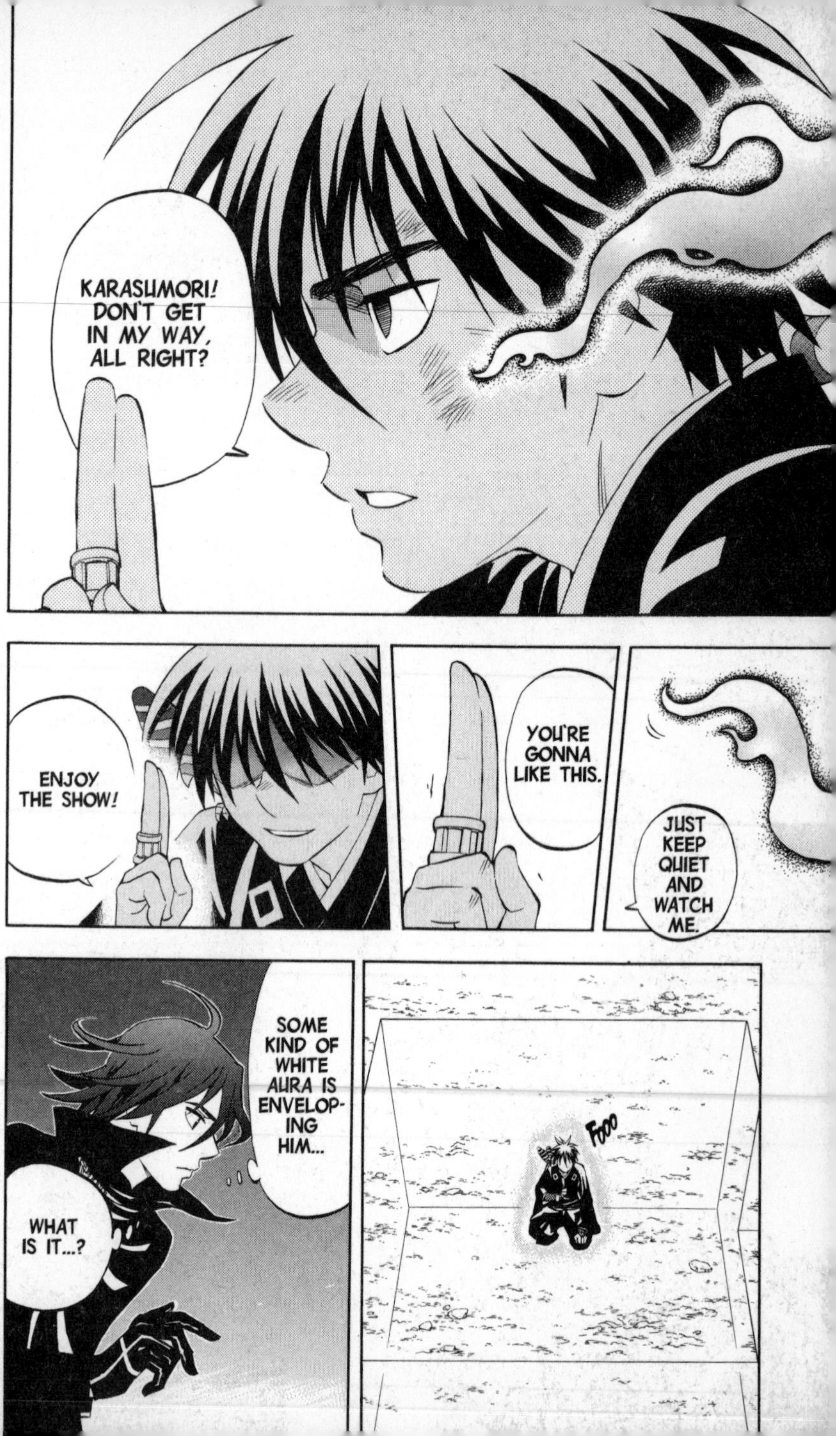
KARASUMORI! DON'T GET IN MY WAY, ALL RIGHT?
JUST KEEP QUIET AND WATCH ME.
YOU'RE GONNA LIKE THIS.
ENJOY THE SHOW!
FOOO
SOME KIND OF WHITE AURA IS ENVELOP-ING HIM...
WHAT IS IT...?

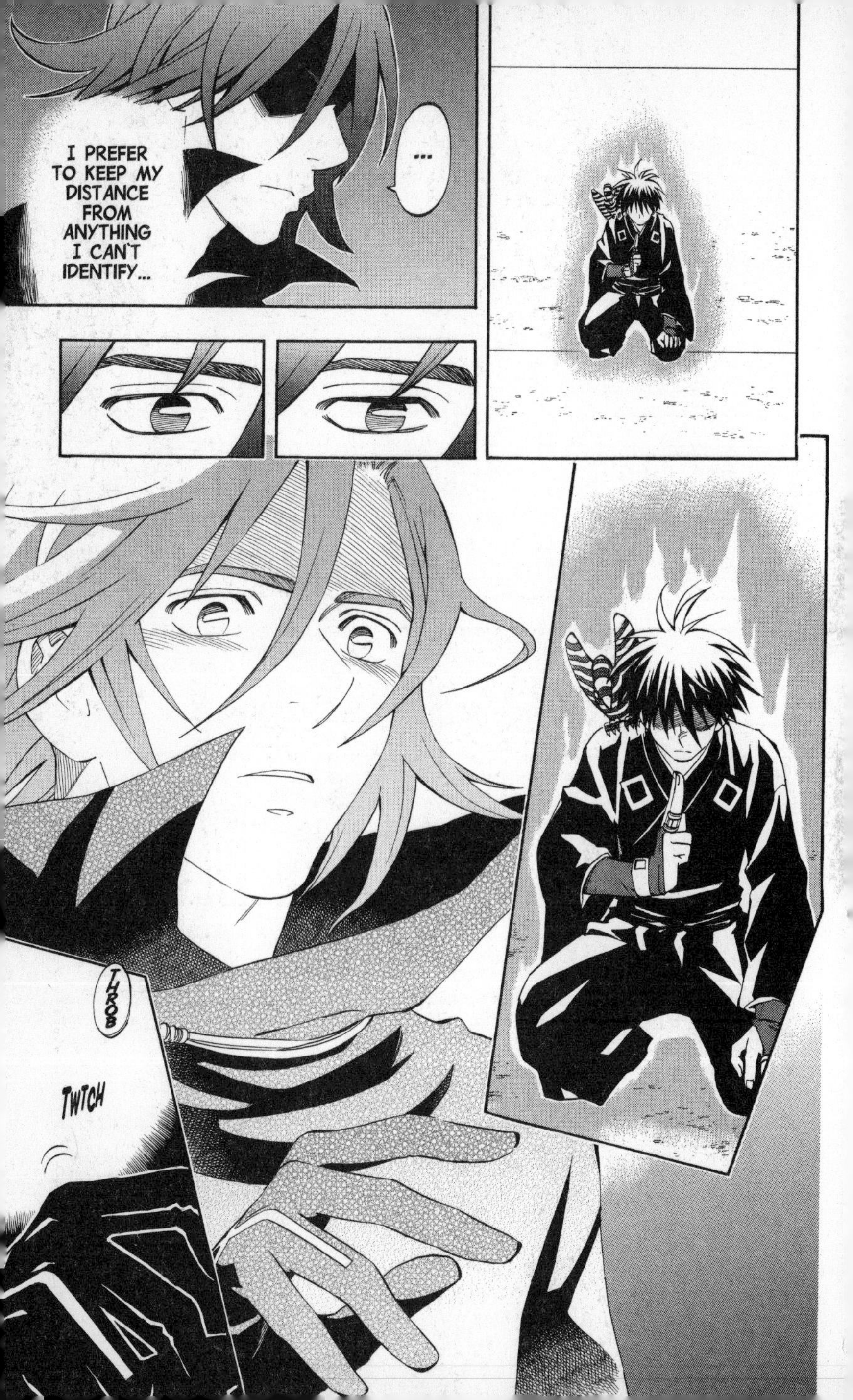
...
I PREFER TO KEEP MY DISTANCE FROM ANYTHING I CAN'T IDENTIFY...
THROB
TWTCH

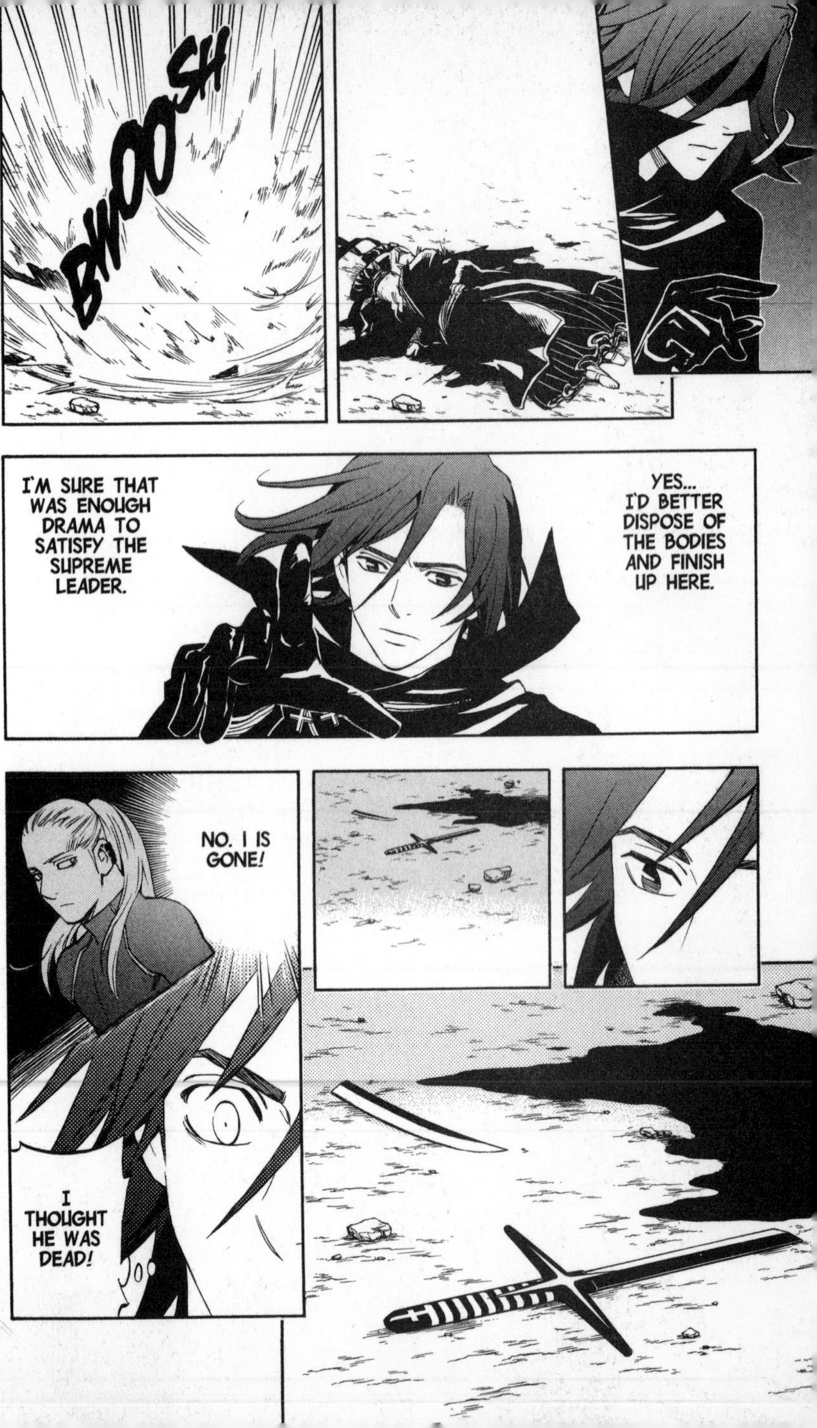
BWOOSH
YES... I'D BETTER DISPOSE OF THE BODIES AND FINISH UP HERE.
I'M SURE THAT WAS ENOUGH DRAMA TO SATISFY THE SUPREME LEADER.
NO. I IS GONE!
I THOUGHT HE WAS DEAD!

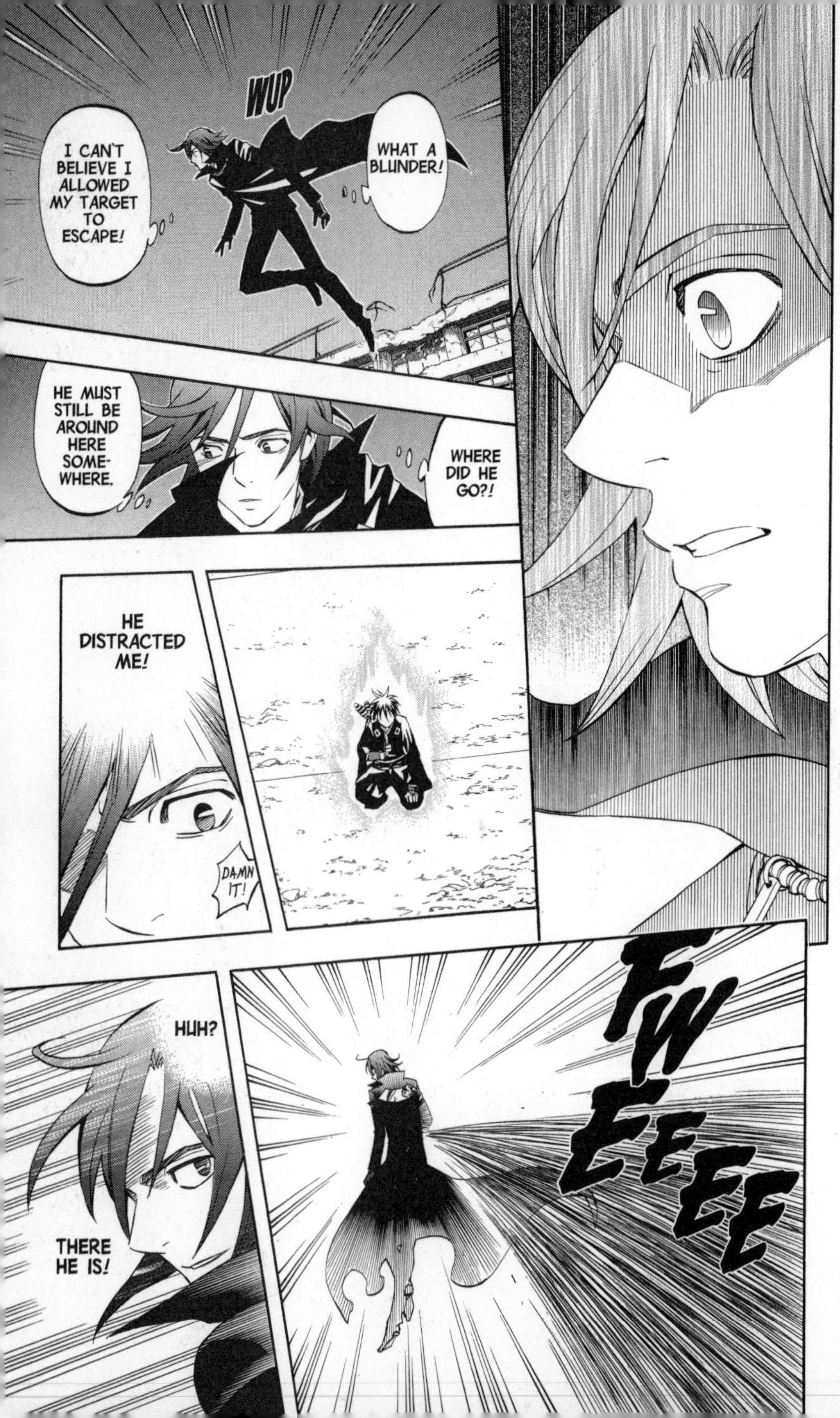
WUP
WHAT A BLUNDER!
I CAN'T BELIEVE I ALLOWED MY TARGET TO ESCAPE!
WHERE DID HE GO?!
HE MUST STILL BE AROUND HERE SOME-WHERE.
HE DISTRACTED ME!
DAMN IT!
FWEEEEE
HUH?
THERE HE IS!

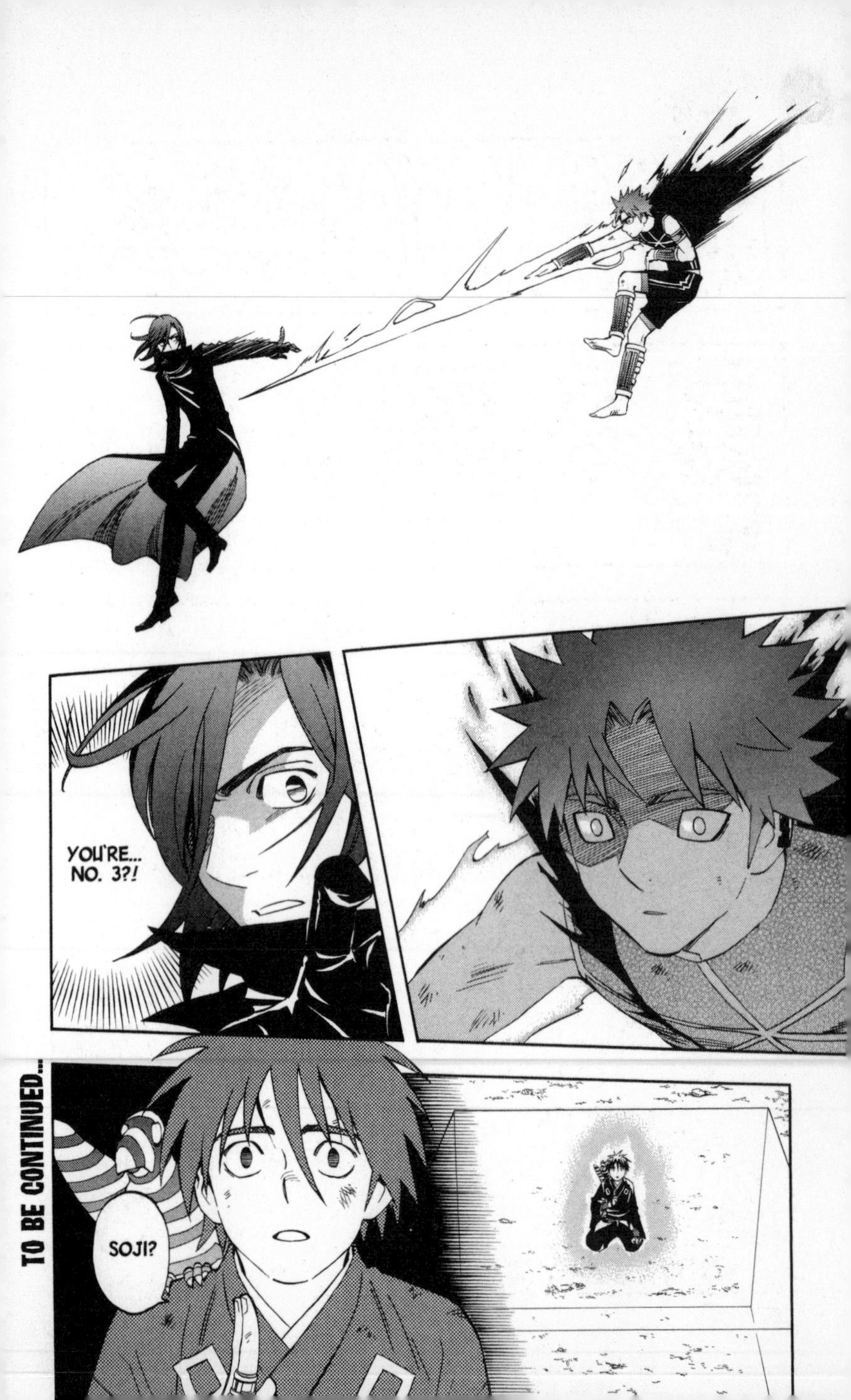
YOU'RE... NO. 3?!
SOJI?
TO BE CONTINUED...

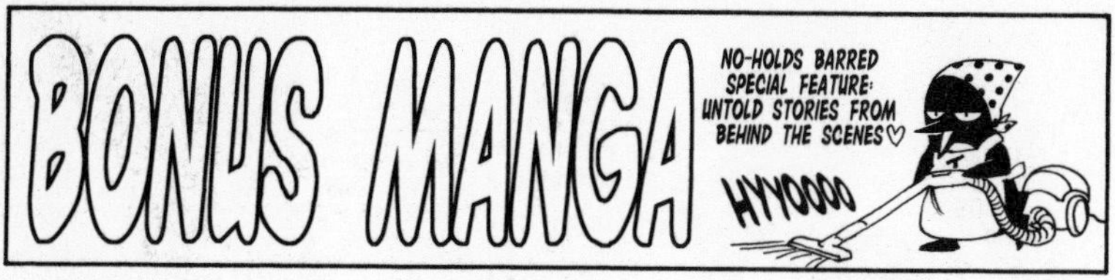
BONUS MANGA
NO-HOLDS BARRED SPECIAL FEATURE: UNTOLD STORIES FROM BEHIND THE SCENES♡
HYYOOOO

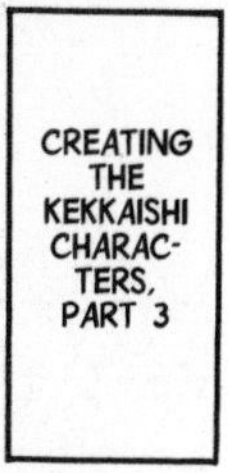
CREATING THE KEKKAISHI CHARACTERS, PART 3

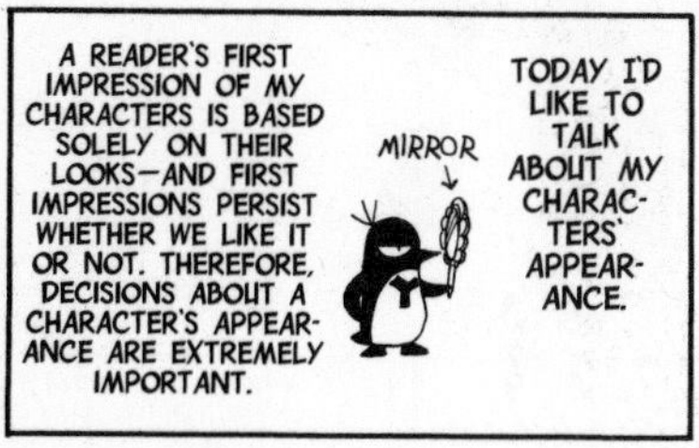
TODAY I'D LIKE TO TALK ABOUT MY CHARACTERS' APPEARANCE.
MIRROR
A READER'S FIRST IMPRESSION OF MY CHARACTERS IS BASED SOLELY ON THEIR LOOKS—AND FIRST IMPRESSIONS PERSIST WHETHER WE LIKE IT OR NOT. THEREFORE, DECISIONS ABOUT A CHARACTER'S APPEARANCE ARE EXTREMELY IMPORTANT.

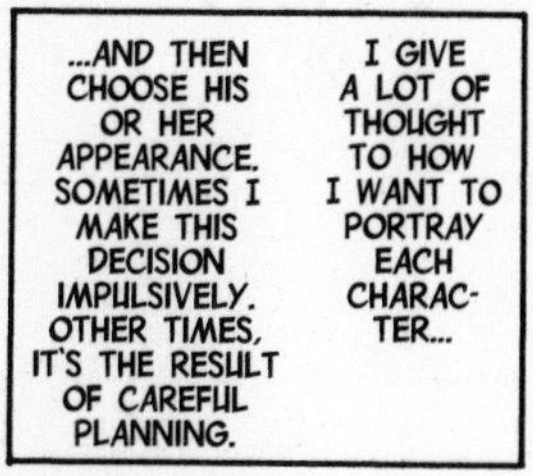
I GIVE A LOT OF THOUGHT TO HOW I WANT TO PORTRAY EACH CHARACTER...
...AND THEN CHOOSE HIS OR HER APPEARANCE. SOMETIMES I MAKE THIS DECISION IMPULSIVELY. OTHER TIMES, IT'S THE RESULT OF CAREFUL PLANNING.

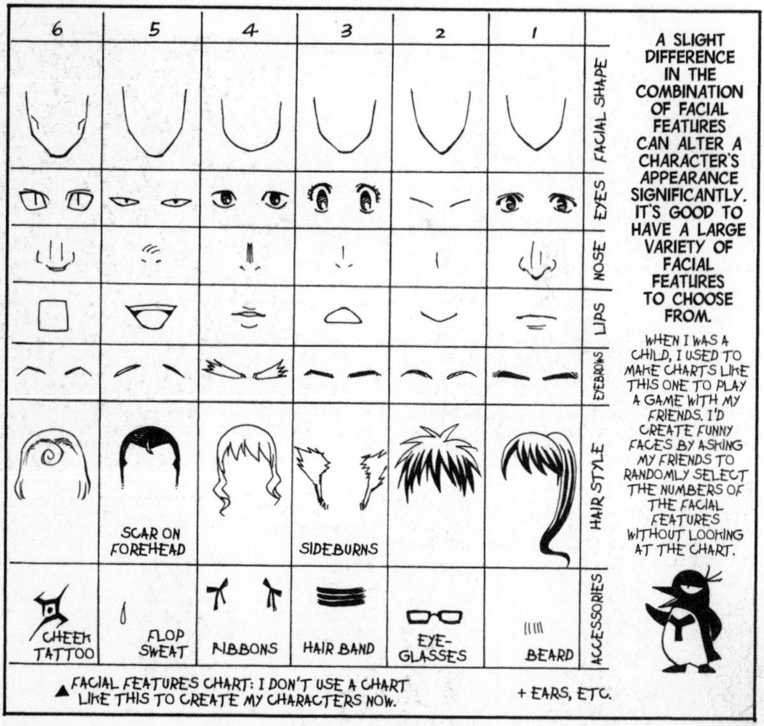
A SLIGHT DIFFERENCE IN THE COMBINATION OF FACIAL FEATURES CAN ALTER A CHARACTER'S APPEARANCE SIGNIFICANTLY. IT'S GOOD TO HAVE A LARGE VARIETY OF FACIAL FEATURES TO CHOOSE FROM.
WHEN I WAS A CHILD, I USED TO MAKE CHARTS LIKE THIS ONE TO PLAY A GAME WITH MY FRIENDS. I'D CREATE FUNNY FACES BY ASKING MY FRIENDS TO RANDOMLY SELECT THE NUMBERS OF THE FACIAL FEATURES WITHOUT LOOKING AT THE CHART.
6
5
4
3
2
1
FACIAL SHAPE
EYES
NOSE
LIPS
EYEBROWS
HAIR STYLE
SCAR ON FOREHEAD
SIDEBURNS
ACCESSORIES
CHEEK TATTOO
FLOP SWEAT
RIBBONS
HAIR BAND
EYE-GLASSES
BEARD
▲ FACIAL FEATURES CHART: I DON'T USE A CHART LIKE THIS TO CREATE MY CHARACTERS NOW.
+ EARS, ETC.

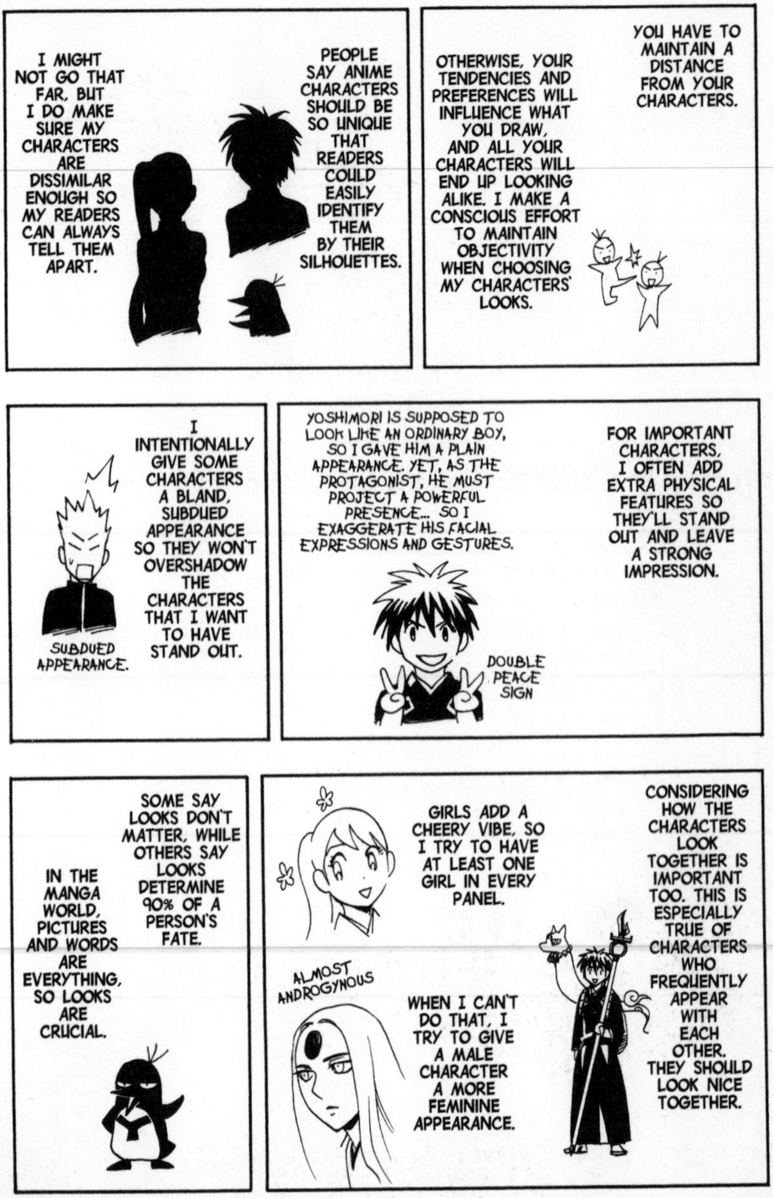
YOU HAVE TO MAINTAIN A DISTANCE FROM YOUR CHARACTERS.
OTHERWISE, YOUR TENDENCIES AND PREFERENCES WILL INFLUENCE WHAT YOU DRAW, AND ALL YOUR CHARACTERS WILL END UP LOOKING ALIKE. I MAKE A CONSCIOUS EFFORT TO MAINTAIN OBJECTIVITY WHEN CHOOSING MY CHARACTERS' LOOKS.
PEOPLE SAY ANIME CHARACTERS SHOULD BE SO UNIQUE THAT READERS COULD EASILY IDENTIFY THEM BY THEIR SILHOUETTES.
I MIGHT NOT GO THAT FAR, BUT I DO MAKE SURE MY CHARACTERS ARE DISSIMILAR ENOUGH SO MY READERS CAN ALWAYS TELL THEM APART.
FOR IMPORTANT CHARACTERS, I OFTEN ADD EXTRA PHYSICAL FEATURES SO THEY'LL STAND OUT AND LEAVE A STRONG IMPRESSION.
YOSHIMORI IS SUPPOSED TO LOOK LIKE AN ORDINARY BOY, SO I GAVE HIM A PLAIN APPEARANCE. YET, AS THE PROTAGONIST, HE MUST PROJECT A POWERFUL PRESENCE... SO I EXAGGERATE HIS FACIAL EXPRESSIONS AND GESTURES.
DOUBLE PEACE SIGN
I INTENTIONALLY GIVE SOME CHARACTERS A BLAND, SUBDUED APPEARANCE SO THEY WON'T OVERSHADOW THE CHARACTERS THAT I WANT TO HAVE STAND OUT.
SUBDUED APPEARANCE.
CONSIDERING HOW THE CHARACTERS LOOK TOGETHER IS IMPORTANT TOO. THIS IS ESPECIALLY TRUE OF CHARACTERS WHO FREQUENTLY APPEAR WITH EACH OTHER. THEY SHOULD LOOK NICE TOGETHER.
GIRLS ADD A CHEERY VIBE, SO I TRY TO HAVE AT LEAST ONE GIRL IN EVERY PANEL.
WHEN I CAN'T DO THAT, I TRY TO GIVE A MALE CHARACTER A MORE FEMININE APPEARANCE.
ALMOST ANDROGYNOUS
SOME SAY LOOKS DON'T MATTER, WHILE OTHERS SAY LOOKS DETERMINE 90% OF A PERSON'S FATE.
IN THE MANGA WORLD, PICTURES AND WORDS ARE EVERYTHING, SO LOOKS ARE CRUCIAL.

GRIND
GRIND

MESSAGE FROM YELLOW TANABE

I've been using the same old pencil sharpener (a manual one) since I was in elementary school. Nowadays, though, I only use it for colored pencils.

I don't particularly like the way it works. If I'm not careful, I end up scattering shavings all over the place.

Nevertheless, I like its size and the way it looks. I guess I'll keep using it until it breaks.

KEKKAISHI

VOLUME 28
SHONEN SUNDAY EDITION

STORY AND ART BY YELLOW TANABE

© 2004 Yellow TANABE/Shogakukan
All rights reserved.
Original Japanese edition "KEKKAISHI" published by SHOGAKUKAN Inc.

Translation/Yuko Sawada
Touch-up Art & Lettering/Stephen Dutro
Cover Design & Graphic Layout/Julie Behn, Ronnie Casson
Editor/Annette Roman

The rights of the author(s) of the work(s) in this publication to be
so identified have been asserted in accordance with the Copyright,
Designs and Patents Act 1988. A CIP catalogue record for this book is
available from the British Library.

The stories, characters and incidents mentioned in this publication are
entirely fictional.

Printed in the U.S.A.

Published by VIZ Media, LLC
P.O. Box 77010
San Francisco, CA 94107

10 9 8 7 6 5 4 3 2 1
First printing, October 2011

www.viz.com

PARENTAL ADVISORY
KEKKAISHI is rated T for Teen
and is recommended for ages
13 and up. It contains fantasy
violence.
ratings.viz.com

WWW.SHONENSUNDAY.COM

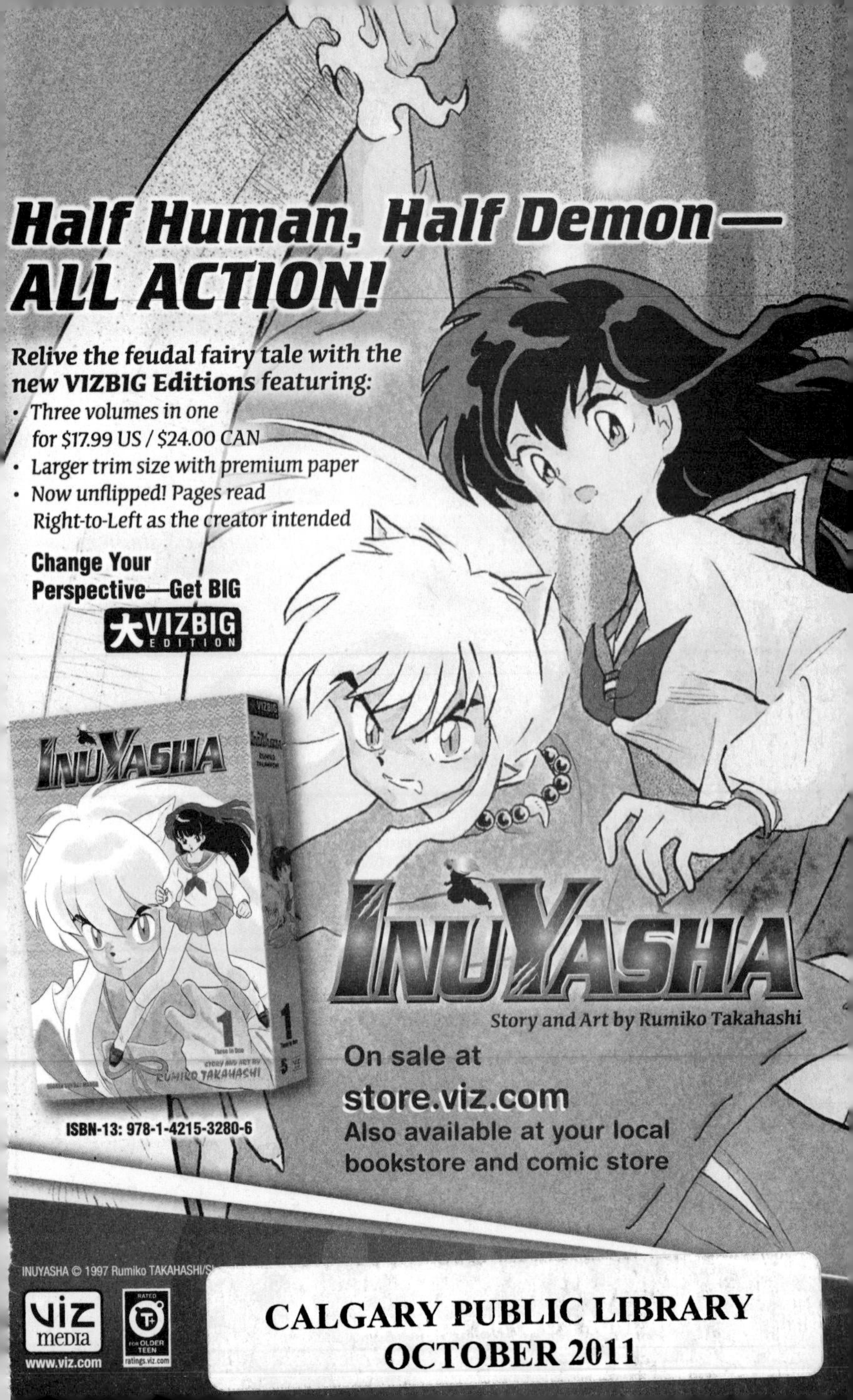
Half Human, Half Demon—
ALL ACTION!
Relive the feudal fairy tale with the new VIZBIG Editions featuring:
• Three volumes in one for $17.99 US / $24.00 CAN
• Larger trim size with premium paper
• Now unflipped! Pages read Right-to-Left as the creator intended
Change Your Perspective—Get BIG
大 VIZBIG EDITION
INUYASHA
1
STORY AND ART BY RUMIKO TAKAHASHI
ISBN-13: 978-1-4215-3280-6
INUYASHA
Story and Art by Rumiko Takahashi
On sale at
store.viz.com
Also available at your local bookstore and comic store
INUYASHA © 1997 Rumiko TAKAHASHI/S
viz media
www.viz.com
RATED T+ FOR OLDER TEEN
ratings.viz.com